LINES OF
SCRIMMAGE

LINES OF
SCRIMMAGE

A Story of Football, Race, and Redemption

Joe Oestreich

Scott Pleasant

University Press of Mississippi · Jackson

Designed by Peter D. Halverson

First printing 2015

∞

Library of Congress Cataloging-in-Publication Data

Oestreich, Joe.
Lines of scrimmage : a story of football, race, and redemption / Joe Oestreich,
Scott Pleasant.
pages cm
Includes bibliographical references and index.
ISBN 978-1-4968-0308-5 (cloth : alk. paper) — ISBN 978-1-4968-0309-2 (ebook)
1. Football—South Carolina—Conway—History—20th century. 2. Conway High
School (Conway, S.C.)—Football—History. 3. School sports—South Carolina—Conway—History. 4. Discrimination in sports—South Carolina—Conway.
5. Conway (S.C.)—Race relations. I. Title.
GV959.53.C665O47 2015
796.3309757'87—dc23
2014049378

British Library Cataloging-in-Publication Data available

For Rose, Kate, Beckett, Eleanor,
and the people of the Independent Republic of Horry.

1989. The number. Another summer . . .

Got to give us what we want.

Gotta give us what we need.

Our freedom of speech is freedom or death.

We got to fight the powers that be.

—"FIGHT THE POWER" BY PUBLIC ENEMY

CONTENTS

LINES OF
SCRIMMAGE

PROLOGUE

NOW

IN A CROWDED POST-GAME LOCKER ROOM ON A HOT SEPTEMBER NIGHT, Mickey Wilson, head coach of the Myrtle Beach High School Seahawks, fans his arms to silence his rejoicing players. The captains *shhh* the underclassmen, and everybody stops hollering and high-fiving. The room is quiet except for the booms of fireworks exploding in the sky over Doug Shaw Memorial Stadium, where the home-team Seahawks have just beaten their fiercest rival, the Conway Tigers. The Myrtle Beach players, assistant coaches, and support staff all angle themselves toward a head coach who at thirty-nine doesn't look much older than the kids staring up at him. They're expecting the same speech they've heard before: *I want y'all to enjoy tonight. Then come back on Monday ready to work hard and get better.* But this win against Conway is especially sweet, so Mickey goes against his normal postgame script.

"Are we alone?" he asks, tapping the gem-studded ring that encases about a third of his right ring finger. "Is the *Sun News* in here?" He scans the room for the reporter that works the local prep football beat. Satisfied that nobody from the press is watching, he picks up a wooden trophy with a silver-plated bell perched on top. "I want y'all to listen up," he says, flashing a devilish smile that runs counter to his usual *yes, sir/no, sir* demeanor. "I'm gonna give you a sound they ain't never heard in Conway." And he whacks his ring against the bell. *Bang.* "Hear that?" he says. Then twice more. *Bing-bang.* "That's the sound of a state championship ring hitting the Victory Bell!"

The team erupts in joyous howls. "That's right! Can't be beat!"

Minutes earlier, after the scoreboard clock struck zeroes, linebacker Octavius Thomas sprinted across the field to liberate the Victory Bell from the Conway sideline. In this, his senior year, Thomas—or "O.T.," as his teammates call the kid with the night-dark skin and the bleach-blonde Mohawk—wanted nothing more than to escort that bell back to the Myrtle

3

Beach trophy case after surrendering it in his junior season to the detestable Tigers. Before tonight's kickoff, O.T. had said, "I'd rather win this one than a region game," because the Bell Game, as the yearly clash with Conway is called, holds much more significance than run-of-the-mill matchups within Myrtle Beach's conference. In Region VII of the South Carolina Class 3A division, the Seahawks are already kings. They haven't dropped a region game in four years, and in that span, they've won two state championships. But coming into tonight, even those fat championship rings couldn't erase the fact that Myrtle Beach had lost to Conway the last time they met. The Victory Bell had spent fifty-two long weeks under enemy control, giving the Tigers a year of football bragging rights here in Horry County, the county that contains both Myrtle Beach (the famous coastal resort town) and Conway (the not-so-famous inland county seat). Tonight, however, the Tigers' claim to the trophy has expired. Tonight, the Seahawks are hoisting it. Tonight, their young coach is smiling. A year's worth of aggravation and swallowed-pride has dissipated with three rings of the bell.

In the visitors' locker room, Conway coach Chuck Jordan also wants to know that he and his team are alone. "Shut the door," he says. And a few seconds later, when he notices it's still cracked: "I told y'all to shut that gotdang door! Now *shut* it!"

The silence in the room is broken by the sniffs and sobs of hunched-over teenagers. For three hours this evening, the Tigers looked strong, stout, like *men*, but now—moments after a heartbreaking loss to their rivals from the beach—these players are boys again, boys who look to their coach to help take away the hurt.

"I know you hate it," Jordan says. "I hate it, too. I hate those guys. Hate the way they run their mouth."

And it's true that Jordan, at age fifty-five, despises mouth running and trash talking—especially when that trash comes from a Myrtle Beach mouth. Later, when he's asked about the recent Seahawk tradition of entering the field from a giant inflatable helmet, through a cloud of smoke, to a looped recording of Jadakiss's "The Champ Is Here" (a song that samples Will Smith's drum-banging boast from his role as Muhammad Ali in the 2001 biopic), Jordan will shake his head and say, "That's what some people choose to do, but I'm just not like that."

For Chuck Jordan, "some people" is a polite way of saying "Mickey Wilson," his younger, brasher counterpart. Maybe Jordan's gesture toward politeness stems from a lifetime spent in the South, where even the worst insults are delivered with a spoonful of sugar, or maybe it's a demonstration of the loyalty he shows to his former players, because as almost everyone in the stadium tonight knows, Mickey Wilson used to play *for* Chuck Jordan, back in the late eighties when Mickey was a quarterback for the Conway Tigers. Twenty-three years ago, in 1989, Jordan promoted Mickey, a white junior, to first string QB over Carlos Hunt, a black senior who had started the previous season. Nearly all of Jordan's black players walked away from the team in protest, and the town of Conway was soon divided along racial lines. One seemingly mundane decision, a coach giving the starting nod to one player over another, incited a storm of racial tension that continues to reverberate in this part of South Carolina.

Right now the stadium is still buzzing, but it's because of a decision Jordan made tonight, at the end of the fourth quarter, with the Bell hanging in the balance. It was a gutsy call, one that observers remarked was out of character for the conservative Jordan. It was the type of call his brazen protégé across the field might make. It was a call that failed.

Chuck Jordan looks around the locker room at the hanging heads and runny noses. As much as he can't stand losing any game, let alone a rivalry game against a trash-talking team coached by one of his ex-players, he knows that he has to find a way to turn this bitter defeat into a teachable moment. His kids are sad and stunned, but if they can find a way to muscle through their disappointment, they will have taken an important step toward manhood.

"Guys," he says. "We all hate losing. But this is what we got." A muffled explosion from the fireworks display pushes past the closed door, and the coach pauses to shake his head, perhaps at the pyrotechnics, perhaps at the thought of the Victory Bell hanging from the hands of his former quarterback. "And now we got to deal with it," he adds.

Jordan has already game-planned how it will be dealt with. He and his players are going back to fundamentals, back to the coach's bedrock philosophy for football and for life: *FIDO. Forget it and drive on.* It's the tenet that has allowed him to thrive for thirty years at Conway, through the winning seasons, the losing seasons, and the 1989 season—the year that will forever link the coach to his ex-quarterback. The loss tonight to Mickey Wilson's squad, disappointing as it is, is already in Chuck Jordan's rearview. And compared to everything else that's also sitting back there, especially the events of '89—the accusations of racism, the marches and picketing, the death threats, the national news coverage, the court hearings, and perhaps most painful of all: loss after loss after loss as he led a depleted team through a miserable season—coming up short against Myrtle Beach is small gotdang potatoes.

-1-

GRAVEYARD/BACKYARD

NOW

THE BLACK BAPTIST MINISTER WALKS ACROSS THE STAGE IN THE CONWAY High School auditorium. A tall man wearing a dark suit, he approaches the lectern and spreads his arms to give himself the appropriate physical presence needed to begin his portion of the afternoon's proceedings. He adjusts the microphone and then clutches the podium with both hands, his torso bent at an angle that would make a chiropractor wince. This is the practiced tilt that gets him physically and spiritually closer to his audience every Sunday, but on this day, it also allows him to steal a look down to the foot of the stage, at the casket containing the Reverend Harry Henry Singleton II—civil rights leader, public school teacher, and this man's mentor and friend.

Jerry Faulk is the minister's name, and at first his remarks come slowly and at a relatively low volume, given the size of the auditorium and the hundreds of mourners seated within it. He speaks with the inflection and intonation the crowd expects from a Southern preacher, including the well-measured pauses not just between but *within* sentences, pauses that give his audience just enough space to slip in an *Uh-huh* or a *Tell it*. He's telling the story of his ordination ceremony, of the day he was called to preach the word not only by God, but by the men who served on the area Baptist Association council. He was drawn to the church most especially by one man on that council, the Reverend H. H. Singleton, the man who, as this fledgling preacher was giving his initial sermon, pointed his long finger at the nervous minister and said, "That's aces, boy," "Preach it, boy," and then, afterward, "Job well done."

The Rev. Singleton taught him to "fight the good fight as an advocate for all humanity" (*Tell it*), challenged him to be a "good soldier and a servant of God" (*That's right*), and reminded him that the "ultimate measure of a man is not where he stands in moments of comfort and convenience, but where he stands in times of challenge and controversy" (*Come on*). Singleton led him on marches through the oak-lined streets of this coastal South Carolina town, through thunder and lightning and a hard rain of hatred and bigotry, and through all those challenging times, the minister walked behind Singleton, asking himself and those around him, "What manner of man is this?"

He's interrupted with applause. "What manner of man is this!" he shouts a second time, and as the acclamation rises in pitch and intensity, he strides back to his seat.

As powerful as this ending flourish is, the line that still resonates even as the next speaker prepares to take the podium is not "What manner of man is this?" but instead one that the minister repeated near the beginning of his remarks. At that moment, just when a more reserved clergyman might have offered a platitude along the lines of "Reverend Singleton has found his reward now. May he rest in peace," this minister raised one hand and yelled, "Fired up! Ready to go!" The pauses between and after these two phrases prepared the crowd to join him in a call-and-return chant, "Fired up!" (*Fired up!*) " Ready to go!" (*Ready to go!*). His cadence brought to mind a drill sergeant's marching call: Fired up! (1-2) Ready to go! (3-4). With the second and third repetitions, the crowd was answering back in full voice, and about half of the assembled bolted to their feet—middle-aged men in suits and ties, Sunday-dressed women wearing hats as ornate as wedding cakes, a few young guys in cornrows and sunglasses. "Fired up! (*Fired up!*) Ready to go! (*Ready to go!*) Fired up! (*Fired up!*) Ready to go! (*Ready to go!*)."

It's likely that most Americans, were they to witness this scene—in this high school auditorium in Conway, South Carolina, on this January Saturday, sixteen days before the nation's first black president is to be sworn in for a second term—would hear *Fired up! Ready to go!* and assume it was a reference to Barack Obama's first presidential campaign. But for this crowd, *Fired up! Ready to go!* has a much longer history, one that stretches at least as far back as 1989. And when blacks in Conway say *1989*, everybody around here knows what it means. It means the 1989 Conway High School football boycott, when thirty-one of the team's thirty-seven black players, for whom Rev. H. H. Singleton was a spokesman, walked away from the squad as a demonstration against Coach Chuck Jordan's decision to start an inexperienced white kid at quarterback over an experienced black kid, a move that many of the players and community members perceived as racist. Soon, the Conway football boycott became the Conway *Movement*, transcending high school sports and growing into a protest against societal injustice, socioeconomic inequality, and the kind of institutional prejudice that many of Conway's white citizens had long assumed was over and done, had it ever existed in the first place.

Fired Up! Ready to Go! is a nifty campaign slogan, but the militaristic rhythm of the chant—*Fired up* (1-2), *Ready to go* (3-4)—is made for marching. And in 1989, with H. H. Singleton leading the way, marching is just what Conway's black population did. In conjunction with the state and national offices of the NAACP, Singleton organized marches through Conway and neighboring Myrtle Beach, including several down Church Street, Conway's main drag, the road the high school sat on then, as it does now. One stormy Saturday, Singleton walked arm-in-arm with fellow civil rights leaders, undaunted by lightning and rain or by the members of Conway's white population who stood at the curb throwing middle fingers. With many of the folks who are in attendance today, plus over a thousand more, following behind him, Singleton called out, "Fired up! (*Fired up!*) Ready to go! (*Ready to go!*)."

Here in the Conway High auditorium, with another speaker now leading the mourners in Singleton's familiar call-and-response, the chant is on, just as it was in 1989. Back then, *Fired up! Ready to go!* echoed through town in marches, meetings, and picket lines. Today, it evokes the moment when many blacks in Conway decided they'd been silent and compliant for too long. They chant to remember a time when they challenged the white establishment and stood up for justice, a time when the national media took notice and spread word of the Conway Movement across America. Even though twenty-three years have come and gone since the football boycott that sparked the movement, and even though H. H. Singleton has passed away at the age of eighty and is no longer here to chant with them, and even though a black man is two weeks from starting his second term in the Oval Office, everybody's still fired up. They're still ready to go. The chant seems to carry past the back row of the auditorium, through the double doors, and out into the hallways, where it rattles the Master Locks against the lockers.

Today's "Homegoing Ceremony" for H. H. Singleton features a twelve-person lineup of speakers that includes clergymen and -women, community activists, and NAACP leaders. Nearly everyone speaks about Singleton's bedrock conviction to do the right thing, not the popular or the easy thing. They speak about his willingness to galvanize the black community against the white establishment despite what it might cost him personally. They hail him as a titanic figure, both in stature and reputation, who led Conway's blacks to hard-fought wins against that establishment. In addition to the spoken tributes, letters from regional and national dignitaries are read, including one from Reverend Jesse Jackson of the Rainbow/PUSH Coalition and one from Benjamin Todd Jealous, the current president of the NAACP. Politics and social justice are the focus of all of these speeches and letters, not the football boycott, and only one of the twelve speakers specifically refers to any of the striking players. Winifred Anderson, a representative of the local branch of the NAACP, tells the crowd, "When I heard the news [of Singleton's death], I called Carlos Hunt, and all he could say was, 'My God. My God.'" Outside of Conway, Hunt's name would be known to very few, but no one in the auditorium today needs to be reminded who Carlos Hunt is.

As everyone here knows, Carlos Hunt was once the starting quarterback for the Conway Tigers. In 1988, his junior year, he led the team to an 8–4 record. The season ended in disappointment, with the Tigers losing in the first round of the playoffs, but with several standout players returning, including Hunt and defensive end Lawrence Mitchell, whom recruiting services were calling one of the top three college prospects in the country at any position, the team was considered a contender for the '89 state title in the top level of South Carolina high school football: the Big 16 Division of Class 4A. Expectations were high that the Tigers would finally, for the first time since the school started playing football in 1923, bring a state title home to Conway. Carlos Hunt had every reason to believe his senior season would be legendary—for him and for his hometown. But a few weeks before spring practice began, Chuck Jordan told Carlos he was moving him to defensive back, while elevating Mickey Wilson, a white kid and son of assistant coach Mickey Wilson Sr., to the starting quarterback position. Later, during preseason practice, after it had become clear that Jordan was sticking with his decision to start the white junior over the black senior, Carlos, Lawrence Mitchell, and twenty-nine more of the team's thirty-seven black players (fifteen of them starters), walked away from their coach, Chuck Jordan, and toward their spokesman, H. H. Singleton. Twenty-three years later, Carlos Hunt has indeed become a legend, at least in the black community, but surely not in the way he originally planned.

Here at the Homegoing Ceremony, no one specifically mentions Hunt's position switch or the walkout that resulted. Nobody needs to retell the story of the boycott any more than they'd need to rehash Noah and the ark. Everybody here knows what happened in that magical year of 1989. And they remember it as the time when their voices could no longer be ignored.

As it turns out, the chanting resonated longer than even they might have expected. When Barack Obama tells the story of his adoption of the *Fired up! Ready to go!* slogan, he mentions that he first heard it at a campaign stop in Greenwood, South Carolina, when a supporter named Edith S. Childs began chanting it from within the crowd. Today at Conway High School, the Rev. Dr. Nelson Rivers III, a vice president in the national NAACP office, reminds the assembled that, yes, Barack Obama borrowed the chant from

Edith S. Childs—but Edith S. Childs, he says, borrowed it from the Conway Movement, and the lion of that movement was Reverend H. H. Singleton.

"The lion sleeps tonight," Rivers says, gesturing toward Singleton's casket, "and the jungle is safer because the lion king did walk, talk, and roar." More *Uh-huhs* and *Tell its* from the audience. "And when the lion roars," Rivers says, "even the elephants have to back down."

Chuck Jordan's office sits around the corner and down a hallway from the auditorium. It's a Wednesday morning in December, exactly one month before H. H. Singleton's Homegoing Ceremony, and in the athletic department's spotless lobby, *SportsCenter* plays on a wall-mounted flat screen that's positioned in front of two leatherette couches, where visitors are invited to make themselves comfortable while they wait to see the head football coach and athletic director for the Conway Tigers. On any given school day, Jordan receives a long slate of visitors: students, players, ex-players, sports reporters, college recruiters, some with an appointment, some not—hence the couches and the television. When ESPN goes to commercial, the visiting eye wanders to the stuffed tiger crouched in one corner of the lobby, or to the other corner, where a bookshelf is lined with scrapbooks assembled by Jordan's mother-in-law, documenting the thirty seasons he's led Conway boys onto the field.

Walk into Jordan's inner office, and you face a cinderblock wall upon which thirty framed team photos are hung, arranged in chronological order, starting with 1983. The uniforms and haircuts vary as the years progress (both the pads and the hairstyles become more streamlined), but the teenage-tough facial expressions do not change. Neither does the man standing in the head coach's spot.

And here he is in person: Chuck Jordan, offering a handshake and then settling behind his desk, ready to field questions about the season that ended a few weeks earlier. He answers in a Carolina drawl, bending "think" into "thank" and pronouncing "going" so that it sometimes comes out as "gonna" but more often sounds like "gone," as in: "I never lined up in a game I didn't thank we were gone win." Between questions, he sips one of the five cups of coffee he drinks every day. "Good for your prostate," he says. And when he's talking football, he's much more cheerful than you'd expect if you only knew him as the serious man pacing the sidelines. In his office he's less like the Chuck Jordan pictured in the team photos and more like the Chuck Jordan who stars in the TV commercials for Conway Ford, in which he's standing inside one of those money-grab booths, dollar bills hurricaning all around him as he says to the camera, "Trust me. This is fun!"

A trim fifty-five, there's no gut ballooning under his tucked-in polo; and maybe it's the caffeine, but as Jordan rehashes this year's heartbreaks and triumphs, he shows none of the weariness you'd expect from a veteran coach who's just taken his team through a fourteen-week season. And the coaching didn't start with game one, either; it started in the summer, with ten days of two-a-day practices, followed by the Fellowship of Christian Athletes Camp and the county football jamboree. Then again, the coaching really started in June and July, with the seven-on-seven passing league; or back in the spring, with the early morning practices; or even earlier than that, way back in the winter, with the weight room sessions. Which means, of course, that the coaching from *last* season never really stopped. Every year bleeds into the next. This never-ending schedule is especially demanding given that, in addition to working with the players and assistant coaches, he's got to mediate the expectations of the fans, defuse the parents who are upset because their sons aren't getting enough playing time, and make nice with the Solid Gold All Sports Booster Club, whose members give his athletic budget a monetary shot in the arm. Not that you'd ever hear Coach Jordan gripe about his job, other than to say, and only when asked, "It's all a management issue."

Coaching sixty teenagers is a challenge, sure, but that's the fun part, the part that feeds his competitive nature. The real "management issue" that Jordan refers to is his role as athletic director, which requires him to track down permission slips and birth certificates, file documentation of medical exams, and monitor transfer status and academic eligibility for every player on all sixteen of Conway's varsity and JV teams, from girls' soccer to boys' golf. In order to do this, he maintains an athlete database of 1,041 students, from the seventh up to the twelfth grade. And when you consider that Jordan has been Conway High's football coach and A.D. not for five or ten years but for *thirty*—and still has the energy of a man half his age—you might do well to have a cup of whatever he's drinking.

As the coach talks and shares stories, he's framed by the large window behind him. Outside, the sun lights up the school parking lot and baseball diamond, and beyond those, the new football field, which is technically called the E. Craig Wall Jr. Memorial Stadium, in honor of a successful alumnus, but is almost always referred to as the Backyard. This nickname is meant to distinguish the new stadium from the old one, the Graveyard, which was on the campus of Coastal Carolina University, five miles southeast of here, across Highway 544 from Hillcrest Cemetery. The Tigers played their home games at the Graveyard for thirty-five years, before moving into their new digs here at the high school. A Conway native and captain of the

CHS football team in 1974, Jordan came home to Conway in 1983, when he was twenty-six years old, accepting a job as a math teacher, head coach, and athletic director. His first team went a disappointing 5–5, and the young coach immediately heard grumbling around town that he wasn't up to the task. He wondered if the Graveyard would be the site of his own demise. At the end of the year, Jordan went to his boss, the school principal, to ask if he should be worried about the tepid fan reaction. The principal gave Jordan a vote of confidence. "If you really want to hear complaining," he said, "just wait 'til you start winning."

The wait, it turned out, was a short one. Jordan's Tigers won ten games the next year, and ten the following year, and ten the year after that: thirty games in three seasons, the kind of success Conway fans felt they deserved but had never seen. Tiger games were some of the biggest and best-attended events in town. But without a state championship to show for it, the talk inside Oliver's Luncheonette and Donzelle's Restaurant was that, yeah, the new coach was good, but was he good enough to win it all?

Jordan commiserated with John McKissick, head man at rival Summerville High, who in 2012 would become the first coach at any level of football—high school, college, or pro—to notch six hundred career wins. McKissick told Jordan that he could choose to live and work in a town where people don't care about football, and he'd never hear any complaining. Or he could coach in a place like Conway, where folks will complain win or lose. "And I've chosen to be in a community where they care," Jordan says. "So I know every now and then I'm gone *get* it."

But a coach doesn't survive thirty years on the job without doing a whole bunch of the *gettin'* himself. On the shelf above Jordan's office window, five commemorative footballs are lined up nose-to-tail, each one memorializing a game when Jordan sent the Conway crowd home happy. There's a ball for Jordan's first win in 1983. One marking a big upset of McKissick's Summerville team in 1992. One for Jordan's 100th career win, another for his 200th win. And then there's the ball from 1989 that reads, *Only Win*. Any visitor wondering what the heck went wrong in '89 and why the coach might display a memorial to a one-win season need only look over at the team photograph for that year. In that photo, unlike every other picture from every other season, almost all of the players are white.

In the spring of '89, Coach Jordan called Carlos Hunt into this same office to tell him that he'd be switching from quarterback to free safety. Mickey Wilson would be taking over the reins behind center. Although Hunt had played well the previous year, Jordan considered his freewheeling style to be at odds with the coach's disciplined offensive philosophy. Jordan pointed to a few instances that year where Hunt decided to run the ball himself rather than hand it off as the play calls were designed. One of those improvisations resulted in Carlos scoring a touchdown, but others lost yardage, and either way, the quarterback's refusal to just run the dang plays as they were called infuriated Jordan and cemented his belief that his quarterback was a showboat rather than the kind of trustworthy, extension-of-the-coach that Jordan expected his signal callers to be. Mickey Wilson, who is a coach's son, seemed to Jordan the more reliable and consistent option at a position that demanded reliability and consistency. To Jordan, the decision to move Hunt to defensive back had nothing to do with race; it was a question of assessing the talent of his players and then putting the right kid in the right position, solely in an effort to give the team the best chance to win. Which is to say it was a management issue, and it struck at the heart of what it meant to be the head coach. Because if there's one thing that a coach—any head coach in any team sport—needs the absolute autonomy to do, it's deciding who plays where. As Jordan says now, he wouldn't bench a black kid for being black any more than he would *play* a white kid just because that kid was, for instance, the son of a wealthy booster. "Bankers and lawyers want their kids to play, too," Jordan says. And when it comes to personnel decisions: "Hey, sometimes you get it wrong, but that's the job."

A few days before the first game of the '89 season, Carlos Hunt and Lawrence Mitchell—the stud-recruit who was being courted by Penn State, Notre Dame, South Carolina, Clemson, and many more big-time colleges— went to H. H. Singleton for guidance. Shortly thereafter, the players formed the Committee on the Concerns of Conway High School's Black Football Players, Singleton was speaking on behalf of the black players at a press conference, and the boycott was on. When the Tigers lined up in that first game, it was with thirty-one fewer varsity players than Jordan had anticipated, and he had to patch the holes left by fifteen striking starters. The protest quickly moved beyond football, spreading out to the larger community and to issues that transcended the quarterback controversy. Despite the picketing and the marches, despite the arrival of the national press, and despite a call from Governor Carroll Campbell, who Jordan says asked him to find a way to settle the strike, the coach refused to reconsider his decision to move Carlos to defense. "Governor," he said, "there are some things you just can't compromise on."

Reflecting on those days, Jordan says the hardest thing was being branded as a racist from both sides. He says he would walk the halls of Conway High and black kids would spit on him and call him, in words he takes pains to cleanse now, "You S.O.B.! You G.D. idiot!" It was equally upsetting when the white community hailed him as a hero and when white parents gave him credit for replacing a black quarterback with a white one. "Until I didn't play their white kid," the coach says. "Then they'd go to the booster club and try to get me fired." From Jordan's perspective, switching Hunt to defense was and remains a football decision, plain and simple. "Carlos was bright," he says, assessing the skills of his 1989 quarterbacks. "By appearances, he was the better quarterback. But Mickey was a leader."

For evidence of the 1989 starter's leadership ability, you need only look seventeen miles toward the shore, to Myrtle Beach High School, Conway's traditional rival, where Mickey Wilson has served as head coach since 2009. For some folks in Conway, being forced to watch Mickey (their guy, their *Mickey*, pride of '89) standing on the Seahawk sideline is a tough betrayal to stomach. Mickey, after all, still lives in Conway. Tiger fans run into him at the Food Lion and at the hibachi joint. But even more painful than Mickey coaching for Myrtle Beach is the *success* he's had there, particularly against Conway, with three wins and only one loss in his first four years as head coach. Most painful of all, maybe, is that Mickey, in just his second year at Myrtle Beach, accomplished what Chuck Jordan hasn't been able to do in thirty years at Conway: win that daggum state championship. Still, some Tiger fans will tell you that Mickey Wilson was no more responsible for the Seahawks' 2010 state championship than Mickey Mouse was. Coach Wilson, they'll say, was supremely lucky in that he inherited a once-in-a-generation quarterback, Everett Golson.

One month from now, Golson will start for Notre Dame as a redshirt freshman in the BCS National Championship game against Alabama. In his four years at Myrtle Beach he quarterbacked the Seahawks to the state title game in '08, '09, and '10, winning two out of three and giving Mickey Wilson more championship hardware than the man who'd once made the controversial decision to name *him* as the starter. In Conway these days, even if some Tiger fans will say that Mickey got a gift from God the day Everett Golson walked into Myrtle Beach High School and without divine generosity Mickey can't coach a lick compared to ol' Chuck, others will whisper that maybe Jordan has passed his prime, and they'll wonder what it might take to convince Mickey to come home to Conway, to take his rightful spot in the very office where Jordan still sits after thirty years.

Here in that office, Jordan is talking about football fans and their expectations versus their knowledge of the game. He's explaining how one thing that makes football unique from every other sport is the huddle. In basketball, for example, the players are running up and down the court and the coaches aren't really making any decisions. They may call a timeout and give some specific instructions from time to time, but for the most part, basketball coaches watch as their players decide what to do with the ball. "But in football," he says, "we get in that huddle, and them people in the stands are going, *What's this idiot gone do now? I tell you what I'd do. I'd run the ball.* So we run the ball and we get ten, and they say, *I told you.* We get stuffed, and they go, *That knucklehead shoulda thrown it.* That's what endears people to football. They're able to get involved on whatever level they can figure out."

What Coach Jordan doesn't say, but appears to suggest, is that some people, people who don't know much about how the game is played, are stuck on a level where the only thing they can see is whether a kid is black or white. Jordan says the only thing he sees is whether or not that kid is a football player.

"Singleton thought he was doing right," Jordan says, but it's clear the coach doesn't understand how keeping a football player off the field could ever be right, especially considering what it cost some of those boycotting players: playing time, practice time, tutoring time, SAT-prep time, and the chance to impress college recruiters. They risked being labeled not just undisciplined but *uppity.* They were fired up and ready to go, but not on the field of play, where they belonged. That's what still stings Jordan about the '89 season: Carlos Hunt, Lawrence Mitchell, and the twenty-nine others who boycotted that year weren't black kids; they were Conway Tigers. And they spent all that time in meetings and on marches—instead of huddled up with their teammates, arm in arm, playing the game they loved.

Then again, if Carlos Hunt were standing here in his old coach's office, staring hard at the photograph of the team he walked away from, he might say the same thing that Chuck Jordan told the governor all those years ago: "There are some things you just can't compromise on."

- 2 -

BITING THE HAND

NOW

ON THE CLOVER-PATCHED FIELD OUT BACK OF THE HIGH SCHOOL, SIXTY-ODD football players and a dozen more hopefuls are readying themselves for practice. Some do wind sprints; some grab their cleats in a hamstring stretch; others hop on their toes to the beat of Guns N' Roses' "Welcome to the Jungle," a song that was released in 1987, six years before even the oldest of these teenagers was born. Organized drills won't officially start until 3:45 p.m., five minutes from now, when the digital countdown clock that is mounted to a tower along the sideline hits 0:00, but the players are already scattered about the grass, doing their individual warm-up routines, helmets on, mouth guards (mostly) in. The assistant coaches gather at midfield, looking serious, shooting an occasional point or a *what's up* nod. The athletic trainer watches from a golf cart. A few parents sit in a set of bleachers that has been placed in the shade of an oak tree. They're all here: players, position coaches, support staff—everybody but Head Coach Chuck Jordan, who is presumably still in the fieldhouse, working through his own pre-practice ritual.

The countdown clock dips under four minutes, and gradually—without having been told to do so, automatic as protons and neutrons—the team rallies in the north end zone, forming columns that run perpendicular to the goal line, everybody ready to move at the chirp of a whistle. Teammates smack each other on the helmet, and the player-hive starts buzzing—not with talk but with energy, with exaltation. "Welcome to the Jungle" is blasting through the P.A. and bouncing off the adjacent school building loud enough to make conversation impossible anyway. Nobody here minds. This ain't the place or time for conversation. This is Conway, South Carolina. This is Conway High School. Home of the Tigers. And this is day one of spring ball.

The heartbreaking loss to Myrtle Beach, the H. H. Singleton Homegoing Ceremony—all of that is still months away. There is no sadness in Conway, not today. It's the first of May, and the sign at the Church Street branch of the Conway National Bank reads 83 degrees, but here at the school, in the afternoon sun, those 83 degrees are playing more like 103. Stand in the same place for too long in the parking lot, and it feels like the soles of your shoes will melt into the blacktop. Luckily the players aren't dressed out in full uniform, just jerseys and shorts. No pads, which means no contact. But one look at the team—lined up in the end zone, bouncing on the balls of their feet as the clock drops toward zero—and it's clear that everybody's itching to lay a hit on somebody. The last time the Tigers were together on a football field was back in November, when they suffered a disappointing loss to Goose Creek Stratford in the first round of the 4A playoffs, disappointing because Conway is a program that has come to expect deep runs in the state tournament, having reached the championship game four times in the last eleven years. From here on the practice field, anybody with decent vision can read the sign on the stadium scoreboard that commemorates those near misses: *AAAA Football, Div. II State Runner-Up, 2001, 2002, 2003, 2006.* Add the Tigers' championship-game expectations to the fact that last year's squad was led by the wildly talented junior quarterback Mykal Moody, a three-year starter who rushed and passed for a combined 3,009 yards, and that team's 8–4 record was a letdown, the exact kind of letdown that'll get players chomping at their mouth guards for *next* season, which, as the clock hits 0:03, 0:02, 0:01, starts right now.

Strength and Conditioning Coach Stephen Burris blows his whistle, and the first players in line high-step down the field. Burris whistles for the next group, then the next, until the whole team is spread across the grass, five yards apart in all directions, in lines as straight as the rows of tobacco that grow just a few miles outside town.

Coach Jordan, having materialized seemingly from nowhere and cradling a football in his arms, cuts through the grid of his stretching Tigers. Sun-safe in a Panama hat and long-sleeved shirt, he stops from time to time to guide a player deeper into a stretch. Under the brim of that hat, his facial expression can change in an instant from all business to sweetness-and-light and back again to business. But right now the coach is smiling, because he's just looked over to the sideline and seen that standing among the half-dozen or so ex-players who have showed up today is Junior Hemingway, a wide receiver who, after graduating from Conway in 2007, went off to the University of Michigan, where, during his senior season, he was the team's leading receiver, earned All Big Ten Honorable Mention honors, and was the MVP in the Wolverines' Sugar Bowl win against Virginia Tech. Perhaps most impressively—especially to the current Tigers, all of whom surely recognize the dreadlocked Hemingway, even if they appear too cool, focused, or intimidated to acknowledge him—is that last Saturday, just three days ago, the Conway legend was picked up by the Kansas City Chiefs in the seventh round of the NFL draft. But instead of spending today celebrating in Kansas City or on some Caribbean island, Hemingway is back home for this annual rite of spring.

Jordan hustles over to Hemingway and puts his arm around him, and for a few seconds they watch the 2012 Tigers together. Hemingway's presence is a reminder to these kids, who don't need much convincing anyway, that the dream is doable. The college scholarship, the bowl wins, the NFL contract—all of it. And this field out back of the high school is where the dream starts.

If you've ever spent any time in Conway, South Carolina, it's probably because you were stuck in traffic here, on U.S. 501, on your way to the beach. Conway is the seat of Horry County (which can be pronounced "Oh-REE" as the natives do or "ORR-ee" as newcomers say it, but never with an H sound at the beginning), the same county that claims Myrtle Beach and approximately two thirds of the sixty-mile stretch of sand known as the Grand Strand. Fourteen million people a year visit the Myrtle Beach area. With no interstate serving the region, a good many of those fourteen million arrive at the coast via Conway, driving right past the school where Chuck Jordan's Tigers roam.

Traffic on 501, or Church Street as it's called within the city limits, can be stop-and-go for seventeen miles or more on a summer Saturday, from the ocean all the way back to Conway High. So if you've ever crawled bumper-to-bumper through Conway, you got a long look at Church Street. And going solely by what you saw on the town's main commercial thoroughfare—the standard strip of Walmart, Applebee's, and McDonalds; a few Southern-based chains like Zaxby's, Chick-Fil-A, and Fatz; the businesses specifically targeting vacationers: Cheap Charlie's Fireworks and Ole Peddlers Sea Shells and Gifts; plus a few title loan joints and pawn shops—you might assume that the Horry County seat is an ugly, impoverished, hick town that leaves zoning pretty much to chance and is best left in the rearview, forgotten except as an excuse to bitch about how bad the traffic was on your drive to the beach.

But you'd be wrong. Take a left turn into Conway's historic district and you'll find the kind of quaint Southern town that a word like *picturesque* was coined to describe, a town of 18,688 that's every bit as charming as Church Street is charmless. First you'll notice the trees: the pine and palmetto, the cypress and myrtle. And the ubiquitous live oaks, whose long branches, hanging with Spanish moss, cantilever out at impossible horizontality. These oaks are so old, and their root and branch systems so complex, that several streets have been paved *around* them. In Conway, the oaks have the right-of-way. Here at the high school, on the day the town's beloved Tigers are running through their first spring practice, the air smells like pine and clover, but across 501, in the historic district, the yards are blossoming with honeysuckle, wisteria, and confederate jasmine. The southern magnolias are just starting to flower big and white, and all this blooming combines to make the neighborhoods near downtown as fragrant as a duty-free shop. Although the houses in the historic district aren't as old or stately as the antebellum beauties ninety miles down the coast in Charleston, some of them date back to the late 1800s, and many of them are impressive in their own right. Folks pay a premium to live here, within walking distance of downtown, which, unlike the central business districts of so many small towns, is thriving. Sure, there are a few empty storefronts, but there are also more and better restaurants, shops, and boutiques than many towns this size can support.

Conway's most salient feature, indeed, the very reason the area was first settled in 1730, is the Waccamaw, a blackwater river that winds through downtown and continues ambling south toward the city of Georgetown, where it empties into Winyah Bay and the Atlantic. Just north of Georgetown is the Waccamaw Neck, a thin strip of land between the river and the ocean that was once lined with the rice plantations that made Georgetown County one of the most prosperous counties in the antebellum United States. The Neck, a mere two miles wide, is the only place where Horry dirt directly touches that of another South Carolina county. Rivers demark the remaining county lines, separating Horry from the rest of the state. This geographical isolation and the fact that the Horry terrain wasn't suitable for rice production or cotton cultivation, thus divorcing the county economically and culturally from the wealthier Georgetown and Charleston Counties, gave rise to the nickname that is still embossed on the Horry County seal, which you'll find affixed to the government buildings in downtown Conway: *The Independent Republic*. Conway was never notable for grand plantations; instead, its genealogy traces back to the yeoman farmers and timbermen who drifted down from North Carolina rather than up from Charleston. It has been said that the stages of Horry County's economic history can be summed up with the four T's: timber, turpentine, tobacco, and tourism. But ever since 1923, the year that Conway High School first fielded a football team, folks in the county seat have pinned their fortunes to the wins and losses of a fifth T: *Tigers*.

• • •

Here at the high school, the clock again hits zero, indicating that it's time to move to another practice segment, and after a series of whistle chirps that are nearly inaudible over Usher's "Oh my Gosh," which is now pumping from the P.A., the players break down by position into smaller coaching groups. The linemen, offensive and defensive, take to the blocking sleds in the south end zone, in the shade of a bank of tall pines. The running backs move through a footwork drill at midfield. The defensive backs and linebackers do a similar-looking drill, but they do it backwards. The upperclassmen run their exercises with the confidence that comes from having already earned a numbered jersey: green shirts for the offense, gold for the defense. The younger guys who haven't yet made the team move with less certainty. They're wearing white shirts and dazed expressions. Roughly half the players are white, half black. The black guys are generally quicker to smile, and many of them, the receivers and backs especially, move with the languid indifference that is the hallmark of speed and athleticism. Most of the white guys, including Chuck Jordan's own son, Sawyer—a senior who starts at receiver and punter and is listed as the third-string quarterback— look like gutsy scrappers.

Coach Jordan, as is his custom, is working with the QBs and receivers, who are winding through a passing drill to the beat of Technotronic's "Pump Up the Jam." Back in the early '80s, when Jordan took the Conway job, folks nicknamed his conservative, run-based offense "Ground Chuck." But now, blessed with returning senior Mykal Moody, who is a gifted runner and passer, the offense is wide open. Less "Ground Chuck," more "Air Jordan."

Coach Jordan simulates the snap by pitching the ball to Mykal, who fires it downfield to his favorite target, 6'2" senior Malcolm Green, who catches the pass cleanly. But something in the play has not met Jordan muster.

"Malcolm!" he yells, as the receiver jogs back to the line of scrimmage. "I'm gone knot-up your head!"

Green stops running and stands next to his coach, waiting to hear what he did wrong.

"You know what I saw on film?" Jordan says. "You keep fading inside. Keep that route *straight*."

"Yes, sir," Green says, not like a military man, but like a polite Southern kid.

Then the coach smiles and gives Green a love-smack on the helmet. "And get your daggum mouthpiece in."

Green flips the ball to Jordan and jogs over to his teammates.

As the passing drill continues, it's clear that Jordan enjoys working with his kids. You can tell by the way he drapes an arm around a player or puts a steadying hand on a shoulder or engages in a playful shadowbox. You can tell by the way he calls Mykal Moody "Mike" or "Mikey" when he's happy with his quarterback and "Moody" when he's not, as in, "Dadgummit, Moody. We cannot put the ball on the ground, you knucklehead. We *cannot win* with the ball on the ground." You can tell by the smack on the helmet he gives his players after they make a nice play ("That ain't bad, 1-3. That. Ain't. Bad.") and by the other, slightly more forceful smack he gives them after they mess a play up ("Catch the daggum ball, Malcolm. You're sticking one hand in there!"). On a practice field, Chuck Jordan is a man in his element.

The clock hits zero yet again, "Pump Up the Jam" fades out, and Jordan has the whole team gathered around him at midfield, all the players down on one knee. He starts talking to them about Genesis 1:27, about how God created them in his own image—but also created them to be men. "And what's most important to me," he says, "even more than winning football games, is helping you *become* men." It's now quiet enough that you can hear frogs croaking from back in the woods. "What does our society say a man is? Money? Power and fame? How many sexual conquests did you have? Shoot, that's not being a man."

Jordan takes off his hat, fans himself with it. "Let me tell you something that's gonna last you your whole life. When it's all said and done, what kind of *brother* were you? What kind of *son*? What kind of *husband*? What kind of *father*? That's what defines you as a man. Those *relationships*."

A few players nod, but most look down at their cleats. Sweat is dripping from everybody's face.

"Let me ask you three questions," Jordan says. "Don't answer out loud; don't raise your hands. Just answer in your head. One. How many of you have a father at home?"

Several players raise their hands.

"No," Jordan says. "No hands. I said answer in your head." He puts the hat back on and continues. "Two. How many of you *wish* you had a father at home? Three. Who do you look to as a father figure? Who is your role model for how to be a man?"

It's impossible to know for how many of these players the answer to that last question is *Coach Chuck Jordan*. But what is certain is that for thirty years, Jordan has happily taken on the role of father figure for Conway boys. With all his helmet-smacking and knucklehead-ing and arm-draping, Jordan is exhibiting an obvious fatherly affection. And his players' responses to that affection, their *yes, sirs* and their rapt attention to his Genesis 1:27 spiel, seem to indicate that most of them respect and admire Coach Jordan as something like a father figure. It should be said that Junior Hemingway is black, as are the majority of ex-players who have come today to observe practice. Mykal Moody, Malcolm Green, and at least half of the current Tigers are black. Jordan has always taken pride in the fact that, be they white or black, he "feeds all [his] boys from the same spoon," as he told reporters back in 1989. Which is why the events of that year felt, and still feel, like such a betrayal. And if you listen closely, in the air over the practice field, bouncing between the school building and the pine trees, you can almost hear the last echoes of "Pump Up the Jam," a song that hit the charts in 1989, the same year that thirty-one of Jordan's kids looked not to their coach as the model for how to be a man, but to the pastor of Cherry Hill Baptist.

THEN

The '88–'89 Conway High School yearbook, the *Mirror*, features a picture of Carlos Hunt on the basketball court, playing alongside fellow Tiger Mickey Wilson. The snapshot captures Carlos, the black shooting guard, standing just outside the lane in "triple threat" position, meaning the ball is in his hands and he can choose to shoot, dribble, or pass. The only other Conway player visible in the photo is Mickey, the white point guard. Frozen by the camera in that critical moment of choice, the Carlos Hunt in that picture forever controls the ball. And true to Coach Jordan's comments on the difference between football and basketball, the choice is entirely his to make. Looking now at that photograph of these two teammates, you can almost hear the clichéd movie voiceover: "It was the calm before the racial storm" or "Nobody knew it yet, but the trouble was already brewing."

Just as today's Tigers—coming off an 8–4 season, led by a talented senior quarterback in Mykal Moody—are entering spring with state championship hopes, so too was Jordan's 1989 squad. That team had also finished 8–4 the previous year, and although they, like the current Tigers, had made a first-round exit from the playoffs, optimism abounded for the new season, at least partially because one of their eight wins had come against perennial power Summerville. Led by the legendary John McKissick—who boasts more wins than any coach at any level of football—the Summerville Green Wave had won the South Carolina 4A State Championship in '78, '79, '82, '83, '84, and '86. Conway had played Summerville three times since 1983, the year Chuck Jordan became coach, and the Tigers had lost all three, by a combined score of 48–7. But in 1988, the Tigers finally took the Green Wave to the woodshed, beating them 27–14 on Summerville's turf, a win that resonated through the off-season and into the start of spring practice.

The Conway team that suited up that spring of '89 was senior-laden, but they were largely an inexperienced bunch, having lost most of the starters from the previous year to graduation. Of the twenty-two players who'd started in 1988, only eight would be returning for 1989—six on defense and two on offense. The good news for Tiger fans was that one of those eight returnees was Lawrence Mitchell, a 6'6", 220-pound blue-chip defensive end who was All-State in both football and basketball. Chuck Jordan has called Lawrence "the best athlete I've ever coached." Mitchell could run a half-mile in just over two minutes, and later that summer of '89, at the Five-Star Basketball Camp in Radford, Virginia, he'd score 42 points in twenty-five minutes of play, shattering the scoring record at a camp that had over the years hosted Moses Malone, Patrick Ewing, and Isiah Thomas. But football was Lawrence's first love, and one recruiting tip sheet, the National Prep Poll, ranked him as the #3 college prospect nationally, at any position.

If Lawrence Mitchell would anchor the defense, it seemed certain that the offense would be led by Carlos Hunt, the 6'3", 175-pound senior who had quarterbacked the Tigers to those eight wins in 1988. His junior-year numbers didn't leap off the stat sheet, but they were good enough to get people excited about another season with Carlos at QB. In 1988 he completed 37 of 92 passes, which makes for a completion rate of only 40 percent. But the 605 yards he notched on those 37 completions amounts to a per-completion average of over sixteen yards—almost five yards per catch better than Joe Montana's lifetime NFL average and higher than the average for any single year in Montana's career as a starting quarterback, pro or college. And Carlos's six hundred passing yards had come on a Chuck Jordan–coached team whose offensive scheme was still being called "Ground Chuck." He averaged less than eight pass attempts per game in 1988, which was just how Jordan had designed the offense to move, almost entirely under leg power—three yards in each cloud of Carolina dust. But in Jordan's pro-set formation, Carlos didn't do much of the ball-carrying. Most of the plays required him to hand the ball off to the fullback or halfback, and in his junior year, Hunt averaged less than six carries per game, including sacks and broken plays. So Carlos didn't pass the ball very often, and he didn't run it much either. What he had done as a junior was steer the offense to wins, including that big win against Summerville. And that's ultimately what coaches ask of their quarterbacks: Don't impress me in the stat sheet; impress me on the scoreboard.

In Conway's black community, Carlos had already assumed a significance that far outweighed his statistics or his win-loss record. The quarterback position—as with all positions of leadership, in and out of sports—is important for reasons that transcend the practical duties of the job. There is more to quarterbacking than the *physical* acts of passing and running. There is also more to quarterbacking than the *cerebral* tasks of reading defenses, assessing their weaknesses, and positioning the offense to best exploit those weaknesses. Much of what makes the quarterback role so meaningful is *symbolic*. Be it a sports team, a corporation, or a nation, any organization's choice of leader reveals much about who makes up that organization and what those members value. So on the football field, no player holds more symbolic significance (or is more highly scrutinized) than the quarterback, who not only leads the offense, but is almost always seen synecdochially as the one piece of the team that represents the whole. But even after it became commonplace in America for blacks and whites to compete in the same leagues and on the same teams, racial prejudice fueled the conventional wisdom that although black players could be blessed with the athleticism to excel physically, they didn't have the mental capacity to excel cerebrally. In football, this view translated to a belief within the dominant (read: white) culture that black players could play (and star) in the "skill" positions like running back, wide receiver, and defensive back but couldn't handle the demands of a position like quarterback, a role that required intellectual gifts and, as the face of the team, a *white* face.

In 1989, 42 percent of Conway's 9,819 citizens were black, and a good many of those black Conwayites spent their Friday nights in the bleachers, cheering on the Tigers. These fans, like black football fans nationally, had spent years frustrated by the fact that all too often a black kid lost out on the quarterback position to a white kid who appeared to have won the job because of his skin color rather than his play on the field. According to Hank Singleton III, H. H. Singleton's youngest son, any black Tiger fan in 1989 could spit out names of white quarterbacks at Conway—he mentions Ward Gatlin, Dirk Derrick, and Rick Smith—who had in the '70s and '80s won the job over seemingly more gifted black quarterbacks.

With the arrival of Chuck Jordan as head coach, however, the pattern of the black kid being overlooked for the white kid was broken. In 1983, halfway through Jordan's first season, he benched Robbie Squatriglia, a white quarterback, and elevated Lavern Reddick, a black player, to the starting position. It was the first time in sixty years of Conway High School football that a black kid was seeing significant time at quarterback, and Jordan says he "caught the devil" from the white community, with folks calling him "nigger lover." Despite the heat from some Tiger fans, and despite a 5–5 record in 1983, Jordan named Reddick the starter the following season, and that year the Tigers won ten games for the first time in school history. Going into the 1989 season, with Carlos Hunt having led the Tigers in 1988, Chuck Jordan had started a black quarterback in three of his six seasons as coach. Combine that fact with the success of Doug Williams—who in 1988 led the NFL's Washington Redskins to the Super Bowl Championship, becoming the first black quarterback to both play in and win a Super Bowl—and by the late '80s, it seemed to Conway's black community that maybe football coaches were starting to recognize that whiteness wasn't a requirement for the QB job after all.

In Doug Williams, Lavern Reddick, and Carlos Hunt, black Tiger fans saw quarterbacks who looked like them, but more importantly these quarterbacks who looked like them *won football games*. And as spring 1989 neared, Conway's black community brimmed with just as much hope for the Tigers as did the white community. In the barbershops and in the churches, the gripes about Chuck Jordan didn't concern race. The complaints were about play calling, about Ground Chuck and his conservative offensive philosophy. But maybe, with the athletic Carlos Hunt coming back for his senior season, this would be the year that Coach Jordan would open up the offense. Let Carlos pass a little more, take advantage of that big arm. And when ol' Chuck did call a running play, maybe let Carlos keep the ball himself instead of making a predictable hand off to an inferior athlete. Better yet, let him run a few read-options to keep the other team guessing. With Carlos steering the offense and with Lawrence Mitchell holding down the defense, it didn't seem to matter that only eight starters were returning. Maybe 1989 was the year that Conway would finally win that state championship. And maybe a quarterback with black skin would take them there.

Nobody was more fired up for football that spring than Carlos Hunt. The '89 season would be his senior year, and he'd be his school's starting quarterback. He'd walk tall in the halls of Conway High during the week; he'd light it up on the field on Friday night; and then, hopefully on a football scholarship, he'd go off to college, where he'd make an even more indelible mark. In order to commemorate this grand senior season, which would lead to an even grander future, he bought a CHS class ring, and on it he had engraved his jersey number, 7, and the letters *QB*.

Carlos's anticipation made it that much more shocking on the day in April, a few weeks before spring practice, when Chuck Jordan called him into the coach's office to tell him that Mickey Wilson would be starting at quarterback that year. Carlos would be moving to the defensive side of the ball, to free safety, the position he would most likely play in college according to the recruiters who had been scouting him. The switch to defensive back would benefit Carlos personally, Jordan said, and would be for "the betterment of the team."

A few weeks earlier, Jordan and his coaching staff had decided that several players would be switching positions, but none of those would become as contentious as the quarterback decision. At first glance it seems odd or even foolish to replace Carlos (an experienced 6'3", 175-pound senior) with Mickey (an untested 5'9", 155-pound junior), but as Coach Jordan would later explain to the *Myrtle Beach Sun News*, his intention was to sacrifice a bit of experience on offense in order to shore up the defense. "When you take a QB and move him to defense because you need some help over there," Jordan said, "that means you've made a commitment to defense, and that's basically where our philosophy is." In addition, the coach suggested, Carlos might see some action on offense at wide receiver. "By using Carlos in that capacity," Jordan said, "we can use him on both sides of the ball. Our quarterbacks play quarterback, and that's it. We just felt like with his talents and our needs as a team, that he would best serve us [as a defensive back and wide receiver]."

Given that Jordan mostly asked his quarterbacks to hand the ball off to somebody else, the coach figured Carlos could make a bigger impact on the game from positions that made better use of his athleticism. Jordan knew that Carlos was initially disappointed with the news of the switch, just as Hunt had been two years earlier when the coach asked him to switch from wide receiver to quarterback in the first place. And just like then, in the days following this switch to defense, Carlos seemed to Jordan and his staff to eventually perk up. "Happy as a lark" is how one assistant described Carlos, and as far as Jordan was concerned, the issue was settled. As Lawrence Mitchell would later tell *Sports Illustrated*, "The way we play, I don't think quarterback is all that important."

But playing quarterback was very important to Carlos. He didn't see himself as just a football player, an X or an O. He was a QB. Those letters were engraved right there on his new class ring. He'd earned that spot by excelling on the field, and he didn't want to move positions, especially not during his senior year. Moreover, he suspected that there was something else motivating Coach Jordan's decision beyond simply the "betterment of the team." He feared that his coach was holding a grudge against him, that the switch to defense was Jordan's brand of punishment, and that the cause of the position switch went back to the ring on Carlos's finger.

Back in November, as football season was ending and basketball season was beginning, Carlos had asked Coach Jordan if he could borrow $80 to help pay for the ring, which would cost $247.50. The coach said sure, okay, and, after drawing up a written agreement—including a repayment schedule—that Carlos signed, Jordan dipped into his athletic department's discretionary fund and handed Hunt the $80. This kind of transaction wasn't against school policy, against South Carolina High School League rules, or even all that uncommon for Jordan. Every year the All Sports Booster Club gave him $200 in cash to use at his discretion. He kept the money in a filing cabinet in his office, and Carlos was one of twenty-five or thirty students who had come to the coach over the years, asking for a small loan from the fund. Jordan always made the students sign a contract. As he'd later tell the *Sun News*, "You've got to hold kids accountable. It's my responsibility to teach kids about life."

Part of the lesson Jordan wanted to impart was that you've got to pay your debts, in full and on time. So after Carlos missed a few payments, Jordan called him into his office to say that he (Jordan, in his role as CHS athletic director) was suspending Hunt for two games from the basketball team, which was coached by Mickey Wilson Sr. Jordan allegedly told Carlos that because of the player's broken commitment he'd "lost all respect for him." And then the coach made one of the few calls in his career that he'd probably like to do over—not that Chuck Jordan frequently admits to second-guessing his decisions. He decided to teach his quarterback a life lesson by reciting a maxim that his own father had once told him. *If you feed a dog, and the dog bites your hand,* he told Carlos, *you stop feeding the dog.*

Jordan reinstated Carlos to the basketball team after one game, but confiscated the ring until the debt was settled, and by January, Carlos had repaid the $80 and reclaimed his ring. But three months later, as Jordan was breaking the news to Carlos that he was no longer the starting quarterback, that he'd been replaced by Mickey—his backcourt mate on the basketball team, a junior who'd completed two measly passes for 25 yards last year as his backup—Carlos couldn't help but think about how his coach had admitted he no longer respected him. And he couldn't help but think about the dog analogy.

We'll never know for certain, of course, but it's possible that everything that happened next could have been avoided if Chuck Jordan had simply not used a metaphor that compared Carlos Hunt to an animal. Or maybe if he'd limited that metaphor to the practice field. Considering how often the coach recycles his favorite turns of phrase, it's possible that by the spring of '89, he'd already spent years telling his players he doesn't reward bad dogs. It's easy to imagine Jordan on a steamy field in August saying something like, "Y'all keep giving me half effort out here, and I ain't gone have it, dadgummit. You practice hard or you don't play! I ain't gone feed a dog that keeps biting me!" He might have said it a hundred times, but the one time he said it to Carlos Hunt laid the kindling. From there, the only thing necessary for combustion was someone willing to strike a match.

Mickey Wilson says now that spring practice came and went for the '89 Tigers with no mention of conflict between Jordan and Carlos. He remembers Carlos getting no reps at QB during spring drills and playing on the defensive side without much complaint. But Carlos's seeming acquiescence to the switch may have stemmed from the fact that because he was a member of the track team, which was still in season, he only practiced with the football squad once that spring. His absences were excused, per Jordan's team rules. Carlos may not have complained on the one day he did take the field, but that didn't mean he wasn't disappointed. When practice resumed in early August, he was angry. And now he was ready to talk. He took his grievance and the dog parable to the pastor of Cherry Hill Baptist Church, the Rev. H. H. Singleton, who was exactly the right guy. Or exactly the wrong one. It all depends on your viewpoint.

- 3 -

RACEPATH

NOW

AT PRECISELY 4:00 P.M., MICKEY WILSON GATHERS HIS PLAYERS AT MID-
field for their first day of spring practice. "I'm not gonna start with a big
talk," he says. "All I'm gonna say is every minute you're out here, I want you
flying around. I don't care if it's a water break or if you're headed to the
porta-potties. I want you runnin.'" His blond hair cropped high and tight
under his Seahawk Football visor, Mickey looks a lot like Val Kilmer circa
Top Gun: strong jaw, proud chin, perfect teeth. It's clear that in the twenty-
three years since 1989, the year he first took the field as the starting QB for
the Conway Tigers, he's done a good deal of running himself. Coach Wilson
is in game shape. His job this spring is to get the Seahawks there.

The Myrtle Beach players are restless, some pogo-ing up and down in
anticipation of the new season. They wear jerseys, shorts, and helmets and
seem relieved not to be in full pads. Even with the sea breeze coming off
the Atlantic, a short mile to the east, the temperature is in the mid-80s. For
teams in colder climates, early May might signal the return of warm weather, but along the Grand Strand, it already feels like summer, and although
these players are teenagers, these aren't boys who are just happy to be out
in the sun after a long winter spent indoors. The Seahawks are anxious to
get down to business. Mickey doesn't need to do a whole lot of rah-rah to
emphasize the importance of spring ball. Everybody knows positions will
be won and lost this month.

The Seahawks play their games in the 4,500-capacity Doug Shaw Memorial Stadium, which is decked out with slick new FieldTurf, the state-
of-the-art surface that many college and pro teams have adopted. From
a distance, FieldTurf looks like real grass springing up from real dirt, but
up close, the plastic blades seem to have been planted in bacon bit–sized
pieces of truck tire. Today, though, the team is working out on the adjacent
natural grass practice field, and from here you can see huge oceanfront

condo resorts towering over the east stands of the stadium. *Myrtle Vegas*, locals call this stretch of beach. At the turn of the twentieth century—back before there were any hotels on the strip, when the shore was thick with wax myrtles and maritime forest—this location was developed primarily as the terminus for the Seashore and Conway Railroad, which was built so that the Burroughs and Chapin Co. of Conway could more easily get their timber to market. Before the railroad came through, Myrtle Beach wasn't called Myrtle Beach; it was known as New Town, to distinguish it from Conway, the Old Town.

And now, looking at the Seahawks' high-tech playing surface, Nike practice shirts, and self-assured young coach, *new* is exactly the word that comes to mind—especially compared to Chuck Jordan's program. The Tigers are solid and stately, like the live oaks that line the streets of Conway. The Seahawks—from Mickey Wilson on down—seem less rigid, less like oaks and more like the palm trees swaying in the breeze over on Ocean Boulevard. But this newness doesn't mean that Myrtle Beach football lacks tradition. A series of jersey-shaped signs hung below the press box reminds everyone that the Seahawks have won the Class 3A State Championship six times (in '80, '81, '83, '84, '08, and '10), which, as every high school football fan in Horry County knows, adds up to six more state championships than Conway has won.

After Mickey's brief opening speech, Strength and Conditioning Coach Matt Moss takes over, telling the players, "I want eight lines every five yards." They know exactly what this command means, and within seconds, Moss has them lined up where he wants them. "Jumping jacks," he says. "Count eight and spell out Seahawks. Then I want five claps." The drill starts: 1-2-3-4-5-6-7-8-S-E-A-H-A-W-K-S. After the claps, he says, "I got a man here who can't even spell. Pitiful!" He doesn't point out the player, but helmets turn toward a kid near the sidelines in gray shorts—shorts that identify him as a member of the junior varsity.

The varsity and JV squads might be separated when summer drills start in August, but for now, they work out together here on the grass. The future B-team (rising ninth graders from the nearby middle school) is having their first session over on the FieldTurf. Their boyish screams filter through the bleachers that separate the stadium from the practice field. "Hear how those ninth graders are gettin' after it over there?" Mickey says, and the implied threat is far from idle: Your position is not safe, because some younger kid is always right behind you, ready to take your spot. No matter who you are, you must prove yourself all over again. Every day. Even if you're the starting quarterback.

In 2007, when he was the Seahawks' offensive coordinator under Head Coach Scott Earley, Mickey made the decision to start ninth-grader Everett Golson at QB over returning starter Andrew Ellis, who was a senior. Golson is black and Ellis is white, and the freshman was so undeniably skilled there was no blowback from the press or the public over the move. Some newspaper articles pointed out the rarity of a freshman starting over a senior, but nobody seemed to pay much attention to either player's skin color. Mickey says now that, while Ellis's mother may have been upset over her son being benched, any doubts among the fans about the decision to go with the younger QB disappeared as soon as they saw "this little kid out there throwing bullets." In fact, he says, if South Carolina High School League rules had allowed it, Golson had had the talent and maturity to start for the varsity team as an eighth grader.

Last season, with Golson off at Notre Dame, Mickey tried to fill the quarterback vacancy with a platoon system. C.J. Cooper and Tyler Keane, both juniors, alternated almost every play, with C.J. taking one snap, Tyler the next, and C.J. the following. They finished the regular season with nearly identical numbers. C.J., who is black, completed 61.9 percent of his 168 pass attempts for 1,485 yards; Tyler, who is white, completed 61.5 percent of his 169 pass attempts for 1,442 yards. They threw for 43 touchdown passes combined, with C.J. completing 19 and Tyler 24. Finishing with ten wins and three losses, the Seahawks had a successful campaign by every standard but one: the ridiculously high precedent they'd set for themselves in recent years. Sure, they won ten games, but they didn't get to the state championship (after having appeared in the 3A title game for three consecutive seasons) and they didn't win the Bell Game against Conway (after having beaten the Tigers four times in a row).

This season, in order to jumpstart the offense, Mickey has installed Tyler as the permanent starter at QB, converting C.J. to wide receiver. Just as Chuck Jordan said twenty-three years earlier about Carlos Hunt, Coach Wilson says now that this move will not only help the team, it will give C.J. a better chance to impress college recruiters. "He's just such a great athlete, we gotta get him on the field," Mickey will tell a local reporter later this spring. "He doesn't need to be standing beside me 50 percent of the snaps on the sideline. Especially when I think he could play [receiver] at the next level." Now on the practice field, as Tyler completes strike after strike to the sure-handed C.J., whose dreadlocks hang down past his helmet, Mickey stands nearby, nodding approvingly.

If it weren't for the metallic flash of braces when he smiles, you might never suspect that Tyler Keane is still at the end of boyhood. A rare left-handed quarterback, Tyler is the kind of player that coaches and sportswriters often describe as *poised* and *confident*. Of course, that same confident attitude from a black player might be called *cocky* or *arrogant*. Next week, on the first day the players are allowed to do full-contact drills, someone will ask Tyler what he wants this season. Without looking up from the shoes he's tying, he'll say, "a ring." No further discussion—just "a ring." It's a response you might expect from LeBron James if you asked him why he took his talents to South Beach. And just as James left the mediocre Cleveland Cavaliers to join the title-caliber Miami Heat, Tyler's family moved after his sophomore year from Carolina Forest High School and their perennially struggling football team to Myrtle Beach and the title-caliber Seahawks.

It's easy to imagine Mickey having this same confidence when he was a high school QB. The position demands it. Quarterbacking requires a level of intelligence and self-assurance that would likely surprise most casual fans if they were here at practice, watching as Mickey shouts to Tyler, "Pro-twin right!" or "What's your read on that play?" Baseball may have the reputation as the cerebral sport, but football is much more complex. The action on a baseball diamond is discrete and usually limited to two or three players on any given pitch. On the football field, twenty-two players move after every snap. The sheer number of formations and alignments can represent a difficult learning curve for even the most gifted players, which is one reason that coaches often favor experienced quarterbacks over new talent, even if the new talent is blessed with superior athletic skills. The complexity extends beyond the quarterback position to all members of the team. This is the first day of practice, and still, when Mickey says, "I want defensive fundamentals on this end of the field and the offense here for team-on-air," not one player needs to ask for a translation. To an outside observer, the mysteries of a routine blocking drill could take hours to get a handle on, but the Seahawks need only the fewest words of instruction to get into the proper lineups and begin executing.

When Tyler hits a well-covered C.J.—his constant companion on the team, the kid with whom he takes water breaks—on a long pass that goes for a touchdown, the two players run toward one another and pat each other's helmets, which doesn't always happen when Tyler throws a TD to Renard "Ray Ray" Pointer or Trell Harrell. And even though you can tell by the sly grin on Mickey's face that he's happy with the result of the play, the coach still reminds Tyler not to force the ball to his favorite receiver, but to make sure he always looks for the open man. And that's part of the complexity of the quarterback position: you can do everything right and still be wrong.

As the first day of practice winds to a close, Mickey gathers his players at midfield and asks them, "Do you know what it means to be common?"

Most of them nod. A few mumble, "Yes, sir."

"Common means being ordinary," he says. "This season I want you to be *un*common. In all that you do: on the football field, in the classroom, at home, everywhere."

More nods, *Yes, sirs.* The theme is resonating, but it's hot, and the players have worked hard. They want to go home.

"All right, now," Mickey says. "Let's be uncommon."

The players bark out a cheer, and when some of them start to stand, thinking that Coach Wilson is finished with them, he motions everybody back down on one knee. "I wanna tell you something else," he says. "Something that I truly believe. And something that no other coach in the state can say." He looks them over, from left to right and back. "We got a great team here. We work harder than anybody else."

The players nod in agreement on both counts.

"And if we do it right," Mickey says, "we can go 15 and 0 and be state champs again this year." It's a closing speech that draws howls of approval from the players and one that his ex-coach, Chuck Jordan, would never give, not if he coached a hundred seasons of football, no matter how talented his team might be. But Mickey's wearing the championship ring that proves this isn't empty talk. And this year he's betting that Tyler Keane—not C.J. Cooper—will be the quarterback that gets him a second ring.

Later this spring, in an interview in his office, when asked if any controversy has originated from switching C.J. to receiver, Mickey says no and then explains the decision by comparing C.J. and Tyler from a purely football standpoint, apparently not realizing that the question was an indirect reference to the players' race. Maybe writers, reporters, and fans are more likely than coaches to notice a player's skin color. Maybe coaches just see Xs and Os, wins and losses. Maybe racial stereotyping plays no part in football personnel decisions. Or maybe stereotyping is so ingrained and systemic as to be nearly invisible—in society and on the field. In any case, it's clear that in making the switch to Tyler, Mickey has not given the least bit of thought to race, and he has to be reminded about the similarity between this year's QB situation at Myrtle Beach and the one he played a part in back in 1989. "Oh, yeah," he says. "Right. I see where you're going with that. No, nobody has said anything. C.J.'s a good boy. He understands what we're doing and why we're asking this of him."

Mickey seems unaware of the possible implications of his use of the term "boy" for C.J., and that's surely because the coach meant the word literally (C.J. *is* a boy, albeit a full-grown one) and he used it with no malice whatsoever. In person, in context, the "boy" comment sounds perfectly un-controversial and innocent—a term of endearment, even. But when he says it, it's awfully hard not to recall Chuck Jordan's "innocent" use of the dog metaphor.

THEN

Carlos Hunt spent the summer before his senior season with relatives in Washington, D.C., sulking about Coach Jordan's decision to move him to defense. He was dejected to be sure, but he also believed that come fall practice, he'd get a chance to win back the QB job. He was confident that he'd beat out Mickey head-to-head, and then Jordan would have no choice but to reconsider. Jordan, however, had no intention of reconsidering. The move was as final as a player personnel decision can be, which is to say the position was Mickey Wilson's to lose. While in D.C., Carlos got a call from his brother saying that word was spreading around town: Carlos was out, Mickey was in. In late July, Carlos returned home to Conway, and after the first day of football practice met with Jordan to ask for a shot at quarter-back, but the coach reiterated that the team needed him on defense. "You've got a choice to make," Jordan said. "Do what you are required to do with this football team, or you don't have to play."

That's when the calls started coming in to Reverend H. H. Singleton—from community members, parents of players, and a few black teachers at the high school. Everybody was asking, "Have you heard about Carlos?" As pastor of the Cherry Hill Missionary Baptist Church, president of the Conway chapter of the NAACP, and an earth science teacher at Conway Middle School, the 57-year-old Singleton had been a leader and advocate in Horry County's black community for over ten years. Among other causes, he'd fought for blacks who'd been victims of unfair employment and hous-ing practices; he'd worked for increased political representation of African Americans by encouraging black candidates to run for office; and he'd ne-gotiated agreements with local businesses in an effort to create more jobs and more upper-management opportunities for African Americans. And just two years earlier, in May 1987, Singleton had served as an advisor to Conway High students who believed they'd been victims of racial injustice at the school—an incident that at that time had nearly led to a boycott by black football players.

In 1987 the complaint was about the racial makeup of the cheerleaders, not the football team. The varsity and junior-varsity cheerleading squads at Conway High were typically selected by two separate judging panels; one panel chose the varsity girls, another the JV. That spring the varsity panel (which featured more white than black judges) selected ten white girls and two black girls. Meanwhile, the JV panel (which featured more black than white judges) selected an *equal* number of white and black girls—six white, six black. The 50/50 ratio on the JV squad was certainly more in line with the racial makeup of the larger CHS student body (which was approximately 40 percent black) than the ten white, two black varsity squad would be. But many whites in Conway didn't see 50/50 as a fair and equal distribution of cheering privileges. After all, these JV girls would eventually become the varsity cheerleaders, and what kind of face would that put on the school? White parents began calling CHS administrators to complain that the JV panel (which, again, was made up of more black judges than white judges) had been racially biased in their selections.

Possibly in response to these complaints from white parents—or possibly not, if you take him at his word—then-Principal Stacy King decided to expand both squads by four members. This, he said, would provide "opportunities for more students to participate." He insisted that the decision was not motivated by the complaints he'd received, but be that as it may, the four additional girls selected for *both* squads were all white. This brought the racial makeup of the varsity squad to fourteen whites and two blacks. The JV squad was now at ten whites and six blacks. King defended the decision, saying, "I have not taken anything away from anyone" because he had "only added additional persons."

Black students, parents, and teachers weren't swayed by King's line of reasoning, and many of them expressed their concerns to H. H. Singleton, who, in his role as NAACP branch president, called a press conference to ask that King rescind his order to add additional members to the squads. This launched a week of student protests at the school. In the commons area, black students sang "We Shall Overcome" in meetings whose attendance ranged from 100 to 300, depending on which kid did the estimating. Foreshadowing similar scenes that would be replayed in 1989, black students and parents held planning meetings at Cherry Hill Baptist Church, and some of the black football players refused to participate in spring practices until the cheerleader issue was resolved. Singleton openly admitted that he was counseling the students and players to engage in these sorts of protests. "What they're doing is as American as hot dogs and apple pie," he said. "I have orchestrated some of the activity. We have to do what is necessary to resolve the problem."

Two years later, Darryl Stanley, who is black and who was a player on the '87 football team, would tell the *Sun News*, "At first I really didn't care about the cheerleaders. But the issue was all the brothers trying to stick together. [Coach Jordan] told us that if you believe in something you should stick with it." Another former player, Scott Thompson, who is white, says the coach told the Tigers they needed to ignore the cheerleader debate, to switch their focus from the sideline to the field. "It's got nothing to do with us," Thompson remembers Jordan saying about the protests. "The cheerleaders are here because of Conway football. Conway football is not here because of the cheerleaders."

Six days after Singleton's press conference, Horry County Schools Superintendent John Dawsey and Principal King met with Mitch Godwin, chairman of the Conway Schools' Advisory Board of Trustees, and decided to remove the four additional white cheerleaders from the JV squad, thus taking the ratio back to six blacks and six whites. The official explanation for the change was that school rules mandated a junior-varsity squad of twelve members and that Principal King had erred in adding four girls to the JV team. However, because school policy allowed for sixteen varsity cheerleaders, that squad remained at fourteen white girls and two black girls. With the JV squad back to its original lineup, H. H. Singleton and the NAACP could declare victory over a white establishment that had seemed to cave too easily to demands from white parents. And with the varsity squad still expanded by four white girls, Principal King and the school system could argue that they hadn't given in to the demands of the protestors. Thus, the outcome of the '87 cheerleading controversy was more or less a draw.

But it was also a prologue. Like the Carlos Hunt incident that would erupt two years later, the cheerleader commotion featured a black activist who was seen by Conway's white establishment as the instigator, black players who were caught between loyalty to their team and solidarity with their racial group, white players who for the most part didn't understand what the fuss was about, a coach who just wanted to play football, and school administrators who seemed irritated by the whole mess—and especially irritated by the black activist.

In the wake of the cheerleader episode, the reverend received a letter of censure from Superintendent Dawsey, who wrote that because Singleton was an Horry County Schools employee, it was a conflict of interest for him to encourage student protests. In the letter, Dawsey warned Singleton that "should I ever again have reason to believe that you have engaged in such unprofessional and inappropriate behavior, I will not hesitate to take appropriate disciplinary action, including recommendation for your dismissal."

One month later Singleton responded in a letter to Dawsey: "if this same or similar situation should arise again, I, as President of the NAACP and as a taxpayer, would not hesitate to duplicate my action or to do whatever is lawfully necessary to expedite the realization of justice and equality for all people."

Now, two years later, accusations of white favoritism at Conway High were again being voiced to H. H. Singleton. This time the reverend was hearing from the community that Carlos Hunt had been moved from quarterback to defense, where his athleticism would be put to better use, and as Hank Singleton III says, "Any black person with a sense of history had heard that [justification] before." Hank is currently a minister himself and a professor of theology at Benedict College in Columbia, South Carolina, but in 1989 he was a recent university graduate, living at home in Conway with his parents. A member of Conway High's 1983 graduating class and a lifelong Tiger supporter, Hank says that as soon as he and his father heard all the *Carlos is a great athlete, but he's not a quarterback* stuff, they thought *here we go again*. As football fans, the switch to an inexperienced, untested Mickey Wilson didn't sound to the Singletons like a decision that was made in the best interest of the team. As community activists, keenly aware of the prejudice against black quarterbacks both locally and nationally, they worried, as Hank says, that "there was something more mean-spirited going on than just a position change." Other members of the community, including several black teachers, seemed to agree. After fielding phone call after phone call, Reverend Singleton told his son, "Find Carlos Hunt."

In a small town like Conway, tracking down the starting quarterback of the football team isn't especially difficult, and Hank needed to look no further than the Smith-Jones Recreation Center, where he and Carlos both showed up often to play pick-up basketball. The next time Hank saw Carlos on the court that August, he asked him how things were going.

"Man, I don't know," Carlos said. "I don't know what's gonna happen."

Hank asked if the change had definitely been made, and Carlos said yes, he thought so. Hank asked how he felt about it.

"I don't like it," Carlos said.

Hank is seven years older than Carlos, so they weren't exactly friends, but they knew each other. Carlos was certainly aware that Hank was Rev. Singleton's son. And everybody in Conway's black community knew who "The Rev." was.

"Would you be willing to talk to Daddy about it?" Hank said.

"Yes, I would," Carlos said. And it would make sense that he'd want to do it sooner rather than later. After all, the annual Sun News Football Jamboree—in which eight schools get together in one stadium to hold four short scrimmages that cap off fall practice and launch the teams into the regular season—was just days away. This year's Jamboree would take place at Myrtle Beach High School, and Conway would be scrimmaging against Loris, an opportunity for Carlos to prove, against a real, live opponent, that he should be quarterbacking the Tigers.

The Wednesday before the Jamboree, Rev. Singleton met with Carlos and Carlos's mother and brother at the Singletons' house, which sat on the corner of Church Street and Racepath Avenue, adjacent to Cherry Hill Baptist. All through practice, Carlos had been working out with the defense, and now Singleton listened as Carlos told him the story of the move to the safety position, including the details of the loan for the class ring and the issue of Jordan's dog metaphor.

When Carlos was finished, Singleton said he wanted to meet with Lawrence Mitchell and all the other players who thought their quarterback had been treated unfairly, so after practice that evening, Carlos, Lawrence, and about thirty more black players plus their parents and a few community members squeezed into the Singleton residence. At first the players were reluctant to discuss the situation, but eventually their parents encouraged them to speak up. The sentiment among the players was that Carlos was the better quarterback and that it would be impossible for the Tigers to challenge for the state championship with Mickey under center. During the two-hour meeting, it became clear that the players were mostly concerned about the possible success (or lack thereof) of the team that season. But to those parents who knew the history of black quarterbacks at Conway High and elsewhere, it was déjà vu—especially given that the switch had been made without Carlos being given the opportunity to compete, via a tryout, for the position. The meeting closed with the Rev. and Hank Singleton advising the players to go back to the team the following day and get ready for the Jamboree. "Just keep practicing," the Singletons said.

The next day, Rev. Singleton, in his official capacity as local NAACP president, called Chuck Jordan to ask for a meeting to, as Hank puts it, "explore the situation with Carlos Hunt being moved arbitrarily to the other side of the ball and replaced with the son of an assistant coach who was white—and the implications involved in that." H. H. Singleton and Coach Jordan were both teachers in the Horry County Schools, and Hank's sister, Leontyne, had graduated from Conway High in 1975, the same year as

Jordan, but the younger Singleton says that his father had never met the coach. At 10:00 a.m. the next morning, the two men were introduced for the first time, as Reverend Singleton, Hank, and Chuck Jordan gathered for forty-five minutes in the coach's office. During that meeting, which Jordan recorded on tape, the coach said he understood that switching Carlos to defense was going to be controversial, but he again insisted that it was the right move for both the team and the individual. He also emphasized that personnel decisions must be made by the coaching staff alone, without the influence of "outside pressure groups." No coach worth his salt is going to yield to interference from parents, booster clubs, or community activists.

"I realize that changes in personnel is your discretion," H. H. Singleton said. "Conversely, you are a public employee. Whatever you do is subject to public scrutiny." To the Singletons, switching Carlos to defense just didn't make football sense, so the reverend asked the coach if he was thoroughly convinced that the Tiger offense "would be better with another quarterback that is not as experienced as the one who has proven a winnable quarterback."

Jordan admitted that when it comes to position decisions, he was never thoroughly convinced. He just made the best call he could at the time. With regard to the current quarterback issue, he said, "I may have made a bad decision; I may have made a good decision; I do not know." And, he said, if it later turned out that he had made the wrong decision, then "I hope you understand that I would take [Carlos] tomorrow and put him back at quarterback, if I was convinced I was wrong, but I'm not [convinced]." Jordan discussed how integral Carlos would be on defense, playing free safety, which he called "probably the most important position on defense." And, he said, "If you know anything about my philosophy of football, we are going to play defense first, because I believe that if you can't score, you can't beat me."

Regarding the offensive side of the ball, Jordan argued that in Mickey Wilson he had a quarterback who was "more than adequate" and who would improve as the season progressed. "And the most important thing," Jordan said, "is that we are good at the end of the season." The coach stressed that the essential quality necessary in a quarterback, even more so than ability, was *loyalty*, and he hinted that Carlos—in missing the ring payments, in changing plays at the line, and in his unwillingness to accept the switch to defense—was short on this fundamental trait. "Players," Jordan said, "don't always approve the moves that we make; but when you are sitting behind this desk and you are making the decisions, you've got to have some degree of loyalty from the people that play for you, that work for you, whether it be in the business world, whether it be in this setting, regardless of the setting; and the decisions the bossman makes isn't always the best decision in the world; it isn't always the right decision; but the intent is important for the bossman."

To the Singletons, this talk of being loyal to the bossman surely struck at the heart of the legacy of race relations in the South—of slavery, of Jim Crow, of paternalism on the plantation. Still, throughout the conversation, Singleton insisted that he was "not about to call [Jordan] a racist," but he did want the coach to understand that "racism is a reality" and that in society and in sports there existed a "subtle racism" which held that blacks were unsuitable for positions of intellect and leadership.

"I cannot see color when I go out there on the field," Jordan said, "and I will defend that to my death."

"I appreciate your openness and your vow [to deal with] people impartially," Singleton said. "My objective is equality for everybody, participation for everybody."

As the conversation drew to a close, Jordan said, "I say to you man-to-man, eye-to-eye, that I made the decision for the reasons I stated to you, and if someone says otherwise and you want to believe otherwise, I have no problem with that. I can't control what you think and what you believe."

"And I appreciate the opportunity to address this matter with you," Singleton said. "It's a pleasure." The reverend closed by insisting he didn't have a personal quarrel with Jordan. "I deal with issues, principalities, not flesh and/or flesh and blood," he said. "And if there's any time that I can be of assistance and you ask, I'll do it; and conversely, if I have to *fight* you, I'll do that, too."

Despite Jordan's explanation of how switching quarterbacks wouldn't slow down his offense and despite the coach's discussion of Carlos's lack of loyalty, the Singletons left the meeting unconvinced that Jordan was justified in moving Carlos to defense. But at that point, according to Hank, "We still expected some sort of compromise. We had no idea that this would escalate into what it would escalate to."

The meeting in Jordan's office took place on the last Friday before the official opening of the season, which, in Horry County, means it took place on the same day as the Sun News Football Jamboree. In later years the Jamboree would get a new sponsor and a less romantic-sounding name: The Conway National Bank Kickoff Classic, but most people in Horry County still call it the Jamboree. A name like "Kickoff Classic" sounds to some ears like just another prefabricated event forged from a corporate mold while "jamboree" hints at something elemental and ritualistic, a celebration of shared identity that can't be contained within the confines of a sponsorship deal.

Back in 1989, in this 13th annual celebration of Horry County high school football, Conway was scheduled to face the Loris Bears at 8:00 p.m. in the third scrimmage of the night, while the host team, Myrtle Beach, was set to take the field thirty minutes later against their perennially inferior rivals, the North Myrtle Beach Chiefs. In the days leading up to Jamboree, the *Sun News* had continued to hype Lawrence Mitchell as the leading player not just on the Tigers, but in the state. The paper had already reported that Carlos Hunt would be replaced at quarterback by Mickey Wilson but hadn't given much attention to the change. To anyone following preseason events through the press, the Tigers were headed toward another season where they'd challenge for the region title and, if fortune broke their way, make a deep run in the state tournament. The pollsters confirmed it: Conway was entering the season as the third-ranked 4A school in South Carolina. There was no reason for anyone outside the team to suspect that relations inside the Tigers' locker room were anything but normal.

That night, during the scrimmage against Loris, the Conway players' fear that they'd have trouble moving the ball with Mickey at quarterback was realized. The junior was sacked several times, and although Conway did manage to eke out a 7–0 win, their lone score came after recovering a Loris fumble on the Bears' three-yard line and running it into the end zone on the next offensive play. Nobody knew it yet, but this would be the Tigers' only touchdown with a fully manned roster all year.

The following morning, coverage of the Jamboree landed on the front page of the *Sun News*—not the front page of the sports section, but on *the* front page—above the fold. Today, page 1A might seem like an odd place for a report about preseason scrimmages that wouldn't count in the standings, but back in 1989, football in Horry County was a major community event. One fan, Adrian Moore, told the paper he was celebrating his eighteenth birthday at the game. On a night when a young man might want to mark his state-recognized entry into majority by shedding his parents and going out with his friends, when the twin forces of peer pressure and biological urgency might have coaxed him into something more rebellious, Adrian attended the Jamboree with his whole family and said, "I can't think of a better way to celebrate than by coming to a football game." The more than 3,000 people who joined him in the stands that night would have agreed.

Seemingly unaware of any trouble on the Tiger squad, *Sun News* sportswriter Mel Derrick referred to the Jamboree as "a reunion of football pals." An annual ritual to mark the changing of the sports seasons and the end of summer, the event was "just fun and games." After the Jamboree, it would be a long time before football felt anything like "fun and games" for Conway.

That Sunday, the Singletons again met with the black Tigers. Deciding that the residence was too small, they moved the meeting next door to the basement of the church. Reverend Singleton asked the players, who were angry about how the Mickey-led offense had performed at the Jamboree, "What would y'all like to do about this?"

According to Hank, one of the players replied, "We should just walk off the team."

"Now, you do understand that there's a risk in doing this," Rev. Singleton said to them. "Are you prepared to stand by whatever solution we come up with?"

The players insisted that a white quarterback would never be treated as Carlos had; this injustice warranted whatever risk came with a walkout.

"If that's what y'all want to do," Singleton said, "then do it. I will act as your spokesman, and I will write up a statement." He instructed them to go to Jordan's office the next day, Monday, before practice, and collectively ask the coach to reinstate Carlos at quarterback. "If the answer he gives you is *yes*," Singleton said, "that's wonderful. If the answer he gives you is *no*, don't argue with him. Don't get angry. Don't do anything."

The next day at 3:30, approximately thirty players showed up in the coach's office, and did exactly what the Rev. Singleton had advised. Jordan again explained why he was moving Carlos to defense and why that move would be in the best interest of the team. He confirmed that the decision was final. "Look," the coach said to them, "you guys have got a choice to make. First of all, you've got to stand up for what you believe in. If you believe I'm prejudiced, then you need to go put your stuff in your locker and go on home, because you don't want to play for anybody, don't ever work for anybody, that's going to look at you different because of the color of your skin. Number two, if you want to play football at Conway High School and you know that I'm not prejudiced, then you need to get your tail on that field; you need to go finish getting dressed, get out there and let's practice football." He added, according to *Sports Illustrated*, "You're going to play on my team, you're going to play on my terms."

Carlos, Lawrence, and the rest of the black players did practice that afternoon, and Carlos took his place among the defensive backs. As he watched Carlos run though drills with the defense, Jordan was feeling good because he "felt like we had confronted our kids up front with it, that they understood where we were coming from, and that they trusted us as coaches."

But after practice, in a meeting with the coaching staff, one of Jordan's two black assistants said, "Don't count your chickens before they hatch. They've got a meeting tonight at the church."

That evening the black cohort gathered at Cherry Hill Baptist, where they were joined by parents and community members. Soon, hundreds of people were there, then over a thousand. The church was jammed, and folks were pressed together in the pews and up against the walls. People were shoulder-to-shoulder back to the door, and out the door onto the steps, and down the steps into the grounds. People were gathering on Racepath Avenue and around the corner onto Church Street. Eventually, Rev. Singleton cleared the church of everyone but the players. Everyone else waited outside while the players and the Singletons conferred inside. After officially voting to boycott, they named Rev. Singleton as their spokesman. When they finally emerged from the church to announce their decision, the crowd erupted in cheers. A thousand people high-fiving and handshaking all down Racepath Avenue, chanting, "Fired up! Ready to go!"

"At that moment," Hank Singleton says, "my father and I didn't see the boycott lasting any longer than a week."

The following day, a scorching August Tuesday, three days before Conway was scheduled to play their first game of the season, Reverend Singleton held a press conference outside Cherry Hill Baptist to announce the boycott. That same day, Black Panthers co-founder Huey P. Newton would be shot in Oakland, California, by a member of the Black Guerrilla Family who felt that Newton had betrayed the movement he had once led. Three thousand miles away, in Horry County, South Carolina, a new movement, the Conway Movement, was beginning with a press conference on the steps of Singleton's church.

A grainy DVD transfer of a videotape of the event shows the striking players, wearing Conway Tigers shorts and midriff-baring t-shirts, surrounding H. H. and Hank Singleton. A few parents stand alongside their sons. A movie version of this scene would probably include a crowd of local blacks on one side, a mob of angry whites on the other, and a throng of flashbulb-popping media members peppering the reverend with questions. In truth it appears that in addition to the Singletons, the players, the parents, and three or four all-white press representatives, there was no significant community attendance, black or white.

But the media-savvy Singleton knew he wasn't addressing the immediate crowd; he was playing to the cameras, phrasing his speech as dramatically as if he were speaking on the National Mall. "This press conference was called by the newly organized Committee on Concerns of Black Athletes of Conway High School," Singleton began. "It is co-chaired by Carlos Hunt and Lawrence Mitchell, and I have been selected as its chief spokesman."

This was a straightforward enough opening, but in a town as divided along racial lines as Conway, even a statement that appears this simple can lead to long-lasting disputes. To this day, if you ask most white residents of Conway how H. H. Singleton became the players' spokesman, you'll hear him described as an unscrupulous deceiver of young men who were forced to participate in a protest they knew was nonsense. The boycott was all his idea, these white Conwayites will say, staged in order to feed his mammoth ego. And it was just another in a long history of unfounded nuisance grievances, including his previous charge of racism in the selection of Tiger cheerleaders. From this perspective, the reverend's role in the cheerleader incident emboldened him, which helps explain how just two years later he worked up the nerve to challenge the leadership of the football team and the school district.

"Carlos, as the once incipient and now salient facts reveal," Singleton continued, his speechcraft honed from years preaching and teaching, "has been flagrantly and blatantly abused and exploited by the athletic director and head football coach of Conway High School, Mr. Charles 'Chuck' Jordan." Hunt was benched, Singleton said, by "an inimical Mr. Jordan" who was motivated by "an incredible compulsion for personal vengeance" and a "callous and racial intolerance that seems to have bordered on racial bigotry."

The "personal vengeance" Singleton spoke of was a reference to the $80 loan for the class ring, the missed payments, and the resulting suspension of Carlos from the basketball team, a suspension that the reverend now said was "for no apparent violation of any rule or curfew" and was "arrogatedly and arbitrarily executed by Mr. Jordan" and handed out "insolently to abuse Carlos for nonpayment of this indebtedness." Singleton claimed that once Tommy Lewis, the principal at Conway High, was "made aware of this disparaging act of suspension," he ordered that Hunt be reinstated to the basketball team after one game. According to the reverend, Jordan was "exasperated by the restoration of Carlos to the team," so the coach decided in April to extract retribution by switching Hunt's position on the football field. "The only reason stated to Carlos," Singleton said, "is that this change would be for the betterment of the team," a claim that the reverend suggested was patently ridiculous. In short, Singleton was arguing that Jordan's decision to move Hunt to defense was racially motivated, that it was an act of revenge for Carlos's missed loan payments, and that it was an attempt by the coach to heal his damaged pride after the principal had reversed his suspension of Carlos from the basketball team.

A fascinating combination of hyperbole, emotional appeal, and heroic adverb usage, Singleton's statement might generate a week's worth of discussion in a graduate-level rhetoric course. Still he comes off as someone who commands a grandiloquence that resonates deeply with his audience. The video shows a man who—with his bushy hair and beard and his intimidating physical size—looked and sounded exactly like the kind of civil rights leader many whites have come to meet with both skepticism and trepidation: a dark-skinned preacher with a large vocabulary and a larger following.

Flanked by more than thirty players, many of them wearing scowls and folding their arms in a posture that suggests defiance and determination, Singleton began to address the assumption that "certain positions—athletic director, head coaches, and quarterback, positions of thought and judgment in football—are indigenous to white males." As he stared straight into a news camera, the reverend must have felt he was speaking not only for Carlos but for every talented black player who'd ever been passed over at quarterback.

Many in the white community who heard Singleton's remarks on the evening news or read them in the paper probably thought, Why's he rehashing this old business? He's the one bringing race into the issue. For a lot of white football fans, the "black quarterback question," if there had ever been one, had been settled two years earlier, when Doug Williams led the Washington Redskins to that Super Bowl victory. However, as many in the black community would tell you, even though Williams's achievement was monumentally important, a championship won by one black quarterback in 1988 didn't flip a switch and instantly cure racism, stop prejudice, and heal four hundred years of black oppression any more than the election of a black President in 2008 would.

Still, in the late '80s newspapers and sports talk shows were announcing that the age of the black quarterback had finally arrived. At last we had moved beyond our outdated notions of black players as less suited to the unique demands of what is often called the toughest position in team sports. A few days after the Redskins' Super Bowl win, the *Washington Post*'s Judy Mann published a commentary optimistically titled "Putting Racism to Rest." In this piece, the Doug Williams victory is given credit not only for ending the long-standing bias against black quarterbacks, but for silencing anyone who might be tempted to agree with the idiotic comments of CBS's Jimmy "The Greek" Snyder, who that same year—just two weeks before the Super

Bowl—had voiced his theory of why black athletes in general, if not quarterbacks in particular, were so successful on the field. According to Snyder,
"The black is a better athlete to begin with, because he's been bred that way.
... This all goes back to the Civil War, when, during the slave trade, the slave
owner would breed his big black to his big woman so that they would have
a big black kid." He later tried to apologize, but comparing blacks to animals
used for breeding was too hurtful and insensitive to recover from. CBS, the
same network that saw no problem in identifying Jimmy "The Greek" by
an ethnically derived nickname, fired him immediately. So in 1988, in the
span of two weeks, racism had allegedly been dealt twin death blows by the
outing of a closet racist in Jimmy "The Greek" and by the fact that a black
quarterback was named MVP in one of the most lopsided Super Bowls in
history. At least that's how the *Post* told the story: nice and clean. But everywhere besides an 800-word newspaper column, the situation was far more
complicated.

In South Carolina, the color barrier for black quarterbacks had already
been famously shattered by Homer Jordan, the starting QB for the Clemson Tigers, who in 1981 took his team to the only national championship
in that program's history. In a postseason retrospective on Homer Jordan,
Sports Illustrated's John Papanek differentiates the barely 6-foot-tall, under-
180-pound QB from stereotypes of both black and white players, writing:
"Little Homer hardly resembles a quarterback, at least in the way the image of a quarterback is fixed in the public mind. Think about it. Is there
any position in any team sport that has a more firmly fixed stereotype than
quarterback? First of all, if the quarterback is black, he's usually not really
what we think of as a quarterback at all, but one of those wishbone-option
juke artists such as Thomas Lott or J.C. Watts. We think of a college quarterback and we think of Jim McMahon or Art Schlichter or John Elway or Dan
Marino. Not only are they white, but they're also big and strong."

Clemson didn't employ the wishbone formation with Homer Jordan
at QB, and many people in South Carolina wouldn't have wanted them
to, because the wishbone looks to some white fans like an inferior, "black
juke-artist" version of the game rather than like football as it's meant to be
played: a golden boy standing tall in the pocket. Jordan was not big enough
to run like the stereotypical black quarterback and not tall enough to stand
in the pocket and pass like a white quarterback, so folks didn't know what
to make of him. There were certainly whites in South Carolina who were
uncomfortable with the idea of a black guy quarterbacking one of the state's
two premier college teams, but it's hard to believe many Clemson fans
cared about Homer Jordan's race on the day he led the Tigers to a victory

against Nebraska in the Orange Bowl, positioning them to be voted national champs. Winning has a way of making people forget little things like skin color. Still, it's not as if racist stereotyping suddenly ended in Clemson, Conway, or anywhere else in South Carolina on the day Homer Jordan hoisted the championship trophy.

The fact is, in 1989, even after the success of Homer Jordan, Doug Williams, and other QBs at the college and pro levels, quarterback was still largely seen as the domain of white players, who, the thinking went, were more likely to have the "head for the position" even if they weren't as "athletically gifted" as black players competing for the same job. According to this line of thought—which still persists today to some degree—playing quarterback isn't just about out-running, out-jumping, or overpowering another player. Instead it requires more brains, more discipline, and more "character," to use a vague buzzword popular with coaches (a word that might, to a coach, be synonymous with "loyalty"), than any other position on the field. A quarterback can get by with less *physical* talent as long as he has that ever-important "intellect." A "smart" QB doesn't have to elude defenders or fight for an extra yard, because he has the ability to "read" defenses and make the adjustments that help him avoid getting pressured or sacked in the first place. Instead of running and juking when he sees that his primary target is covered, this "astute game manager" has the good sense to check down to a second or third receiver, or if that doesn't work, to throw the ball away. Thus, the argument goes, a smarter player—which is to say, usually a white one—can outperform a player with superior physical skills—which is to say, usually a black one.

Even today, white athletes are often praised for their devotion to learning the principles of the game, and black athletes tend to be described as "natural" athletes, sometimes with freakish or animalistic physical talents ("He's a monster," a fan might say of a black player, or "He's a beast"), all of which hearken back to the asinine comments of Jimmy "The Greek." There are exceptions to the rule, of course, but odds are that any player described in reverent tones as "heady" is going to be white, while players praised mainly for their raw athleticism are almost always black.

Chuck Jordan admits that Mickey Wilson didn't appear on the surface to be a better QB, but when it comes to player decisions, he says, "You have to go with your gut." What was in Coach Jordan's gut that led him to pick Mickey over Carlos? Whatever it was, it couldn't have been rooted solely on the players' on-field performances. When Mickey was a freshman, he had led the JV team to 9–1 record, but in 1988, his sophomore year, he didn't get many chances to play with the varsity squad, and on the rare occasions when he did get into the game, he didn't do much to suggest that he was ready to overtake Carlos the following year. After all, he completed just two of eight passes. Maybe the money that Jordan had loaned Carlos for the ring was as much a test of Hunt's maturity as it was a helpful gesture, and if it was, Carlos's missing payments (his failure of the test) might have been just as important a factor in promoting Mickey over him as anything that had happened on the field.

Coaches' guts sometimes steer them toward a player's "intangibles," a combination of unquantifiable factors that can mean more to a coaching staff than the statistics a player compiles or the physical prowess he demonstrates. Perhaps there is no greater intangible for a quarterback than for him to be a "student of the game," a qualification that transcends even intellect. To be a student of the game means having at least a fair amount of smarts and talent and then spending years under the tutelage of a mentor who imparts the finer points and nuances of the position—not just intelligence but wisdom. The way this quarterback creation myth goes, the mentor is typically a father, ideally one who had also played the position and can now pass the sacred knowledge down to the next generation of field general. As the white son of a football coach, Mickey Wilson fit this mold. With only one year of starting experience to judge Carlos by, maybe the "disloyalty" of changing the coach's play calls at the line was enough to make Jordan see the "intangible" benefits of having a disciplined coach's son at the helm. And since most coaches were and still are white, the odds that that coach's son would be white are obviously pretty high. Thus, even if Chuck Jordan's heart and mind were free from even the slightest hint of overt racism, the very social situation he was working in was rigged in favor of a white QB.

In his remarks to the press at the time and in interviews today, Jordan maintains that switching Carlos to defense was motivated by two interests: putting the best team on the field and offering Carlos the best chance at a college scholarship. And given the prevailing assumptions about black quarterbacks in 1989, Jordan may have been correct in believing that colleges would be more interested in Carlos at defensive back or wide receiver, positions that, according to the conventional wisdom, better suited his athleticism. Jordan has steadfastly claimed, after all, that a few college coaches had specifically *told* him as much: Carlos wasn't a college quarterback, but he was a great athlete.

The day after the boycott began, Mel Derrick of the *Sun News* described Carlos Hunt as "an outstanding athlete, no question." What he doesn't say, but certainly implies, is that there may have been questions about him beyond the issue of physical talent. Sports commentary may be one of the last arenas where racial consciousness has yet to be raised above the principle of inclusion. As long as black players have a chance to play—and they did in 1989, whether that chance was exactly equal or not—the issue, for the most part, is considered closed. "Ten years ago, maybe even five," Derrick wrote, "the charge that coaches were prejudiced against black quarterbacks might have held up. Today, it's dated." His optimism was probably at least ten years premature. Still, for many white people in Conway, the fact that Carlos had played quarterback the year before was proof positive that racism on the football field was a thing of the past.

It's possible—to the extent such things are possible for any of us—that Jordan made the decision to replace Carlos with Mickey without any cognizance of race. And it seems evident that Jordan never consciously took the view that black players were primarily physical athletes who lacked the mental abilities to play the QB position. After all, in addition to starting black quarterbacks in three of his previous six seasons as the Tigers' head coach, he had hired several black members to his coaching staff, all of whom remained loyal to him during the boycott. If Coach Jordan was a stereotypical Southern bigot (and all the evidence indicates that he was not even remotely bigoted), he'd done an awfully good job of hiding it. But it's also possible that Jordan, along with thousands of other coaches and millions of football fans, was unconsciously influenced by the prejudices inherent in the prevailing attitudes of the game. Even if he was earnestly trying to help Carlos succeed within the system that funneled high school players to college teams, it seems clear that the system itself was biased against black quarterbacks.

Standing at the podium in front of Cherry Hill Baptist, at the corner of Church Street and Racepath Avenue—the street that runs from the traditionally black part of town (west of Church St.) to the traditionally white part of town (east of Church St.)—H. H. Singleton surely knew that his message would be heard very differently on the two ends of the avenue. In the black community, the idea that Carlos had been moved to defensive back to give him a better chance at a college scholarship was, as Singleton said during the news conference, "the sheer epitome of a pretext." But many local whites also saw a "pretext." To them, Singleton wasn't an activist; he was an agitator who'd found in the Carlos Hunt situation an excuse for the kind of protest he was always looking for a reason to make. Move Carlos from linebacker to safety, and nobody would have had a complaint worthy of a press conference. But move him from quarterback to any other position, and you had the ingredients for a *movement*, one that seemed long overdue to Conway's black population and positively absurd to most of the town's white residents. When news of the striking black players hit the front page the next day, whites may have seen the boycott as the first step down an incendiary path—the same race path that Conway's blacks knew they had been traveling for a long, long time.

- 4 -

WEEK ZERO

NOW

FRIDAY NIGHT IN CONWAY, SOUTH CAROLINA. AT THE E. CRAIG WALL JR. Memorial Stadium, with the scoreboard clock counting down the minutes until kickoff, Chuck Jordan's current Tigers are pent up in the home team locker room, waiting for their coach to deliver the pre-game speech that will launch his thirtieth season. After three and a half months of preparation—after starting up spring ball back in May; after temporarily losing Mykal Moody to a collarbone injury (broken at the Nike SPARQ camp in Charlotte less than a week into spring practice); after substituting for Mykal with rising sophomore Ethan Smith; after the intra-squad spring game in which Smith threw three touchdown passes to Malcolm Green; after the end of the school year and the start of summer break; after the Backyard BBQ fundraiser and the Fellowship of Christian Athletes Camp; after the 7-on-7 summer passing league; after Mykal's collarbone recovery, rehab, and return; after sixteen days of preseason practice in 90-degree heat and lung-crushing humidity; after two full-contact scrimmages against other schools; and lastly, after hosting the CNB Kickoff Classic, which everybody still calls the Jamboree—it's finally, *finally*, game night. Time to snap on the chin-straps, lace up the cleats, and cut somebody's daggone butt.

The butts to be cut tonight belong to the Georgetown High Bulldogs, a 3A school that sits thirty-five miles south of here, just across Winyah Bay from the southern tip of the Grand Strand. Conway competes in the 4A class of the South Carolina High School League (SCHSL), Division II, Region VI, which is an administrative way of saying that the Tigers, as the school with the larger enrollment, might be expected to win handily if this game were played on paper. But on the field, nothing's foretold. The Myrtle Beach Seahawks are a 3A team, one notch smaller than Conway, and yet they've dominated the Tigers of late, winning four of the last five matchups. So even if Georgetown is literally not in the same class as Conway, you can tell by the determined looks on the Tigers' faces that they are taking this game seriously. Not only is it a chance to rinse away the bitter taste of the playoff loss Conway suffered to end last season, but tonight's game puts both the Tigers and Bulldogs in the local football limelight, because less than half of the state's schools have scheduled a game this early, mid-August, with classes not yet in session. Myrtle Beach isn't playing tonight; Summerville isn't playing tonight. The SCHSL has dubbed this week of the season "Week 0," but despite the seeming nothingness inherent in that name, the players, coaches, and fans here in the stadium all know that this game matters.

The clock in the south end zone says ten minutes to game time, which means it's 7:20 p.m. and still daylight savings bright. Out on Church Street, vehicles are lined up in the turn lane, waiting to be funneled into the parking lot that's already packed tight with pickups and SUVs, some outfitted for tailgating on the asphalt, some left haphazardly in the grass. Because the school year won't start until Tuesday, tonight marks the first time in months that so many CHS students have found themselves together in one place. The kids that spill from these cars and trucks are buzzing with the kilowattage that such high teenage density generates. The adults, too, are fired up—because it's the end of the workweek, because it's the first night of football season, and because of the communal nature of a big gathering in a small town. This isn't the homecoming game, but it feels like one. Or a family reunion. People wave and say hey. You hear snippets of "What you up to?" and "How's your mama doin'?" All the while, everybody's moving en masse toward the ticket booths and the security checkpoint where, after handing over the six-dollar admission, they'll be asked to remove the keys, cellphones, and loose change from their pockets in preparation for the metal detecting wand—standard procedure at high school football games in Horry County. But just before everybody arrives at the gates, they'll have to cross the border from parking lot to stadium grounds, and in doing so they'll walk over a two-foot-wide, thirty-foot-long red stripe that has been painted on the concrete. WELCOME TO THE BACKYARD, it reads. Tonight, in the merchandise booth, you can buy a Conway Football t-shirt that proclaims WE GUARD THE BACKYARD. And this whole event does have the intimate feel of a backyard get-together—down to the fried chicken (sold out of the mobile Bojangles trailer) and the pulled pork sandwiches (served at the concession stand).

As kickoff nears, the oldest and youngest Tiger fans make their way up the home-side bleachers, where they'll sit and cheer and actually watch the game. The middle- and high-schoolers, who'll spend most of the evening eying each other, stand on the hill behind the north end zone, in groups of five or six. They're wearing Abercrombie, American Eagle, and—this being the coastal plain in the run-up to waterfowl season—a healthy smattering of Drake brand camouflage. The CHS cheerleaders are bounding up the hill, readying themselves for the big moment, just before kickoff, when the players charge down the hill and onto the field. Some of the younger kids are already forming the human tunnel the team will run through. The cheerleaders—wearing conservative white outfits, each member's hair tied back in a bow—shake their pom-poms and shout in unison to the kids: *We say green, you say gold! Green!* Gold! *Green!* Gold!

Back in the locker room, which is about half the size of a tennis court and smells like wet cheese ripening in a work boot, the Conway Tigers are taped up and dressed out, chattering about football and girls. The coaches are still holed up in the adjacent meeting room, so the players are solely under the leadership of the four senior captains. Still, even without direct coach supervision, there are no door-slamming shenanigans, no horseplay. Coach Jordan's warnings about the hazards of locker room grab-ass have been burned into the team's collective psyche ("I've had more players hurt in the locker room, horsing around, than I have out on the football field," the coach says at most practices). Sporting their green jerseys and gold pants, most of the players have taken to the benches that run in front of the lockers. A few bounce their feet on the floor, cleats tap-tapping the polished concrete like drumrolls. Every now and then, somebody gets up and walks over to the drinking fountains that are tucked away in the corner.

Suddenly, the door to the coaches' room opens, and Chuck Jordan comes out, wearing a cream-colored polo and khaki shorts. He walks to the center of the floor, staring hard at the sheet of notes he's holding. If the players notice him, they don't give an indication; they keep up the chit-chat. Jordan, still looking at his notes, begins to pace the concrete, about fifteen steps in each direction. The players start to quiet down, gradually, over the course of a couple of minutes, during which the coach hasn't said a word. He just walks and turns, walks and turns. The players have now fallen totally silent. There are sixty beating hearts in the room, but the only discernable sound is the hum from the cooling unit of one of the drinking fountains. Eventually that too goes quiet. Jordan keeps walking—head bowed, notes in hand. A full minute of absolute silence passes. On the wall hangs a poster with a three-word passage from Proverbs 27:17 on it: IRON SHARPENS IRON.

"Football," Jordan finally says, so softly as to be almost inaudible. He's still pacing, his gaze still aiming down. "Greatest game in the world." He looks up and shakes his head as if in awe of the sheer wonder of the sport. "You guys are lucky you get to play this game." His voice is stronger now, rising in volume and pitch. "Seniors. Help me out. What are the three things I always say?"

As their coach lists them, Mykal Moody, Malcolm Green, Sawyer Jordan, and a half dozen more voices join in.

"One," Jordan says, "Play with passion. Two: Expect to win. Three—" and here the coach smiles ever so faintly, his demeanor softening from iron to gold "—enjoy the ride." The players nod at the familiar refrain.

Jordan curls his notes into a roll and smacks it against his palm. "*Play with passion,*" he says. "That means we intimidate by *effort,* not by running our mouths. *Expect to win.* Expect good things, and good things will come to you. One day you'll understand that. *Enjoy the ride . . .*" Jordan shrugs at the self-explanatory nature of the rule. "Well, let's just remember how lucky we are. Okay." He signals for them to stand up, and they do. He bows his head and begins, "Our father, who art in heaven," and he leads the team through the Lord's Prayer.

"Let's *do* it!" somebody yells after the Amen. "Let's *go!*" The players pop each other on the shoulder pads and swarm toward the double doors that will open up to the stadium, the hill, and the crowd.

Jordan is holding the doors shut, pressing his players back. "I want you gang-tackling out there!" he says. "We gotta put some hats on that ball!" And with that, the doors swing wide, and the Tigers explode from the locker room and run across the top of the hill, where the CHS cheerleaders and a human tunnel await them.

Now surrounded by friends, fans, and their families, they're stomping their feet like bulls ready to charge. If they look out into the stadium, they'll see that the home stands are maybe half full, a good-sized crowd but much smaller than those that regularly packed the Graveyard back in its heyday—not that these players have many memories of the Graveyard. If any of the current Tigers ever attended a game there, they would have been preschoolers. Maybe the falloff in attendance is because in Horry County these days, there's a lot more to do on a Friday night than to head over to the high school. Conway's population has nearly doubled since 1989; so has the population of the county. And with the influx of people, the entertainment options have grown. Or maybe it's because, as Hank Singleton says, after the '89 boycott, many members of the black community lost interest in Tiger football. Sure, he says, if your son is suiting up for the team, you'll go to the games, but gone are the days when local blacks would throw down six bucks for a ticket on a Friday night just because it was the thing to do.

Right now, behind the home bleachers, up against a chain-link fence, there sits a gravestone that's the size, shape, and composition of the markers you'll still find in Hillcrest Cemetery, the burial ground that inspired the old stadium's nickname. On the stone, in the spot where the deceased's last name would typically go, it says CONWAY. Underneath, an inscription reads: THE GRAVEYARD. 1964-1999. A CONWAY TIGER FOOTBALL TRADITION. Not that ancient history means spit to the current Tigers. Like the 1989 players, who may not have known much about the history of black quarterbacks, these players are kids, and as with all kids, they're blessed with myopia and short memories. Tonight, they're just trying to win a football game. So when they look down to the bottom of the hill, where eight cheerleaders have stacked themselves into a living, breathing set of sign posts, holding a giant banner that reads RESTORE THE ROAR, the only thing it means to these players is that the team flat-out hasn't been good enough lately. Over the last three years, they've won seventeen games total. The previous three years, the Tigers won a combined thirty-three. But again, that's history. As far as these players are concerned, this is their team. This is their time. Conway High School football belongs to them.

From the top of the hill, Sawyer Jordan—the coach's son, the senior captain known as "Sawdawg"—barks out to his gathered teammates a call-and-response cheer that he brought home from this summer's Fellowship of Christian Athletes Camp. "Who runs this ship?" he yells.

"WE run this ship!" comes back sixty Tigers strong.

"Who the captain of the ship?"

"WE the captains of the ship!"

"Click."

"BOOM!"

"Click-click."

"BOOM!"

"Click-click-click."

"Reeeelooooad . . . BOOM!"

With that resounding BOOM, it's game time. The Conway Tigers storm down the hill, tearing the banner in two.

THEN

The day after H. H. Singleton's press conference, the Myrtle Beach *Sun News* led with the story of Huey Newton's murder. BLACK PANTHERS CO-FOUNDER SHOT TO DEATH read the headline. Immediately underneath that article, above the fold, ran the piece announcing the football boycott, one of three stories about the walkout the paper published that day. In one article,

Jordan is quoted as saying that his job as coach is to "do the right thing," an interesting, and probably unintentional, use of the title of the Spike Lee film that had been released on June 30 of that year, less than two months before the coach's quote appeared in the paper. "I think the people in this community," Jordan says, "black, white, blue, or orange—want to see me do the right thing." Up until this moment in his career, the right thing had been fairly clear-cut for the coach: impart the life lessons that help boys become men and hopefully win a mess of football games while doing it. But now, people from different facets of the community were holding very different ideas about what the right thing was. This situation was unheard of for Conway and for the coach. Everybody in the Carolinas was at least a little familiar with the lunch counter sit-ins and the boycotts of white businesses that had taken place during the civil rights movement of the '50s and '60s. But what the heck does a coach do when more than half of his football players are telling him they aren't going to play football?

In his office, Jordan may have feared a protracted conflict that would put him at the center of a larger debate on social and racial issues, but on the practice field, three days from having to suit up and play a game, the coach decided to treat the strike as a simple matter of team discipline. The thirty-six black players who'd skipped practice on Tuesday, the day of the press conference, would be charged with an unexcused absence, which, according to team rules, would result in a "disciplinary action," like running laps or doing pushups. A second missed practice would result in a one-game suspension, a third would bring about more "disciplinary action," and a fourth would trigger automatic dismissal from the team. These kinds of measures had been working for football coaches since the advent of the game, so they were familiar to Jordan, a precedented method of handling an unprecedented situation. The boycotting players—despite their threats and accusations, despite their committee and their spokesman and their press conference—had so far broken only one rule: They'd missed a football practice. And for that there would be repercussions. Jordan would stand on policy. This was the fair thing. This was the right thing.

But most important, this was the stance that would allow the coach to do his job, which was to get his squad, whoever was left, ready to play the season opener on Friday, against the Dalzell-Hillcrest Wildcats, a school that under ordinary circumstances Conway would have been expected to dominate. Hillcrest was perhaps the weakest team in all of South Carolina, going 0–11 the year before, and coming into the '89 season riding an eighteen-game losing streak, the longest active run of futility in the state. The Tigers could probably beat the lowly Wildcats with less than half a team, but it's safe to say Jordan didn't want to be forced to find out. Not that he'd ever admit to any sort of pre-game anxiety in the press. After all, this is a man who has said on many occasions that he never once lined up in a game he didn't expect to win. "If we have to," Jordan told the paper on Tuesday, "we're prepared to go with what we've got. We might not be as good as we could be, but we'll get fired up and go after them."

Jordan's word choice was oddly similar to the "Fired up! Ready to go!" chant that was already in use among the boycotting players and their supporters, but his meaning couldn't have been more different. In the black community, "Fired up! Ready to go!" put voice to the urgency many felt to follow through with the boycott, no matter the consequences. For Jordan, though, getting *fired up* and being *prepared to go* meant practice, discipline, and making the most of whatever players you've got handy: in short, doing what football teams always have to do and saying what football coaches always have to say. In promising the fans that he could get a depleted squad *prepared to go*, the Conway coach sounded like a guy who wasn't convinced it would come to that, like a disciplinarian father who was confident his rebellious sons would see the error of their ways and wise up. Looking back on it now, Jordan says he's pretty sure the striking players were misled into thinking he would immediately cave in to their demands. And while H. H. Singleton and the black players were wrong if they thought Jordan would quickly back down, the coach probably underestimated the will driving the boycott. The Conway Tigers, it seemed, were locked in a game of chicken.

On Wednesday, though, Jordan had reason to hope the dispute was already over. That afternoon, a few hours before practice, which was scheduled to start at 3:30, two black players (Lawrence Mitchell and linebacker Julius Spain) met behind closed doors with the coach. According to Jordan's records of the meeting, they told him that all the black players would be returning to practice. But first they needed to break the news to Reverend Singleton, and they'd already committed to a 7:00 meeting at Cherry Hill Baptist.

"Well, then, I'll tell you what," Jordan said. "Let's make it 7:30; you all go to the meeting, get the guys, come on to football practice." After leaving the meeting with Mitchell and Spain, Jordan called the white varsity players together and announced that he was postponing practice until 7:30. Once Lawrence and the rest of the black players voted to end the boycott, they'd have just enough time to hustle from Cherry Hill back to the high school and thereby avoid missing a second practice and the one-game suspension they'd face for two unexcused absences. Maybe Jordan would be able to suit up a full squad against Dalzell-Hillcrest after all.

When 7:30 p.m. came and went with no sign of the black players, Jordan moved the start back to 8:00. This, he said, would give the grounds crew time to mow the baseball field—which in '89, eleven years before the Backyard was constructed, was the school's only field equipped with lights, and lights would be an absolute necessity for a practice that started so late. But at 8:00, with the lights on and the baseball field mowed, it was clear that the black players wouldn't be practicing that night.

At 8:45 p.m., as Jordan and his coaches were running the twenty-five white varsity players through drills and game prep, Carlos Hunt, Lawrence Mitchell, and a few more black players finally showed up at the school. They walked from their cars up to the hurricane fence that encircled the baseball field. Fingers wrapped around the chain-link, they watched practice from the other side. When reporters asked them questions, Carlos and Lawrence responded with "No comment." Eventually, Bob Parker, a black assistant coach, broke away from practice and came over to the fence. He talked to Carlos and Lawrence about what a boycott might cost them in terms of scholarship opportunities and attention from college scouts. Then Chuck Jordan walked over to the fence. The black players listened as their coach told them that play or don't play, he'd understand their decision. For now anyway, their decision was to watch rather than practice, and as they watched, according to the next day's newspaper, "there was a wistfulness in their eyes."

"Sure they want to play football," Rev. Singleton had told reporters earlier that evening. "But they don't want to play football at all costs."

On Thursday, there again seemed reason to hope. As on the previous day, the coach met with two players during the afternoon, this time Hunt and Mitchell. According to Jordan, the players told him that they knew his decision to replace Carlos with Mickey was not racially motivated, and they told him they wanted to play football. But, said Lawrence, "we have to at least show our respects to the Rev. and let him hear it from us and not from somebody else."

So again Jordan postponed practice in order to give the players time to attend the meeting at Cherry Hill, break the news to Singleton, and make it back to the school. If they did, the season could still be salvaged. Carlos, Lawrence, and the other striking players would be benched tomorrow night for missing two practices, but the Tigers might be able to win the Hillcrest game anyway. And if the scrappy, under-experienced white kids pulled off that win, then with their formerly-rebellious-but-now-penitent black teammates back and eligible for game two against John McKissick's Summerville team, all would again be right in Conway.

Early that evening, however, about an hour before practice was scheduled to start, Carlos and Lawrence again showed up to speak with Jordan, who was sitting in his office, talking with Mickey Wilson Sr.

"Coach, we've got some problems," Carlos said. "When am I going to start taking snaps?"

Jordan reiterated that Carlos wouldn't be taking snaps at quarterback, not unless the coaching staff decided it was best for the team.

"But, Coach, you got to understand," Carlos said, "the NAACP can't come out of this looking bad."

"Well, son," Jordan said, "let me tell you something. If the need arises for you to be backup quarterback, then you'll be backup quarterback. If the need arises for you to be the quarterback, you'll be the quarterback; however, it's going to be when I decide and when my coaching staff decides, and not when your mama decides or not when you decide or not when any pressure group decides."

"Well, Coach," Carlos said, "I'm not going to be able to play. If I can't be a quarterback, I'm not going to play." Clearly upset, he shook his head, stood up, and wandered into an adjoining office and then out into the hallway. Now it was just Jordan, Wilson Sr., and Lawrence.

"Don't go back to the meeting," Jordan said to Lawrence. "Because if you go back, it's going to be tough. You know you're not going to get back out here."

"Yeah, I know, Coach," Lawrence said. "I know." The stud defensive end then told Jordan he was heading to the locker room to get dressed.

A few minutes later, Jordan received a call from H. H. Singleton who said that it was his understanding that Jordan and Carlos had reached a compromise wherein Carlos would be the backup quarterback and that he'd be allowed to compete for the starting position.

"No, sir, I did not make that compromise," Jordan said. "I simply stated to Carlos that when I saw fit and when our staff decided that he would be a quarterback, then that is when it would take place."

At that point, Reverend Singleton said, according to Jordan, "Sir, you have a dictatorship mentality. You have not heard the last of me. I will get you yet."

By about 7:00 p.m., as many as fifteen black players had shown up at the practice field, but only six of those were dressed and ready to participate in drills. The rest of them, including Carlos and Lawrence, were standing against the fence, still in street clothes. Reporters asked Carlos how he was feeling. "Not too good," he said, wearing a tearful expression. "There are a lot of things on my mind."

A few minutes later, a woman drove up and escorted Carlos away, saying to him, "You're supposed to have a meeting at the church." Shortly thereafter Lawrence and the rest of the players who were in street clothes also left for Cherry Hill.

As the whistle blew to start practice, the six black players who had showed up in uniform were still there, appearing ready to play. One of them immediately reported to the field, and then, over a period of few minutes, "by ones and twos," the *Sun News* reported, "the other five joined the drills." Jordan decided that they'd be eligible to play the following night against Hillcrest. Carlos, Lawrence, and the others had officially been suspended. The six black players who stayed with the team—none of whom had been varsity starters before the walkout began—would eventually become known by the boycotting players as the "Zebras."

On Friday morning, the first mention of the Conway football boycott hit national papers, as the Associated Press and *USA Today* picked up the story. Coach Jordan awoke that day finally knowing, for better or worse, which guys he'd have available that night. He'd begun fall practice with 55 varsity players, 31 black and 24 white, a fact he'd learned only after being asked by a reporter how many of each race were on the roster. "I'd never thought about how many white players and how many black players we had until the situation came up," Jordan said. "The only way I figured it out was to get a team picture and count." Now, even with the addition of the six black players who'd decided not to boycott, he was still playing with half a team. The gaps would be filled by JV kids. Still, said Jordan, "We're going in with the attitude that we're going to be successful."

Not everyone shared his optimism. Mark Johnson, the *Sun News* sportswriter who ran game predictions in his weekly "Prep Football" feature, wrote of the Conway/Hillcrest matchup, "Talk about tough games to pick. . . . But with all the turmoil going on this week, I'll have to say Hillcrest will win its first game in two years."

That evening, Jordan loaded his players onto the two school buses—a short bus for the seniors and a regular bus for everybody else—that would take them from Conway High to Thorny's Steakhouse, where they would eat their traditional pre-game meal. After dinner, the two buses and the equipment van would travel the next five miles to the Coastal Carolina branch campus of the University of South Carolina, home of the Graveyard. Just like always, they'd take a right turn on Highway 544, and as they came up on a convenience store called the Jiffy Shop, they'd be able to see the stadium lights burning in the distance, glowing high over the pine trees. Riding in the first row of the long bus, Jordan would turn back toward the underclassmen. "All right, boys," he'd say, clapping his hands together just as he always did, "the lights are on."

But first, in order to get from Thorny's to the Graveyard, the buses would have to roll down Church Street, passing directly in front of Cherry Hill Baptist, where the striking players where gathering for a 7:00 p.m. meeting. And wouldn't you know it, when the convoy arrived at the corner of Church and Racepath, it was stopped at the intersection by a red light. Now Chuck Jordan's remaining Tigers were sitting within twenty yards of the church. The boycotting players, seeing the buses idling at the light, quickly lined up along Church Street. Inside the underclassmen's bus, Mickey Wilson and the white Tigers looked out the windows and saw their black teammates—some in their game jerseys, some in identical white shirts—staring in silence back at them. "They were waiting on us," Mickey recalls now. When the light turned green, two buses filled with mostly white players slid past the gauntlet of striking black players in what must have felt like slow motion.

After the team passed by, Carlos, Lawrence, and the rest of the boycotting players filed into the church for the meeting, just as they had every evening since Monday. These "mass meetings," as Singleton called them—employing the same term that had been used for planning sessions during the civil rights movement—would be held nearly every night, as long as the boycott continued. On this night, game night, the striking players made it known that they wanted to attend the Conway Tigers' season opener, not as participants but as spectators. Reverend Singleton said he didn't think that was a smart idea. No good could come of it. His attention was focused on the overnight bus trip he'd be leading later that evening, taking a large group to Washington, D.C., for the NAACP's Silent March, which was scheduled for the next day. Inspired by the 1917 silent parade in New York City—which had been organized by the NAACP and led by W. E. B. Du Bois to protest lynching and segregation—this new Silent March was staged to voice opposition to recent decisions by the U.S. Supreme Court on affirmative action and minority set-asides. Singleton was much more interested in seeing the striking players attend a civil rights march than a football game, and some of them, including Carlos and Lawrence, were already planning on riding the bus to D.C. But when it came to the game, the reverend was outvoted. The players had decided to visit the Graveyard.

"If you're going to go," Singleton said, "go together and sit in a specific area." He was worried about the boycotting players' safety. You never knew what might happen if somebody was caught alone by a gang of people who were angered by the boycott, maybe angered to the point of violence. The school year wouldn't start until Monday, so this game marked the first time in several months that so many Conway students, black and white, would be together in one space. Couple that with whatever aggravations might be boiling in the community, and you had all the makings for clashes and hostility. As the game began, twenty police officers—more than double the usual number—were positioned in and around the stadium.

Carlos, Lawrence, and the rest of the boycotting players arrived during the first quarter, and as instructed, they all sat together. According to Hank Singleton, who attended with the players that night, "One of the things that was very easy to do at a Conway High football game was to sit in a specific area, because on the home side, the whites sat on one side of the stands and the blacks sat on the other. That's just the way it had always been." The players, however, isolated themselves even further by congregating in separate set of bleachers near the south end zone, the end closest to Highway 544 and the cemetery across the road. If you hadn't been reading the newspaper all week, you might have thought, for a while at least, that you were watching a regular old football game. Sure, there were a few oddities: a beefed-up police presence, the fact that one team fielded white players almost exclusively, the block of black kids wearing game jerseys sitting together in the small set of bleachers. But for most of the first quarter, the atmosphere was pretty typical, perhaps even a tad sedate.

A few minutes after the striking players arrived, however, everything changed. The Conway offense, which had been sputtering all game, was backed up on the south end of the field, the end where the protesting players were sitting. Then Mickey Wilson was sacked. Hard. By a vicious hit that knocked the ball loose. And Dalzell-Hillcrest recovered the fumble. In the stands, some of the white fans shook their heads in both frustration and sympathy; some of them gave keep-your-chin-up claps in support of the Tigers. The boycotting black players, however, rose to their feet in support of *Hillcrest*. When the ball popped from Mickey's grasp, they cheered and started chanting, "We want Carlos!" Many of the white Conway fans were shocked. The striking players were heckling their teammates, kids they had, as recently as Monday, sweated with and celebrated with and battled alongside.

From there it only got worse, both on the field and in the stands. Every time Hillcrest made a good play, the striking players cheered, and if you happened to be rooting for the Wildcats, there was much to cheer about. Hillcrest scored on a 22-yard touchdown pass. The black players erupted. Hillcrest scored on a 70-yard punt return. The black players mocked their fellow Tigers. Hillcrest scored on a 65-yard run. The black players stood on the bleachers, arms raised high in the air. The score at halftime was Hillcrest 20, Conway 0. And the chanting continued, "We want Carlos! We want Carlos!"

The louder the striking players chanted, the louder the white fans hollered back at them. The white fans were angry—*infuriated* is how Hank Singleton remembers it: "Because it [the black players rooting for the other team] looked like something that was orchestrated, and there was only one person in the black community who could have orchestrated something like this."

According to Hank, this kind of disruption was one of the reasons his father hadn't wanted the players to attend the game in the first place. The display threatened to undermine the legitimacy of the complaint against Coach Jordan, and it took everybody's eyes off the prize. Hank and several older folks tried to quiet the players, but, even as he was doing it, he understood that what sounded like maliciousness to the white side of the bleachers was really frustration coming from the black side. "It's tearing these guys apart that they can't be out there," he told the *Sun News* at the time.

Rudolph Brown of the NAACP stressed that the protesters were not cheering for Hillcrest or against the Tigers, but were instead "cheering for the defense that's not out there and the offense that's not out there," a distinction that was surely lost on the kids who actually played that night and lost on the white fans who, according to reports, became increasingly agitated by what they saw as the black players' disloyalty. Conway High Principal Tommy Lewis told *Sports Illustrated*, "It was tough not to send in the police. But [the striking players] had paid their four dollars."

Reminded now of the black Tigers cheering for the Wildcats in 1989, Mickey Wilson says, "That was probably one of the toughest things about the whole boycott."

During the halftime intermission, Hank Singleton pulled Carlos Hunt and Lawrence Mitchell out of the bleachers and drove them back to the church. He did this for two reasons. One, they needed to pack up for that night's trip to Washington; and two, he wanted to get them out of that volatile atmosphere before they could be goaded into a fight.

When the clock finally hit 0:00, the scoreboard read Dalzell-Hillcrest 34, Conway 6. It was as thorough a defeat as a Chuck Jordan–coached team had ever suffered. Still, as he told reporters, the overmatched kids from Conway "played their hearts out." Jordan mentioned that a spectator came up to him after the game and told him that as a thirty-three-year fan of the Tigers, he'd never been more proud of a group of kids. "And that's the same way I feel," the coach said.

Who could blame Jordan and the Conway faithful for grasping the silver lining? The cloud itself was gray as could be. The skeleton crew Tigers had gotten their butts cut by one of the worst teams in the state. Conway lost by four touchdowns. They were outgained in total yardage 349 to 62. The Ground Chuck running offense put up only 37 yards (to 291 for Hillcrest). And if Mickey Wilson had been promoted to starting QB on the basis of his potential as a passer, that potential wasn't evident in this game. He connected on two of three throws for a total of one yard. Mickey's only highlight in the game—and the only real highlight for the team, period—was his one-yard plunge for a touchdown in the south end zone, the end nearest the striking players, long after the game had been settled.

"You know, we got beat, of course," Mickey says now. "We got beat pretty good. But I scored on a quarterback sneak in that end zone down there, and I remember when I got up, I looked over there [at the striking players], and I was extremely, extremely *pissed.*" He lets out a good laugh. "I used to have a really bad temper, and for a brief second, I thought about running over there and just, you know. . ." He makes a shaking motion with his right hand, scolding an imaginary foe with an imaginary football. "But I remember thinking, no, no, just go to the sideline." His smile fades, all traces of laughter now gone. "That was tough. That was definitely tough."

It must have also been tough, on the bus ride back to the school, to have to drive right past Cherry Hill Baptist again, this time after a humiliating defeat. When they hit the intersection of Church and Racepath, if Mickey Wilson and his teammates looked out the windows and into the darkness, they might have seen Reverend and Hank Singleton readying the Cherry Hill bus for the trip to D.C. They might have seen Carlos Hunt and Lawrence Mitchell walking across the parking lot and loading their bags and themselves onto that bus.

Mickey Wilson and the white Tigers rolling in one direction.

Carlos, Lawrence, and the Cherry Hill folks rolling another.

Out past the headlights of the football buses was a game next week against Summerville, then a whole season of who knew what. More ass-whuppings? More mouthing off and trash talk from the striking players?

On the church bus, the Cherry Hill contingent looked forward to spreading word in Washington of what was happening in Conway. Because something was most definitely happening in Conway. Nobody, not even H. H. Singleton, knew exactly what—except that the powder keg that had been fueled by years of perceived inequity, on the football field and in the community, had finally exploded.

Other explosions of black empowerment were detonating that summer of 1989, some the people on the Cherry Hill bus were aware of, some they probably could have predicted, and some they might not have seen coming. As they eased out of the church parking lot, they may have known that the next day—in addition to the Silent March they'd be attending in D.C.—the Rev. Al Sharpton would be leading a march through the Bensonhurst section of Brooklyn to protest the murder of Yusef Hawkins, the sixteen-year-old who'd been shot a few days earlier after he and three friends were attacked by gang of white kids. The Cherry Hill group couldn't have known for certain, but they may have guessed correctly, that during the Bensonhurst march, the black protesters would be greeted by whites who were carrying watermelons and chanting, "Niggers go home!"

They wouldn't have known, but perhaps could have predicted, that in just over a week, during Labor Day weekend, Virginia Beach police would clash with black college students who'd come to the shore for their annual Greekfest celebration. The resulting protests (or "race riots" depending on your point of view), led to billy-clubbed faces, broken storefront glass, and phalanxes of machine gun–wielding National Guardsmen.

And although Carlos's and Lawrence's Walkmen may have been loaded with the cassette single of the song, they and the other members of the traveling party probably wouldn't have been able to accurately gauge the profound cultural influence of Public Enemy's "Fight the Power" or the Spike Lee film *Do the Right Thing*, for which that song served as the theme.

But on the drive out of Horry County and up I-95, Reverend Singleton's group surely understood that something real and powerful was building in the black community—in Conway, in South Carolina, and nationally. For the generation of black kids who had grown up listening to stories about the civil rights movement of the '50s and '60s, the summer of '89 marked the moment when acquiescence, complacency, and "go along to get along" weren't going to cut it anymore.

- 5 -

WORK TOGETHER, WALK TOGETHER

NOW

LATE-SUMMER WEEKENDS IN HORRY COUNTY TEND TO BE PRETTY RELAXED affairs. Beaten down by the heat and weary after a season of tourist traffic, locals know better than to drive to the beach on these days when last-chance day trippers from inland towns clog Highway 501. Easier to stay close to home for burgers on the grill and a splash in the kiddie pool. Maybe drop the jon boat in at Pitch Landing and do a little bass fishing on the Waccamaw and then deeper back into Cox Ferry Lake. Maybe head out to Punch Bowl for a dip in the Little Pee Dee. Better yet, stay cool inside in the AC, crack a beer, and catch a few innings of the Braves game. On this particular late-August Saturday, however, there's high school football to be played—a doubleheader, even. Down at the beach, in Doug Shaw Stadium, Mickey Wilson's Seahawks are hosting a special event called the Derrick Law Firm Kickoff Classic. In game one, the Conway Tigers will take on Northwestern High School, a team out of Rock Hill, South Carolina. In the nightcap, Myrtle Beach plays their season opener against Irmo, a school from up near Columbia. It's rare for high school ball to happen on a Saturday, rarer still to get the chance to see two of Horry County's more prestigious programs in one night, for one ticket price. And although Conway and Myrtle Beach won't be going against each other tonight (the Bell Game is scheduled for Week 5, right here at Doug Shaw), any time you get the Tigers and the Seahawks on the same field, that's the sort of thing that will pull several thousand Horryites out of their easy chairs and into the stadium—tourist traffic be damned.

For Mickey Wilson's team—who sat idle last Friday, Week 0—game day starts more than four hours before kickoff when the players gather for a team meal of Italian food at a chain restaurant. There's a big crowd here even before two school buses' worth of Seahawks and their entourage pile

in. But because a former Myrtle Beach player's father is a regional manager in the restaurant chain, there's plenty of room set aside for the sixty
or so players, a coaching staff of six, and a few affiliated personnel. When
the buses arrive back at the school, Conway and Northwestern are getting
set to kick off, which means the Seahawks have another three hours to kill
before taking the field. The wait must be excruciating for the players, who
know that Conway will have finished their second game of the season before Myrtle Beach has even begun their first. Walking through the halls on
the way to a team meeting in the school auditorium, the players show every
bit of the pressure and anticipation they feel, though they show it in different ways. Some release the accumulated energy by play fighting whenever a
coach isn't nearby to witness it. A few bark out verses from rap songs whose
bitches-and-hoes lyrics the coaches pretend not to notice. Others appear
to be getting in the zone by practicing an exaggerated state of calm, but it's
hard to maintain game face for three hours, so most of these budding Zen-
masters revert periodically to the giggling and scuffling of the first group. If
the aim of preseason and pre-game preparations is to get the Seahawks fired
up and ready to go, Coach Wilson and his staff have succeeded.

For the last four months, Mickey's players have spent far more time
in the weight room than on the football field. All high school teams do
strength and conditioning training, and all coaches try to make the off-season weight regimen a point of pride among their players. And come game
time, when the scoreboard flips to the fourth quarter, players on every team
will raise four fingers in the air to signify that their school and their school
alone owns the final twelve minutes of play, specifically because of all the
work they put in during the off season. But the fact is, every team can't
own the fourth quarter; somebody's gotta win, and somebody's gotta lose.
Mickey Wilson has hung the championship banners that prove his players
already know what it means to be the last team standing at the end of the
season. So his kids buy in to his strength-training regimen at the beginning
of the season, as early as spring semester, when his Seahawks start hitting
the weights in preparation for games that are still six months away. In June,
when the school year ends, the mandatory ninety-minute morning sessions
begin. A typical summer schedule will have the players in the weight room
at 7:00 a.m. almost every weekday all through June and July before official
team practices start in August. Mickey points to these intense, early morning workouts as one of the secrets of Myrtle Beach's success.

Headed into tonight's opener against Irmo, despite all his players' individual and collective preparations in the preseason, Mickey's team is at far

less than full strength. Four starters will sit out with injuries, including the Seahawks' best defensive player, D'Andre "Chocolate" Wilson (no relation to Coach Wilson), a senior who is being scouted by N.C. State, Ole Miss, and Missouri, but is currently on crutches after undergoing surgery to repair a torn meniscus. Two other starters were injured in separate pickup basketball games. Now, as Mickey opens the double doors that lead to the auditorium, he is asked about his chances against the Irmo Yellow Jackets. "If we can pull this one off," he says with a nervous laugh, "you can go ahead and give me the coach of the year award."

The players walk through the doors and are immersed in near-total darkness. Mickey has brought his team through the side entrance, which means that in order to get to their seats, they have to negotiate a short flight of stairs. The slow descent of the first few players on the darkened staircase has the rest of the team crowded outside the entrance, wondering what has caused the line to back up. "Shut up, y'all," the seniors whisper-shout to the underclassmen. "Take your hat off." Whether this plunge into a darkened traffic jam was planned or not, it has the effect of focusing the players on what is about to happen: a brief speech from the head coach, followed by a longer one from team minister Ronny Byrd, pastor of Palmetto Shores Church. Mr. Byrd—that's what everyone calls him, not Reverend Byrd or Pastor Byrd—is a former high school player who often uses Biblical metaphors when talking football and football metaphors when talking religion, which is fitting because his devotion to the Seahawks appears to be about as deep and sincere as his devotion to the Lord.

With his players finally assembled in the auditorium, Mickey takes the stage and, as is his custom, says very little. "What can I say to them at that point that they don't know already?" he says when asked about his brevity. "If we've done our job as coaches, they already know what to do." Besides, the long wait for game day has done more to get the team psyched up than anything he can say to them now. During his comments, he ignores a few guys glancing at their cell phones, and for the moment he allows the players to scatter throughout the auditorium, which gives them space to relax. Designed for students who are, on average, a good bit smaller than the members of the football team, the seats in here would make anyone yearn for the relative comfort of coach class in an oversold 737, but before introducing Mr. Byrd, Mickey makes the kids in the cheap seats get up, and everybody wedges into the first four rows. Given the subject of his impending remarks, this enforced closeness seems like an organic choice.

Ronny Byrd shares with Mickey a manner that's hard not to describe as folksy. He's a perpetual grinner, and he speaks with the kind of glad-to-see-you casualness that charms people into responding to him in the same manner. The players mostly come from churchgoing families, so it's not surprising that they hold a reverence for him that rivals the respect they show for Coach Wilson. And even if they didn't, Mickey would insist that they appear to.

Aware of Chocolate Wilson and the other injured players who will miss tonight's game, Mr. Byrd begins his comments with the obligatory David vs. Goliath reference, stressing that David achieved victory because he knew that as long as he had faith in the Lord, defeat was impossible. Then, glancing at his notes, he transitions to the heart of today's message, which comes from Ephesians, Chapter 5. He draws five lessons from the chapter, all of which amount to nuggets of conventional football wisdom supported by Biblical imperative. First, he focuses on the clause "walk in love" from Verse 2 ("And walk in love, as Christ also hath loved us, and hath given himself for us an offering and a sacrifice to God for a sweet-smelling savour"). A team, he says, isn't just a group of guys who happen to play together. They have to work together, *walk* together, in all they do, and only when they are joined "in love" can they truly play together. Next, he selects an injunction against "foolish talking" from Verse 4 and another against "vain words" from Verse 6 ("Let no man deceive you with vain words: for because of these things cometh the wrath of God upon the children of disobedience"), a warning to avoid wasting energy on trash talk before, during, or after the game. Apparently, even the Bible coaches you to "let your play do the talking," a dictum that many of Myrtle Beach's rivals might argue the Seahawks have yet to learn, considering their showy tradition of taking the field by running through that inflatable helmet to a looped recording of "The champ is here! The champ is here!"

To biblical scholars, Ephesians 5, a New Testament chapter on topics like sexual purity, marital life, and the dangers of strong drink, might seem unrelated to high school football. But as a preacher whose rhetoric parses sentences down to their phrasal molecular structure, Mr. Byrd makes this chapter seem like it was written not just about football, but specifically about the situation the Seahawks find themselves in tonight: up against a superior foe in the Yellow Jackets and needing a "team effort" even to have a chance. He isn't nearly the disciple of brevity that Mickey is, though, so he doesn't finish the last of his five lessons from Ephesians until nearly twenty minutes have passed. Then he announces that he will now say a prayer, and Mickey asks everyone to huddle together and "touch a shoulder."

After praying for a safe and fair contest, Mr. Byrd closes with "And these things *I* pray in Jesus' name." The over-stressed *I*—which seems to emphasize for the record that he's only speaking for himself and that the prayer doesn't necessarily represent the views of the players—feels more than a little forced, as in forced by the political and legal powers that insist on at least some separation between the church and public school, even in the Bible-belt state of South Carolina. Not that there's anyone in this room who would object if he had said instead, "And these things *we* pray." In Myrtle Beach and all over the South, football and Christianity are linked so strongly that one is seen as having an obvious and natural connection to the other. And this connection isn't restricted to the school auditorium or the locker room; it will often be voiced over the P.A. system, to the whole stadium. Before tonight's kickoff between Conway and Northwestern, the crowd will be led in a prayer thanking the Lord for two things: the ways he loves us and the great game of football. Similar themes can be heard every home-game Saturday in stadium-wide prayers at the University of South Carolina and at Clemson University. In the Palmetto State, religion isn't something that people attach to football. It's a necessary part of game preparation.

After the amens, the players move to the fieldhouse to receive their final pieces of equipment. They line up methodically at the window joining the laundry room to the locker room, waiting to receive their compression shirts, athletic supporters, socks, and other personal items that make football possible or at least a little safer and more hygienic. Outfitting sixty players is not a quick or simple process, so Mickey's staff has adopted a seniority system: seniors first, then juniors, and so on. The coaches approach this annual duty with a stateliness that some might find odd, considering that they are essentially passing out underwear. But this is one of the last rites in an offseason ritual that culminates in the elevation of a group of boys into something like manhood. If Myrtle Beach were a tribe, these would be the new warriors sent out to fight. Handling the battle garments for these anointed few is an honor.

While the players change into their new gear, including the white pants that signify their membership on the varsity team, Mickey and his assistants gather in the next room, where they talk about deer hunting and watch a comedy DVD on the screen that's usually reserved for viewing game footage. They have left the players unsupervised in the locker room in the hope that the captains and other seniors will take charge. Eventually, Mickey receives a text message saying that halftime of the Conway-Northwestern game is almost over. He asks the coaches to gather the players and walk them the short distance from the fieldhouse over to Doug Shaw Stadium. Work together, walk together.

• • •

While the Seahawks are going through their pre-game prep, the Tigers are getting the snot knocked out of them by the Northwestern Trojans. Last week against Georgetown, it seemed that, for one night anyway, the Conway Tiger roar had indeed been restored. Chuck Jordan's boys dominated the Bulldogs, building a 35–6 lead at the half before easing up and cruising to a 42–25 win. Mykal Moody completed ten of twelve passes for 185 yards and 3 touchdowns and then rested for most of the second half. In short, Conway did to Georgetown what a 4A team is supposed to do to a 3A team. Coach Jordan, in his halftime speech last week, told his players: "Okay. This is your opportunity to learn to play *ahead*. But, believe me, there will come a time this season when you're gonna have to learn to play *behind*."

And now, one week later and just as their coach predicted, the Tigers find themselves *way* behind, down 34–12 at the half against Northwestern, a strong 4A team that has just come off of a win against perennial power Gaffney. The Trojans arrived at tonight's game armed with a stud quarterback named Mason Rudolph who is being recruited by Oklahoma State and who leads a passing attack ominously nicknamed the "Air Raid." As it turns out, the Northwestern offense will be good for more than six hundred yards tonight, a total that might have been more like eight hundred if they hadn't sat their starters in the fourth quarter. As the Trojans were running up and down the field in the first half, one angry Tiger fan shouted from the stands, "Does anybody in Conway still like to *hit*?"

Late in the second quarter, the Tigers had a chance to cut the lead to ten, but while attempting to dive across the goal line, Mykal fumbled the ball into the end zone. The Trojans recovered, took over on their 20, and on the very next play, scored a touchdown on an 80-yard run that put the score at 34–12 going into the half. Moody got a hard lesson in the maxim his coach never tires of preaching: You can't win if you put the daggum ball on the ground.

Now, with halftime over and the Myrtle Beach Seahawks watching from the visiting stands, Mykal is sitting on the bench, getting worked on by the trainers for leg cramps. With 9:38 left in the third, his backup, sophomore Ethan Smith—a white kid with the type of tall body frame that often gets called "prototypical" for a quarterback—throws a touchdown pass to cut the lead to 34–19, but that's as close as the Tigers get. Before the end of the third quarter, the Trojans are up 55–19, which will turn out to be the final score. For Conway, the pain of losing is magnified by the fact that it happened in Myrtle Beach's stadium, in front of Seahawk players and fans. But there's one final indignity: In order to exit the field, the Tigers have to walk the wrong way through Myrtle Beach's damn inflatable helmet, and as they do, it looks like they're being swallowed whole.

• • •

With the clock winding down on the Tigers, the Seahawks walk back to the fieldhouse, where they make their final preparations and then board the buses that are their official transportation to the game. The distance between the fieldhouse and the stadium is only about 150 yards, but the Myrtle Beach players will not arrive on foot. Instead, with a police cruiser leading the way, sirens blaring and lights flashing, the buses take a slow ride past the high school, turn left onto Grissom Parkway, left again on 29th Ave, and left again on Oak St. before making yet another left at the stadium entrance. In this three-quarter mile journey that draws a nearly perfect square on the map, the buses roll through a neighborhood that doesn't feature prominently in the Grand Strand tourism brochures, which is to say a neighborhood where locals actually live. They pass a bank, a flower shop, and several small houses and duplexes. As they pull into the parking lot, the police escort adds a couple of extra siren blasts to alert everyone that the Seahawks have entered the facility.

After stretching and working up a good sweat on the field, the entire team retreats to the tiny home locker room under the bleachers, where they drink water and await Mickey's final words. Entering the double doors, the coach surveys his team for a moment, and says, "Okay, hats off."

The players still wearing their helmets unstrap them and put them in their laps.

"Here's all I'm gonna say." Mickey doesn't pace the room because it isn't large enough for pacing. Instead he stands near the doors, wearing a white polo and khaki pants. "We're better prepared than they are. We work harder than anybody else in the state."

Some players have already heard talk about Irmo's relatively weak off-season preparation regime, and, right or wrong, a consensus has developed among the team that the Yellow Jackets are soft, that they have great talent but aren't yet ready to play. With or without Chocolate Wilson and the other injured starters, the Myrtle Beach players believe they can win.

"If you can get this game into the fourth quarter," Mickey says, "you *will* win!"

With a mighty whoop, the players leave the locker room and gather inside the inflatable helmet in a cramped pack. Metallica's "Enter Sandman" thunders from the stadium P.A. Two students wearing green body paint use fire extinguishers to create a dense fog at the facemask of the helmet, and the Seahawks begin a group prayer, so silent at first that it's nearly impossible to hear them over the stadium music. "Dear Lord," they say in unison, beginning what has become known as the Cornhusker Prayer, named for the University of Nebraska Cornhuskers, who also recite these words before every game, "in the battles we go through in life, we ask for a chance that's fair, a chance to equal our stride, a chance to do or dare. And if we win, let it be by the code, with faith and honor held high. But if we lose, let us stand by the road and cheer as the winners go by. Day by day, we get better and better. A team that can't be beat, won't be beat. WON'T BE BEAT!"

And then suddenly the team bolts from the helmet, and they're onto the field. The music has now crossfaded to "The champ is here! The champ is here!"

It's go time.

The game starts well for the Seahawks. After an Irmo fumble on the Yellow Jacket side of the 50, Myrtle Beach kicker Max Huggins nails a 47-yard field goal to put the home team up by three. Later in the first quarter, an interception sets up a scoring pass from Tyler Keane to Sean Michael Orcutt, who, one series later, has to leave the field after a massive helmet-to-helmet hit. Midway through the second quarter, Huggins drills another field goal to take the score to 12–0. It's a nice start, but with the versatile Orcutt—who plays both ways, offense and defense—sitting on the bench, Myrtle Beach now has five injured starters, and the lack of experience starts to show. Irmo scores two quick touchdowns to take a 14–12 lead at the half.

Instead of tearing into his kids for giving up two scores and the lead, Mickey tells them, "We're in great shape. They were getting tired out there. I think you saw that." He says little else other than to tell his players to get out of the absurdly hot locker room and drink a lot of water. Just before they leave, he says, "Now bow your neck and fight like heck!" The Seahawks howl in response.

But as the new half begins, it appears that Mickey has misjudged the Irmo team's fitness. The third quarter sees two long Yellow Jacket touchdown passes, the second coming on a 61-yard double pass play with the QB throwing a backward screen to a receiver, who then fires to another receiver wide-open down the field. With his team now behind 27–12, Mickey must somehow re-energize a group of players who have given up 27 unanswered points, players who a few hours ago watched Conway fail to come back from the same fifteen-point deficit.

Early in the fourth quarter, after Tyler Keane's 38-yard touchdown pass to Ray Ray Pointer brings the score to 27–19, a Seahawk assistant points to a Yellow Jacket lineman who is hunched over with his hands on his knees. It's a clear sign of the Irmo fatigue that Mickey predicted his team could exploit.

And they do.

Down 27–25 with four minutes left to play and Irmo back to punt deep in their own territory, C.J. Cooper, the kid that Mickey moved from the quarterback position, races around the edge and blocks the kick. Linebacker Octavius Thomas scoops the ball and runs it in for the touchdown to put the Seahawks up 31–27. A successful two-point conversion makes it 33–27 with 3:21 to go. It's a score that becomes final when Cooper, substituting for Keane at QB on the last drive of the game, lets the clock run out by taking a knee. The first player to greet C.J. on the sideline is Tyler. They smack one another on the helmet, and together they move toward the midfield stripe, where the Seahawks and Yellow Jackets march past each other in long lines, offering up good-game high-fives.

THEN

Even after the Dalzell-Hillcrest disaster, Conway's season still could have been saved. The loss was humiliating for Chuck Jordan and his boys (and watching half the team cheer for the opponent was even more infuriating than the final score), but, if you could reduce the ramifications of the blow-out down to dispassionate rules and numbers, getting hammered by the Wildcats didn't mean all that much. For a team like Conway, whose goal was always to compete for a state championship, what really mattered was the postseason, which wouldn't start until November, and, because every school in the Big 16 Division of Class 4A qualified for the playoffs, the Tigers were assured of making the tournament. Still, Jordan knew that his guys wouldn't survive the loser-goes-home postseason without piling up some regular season victories. Not only would the regular season determine the playoff seeding, it was where teams learned how to win. For Conway to be competitive, they needed the boycotting players back, and if that wasn't clear before the Hillcrest game, it certainly was now. Team rules dictated that the striking Tigers could avoid being cut from the squad (for missing four practices) if they showed up for drills on Monday. Having served their one-game suspensions against Hillcrest, they could conceivably play on Friday against Summerville. But even if Carlos, Lawrence, and the others did decide to come back, how the heck would Jordan handle the return of players who just a few days earlier had cheered against their teammates? He'd simply have to find a way. As angry as the coach and most white Tiger fans were, they knew that in order for Conway to compete with John McKissick's Green Wave, the team had to be made whole.

In the meantime, what concerned everybody in town, white and black, was that Monday was the first day of the school year. How would the Conway High students behave? What would the atmosphere be like at Conway Middle, in H. H. Singleton's earth science classroom? "I have a son in jeopardy," Carlos Hunt's father told the *Sun News*. "So do the other parents, black and white. This situation has gone beyond football, far beyond. When school opens on Monday, there is going to be fuel for a fire."

Some of that heat had already been aimed at Horry County Schools Superintendent John Dawsey, who was busy navigating the delicate fact that Singleton was both an employee of the school district and its most prominent critic. During the week leading up to the Hillcrest game, Dawsey had begun to hear complaints from the white community, including from white Horry County Schools employees who argued that Singleton was getting preferential treatment, because if they had behaved similarly, they would already have been disciplined. The superintendent told the press he was receiving phone messages saying that he didn't deserve his salary, because Singleton was "already running the school district free of charge." On the Friday of the Hillcrest game, after a school board meeting in which a "personnel decision" was discussed, Dawsey—who, during the '87 cheerleader controversy, had reprimanded Singleton and told him never again to engage in such "unprofessional and inappropriate behavior"—announced that the district was not immediately planning to discipline the earth science teacher for his role in the football boycott. However, Dawsey said, "If Reverend Singleton's behavior or his involvement creates such a disturbance that he cannot be effective as a teacher, then it could become a problem to be dealt with."

The first day of school was charged with uncertainty, but the answer to the "How would the Conway High students behave?" question turned out to be surprisingly positive. Carlos, Lawrence, and most of the other striking players came to school, and although Superintendent Dawsey had promised to bring in police if necessary to quell violence, the day passed without any major incidents and no additional security was needed. Principal Tommy Lewis said, "I can't tell any difference in today and any other day." One student was quoted in the paper as calling the school day "boring." It seemed that Conway's young people had, for a day at least, forged an uneasy détente.

Looking back now, Larry Biddle, who was an assistant principal at Conway High in 1989, says he wasn't surprised by the relatively peaceful beginning to the school year, and he credits the implementation of an innovative educational program for that peace. The "Renaissance Program," which had been in place for five years, centered on a combination of rewards for student achievement and consequences for negative student behavior, and by early '89 it had received national attention—in the form of a special cover wrap for *Life* magazine—because of its success at Conway High. Interestingly, in the *Life* cover, one of the parents offering a testimonial to the effectiveness of the program was Carlos Hunt's mother, Kathy Thomas. "My son's attitude has improved so much in the past two years," she said. "He cares more about school now than he used to."

Although there were no significant disturbances at the high school that day, across town, at Conway Middle, the year hadn't launched quite so smoothly. A group of white parents complained to Principal Gil Stefanides, demanding that their children not be forced to attend Singleton's earth science class. They were afraid that Singleton would turn his classroom into a forum for his views on race and that he'd be unfair to his white students. They wanted their kids transferred to another teacher. One parent, Sylvia Housely, was quoted in the *Sun News* as saying, "I do not want his racial views and bigotry imposed on my daughter." Yvonne Tyler, another parent, put it bluntly: "He's prejudiced. No doubt about it. He makes me sick." That afternoon, after Stefanides told them that Conway Middle didn't employ enough science teachers to accommodate change requests, approximately twenty-five parents showed up at the school district offices, where they met with Superintendent Dawsey and asked that their children be transferred to another classroom. Some went further, demanding that Singleton be fired. Again they were told that there simply weren't enough teachers. Students could choose to skip the class, but they would lose their science requirement for the year. As upset as these parents were at the prospect of H. H. Singleton corrupting their kids, when the dismissal bells rang on Monday afternoon, the earth science teacher was still holding on to his job. The white parents' fears that their concerns wouldn't be addressed led some of them to threaten to picket at the school—a counter-protest. "We are trying to teach my daughter that people are people," parent Cindy Dexter said, "no matter what color."

When racial issues arise in the post–civil rights movement era, many whites take this "people are people" stance, which, though tautologically true and undoubtedly hopeful, usually amounts to denialism—denial that race matters, sure, but also denial that cultural differences and racial prejudices (especially their own) exist at all. Statements such as "I'm colorblind" or "I treat everybody the same" derive from the optimistic, but premature, assumption that we are already living in a post-racial world, and they sound like a call for assimilation rather than an appreciation of ethnic diversity. It's tempting to argue that the parents accusing H. H. Singleton of bigotry and of being prejudiced were motivated to do so by their own bigotry and prejudices. But rather than being an example of overt racism, the backlash to the boycott might best be described as a white weariness with the issue of race—a kind of haven't-we-dealt-with-this-already roll of the eyes that isn't racism exactly, but is probably just as bad in the aggregate.

Although Singleton stressed that he never taught anything in his classroom other than earth science, the white parents who complained that he was letting his activism color (pun intended) his teaching were expressing a belief that in 1989, race had already become a societal non-issue. Therefore, discussions of race were inappropriate and outdated—and maybe even dangerous. These parents might not have had any hard evidence of Singleton misleading or mistreating their children, but that's not the point. A common white view of race relations is that anyone—black or white—who openly discusses differences between the races is already making evaluative judgments based on race and is therefore guilty of racism. When the person pointing out differences in how races are treated happens to be a black activist, he is often accused of "reverse racism." Because one lesson many whites have learned is that you are not supposed to discuss race openly, especially if you are claiming that race is the primary cause of something—be it a hiring decision, school choice, or who starts at quarterback. This fear of discussing race *at all* is perhaps why, even today, a white person might whisper "He's *black*" when talking to another white person about a third person who is, in fact, obviously and proudly, black.

After all, by 1989 whites had seen what happened to people like Jimmy "The Greek" Snyder, who was dumb enough to be caught on TV casually citing race as a factor in performance. Snyder's firing by CBS came less than a year after Al Campanis, the general manager of the Los Angeles Dodgers, was interviewed by Ted Koppel on *Nightline* on the 40th anniversary of Jackie Robinson breaking baseball's color barrier. Campanis told Koppel that there weren't many blacks in important positions in Major League Baseball because black people "may not have some of the necessities to be, let's say, a field manager, or, perhaps, a general manager."

"Do you really believe that?" Koppel said.

"I don't say all of them, but they certainly are short . . . how many quarterbacks do you have? How many pitchers do you have that are black? The same thing applies."

"I gotta tell you," Koppel said, "that sounds like the same kind of garbage we were hearing forty years ago about players."

Even when pressed, Campanis continued. "Why are black men or black people not good swimmers? Because they don't have the buoyancy?"

"It may just be," Koppel said, putting the period on the interview and on Campanis's baseball career (he resigned from the Dodgers two days later), "that they don't have access to all the country clubs and the pools."

After seeing Snyder, Campanis, and others get in high-profile trouble for citing race itself as a direct cause for inequalities between the races, many whites seem to have taken away an oversimplified message from the public humiliation of these figures. If Jimmy "The Greek" can't say that blacks have an advantage because of their alleged "breeding" and Al Campanis can't say that blacks lack the "necessities" to be in management positions, the logic goes, then the safest bet it is never to use race to explain anything. Instead of directly referring to race, then, whites—even supposedly liberal whites—tend to speak in code. When looking for a new house, a white couple won't come right out and say they want to raise their kids among other white children, but they're perfectly willing to reject certain neighborhoods because they're looking for "a safer place to raise our kids—you know, where we could let them play outside and not worry about them so much." When real estate agents show houses to potential buyers, they know to use the code of "It's in a good school district" to get the message across without mentioning race. After all, no one but a bigot is going to buy a house from a real estate agent who says, "Good news! Gentle Acres is 93 percent white and so is the elementary school around the corner." If that agent says, "This neighborhood feeds into one of the best elementary schools in the state," however, she just sounds like someone who cares about her clients and their kids. Never mind that the meaning might be pretty much the same. Too often, the goal isn't to avoid thinking about race; it's to avoid *talking* about it. And in 1989, who was talking about race? Not Chuck Jordan. Not John Dawsey. Not white parents. They were the ones saying race didn't matter, that skin color wasn't the issue. The ones saying race *was* the issue were people like Jesse Jackson, Al Sharpton, and H. H. Singleton. Therefore, in many white minds, these black leaders were the true racists.

Between the extremes of white guilt and white superiority lies a middle ground where many, and perhaps most, whites live. They accept the notion that blacks are, theoretically at least, equal to whites, and for them, the issue ends there, on the theoretical level. The practical realities of a world where blacks clearly aren't achieving as much, on average, as whites don't matter nearly as much as the fact that individual blacks are technically capable of achieving anything whites can. It's easy for whites to point to a few successful black professionals or business owners or even a black president and say, "See. Nobody's stopping them. Blacks have the same opportunities we do." For many whites, the conviction that neither they nor anyone they personally know would stand in the way of an upwardly mobile black man or woman is enough to silence the debate.

On the Sunday before the first day of school, the *Sun News* printed five articles related to the boycott, and all of them, in one way or another, address race relations in Conway. "Until last week," begins one article, "the often separate worlds of whites and blacks in this town seemed to merge easily on the football field." Later, the author writes that "the issue is best illustrated by the fact that many blacks believe [racism exists in Conway] and many whites do not." But a question like "Do you think this town has a problem with racism?" can't really be answered, and that's because the question itself is wrong. The right question isn't "Is there racism here?" but something more like "What's the next step?"

Imagine an obese man who has already lost fifty pounds—and is justifiably proud of that fact—being told by his doctor, "Listen, you still have serious health issues you need to work on." The doctor is correct, of course. Clogged arteries and joint injuries don't go away the instant the weight is gone. The damage has already been done, even if you eliminate the most obvious and visible signs of the problem. But if the doctor were to be that blunt and brutally honest, the patient might wonder why he bothered to lose any weight to begin with. A guy who loses fifty pounds wants to be praised for his commitment to health. He doesn't want to hear, "You're still almost as unhealthy as ever. You've got a lot of work to do." He might pay attention, however, if the doctor told him, "Now that you've lost that weight, you can handle more strenuous exercise." *What's the next step?*

The white establishment is like that theoretical patient, because the truth is, the progress that has been made since the time of Jim Crow is remarkable in many ways. Whites, and especially older whites in the South, want a little credit for that transformation, whether they deserve it or not. After going along with the integration of schools and professions, after cleaning up their language, after resisting the urge to flee the neighborhood as soon as the first black family moves in, after smiling politely when a cousin marries a black man—many whites want some acknowledgment of the transformation they've already made. It's painful to them to be told that there's still work to do, and it's even more painful when it sounds to them that they, despite all the steps in the right direction, are still being called racists. Ike Long, the white mayor of Conway in 1989, said, "I'm in touch with 100 people every day, and I just don't see a racial problem. I think maybe there are some groups that try to make a racial problem, but I think they're cultivating something that's just not there." The day the boycott began, one of the white players told the *Sun News*, "I don't really think it's the players doing this. I think it's other people in the community." Another echoed that sentiment, saying, "I don't think there's any racial problem on this team. The players get along. I think it's outsiders behind this." In making these statements, these whites were doing what the Conway Middle School parents and many others in the white community were doing: dismissing H. H. Singleton as a race-baiting agitator looking for problems that just weren't there. To many white Conwayites, not only was racism not to blame for Hunt's removal from the QB position, racism itself was a thing of the past—at least until Reverend Singleton had gone and stirred everybody up.

But on the other side were thirty-one players—along with their parents, their families, and nearly half a town's worth of supporters—looking at the quarterback issue not as singular and isolated but as another example of racial bias and intolerance in a city and state that had a long, violent history of racial bias and intolerance. Former Conway city councilman Cleveland Fladger, who was black (and who, in his days as a football coach, had coached Chuck Jordan), stood with the boycotters, saying, "Racial tensions still exist. A lot of people are undercover about it, but then it leaks out." Earlier that summer of 1989 (not 1969 or 1949), it had already leaked out that a swimming pool in Saluda, South Carolina, was still enforcing a policy that barred blacks from attending. And it would leak out again, on September 5, 1989, approximately a week after the first day of school at Conway High, when the Buffalo Room, a tavern in North Augusta, South Carolina, would make national news for its refusal to serve blacks. Bruce Salter, the seventy-five-year-old owner of that tavern, would ultimately change his policy when he was sued not just by the NAACP but by the U.S. Justice Department. He never denied that he had had such a policy, but still, he would maintain, "I am not racial" and claim that he was "set up" by the NAACP when "[t]hey came to harass me." Given this context—given not just South Carolina's history but its present—how could Conway's black community *not* suspect that race was a factor in the Carlos Hunt situation?

After school that Monday, the focus shifted to the practice field, where Chuck Jordan would be trying to get his team, whoever showed up, ready for Friday's game against Summerville. Once again, the coach found himself in the same position he'd been in two times the previous week: about to start practice; hoping that Carlos, Lawrence, and the others would participate; and girding himself against the probability that they wouldn't. Optimism followed by disappointment: he'd ridden this rollercoaster before. Earlier that morning, in fact, there had been another glimmer of hope, when Carlos Hunt's mom, Kathy Thomas, met with Superintendent Dawsey. Perhaps this was a step toward reconciliation. But nothing was resolved at the meeting. Thomas asked Dawsey to overrule Jordan's decision to move Carlos to defense, arguing that because her son was not given a chance to compete for the QB position, his civil rights had been violated. Dawsey refused. Later, when asked by the press if any progress had been made in the meeting, the superintendent said, "We're back to square one."

When practice started, Jordan had a sheet of paper tucked into his pocket, a sheet with two statements written on it. At the top of the page was the statement he'd deliver to the press in the event the striking players skipped practice. At the bottom was another one, for use if they showed. And just like on two occasions the week before, Lawrence Mitchell and a few other black players did come to the high school. This time, however, instead of watching from the fence, they stayed in the parking lot, taking questions from the media. On the field, several policemen were lined up, there to ensure that reporters stayed on the other side of the white lines. Then, with about a hundred (mostly white) Tiger fans watching, Jordan took his squad through a three-hour session. Sixty-five varsity and junior varsity players participated in drills that night; only eight were black. Carlos, Lawrence, and all the black players who just two short weeks ago Jordan had assumed would make up much of the core of his team were gone.

After practice, in front of a crowd of reporters and fans, Jordan read his statement. The one at the top of the page. "This is our football team for 1989," the coach began. "We will play with the individuals who practiced with us today."

The Tiger fans cheered. Jordan hadn't used the words "cut" or "dismissed," but everyone in attendance understood the message: The boycotting players were no longer members of the football team.

Jordan continued, "I do want to say that it is an opportunity and a privilege to play football at Conway High School. We are proud of our young men and will continue to be. We will play hard and be the best team that we can be." The *Sun News's* Mel Derrick noted that at this point Jordan seemed to relax, now with a clearer picture, for better or worse, of what his team would look like. But still the coach left the door cracked for a possible return of the striking players by adding, "From this point on, we will deal with any appeals on an individual basis." With the crowd chanting "Let's go Tigers," Chuck Jordan folded up the paper and slid it back into his pocket.

The following morning, Tuesday, H. H. Singleton left his family's residence at the church and pulled into the parking lot at Conway Middle School. Talk from the group of white parents about a counter-boycott of his classes was heating up, but Singleton had a job to do, so he showed up for work, just as he'd been doing, at one school or another, for the last thirty years. The criticism from certain members of the white community was the kind of flak he'd become accustomed to taking, the kind of flak that in his role as president of the Conway branch of the NAACP it was his job to take. Granted, he was less accustomed to feeling this particular pressure here on the grounds of the middle school—where, from his point of view, he taught nothing that might be considered controversial, unless you thought plate tectonics and erosion and deposition issues were controversial—but still, because he compartmentalized, because he never talked about race or civil rights inside the classroom, he was confident that he'd be allowed to keep making the daily drive from the church to the school until he was ready to retire. So H. H. Singleton walked into his room and up to his desk, where he started taking his papers and materials from his briefcase.

Suddenly Gil Stefanides appeared in the doorway. "Mr. Singleton," the principal said, "the superintendent wants to see you."

The specific details of what happened next vary depending on whose account of the events you get, John Dawsey's (via sworn testimony) or H. H. Singleton's (via his son Hank). What's certain is that Stefanides escorted the earth science teacher to the principal's office. When they got there, according to Dawsey, the superintendent was waiting at the door (Hank Singleton says his father told him that Dawsey was sitting in the principal's chair).

"I guess you know what this is about," Dawsey said, according to Hank.

"No," Singleton said. "I have no idea what this is about."

Dawsey asked Singleton and Stefanides to sit down. "Reverend Singleton," the superintendent said (Hank says that Dawsey usually called his father "Harry"), "this is something I don't enjoy doing."

Then Dawsey read from a statement he'd prepared the previous evening. That night—after meeting with the angry white parents earlier in the day and after consulting with Bruce Davis, an attorney with the school system— he sat down in his favorite chair, and thought about what he was going to say to Singleton the following morning. He knew that after he said it, "all hell was going to break loose, and John Dawsey was going to catch it." But while sitting in that chair, he made up his mind that, as he would later testify, "I was willing to bear any burden or pay any price to see that this man didn't teach children in Horry County again." Then he took out a legal pad and wrote up his statement.

Now, in the principal's office, he was reading from that statement. "Reverend Singleton," he read, "your presence at Conway Middle School has become a disruptive force in the orderly process of providing a quality education for the students in the Horry County Schools. For this reason, I am suspending you with pay, and will recommend to the Board that you be terminated. You are hereby directed to go to your room and get your personal belongings and leave the campus immediately. You will receive written confirmation of this at a later date."

"Mr. Superintendent," Singleton said, according to Dawsey, "did you say you *enjoyed* doing this?"

Dawsey would later testify that he looked Singleton in the eye and said, "Reverend, you know that's not what I said. You know I told you that this was something I *didn't* enjoy doing."

H. H. Singleton would later tell the *Detroit News* (and Hank Singleton confirms this in an interview) that Dawsey said, "I have the greatest pleasure this day in telling you that you are suspended from your job." Principal Stefanides, on the other hand, recalls Dawsey indicating during this exchange that he did not take pleasure in suspending Singleton.

However the news was conveyed, the result was the same: suspension with pay and a recommendation that the earth science teacher be fired. Singleton was stunned. He knew that the superintendent and the board didn't look upon his brand of advocacy with favor, but still, to his thinking, they didn't have grounds to suspend him. In acting as a spokesman for the striking players, he had been well within his First Amendment rights.

Both men stood, and before Singleton could say anything, Dawsey said, "I expect you to go to your room and clean out your desk and leave immediately." He later testified that he wanted Singleton off campus before the students arrived. Then, according to Hank Singleton, Dawsey said, "I guess I haven't heard the last of you."

"No, Mr. Superintendent," Singleton said, "you haven't heard the last of me."

"I figured that." Dawsey walked out from behind the desk and escorted Singleton out the door. "All the way up to the top?"

"If need be," Singleton said. "All the way up to the top." The meaning, according to Hank, was clear to both men. "The top" meant the very top—the U.S. Supreme Court.

When Singleton got back to his classroom, he was met by two police officers. Under their supervision, he packed up his briefcase and drove back to the church.

Hank Singleton was home that Tuesday morning, sitting in the den, working on a story he was writing for a newspaper based in Florence, South Carolina. At about 8:45 a.m., he heard the back door open. Soon, his father walked into the room. The elder Singleton appeared visibly shaken. Hank had never before seen his father looking quite so alarmed. "What are you doing here?" Hank said, knowing, of course, that his father should be at school.

"Son," Reverend Singleton said, and he sat down on the arm of the chair in which Hank had been writing. "Now we got to get 'em."

- 6 -

FROM THE SAME SPOON

NOW

AFTER GETTING SHELLACKED 55–19 BY THE NORTHWESTERN TROJANS, Chuck Jordan's present-day Tigers fall to one win and one loss, and among Conwayites, there's no consensus about what this middling start means. Glass-half-full types will tell you that the Tigers ran into a buzz saw against the Trojans, a talented Big 16 school that played a perfect game, especially on offense. Northwestern had already proven themselves the week before by beating Gaffney, and on the night they met Conway at Doug Shaw Stadium, their Air Raid offense was cruising so smoothly, they might have put up 30 against a small college program. Still, Conway was playing them pretty even until Mykal Moody's fumble into the end zone just before halftime. Chuck's boys have got all the talent they need, the glass-half-full folks are saying. Mykal is still out there running and throwing, and Malcolm Green is still there to catch passes and return kicks. They'll be all right. Getting spanked by Northwestern might be just the thing to toughen 'em up for the rest of the season. The negativity from the glass-half-empty crowd, though, always seems to resonate a few decibels louder, especially after a loss. And to the naysayers, the fact that Conway gave up 55 points to Northwestern is the sign of a defense that breaks as easy and as ugly as a five-dollar beach umbrella caught in the sea breeze. Looking back now, even the win against Georgetown wasn't exactly dominating. The Bulldogs had no business chalking up 24 against the Tigers. Sure, Mykal and Malcolm are the real deal, but Chuck's offense ain't never gonna outscore a good team unless he gets his defense stiffened up.

For his part, Coach Jordan, furious as he was in the minutes after the game, quickly pivoted to his go-to sermon—forget it and drive on—a maxim that is often condensed into FIDO, which, like SNAFU and FUBAR, began in the military as a sardonic acronym. The "F" in FIDO would normally

stand for an expletive, but Jordan prefers the polite version. In the team
circle on the field, he confirmed the obvious for his players: The Trojans had
whupped 'em good. There wasn't much else to say except to remind them—
again—that turnovers'll kill you. Other than that, drive on.

There's still a lot of football to be played this year, so now, in the week
leading up to game three, it's time to focus on the positives, to keep everybody's head high. The head Jordan is most concerned about is his quarterback's. A handsome kid with a mischievous smile that surely gets the
girls talking, Mykal Moody has held the starting position since he was a
freshman, and in his three-plus years behind center he's made his share of
knuckleheaded mistakes and YouTube-worthy highlights. But even though
his QB is a four-year starter, Jordan knows that Mykal, like all prep quarterbacks, is still learning the game.

"In high school football," the coach says by telephone after the Northwestern loss, "you're always battling confidence. Either overconfidence or
the lack of." Asked about Moody's back-breaking fumble, Jordan says he's
pleased that his quarterback made the extra effort to stretch for the end
zone with the ball, but he's disappointed that Moody didn't have the savvy
to understand that because it was first down, reaching out with ball was an
unnecessary risk. "We had three more shots," Jordan says. "There's a time to
extend it, and a time to secure it. On fourth down, extend it. But on first, secure it." His frustration is evident over the phone. *Forgetting it* is easier said
than done, even for the coach. "But I try not to blame kids when they make
a mistake," he says, slipping back into a more composed voice, the same one
he uses when tutoring students in the finer points of the quadratic equation.
"After all, I'm the one who taught 'em." This week, his job is to teach Mykal
not to make that same mistake again. *Forget it and drive on* is what Jordan
says, but it's clear that he really means, *Learn from it, dadgummit.*

On Friday, an evening that has finally brought clear skies to Horry
County after four days of rain, the Tigers charge down the hill and onto the
field, anxious to right the ship after last week's disaster. Conway fans—the
optimists and the naysayers—file into the Backyard, hoping that tonight's
game will alleviate any doubt about this year's squad. The opponent tonight
is Rock Hill, who, like Northwestern, is a Big 16 school from the Upstate.
Back in 1989, Conway played in the Big 16 (4A, Division I) class of the South
Carolina High School League, but in the years since, due to a decrease in enrollment relative to other schools in the state—thanks in part to the creation
of Carolina Forest High School, which sits between Conway and Myrtle
Beach and draws students from both areas—Conway has been moved to

Class 4A, Division II. Even with an enrollment of approximately 1,500 students, Conway High is no longer big enough for the Big 16.

Rock Hill is, however, and they get off to a quick start tonight, taking a 14–0 lead before the Tigers can notch a single first down. The field is muddy, the grass is nearly three inches long, and Jordan's offense is mucking through drive after futile drive. Punt. Fumble. Punt. Punt. Punt. The only player doing a dang thing is Jordan's son Sawyer, who, in addition to being the starting slot receiver and third-string QB, is also the punter. The offensive scheme mostly consists of Mykal running quarterback keepers for minimal yardage behind offensive linemen whose gold pants are flecked with dirt, their thighs looking like the side panels on a Chevy Z-71 after a day of mud-boggin'.

Annoyed by the offensive impotence, somebody shouts from the crowd, "Let the cheerleaders play!" A more optimistic somebody else yells, "Throw it downfield, Chuck!" But Mykal's got no time to throw. He's not getting any protection from his line. After the sixth consecutive failed drive, Coach Jordan is spitting mad. He sends in Sawyer and the punt unit yet again, and as the offense returns to the sideline, he jabs the brim of his visor up against the facemask of senior tight end Nathaniel Nesbitt and yells, "You gotta block! We need that edge, but we can't get outside, 'cause you won't block!" Jordan points to one of his assistants, Carlton Terry, who coaches the tight ends. "Coach!" he barks. When he's this angry, Jordan stares daggers that'd make Clint Eastwood blink. "Give me a different H-Back if that's what it takes." Another player walks up and puts his arm around Nesbitt, as if to shield him from the tirade.

With the full moon rising big and orange over the fieldhouse, the players head to the lockers for halftime. The scoreboard reads Rock Hill 21, Conway 0. The cameramen and sports reporters from the local news stations hustle off to another game. The P.A. announcer says to the crowd, "Let's see that Tiger pride!" And in the second half, the Conway offense does begin to get a push from the line, and the Tigers cut the lead to 21–13. But that's as close as they get. Rock Hill buses back upstate with a 34–13 win.

On the field after the game, Coach Jordan again has his players down on one knee. "Right now this season can go one of two ways," he yells. "And I don't know which it's gonna be. I really don't. One: You can pack it in and give up." He's screaming now, loud enough that his voice can surely be heard in the visitor's stands. "Two: You can suck it up and decide to do something about it!" He takes off his visor and whacks it against his leg. "Somebody's gotta step up and say *I'm* gonna *do* something about it!" He pauses for a minute, and the silence is more intimidating than the noise. "You guys keep playing dead, and we're gonna have a terrible year." The coach is calm now. Frighteningly calm. He shakes his head. "I can't tell you any more," he says, pointing at his heart. "It's gotta come from *inside*."

Conway is now sitting at 1–2, and the defense—which is coached by Kelly Andreucci, who happens to be Mickey Wilson's brother-in-law—is yielding an average of 38 points a game, but still, if you're an exceptionally sunny Tiger fan, you can probably write off these two losses to Big 16 schools as character-builders. As Rich Chrampanis, sports anchor for Myrtle Beach's WPDE, says after presenting the Conway/Rock Hill highlights on the evening news, "It would be foolish to think that Conway is going to struggle this year." Chrampanis closes the segment by assuring Tiger fans, "Conway is a good football team. Do not be fooled by that 1 and 2 record," but until they see some quality wins from their guys, most Tiger backers are going to be skeptical about this team's chances to bring home a title.

And again, as irate as Coach Jordan is after the Rock Hill game, by Wednesday afternoon, he's back in good spirits. FIDO. "Kids are going to emulate the people around them," he says. "Coaches, teachers, parents, whoever. So I don't like to cuss and fuss. Now don't get me wrong, I *hate* to lose. But I get over it quicker than I used to." He goes on to explain that during a football season, each subsequent game comes along so fast, he and his coaches have no choice but to get over it. "We start looking at film on Saturday afternoon," he says. "By then we're done with the last game, and we're starting to get fired up, because now, we're thinking about the *next* game." For Conway, a team that desperately needs a win, the next game—at Socastee—looks to be about as close to a guaranteed W as the schedule ever gives up, not that Jordan would admit as much. Still, the last time Conway lost to Socastee was 1998. Going into Friday night, the Tigers have won thirteen straight against the Braves.

And that's why it's so shocking when Socastee beats Conway 35–21. The Tigers played it close for a while, tying the score at 14, but behind quarterback Hunter Renfrow, Socastee Head Coach Tim Renfrow's son, the Braves run away with the game in the second half.

Now Conway is 1–3, and glass-half-full is becoming an increasingly untenable position. Around town, in places like Stalvey's Cleaners, you hear conversations like this:

TIGER FAN #1: I know Moody's started since he was a freshman, and, yeah, he's a great athlete and all, but maybe Chuck ought to give the white kid, that Ethan, a shot.

TIGER FAN #2: Man, the game has changed from back in Chuck's day. We need new blood at coach. I tell you what, Conway High School ought to give Mickey Wilson a shot.

TIGER FAN #1 (laughing): That's crazy. You know Chuck Jordan ain't never leaving except in a box.

After thirty years, Jordan, like all coaching legends, has risen to a height that makes him a fat target for criticism—but also impervious to it. And this imperviousness was forged and hardened during the 1989 season, in the way much of the town rallied around him during the strike. "The Cult of Jordanism," as one local resident calls it, lives on. The question is, how many seasons does the coach have left before the pressure to win that elusive state championship outmuscles the admiration so many Conwayites maintain for him? And when he finally does retire—or, unlikely as it may seem, gets fired—might Mickey Wilson come home to replace him?

This season, beyond the three losses the Tigers have racked up, Chuck Jordan is frustrated because he's just not seeing enough passion in his kids, especially his defense. It all goes back to the locker room speech he delivered before game one. Three rules: Play with passion. Expect to win. Enjoy the ride. Coming out of the Socastee game, the Tigers are failing on all counts. Still, Jordan insists that all is not lost. Conway's got two more games before region ball starts. If they finish high enough in their region, then they'll make the 4A playoffs. And one of the coach's maxims is that he's never simply preparing his team for the fifth game or the sixth game or for whatever game happens to be next; he's always working to get them ready for the *twelfth* game, which is to say, for the first game of the state championship tournament. So, yeah, the Tigers still have everything to play for. But they'd better show some improvement this week against Marlboro County. Because they'll need to build all the passion and confidence they can muster to be ready for the game after that—the Bell Game—against Mickey Wilson's Seahawks, who are currently the #1-ranked 3A team in the state. Coach Jordan won't say it out loud, but deep inside, he surely knows that for him, his Tigers, and their fans, beating Mickey and Myrtle Beach is a must.

THEN

News of H. H. Singleton's suspension spread quickly through the black community. By lunchtime on that Tuesday, a couple hundred people, including several of the boycotting players, had shown up at Cherry Hill Baptist. They gathered in the parking lot and on the church steps, everybody asking each other, "Is it true? Did they really fire him?" Reverend Singleton hadn't been fired—yet. Just suspended, with a recommendation from John Dawsey that the school board should go ahead and fire him. But the difference scarcely mattered to the folks who were congregating at Cherry Hill. Fired, suspended—either way, they were livid.

As the crowd assembled outside, Singleton was in his office in the basement of the church, making calls to the board members with whom he had better relationships than he had with Superintendent Dawsey. Many of these members, according to Hank Singleton, weren't aware that Dawsey had suspended the earth science teacher. The superintendent had apparently made the decision in consultation with the school district's attorney, Bruce Davis, but not with the full participation of the board.

When Singleton got off the phone, his son was standing in the office doorway. "You need to come out here and say something," Hank said to his father. "We've got two or three hundred people outside. We've got players who've left school."

"I can't have that," Reverend Singleton said, meaning the truant players. He went out and talked to the crowd, telling the kids to go back to school for their afternoon classes (some did, some didn't) and asking everybody else to come back at 6:00 p.m. for a mass meeting.

Reporters weren't allowed in the church that night, but newspaper articles put the attendance at approximately seven hundred people; Hank cites a figure more like 1,300. What's certain is that when the pews filled up, the ushers had to get more chairs from the basement. When the chairs filled up, folks stood in the aisles. When the aisles filled up, they opened the doors so everybody who was left standing outside could see in.

That evening, Hank says, marks the moment when "It was on."

There's no way to know this, of course, but if John Dawsey had not suspended Singleton, the boycott may have fizzled. Six or eight black players had already crossed the line to rejoin their white teammates. With their positions on the team and possible college scholarships at stake, would the rest of the players really have continued to protest Carlos's position switch if not for Dawsey's upping the ante by suspending Singleton? The fact that between 700 and 1,300 people squeezed into Cherry Hill that night is a clear indication that, for most blacks in Conway, the suspension of a teacher who had spoken out against the football coach was a much bigger issue than who started at quarterback. Dawsey's suspension of Singleton was further proof that the white establishment, this time in the form of a white superintendent and an all-white school board, was working against the town's minority residents. The Conway football boycott had become more than a sports story.

One attendee at the Cherry Hill meeting that night was Preston McKever-Floyd, who, in 1989 as he is now, was a professor of philosophy and religion at Coastal Carolina. For most of his life, he'd been mediating the distance between Conway's black community and its white establishment. As a young man in 1968, McKever-Floyd and four other black students became the first African Americans to graduate from Conway High, which hadn't desegregated until 1967, thirteen years after the landmark *Brown vs. Board of Education* decision mandated that school desegregation happen "with all deliberate speed." He remembers his father telling him, in the years between *Brown* and his eventual entrance into the previously all-white school, that whites in town were saying and, worse still, *believing* that "If blacks are ever allowed in Conway High School, blood will run in the streets." Given that his father was a member of the Conway Police Department—and had been since 1947, when he became the first black police officer in the state of South Carolina—McKever-Floyd had reason to suspect his dad knew quite a bit about what could happen in the streets of Conway. But, McKever-Floyd says, despite the slowness with which desegregation occurred in Conway (or perhaps because of it), he and the other black students entered the white schools without incident. No bullying, no protests, no blood. For this peaceful beginning of a new era, he credits a group of Conway's forward-thinking white leaders—especially Reverend George Lovell, pastor at First Baptist—who sent the message to the white community that desegregation had not only arrived, it was the right thing to do. Still, McKever-Floyd doesn't look back on the relative smoothness of this transition as evidence that race issues had been definitely resolved in Conway. In fact, he's always careful to make the distinction between "desegregation" and "integration." *Desegregation* happened in 1967. The kids were going to school in the same building, nothing more. *Integration*, he says, still hasn't happened. Not in the schools and not in Conway generally.

McKever-Floyd first heard about the football boycott when he was attending a college faculty party and a colleague asked him what he thought of the situation. He said he wasn't especially concerned. "I wish *all* African American men would stop playing football," he told his colleague, "and concentrate instead on their SAT scores."

In the days that followed the announcement of the boycott, members of the black community tried to convince McKever-Floyd to publicly support Carlos Hunt and the other striking players, but he didn't feel the need to protest for one student's preferred position on the football field. Everything changed, however, the day Singleton was suspended. "I had very serious problems with that," he says now, "because it was a matter of First Amendment rights. Suddenly the school superintendent could just do whatever he wanted, like we don't have a constitution. And if we do, then it doesn't apply to H. H. Singleton—because we don't like him." So McKever-Floyd, along with several more black community members who had not been driven to action by the quarterback controversy, wedged into the church that Tuesday night.

Singleton had been suspended because his support of the boycotting players had allegedly become a disruption in the classroom, but to everyone at the mass meeting, the real message from the white community was clear: Don't rock the boat. And in Conway, messing with the football team was about as hard as the boat could be rocked. Everybody in the black community knew football was a big deal, but was it so important that a veteran educator could potentially lose his job over it? You're gonna fire a teacher, people asked, over *football*?

During the meeting, speaker after speaker echoed the same message: *We can't take this lying down. We can't let them do this to our leader, a man who has for so long spoken up for those not in a position to speak up for themselves.* Like many black clergy in communities all over America, H. H. Singleton had often taken a leadership position on civic and civil rights issues. Because church leaders are positioned at the center of an important social and cultural institution, they are keenly aware of the matters affecting their members, and because they are often economically independent from the white establishment (i.e., not working for a white boss), they risk less than the average black citizen does when they speak up against that establishment. The clergy are often among the few members of the black community who can afford, literally, to speak out against the socio-economic power structure. Singleton, however, was employed outside the church, by the establishment. He reported to a white principal, white superintendent, and all-white school board. So when he advocated for blacks—not only in his role as pastor but also as Conway's NAACP president—he did so at considerable risk, economic and otherwise, to himself. His suspension made that all too clear. In a statement that would be released three days later, William F. Gibson, chairman of the national NAACP board and president of the NAACP's South Carolina conference, crystallized what many who packed into Cherry Hill Baptist must have been thinking: that Dawsey's suspension of Singleton was "the classical knee-jerk reaction by whites when blacks challenge injustice," an attempt to "put this uppity colored boy in his place."

Former Conway councilman Cleveland Fladger—the man who had once coached Chuck Jordan and who was now head of a group called the Black Coalition of Horry County—summed up the sentiment in the black community like this: "There is anger now. Here [in H.H. Singleton] you have a champion of justice for the black people, and they are going to try and get him like that." Fladger's use of "they" may have been a reference to the school system, but it's perhaps more likely that "they" meant the entire white establishment, as in this statement by Herman Watson, president of an Horry County civil rights group called Operation Reach Out: "If they think they've had a problem before, now they're really asking for it. Conway's in for the fight of its life."

The next two mornings, Conway's black community took the fight to the streets, picketing in front of the school district offices, demanding that Singleton be reinstated. Noting that the teacher's suspension came after whites had objected to having their children in his class, they asked that Chuck Jordan also be suspended from his teaching duties because some black parents didn't want the coach teaching math to their children. Dawsey wouldn't yield on either demand. He wrote in a letter to Fladger—who had become a spokesman for the protestors picketing on Singleton's behalf—"I have determined to neither suspend Coach Jordan nor reinstate Rev. Singleton. I simply have no compellingly responsible reason to do either."

In response, the protestors presented a petition to Dawsey, signed by more than two hundred people, asking him to resign from his position as superintendent. Picketing every morning, mass meetings every evening. *You've had our backs for a long time,* Conway's black community was saying to Reverend Singleton. *Now we've got yours.*

The football calendar doesn't capitulate to the changing social landscape; convenient or not, Friday night is going to come. And on the Friday after the Singleton suspension—the Friday of Labor Day weekend—Chuck Jordan's Tigers were slated to meet perennial power Summerville, a team that could whup you silly on a week when everything had gone right, let alone if you were dealing with a split squad and town torn in two. "It's been hell," Jordan told the *Atlanta Journal-Constitution* on Friday morning. "You have to remember, it's more than just a job here. This is my home. And here I am, in the middle of a town that has been torn in half because of . . . well, football. It's ugly."

And on paper, at least, it looked like the game might be just as ugly. After moving so many junior varsity kids up to the varsity team to fill the holes left by the boycotting players, Jordan was forced to eliminate the JV team entirely. There was still a B team made up of kids way too young and inexperienced to line up with the varsity squad, but clearly, the Tigers were in no way equipped to play one of the state's premier programs. Before kickoff, Jordan told his team that in order for them to even have a chance against the Green Wave, Summerville would have to play badly and the Tigers would have to play well. This was the understatement of the season.

On the heels of the previous week's game against Hillcrest, when the black players cheered against their teammates to the ire of white Tiger fans, the Conway and Horry County Police Departments again doubled their presence at the Graveyard. But the boycotting players wouldn't be cheering for Summerville that night. In fact, they wouldn't be attending the game at all. By now the boycott had spread from the black players to the black cheerleaders to the black band members, and none of them showed up at the Graveyard for Conway's second matchup of the season. Instead, most of them, along with a large contingent from the black community—several hundred people total—attended a rally at Cherry Hill Baptist, making it the twelfth consecutive day in which a meeting, rally, or press conference was held at the church.

As the Cherry Hill crowd was meeting in support of the boycotting players, cheerleaders, and band members, the Graveyard was filling with approximately 3,500 fans, almost all of them white, who were squeezing hip to hip on the bleachers to cheer on the overmatched Tigers. Looking only at the final score of 42–14, you might guess that there wasn't much on the field to cheer about, but for the Conway fans who attended that night, there *was*. There was effort and scrap. There was participation. And that season, participation itself was worth applauding. Every time the Green Wave scored, the crowd gave the Tiger defense a standing ovation. Every time the Conway offense sputtered to a three-and-out, the crowd clapped with encouragement. By halftime, the score was Summerville 35, Conway 0. Down to merely twenty members, the Conway Tiger Pride Marching Band didn't have enough bodies to perform the halftime routine they'd planned. So the Summerville band hit the field with more than a hundred members, and the Conway crowd cheered that, too.

Mickey Wilson completed only five of twelve passes for 56 yards that night, but the game wasn't entirely devoid of highlights for Tiger fans. The crowd especially appreciated the play of Cleveland Sanders, one of four black kids who saw action for Conway. An undersized defensive lineman at 5'4" and 152 pounds, Sanders was switched to fullback for the Summerville game, and he excelled in his new position. Where there wasn't running room, he made room himself, tallying four carries of over 15 yards each, often pulling several tacklers along with him for extra yardage. He was given a standing ovation when he finally went to the bench, having racked up 117 yards and one touchdown on thirteen carries. "He's a tough little ol' rascal," Coach Jordan said after the game. His gutsy performance against Summerville would make Sanders—a junior who wouldn't have seen the field if not for the boycott—something of a superstar to Tiger fans and boosters. Here was a black kid who was still playing and playing well. Sanders says now that his loyalty to the team was rewarded not just by the increased attention he received (pats on the back, rides to and from school) but also in the form of white fans who would walk up to him, shake his hand, and say, "Good game. Go get yourself a steak." The running back would then find a 20-dollar bill folded in his palm.

Most of the Tigers' limited success came after halftime, when Summerville's Coach McKissick, sitting on a 42–0 lead, sent in his second and third stringers. Resting the starters was the kind of restraint you'd expect from a smart coach with a big lead, but it was also an act of respect for the Conway program and for Chuck Jordan. When they met at midfield after the game, McKissick told Jordan, "We've got some good fans, but you've got the best damn fans I've ever seen." And McKissick wasn't the only one from Summerville to pay homage to Jordan. Green Wave quarterback Louis Mulkey made it a point to shake the Conway coach's hand, and as he did, a towel was hanging from his belt with the words COACH JORDAN printed on it.

Coaches in general—and football coaches particularly, even in high school—enjoy a level of respect that few other professions can match. For people who didn't grow up in a football state like South Carolina, Florida, Texas, or Ohio, this reverence for the coach might seem bizarrely off base, especially considering the academic fraud and recruiting violations that frequently plague the sport. But this veneration of coaches endures, even in the face of especially shocking episodes such as the Jerry Sandusky sexual-abuse-and-coverup scandal that led to the ouster of Penn State's president, Graham Spanier, and their legendary coach Joe Paterno. Why, some people will ask, should a guy who wears a whistle be the highest paid public employee in the school district (in the case of high school football) or in the state (in the case of college)? Often, it's because football, like it or not, is one of the most galvanizing forces in that school district or state. More precisely, though, it's not the football coach who is valued, so much as the *position* of football coach. In much the same way that ministers are merely citizens until they put on their robes and take their spots at the altar, where their words are only a breath removed from God's, football coaches live a dual existence—ordinary people at home, but something greater and more symbolic when they don their ball caps and lead their teams onto the field.

In 1989 Conway was a place, as characterized by the *Sun News,* "where high school football is almost its own religion." And if football truly does function like a religion, then the coaches are the prophets of that faith. Thus, like any holy messenger, a coach is revered for what he says and how he says it. And like any prophet, the coach's words are not simply his words, but represent a larger Truth, with a capital T, that was true before he said it and will be true long after he has quit the game. Football coaches know better than to promise victory, so instead they talk about instilling character and communicating values. Character and values, unlike wins and losses, are difficult to quantify, so if a coach pledges that he can teach your son the virtue of hard work by playing football his way, it's tough to prove he hasn't succeeded. Coaches interact with many players simultaneously, and those players are too busy running through drills to take notes, so instead of making nuanced and multifaceted arguments, coaches are pithy, speaking in catch phrases and reducing complex ideas down to a few clear and unequivocal points ("Forget it and drive on"). In coach-speak, issues are black and white, and the language, especially in the South, is heavy on statements about the "right" way to approach not just football but life. This kind of rhetoric, of course, makes coaches sound a lot like preachers, the only other people in most Southern towns who are given a comparable level of automatic respect.

In many minds, when Reverend Singleton questioned Coach Jordan's decision to move Carlos to defense, it was the equivalent of Jordan questioning one of Singleton's sermons. The preacher's position demands that—even if you feel the sermon could have been better and even if you second-guess his decisions about style and substance—you don't question his authority to make those decisions. Not publicly, anyway.

In the face of pressure from Singleton and the black community to reconsider his choice of QB, Coach Jordan continued to insist that it's the job of the head coach to decide who plays where. As Summerville's John McKissick said, "You can't have outside interference. A coach has to be captain of his ship. That's all there is to it." The unquestioned authority of the head coach is an unwritten rule in all tiers of football, even at the professional level, where the presumption of the coach's unqualified control of player personnel decisions is so bedrock to the game, it's considered a scandal when even a team owner tries to chime in—for example, the Dallas Cowboys and their famously meddling owner Jerry Jones. Granted, for an NFL franchise, the owner and the general manager, under the constraints of the team budget and the salary cap, are going to work together to determine the team roster; however, as soon as it's time to strap on the helmets, the coaching staff is supposed to enjoy the unquestioned right to choose who takes the field. In the college game, it's unthinkable that the athletic director or the school president would insist that the coach start a certain player and sit another. Boosters may contribute huge sums of money to the school's athletic department, and they have been known to get involved—sometimes illegally involved—in the recruitment of players, but a solid and unbreakable line is drawn around a coach when it comes to his right to make game-day decisions. You won't find that commandment in any rulebook, but it's a law of football that's no more controversial or up for discussion than a decision to punt on fourth and 15. Randy Beverly, who played for Conway High in the '60s, spoke for many Tiger fans when he told the *Sun News*, "When I played ball, the coach was the coach. The minister of First Baptist, United Methodist, or Cherry Hill didn't get involved. A minister doesn't know how to run a football team—that's absurd." The football team may belong to the school or the town or the owner—but the players answer to the coach. The vast majority of the whites in Conway agreed: Chuck Jordan's calls may be subject to dispute, but his prerogative in making them was absolute.

The motivation behind this particular call, Jordan insisted, was a need to shore up his defensive unit. "I moved Hunt because I wanted his athletic ability on defense," Jordan told the *Atlanta Journal-Constitution*. "I win with defense." And many of Jordan's former players, including a slew of black former players, rushed to defend the coach, stating that Jordan cared only about winning, never race. John Avant, an African American who was a member of the advisory board of trustees for Conway High, was critical of Singleton's implication of racism in the Hunt switch, telling the newspaper, "The public has ruined Chuck's credibility as a coach." Avant's word, *credibility*, offers a key to understanding how many Tiger fans (most of the white ones, but some blacks, too) felt about the boycott. Avant wasn't necessarily saying that Jordan had made the right decision when he promoted Mickey over Carlos, but he was saying that the players had to believe in the decision, to have faith in their leader's vision. Without credibility, a coach can't lead his team—any more than a sergeant on the battlefield can lead soldiers who don't have confidence in his commands.

Even today, Jordan won't claim that Mickey Wilson was a better player than Carlos Hunt; instead, he simply insists that moving Carlos was his call to make. These days, when he talks about making such tough decisions, you get the sense that he feels the burden of leadership keenly, but knows he can never admit that he does. Football coaches are no more allowed the luxury of self-doubt, especially self-doubt expressed publicly, than religious leaders are. Coaches and clergy must give the impression that they have absolute confidence in their own convictions. Otherwise, they risk losing the faith of the flock.

Again, we can't know if the boycott might have ended had Dawsey not acted so quickly to appease a group of white parents. What we know, though, is that his suspension of Singleton made matters more intractable on both sides, hardening the "us" and "them." Even if the superintendent's motive had simply been to minimize disruptions at Conway Middle, after the suspension, many local whites were emboldened to say loudly and openly that "we" (as represented by Dawsey) won't put up with agitation from "them" (as represented by Singleton). Amid polarization so deeply entrenched, the odds of reconciliation were low—perhaps even more so in a county whose seal reads THE INDEPENDENT REPUBLIC. Folks in Horry come by their stubbornness honestly. So it's no surprise that attempts at a compromise during the early weeks of the boycott were unsuccessful. On the Thursday before the Summerville game, John Dawsey, Chuck Jordan, and Cleveland Fladger met in an attempt to reach some sort of agreement, but nothing came of the meeting. Such negotiations were doomed from the start because in Jordan's mind there was no deal to make, not if that deal would undermine his authority as coach. Dawsey described the meeting as cordial, but said, "There wasn't any give and take." Fladger came away disappointed, saying, "I thought we would make a compromise, but Chuck Jordan and Superintendent Dawsey would not budge an inch."

The compromise Fladger had in mind was that Carlos Hunt be given a chance to try out for the quarterback position, to compete on the field. As an example of how this chance might work, Fladger shrewdly cited a case from his coaching career years earlier, in the 1970s, when an undersized Chuck Jordan had come to him wanting to play defense. "I bet he didn't weigh 125 to 135 pounds," Fladger said. "He was too small to play defense, but we gave him a chance." Giving Carlos a tryout seems like a reasonable request on the surface, and the idea that Jordan denied Hunt the opportunity to compete is still the source of much of the anger that blacks in Conway feel about 1989. Carlos, they say, wasn't asking for special treatment. Mickey is the one who got special treatment when he was handed the job. Of course, the coach's supporters can counter that Carlos had already had a season-long tryout the previous year, which he'd failed by changing play calls at the line and being difficult to coach. According to this view, Jordan hadn't acted too quickly in moving Carlos; if anything, he'd waited *too long* to make the switch. With the two sides divided along such clear lines—and with each having claim to a reasonable point of view—maybe it was a foregone conclusion that "no progress" (which is the wording the *Sun News* used in its headline of the story about the failed meeting) would be made at the bargaining table.

But *progress* is a relative term. The newspaper could find "no progress" because none of the negotiations to that point had brought the boycotting players back on the field. To the white majority, progress would be measured only by a return to the status quo, to how everything had been before the boycott, with Chuck Jordan back in command of a whole, championship-contending squad. But this limited definition overlooks the fact that, from another perspective, a great deal of progress had been made. If the goal of Singleton and his supporters was to destabilize the power structure in Conway in order to increase awareness of racial inequality, then they were succeeding, big time. The mere fact that Superintendent Dawsey and Principal Lewis were regularly fielding questions from the press about the boycott testified to the effectiveness of the boycott.

There were other signs of progress, too, most importantly including the fact that Conway's black community had begun to unify around a larger movement, one that transcended football and was more concerned with equal employment opportunity and economic equality. Even if many blacks—like Preston McKever-Floyd, the philosophy and religion professor—couldn't have cared less about the quarterback issue, they understood that a sleeping giant of discontent had awakened. The time had come for Conway's blacks to be heard. Two letters to the *Sun News* editor on the Thursday before the Summerville game captured this feeling. Jimmy Sherman, a graduate of Conway High School wrote, "To say that there are no race-related problems at Conway High is just not true. It's just being swept under the rug. I am very glad these kids took a stand for what they believe is right, even if it may have been by the Rev. Singleton's hand." George Latimer, also of Conway, accused the newspaper of racism because in the previous Sunday edition, "no black opinionated letter was chosen." Latimer suggested that the paper was trying to "cast the problem off as a trivial matter and blame the black community" for the boycott. Immediately after the letter, the editor added a note that explained the newspaper had printed all the correspondence it had on file when the Sunday issue was printed, but the point remains. Blacks felt that their voices were being ignored. The football issue may have been "trivial," but the larger cause sure wasn't.

On the Friday of the Summerville game, Mayor Ike Long selected six community leaders to serve on a biracial committee to examine race relations in Conway. Several years earlier, Mayor Long had commented that the town of Conway wasn't ready for a black mayor, and in the wake of that statement, Singleton asked Long to form exactly such a committee. The mayor refused then, but now, in light of the boycott, it was finally happening. Ralph Wilson, a successful black professional and deputy solicitor for the Fifteenth Judicial District, would chair the committee that also included Ron Eaglin (chancellor of Coastal Carolina College), Professor McKever-Floyd, a local attorney, and two prominent business people. Six days earlier, Mayor Long had said that Conway didn't have a race problem, and anyone who felt there was a problem was "cultivating something that's just not there." Now, he was charging the task force with the goal of looking for ways to "ease tensions," and he was admitting that, "During the last 11 days, our community has experienced confusion, frustration, hope, anticipation, anger and division as the result of issues concerning the Conway High School football program."

Local blacks may not have held much faith that the committee could "fix" race relations. Still, anyone supporting either Singleton in his quest to be reinstated or Hunt in his attempt to win back the QB position could see that the boycott had caused many Conwayites to finally take notice of issues that had seldom been discussed openly in the past. The state and national NAACP were mobilizing, as South Carolina executive director Nelson Rivers joined national board chairman William F. Gibson in promising to support Singleton "1,000 percent." A civil rights group called Operation HELP from Mullins, a town in neighboring Marion County, filed a complaint with the U.S. Equal Employment Commission and the South Carolina Department of Education alleging race discrimination in the Singleton case. The group's president, the Rev. Franklin Reaves, suggested that he had larger concerns about racial injustice in Horry County Schools, on issues like corporal punishment, student suspensions, and placement in the district's special education and gifted and talented programs. There'd been twelve consecutive nights of mass meetings at Cherry Hill. NAACP membership was expanding. Young people were taking an interest in civil rights activism.

In the black community, there was progress.

After Singleton's suspension, the Conway football boycott was no longer a news item with merely regional appeal. The flare-up gained the attention of *Sports Illustrated* and *USA Today*. ABC News was making calls into town, and the Associated Press was sending out stories on the national wire. A hundred and thirty miles west of Conway, in the state capital of Columbia, a spokesman said that Governor Carroll Campbell was maintaining "an active interest in the situation," and the head of the SC Human Affairs

Commission, James Clyburn—who in 1993 would become a member of Congress, eventually rising to the position of assistant minority leader, making him the third most powerful Democrat in the House—had already sent representatives from his department to Horry County to investigate the allegations of racism.

Over the Labor Day weekend, the governor's monitoring of the events in Conway surely became more intense—not because of any new incidents in Horry County, but because of what was happening 300 miles up the eastern seaboard, in Virginia Beach. That weekend, during a Greekfest celebration that had brought a huge crowd of students from historically black colleges and universities to the coast, police clashed on two successive nights with as many as 100,000 young people who had taken to the streets. There was looting. There were injuries and claims of police brutality. To quell the violence, 150 National Guardsmen were called in and a curfew was imposed. While they were protesting, some of the young African Americans chanted "Fight the Power." As Governor Campbell of South Carolina was surely aware, there would soon be headlines that put the words "Virginia Beach" and "Race Riots" together on the front pages of newspapers all over the country.

Given that tourism was and remains the number one industry in South Carolina; and given that in 1988 Horry County by itself generated nearly $1.6 billion in tourism dollars, which amounted to approximately one-third of South Carolina's entire tourism revenue that year, making Horry the state's overwhelming tourism leader; and given that reporters were already on the Grand Strand, asking about an increasingly high-profile incident with racial implications; it seems safe to assume that the governor would be highly motivated to see that the Conway situation was resolved before the events—and the headlines—turned ugly.

On Wednesday—two days before Chuck Jordan's Tigers would play their third game of the season—Gov. Campbell dispatched Human Affairs Commissioner Clyburn to Conway to meet with Jordan in person and see if some resolution might be found. The commissioner's first decision was that the football boycott and the Singleton suspension should be handled separately. The suspension, he determined, would need to be settled by official administrative or legal processes. The boycott, however, might best be resolved through mediation and old-fashioned give-and-take.

That evening, Gov. Campbell called the coach personally, asking if there was any way to resolve the dispute before, as Jordan recalls, the state started to become "perceived in a certain way." Jordan told the governor that there would be no compromise, at least not one that undermined the coach's authority to make player decisions. But Jordan did agree in principle to the idea of extending an invitation to the striking players, allowing them to return to the team.

The next day, the coach sat down with Clyburn, school officials, and a few members of the black community to begin working on a statement in which Jordan would officially ask the striking players to come back. The coach refused to sign an initial version of the invitation, drafted by Clyburn, because it included a passage that mentioned Hunt specifically: *Carlos Hunt will be given an opportunity to compete for any position he feels his abilities can be best utilized,* it read, *including that of quarterback.*

Jordan insisted that the statement not single out any specific player. Instead the coach would invite all the players to return. He told Clyburn, "I'm going to feed all my players from the same spoon."

"I applaud him for that," Clyburn said.

Jordan then decided to write up his own statement.

The final version of the invitation was reportedly assembled from three separate drafts written by Jordan, Clyburn, and school district attorney Bruce Davis. The Carlos Hunt passage was struck, and added was a line affirming the coach's unquestioned right to determine who played where: *These decisions cannot be influenced by players, parents, pressure groups or administrators,* it read, because *[t]he coach must be the coach.*

After settling on the final draft, Jordan ran the invitation by the thirteen white seniors on his team. All of them agreed: Let's ask the black players to come back.

But even once the official invitation was extended, that didn't mean that Carlos, Lawrence, and the other striking players were going to accept it. In fact, it's not clear if all of the boycotters were even aware of the invitation. Striking player Michael Pickett says now, "Nobody gave any invitation to me. I didn't hear anything about it. It may have been in the paper, but I never heard anything about that." Pickett may not have read in the paper about the coach's invitation, but a lot of people in Conway would have. And when blacks read about the deletion of the passage that mentioned Carlos could try out at quarterback, they would have seen the removal of that line as just another indication that nothing of significance had changed. Coach Jordan wanted the players to come back? So what? Given the raggedy team he was left with, of course he wanted the black players back. Who wouldn't? The question was: What was he going to *do* about it?

From Singleton and Fladger's perspective, apparently nothing. There was no real compromise in the invitation. No promise of a chance for Carlos to try out behind center. No admission of wrongdoing by Jordan. So while the boycotting players were weighing the decision of whether or not to break the strike, Singleton and his followers were continuing the daily picketing at the school board offices. Moreover, they'd scheduled for Saturday an NAACP march right down the middle of U.S. 501, Church Street. A permit was applied for and granted. The march was expected to draw 2,000 people from Horry County and beyond. William Gibson, Nelson Rivers, and other NAACP leaders were on the way to Conway, and they were bringing busloads with them.

On the Thursday that Jordan and his white seniors invited the boycotting players back, Singleton and his supporters held another meeting at Cherry Hill, just as they had every night since the strike began, a little more than two weeks earlier. In many ways, this meeting was like all the others. Speeches were made. Protests were planned. Folks chanted that they were fired up and ready to go. On this night, however, one thing did change, and it was a big one. Six-foot-six, 220 pounds of big. All-state defensive end big. Number three college recruit in the nation big. Lawrence Mitchell, the single best player in the state of South Carolina, unfolded his massive body from a pew, stood up, and walked with the other black boycotters down to the basement, where they held a players-only meeting. "No point is going to be proven by this," Lawrence said to the others, "nothing is going to happen, and I want to go back." That was it. He was returning to the team. For Lawrence and anyone else who was ready to follow him, the Conway football boycott was over.

- 7 -

SHAKEN UP

NOW

MICKEY WILSON LIKES TO PUNCH ABOVE HIS WEIGHT, ESPECIALLY EARLY IN the season, when he front-loads the schedule with 4A opponents. This year, the Seahawks' first five games are all against teams from the big-school class, and Mickey's counting on this 4A-level competition to toughen up his guys for the smaller schools the Seahawks will play in region ball and in the 3A playoffs. It's like swinging two bats in the on-deck circle: Once you get through a few 4A bruisers, then 3A teams like St. James and Georgetown feel like featherweights. The goal, of course, isn't just to compete with but to *beat* the big boys, and in week one, Myrtle Beach did just that, knocking out Irmo 33–27. Tonight, in week two, the Seahawks travel seventy miles inland to meet another 4A team, the West Florence Knights, defending champs of Region VI, the same region Conway competes in.

Tonight's game is a rare Thursday contest, and coming on the heels of last week's Saturday matchup, it means that Mickey's squad has had only five days to prep, their sore muscles only five days to heal. But the Seahawks are resilient. They're kids, and they bounce back quickly. During pre-game warmups, the mood among the players is high-spirited, confident. And that confidence carries over to the opening kickoff, which Myrtle Beach's Trell Harrell returns untouched for a 94-yard touchdown to put the Seahawks up 6–0. West Florence is a good team, though, a team that knows how to win, and they answer with a TD to take a 7–6 lead. Later in the opening quarter, Myrtle Beach jabs right back when Tyler Keane finds tight end Sean Michael Orcutt on a 32-yard scoring strike that puts Myrtle Beach ahead 13–7. In the visitors' bleachers, the Seahawk fans who've made the drive to Florence stand and cheer, partly for the touchdown but mostly for Orcutt, who, given the wrecking ball of a hit he absorbed last week, seemed unlikely to even suit up tonight.

Five days ago, midway through the second quarter of the Irmo game, Orcutt caught a short pass from Keane on third and 15. He turned up field and had room to run, maybe enough to make it to the first down marker, which was planted at the Yellow Jacket 25. The players on the Seahawk side-line stood on their tiptoes to see over each other. Fans yelled, "Go, baby, go!" And just when it looked like Orcutt would make the first down and keep the drive alive, an Irmo defender leveled him with a helmet-to-helmet blow that sounded like a blast from a deer rifle. Orcutt fell one yard shy of the marker. Even the fans that hadn't been paying attention turned their heads toward the field, where Sean Michael was knocked flat.

Instances like this happen once or twice in every football game, but usually the player pops right up. Walks it off. Shakes the cobwebs and goes back to the huddle. Or, even if he doesn't rise to his feet immediately, as long as he's clutching a body part to indicate where the pain is, his parents, coaches, and teammates, can exhale in relief. If a player can tell the training staff where it hurts, he usually hasn't been injured all that terribly. Maybe a collarbone, maybe an ankle. Worst case: a knee. But not, God forbid, head, neck, or spine.

Every so often, though, the silence deepens when the player lies mo-tionless for a few beats too many. For Sean Michael, this was one of those occasions. Coaches who'd been berating the officials for not throwing an unnecessary roughness flag suddenly stopped yelling. The band stopped playing. On the field, Seahawk players gathered in a circle around their in-jured teammate. On the sideline, they stepped onto the bench to get a better view. The Myrtle Beach trainers were now attending to Orcutt, and over by the ambulance, the EMTs began scrambling. A few players from both teams appeared to be praying. Kicker Max Huggins, who'd been warming up for a possible field goal attempt, left his ball on the tee and gathered with his teammates near the bench. The steady *thunk-swish* of the ball coming off of his left foot and into the practice net was now gone, replaced by a quiet more frightening than if Sean Michael had been screaming in pain.

"Number 32, Sean Michael Orcutt," the P.A. announcer said, breaking the silence, "shaken up on the play."

The brutal social calculus of football—especially at the high school lev-el—holds that the benefits of competition outweigh the risks. Those benefits sometimes come in the form of college scholarships, but everyone knows that only a small percentage of high school players will go on to play at "the next level." The more universal and enduring rewards are supposed to come in the form of values and work ethic and the transformation of boys into men. Any competitive sport might build character, but for many parents in South Carolina and other football states, if you want your boy to grow up right, he's got to don the pads. To some degree, then, the pain and danger are seen as positives, as chances to overcome adversity—provided, of course, we're not talking about permanent injury or death, and usually, we're not.

According to a 2006 report by the Centers for Disease Control, football is statistically the most dangerous of the nine sports the authors studied, but the differences between football and other sports aren't as radical as you might expect. The report looks at injuries sustained during practice sessions and during actual competition, and not surprisingly, football leads the list in both categories. However, the rate of injury during practice drills is only slightly higher than the rate for wrestling, which is the second most danger-ous sport to practice. Even compared to a supposedly non-contact sport like girls' volleyball, there's a smaller difference than one might guess in the rate of injuries per 1,000 "athlete exposures," a term that refers to the num-ber of players on a team multiplied by the number of practice sessions or games (e.g., a 15-member volleyball roster that practices four times per week will have 60 athlete exposures every week). The rate for football practice is 2.54 injuries per 1,000 exposures. For girls' volleyball it's 1.48 per 1,000. Ex-pressed another way, these statistics mean that a football player has about a 0.25%—one quarter of one percent—chance of injury at any given practice, while a girls' volleyball player has approximately a 0.15% chance. This tenth of a percent difference is measurable and important to be sure, but the point is, the chance of injury during football practice is rather small—perhaps be-cause these sessions generally consist of skill-building exercises that barely resemble the game itself. Football practice is like shadowboxing. Linemen block imaginary opponents, defensive backs cover invisible wide receivers, and running backs brace for rib-crunching hits that never come.

The risk of injury rises dramatically during actual games, however, where football players are hurt at a rate of 12.09 per 1,000. And this number considers every player on the team equally. While some kids spend their Friday nights riding the bench, some, like Sean Michael Orcutt, start on both offense and defense. Because Orcutt rarely leaves the field, his risk would obviously be much higher. Compare football's in-game injury rate of 12.09 per 1,000 to the rate for baseball (which is the safest sport in the study at 1.77 per 1,000) or girls' soccer (which is the second most dangerous at 5.21 per 1,000) and it's clear why football can't be practiced the way it's played.

But nobody who is truly invested in high school football wants to see it reduced to two-hand-touch or flag or some other weak-kneed imitation. Football without contact would be like the Flying Wallendas doing their high wire act over a net. It might be comforting to know that the perform-ers couldn't get seriously hurt, but without the threat of catastrophic injury, the Wallendas would no longer be *daredevils*; they'd be gymnasts in the sky. The risk of injury isn't just a regrettable consequence of football; it's an im-portant part of the game. For some positions, intimidating the opponent via the threat of injury *is* the game. Linebackers and safeties, for instance, take pride in leveling an opposing receiver, so that the next time the receiver cuts through the middle on a pass route, instead of fully extending to catch the ball, he'll keep his arms close to his body in a defensive posture. Alligator arms, it's called. In a sport where one dropped pass can be the difference between a win and a loss, a big hit delivered on an earlier play can influence whether the game-winning ball is caught or not. A player who's been flat-tened—like Sean Michael—is going to remember what that feels like. And maybe the next time he scrambles toward the first down marker, he'll do so more timidly.

After another long minute, as if his body and brain had simply needed to go into sleep mode before rebooting, Orcutt was sitting up, saying he was okay. In both the home and away stands, fans clapped in encourage-ment. The player circle cinched a little tighter. "Stay back, y'all," a coach said. "Give him some room." The trainers shone penlights in Orcutt's eyes and asked him the kinds of questions first responders are taught to ask when they suspect brain trauma. What's your name? Where do you live? Who's the president of the United States? Wearing a facial expression that fluctuated between a forced smile and an honest wince, he answered the questions and passed the tests, even after admitting to some dizziness.

Sean Michael was taken to the sideline, where he was told that he was fin-ished for the night. Sitting on the bench with his helmet off, he still looked a little rattled. But more than that, he looked disappointed—disappointed that he hadn't made it to the first down marker, disappointed that he'd be sitting out the rest of the game. A few at a time, his teammates wandered over to bump fists. "Is it as bad as last time?" one player asked him, referring to the serious concussion Sean Michael had suffered the year before. The verdict this time, according to a television news report, would be "mild concussion," later downgraded to "concussion-like symptoms," according to the coaching staff.

Orcutt's gutsy run left the Seahawks with fourth down and one. In-stead of kicking the 43-yard field goal, which was well within Max Hug-gins's range, Mickey Wilson kept the offense on the field. He and his players were determined to make sure their senior tight end's sacrifice was worth the headache he'd wake up with the next day. With a short yard to go, C.J.

Cooper lined up at quarterback, took a shotgun snap from center, and ran the ball 7 yards to the Irmo 19 for the first down. Sean Michael shook his fist in the air and then helicoptered a towel over his head. The home stands went wild.

Now, five days later, Seahawk fans are again on their feet and cheering for Orcutt. Sean Michael avoids taking any serious shots to the head this week, but his quarterback, Tyler Keane, doesn't escape West Florence without injury. Midway through the fourth quarter, with Myrtle Beach ahead 21–14, Tyler is forced to leave the game with an ankle sprain. Then, with under two minutes left and the Seahawks still up by a touchdown, a West Florence player goes down hard after a run. He stays down. A family of Myrtle Beach fans laughs, thinking the injury is a ploy by West Florence to stop the clock. "Don't fall for it!" one member of the family yells in the direction of the referees. But the player hasn't yet moved, and the crowd turns quiet—a silent echo of the play that Orcutt was shaken up on five days earlier. This time, when the trainers shine their penlights and ask their questions, the player doesn't pass the tests. The ambulance backs onto the track encircling the field. The EMTs strap the player to a backboard and put him in a neck brace. As the ambulance pulls away, the family that had been laughing forms a circle and holds hands in prayer.

Twenty minutes after the West Florence player first went down, the game resumes, and when the clock hits zero, the Seahawks have improved their record to 2–0. Sitting alone at the end of the bench and wearing an air cast to support his injured ankle, Tyler Keane doesn't participate in the postgame rituals. Rather than limp through the handshake lineup, he watches from the bench as his teammates walk across the midfield stripe, slapping hands with the Knights. Some say "good game" or "nice hit," but most just walk and slap, walk and slap. When the lineup is over, the players pull off their helmets and run toward the team buses, jumping and hollering, now in full celebration mode. The trainer turns to two Seahawks and says, "Aren't you forgetting your quarterback?" They walk back to the bench and drape an arm around Keane's shoulders, turning themselves into a set of human crutches. As he limps off the field, Tyler puts his weight onto his teammates.

The buses are idling, but before the Seahawks ride back to the beach, Mickey assembles his players in the grass, in the shadow of the bleachers. He calls Mr. Byrd over and says, "Okay, everybody. Hats off. Down on one knee so we can pray for that kid that got hurt." He's not talking about Tyler, of course. He's talking about the player who was carried away in the ambulance.

"Father," Mr. Byrd begins, "we want to ask you to look over the young man who was injured tonight and protect him and bless his family." And this time, he ends with "In Jesus' name we pray," choosing not to bow to any outside pressure to differentiate his own beliefs from those of the players. When an injury is serious enough to stop the game for more than twenty minutes, there are bigger issues to worry about than pronoun choice.

In the week following tonight's game, Mickey will get word that the West Florence player suffered a neck sprain—serious and painful but not the debilitating injury it had appeared to be. A truth about football injuries: It's usually not as bad as it looks.

Usually.

A month from now, Ronald Rouse, an 18-year-old, 320-pound lineman for nearby Hartsville High, a team that competes in Region VI along with Conway and West Florence, will die during his team's homecoming game. He'll stay on the ground after assisting on a tackle, and after being helped to the sideline, he'll collapse a second time. The EMT crew will try to revive him, and they'll cart him away in an ambulance, but he'll be pronounced dead in the emergency room. The Hartsville principal will tell the crowd over the P.A. that the game won't resume after halftime. With heavy hearts and teary eyes, they'll crown the homecoming king and queen and head for the parking lot. The mayor will order the town's flags to be flown at half-mast and ask residents "to take a moment and ask God to be with this family, to help them find peace in this chaos, and to help this team deal with the grief and shock of losing a brother."

THEN

Lawrence Mitchell had already been tempted to break the strike. He was an athlete, after all, built for competition. He wanted to spend his afternoons that fall on the practice field, chasing down running backs. He wanted to spend his Friday nights under the lights, bulldozing the other team's quarterback. He wanted to spend his senior year playing football, and yet somehow it had worked out that football was the one thing he wasn't doing. While his white teammates were popping pads and gathering grass stains, he and the rest of the striking players were sitting in meetings, forming committees, planning protests. Neither he nor his grandmother—Gussie Lee Pertell, the woman who was raising him—was a member at Cherry Hill Baptist, and yet there he was every night, at the church, in the mass meetings. Lawrence knew that every time he spent an evening at Cherry Hill instead of on the practice field, he was one day closer to losing the whole season, and a season is a precious thing for any football player. But Lawrence wasn't just any football player, and this, his senior year, wasn't just any season. If he missed the remaining games on the schedule, he'd be making a sacrifice that was as outsized as his talent. Earlier that year, a recruiter from Notre Dame had walked into Conway High, watched game footage of Lawrence, and told Mickey Wilson Sr., "That kid could play on Sundays right now." His status as a top recruit, his college choice and eventual career, heck, even his chances of one day playing in the NFL—all of it was riding that picket line. As loyal as he was to his buddy Carlos, he didn't necessarily want to bet his future on that friendship. But still, he wanted to do the right thing. And that was the trouble. What *was* the right thing? And for whom was it right?

From the beginning of the boycott, Lawrence had felt pressure to play—and pressure not to play. H. H. Singleton's supporters needed Mitchell on their side, because if the stud recruit went back to the team, there was a good chance that the rest of the striking players would join him. After all, as James Clyburn mentioned in the press, "[Lawrence] seems to be the one everyone listens to." If the boycott lost Mitchell, it might crumble. And if the boycott crumbled, then the larger Conway Movement, suddenly without the spark that had launched it in the first place, would surely lose momentum. The black community risked sliding back to acquiescence, back to "go along to get along." And that's also in part why Coach Jordan's supporters wanted Lawrence back on the field. If all the boycotting players followed him and the strike fizzled, not only would the team suddenly be in contention for a state championship, but the town would ease back to the relative peace it had known before all this ugliness, and on some level, Jordan, the school system, and, by extension, Conway's white establishment would be vindicated. If, on the other hand, Mitchell could be persuaded to stay with the protest, the strike would continue to be the galvanizing force behind a movement that had transcended football. And the white community would finally have to confront the issues of racial inequality that had been all too easy for them to ignore right up until the moment their beloved football team fractured.

For both sides—for those who applauded the walkout and for those who wished to end it—Mitchell represented a strategic advantage that was both real and symbolic. As he told *Sports Illustrated*, from the minute the boycott was announced "everybody was coming to my house, telling me do this, do that. The white community was saying, 'If you don't play, you won't go to [college].'" From the black community, he heard: "You don't have to play, you've already proved yours." He didn't play the first two games, and to lots of folks, this abdication confirmed his loyalty to the cause and the community. But Lawrence admits now, twenty-five years later, that he never felt much dedication to the larger movement. He was a football player, and his allegiance all along was to the football team. He agreed to the protest at first, he says, not knowing what he was getting into. He'd assumed that the adults on both sides ("grown folks" is the term he uses) would quickly figure a way out of the mess and he'd be back on the field.

Two weeks into the boycott, it dawned on Lawrence that continuing the walkout would mean missing the Bell Game. He looked around at his striking teammates, sitting for those mass meetings and, at least on the inside, he was incredulous: *We're not playing against Myrtle Beach?* The thought of skipping the Bell Game during his senior season, his last shot, was crushing. "This is what I live for," he says now, "playing for the Bell."

He said as much to his grandmother, but she told him there were issues involved that were larger than football. "If you start a fire and don't put anything in it," she said, borrowing a line from her father, "it'll soon go out." When it came to the boycott, the right thing was for him to "stick with it."

Lawrence was a loyal grandson, but he wasn't convinced. To him, football had always felt like the right thing. He'd kept in conversation with Coach Jordan throughout the strike, and on the day when Jordan and the white seniors formally invited the boycotting players to come back, Lawrence decided he was going to accept their invitation. As he walked into Cherry Hill Baptist that Thursday night, he was ready to say to Carlos and everybody else, to his grandmother and Rev. Singleton and the larger black community: "I'm going back to the team, man. Enough of this foolishness."

The players headed down to the church basement for a private meeting. Now that the assembly was much smaller, Lawrence, Carlos, and their teammates could talk without input from outside voices, which was what many people had seen as the key to a resolution all along. Lawrence told his fellow players that no point would be proven by the protest. Nothing would change. "I'm not with this boycott no more," he said.

These days, when he's asked about the difficulty of announcing that he was breaking the strike, he says, "It was hard, man. It was real hard to do that. To see the look on everybody's face." After the players-only meeting, it was time to break the news to the parents and the larger community. Lawrence told *Sports Illustrated* that when he walked out of the church, "All these ladies were saying, 'Ahh, please don't go back.' It was crazy, people talking to me for about three hours telling me, 'Don't go back.'"

But Lawrence had made up his mind. "I made the decision by myself," he says now. "To do it by myself. Not nobody else's feelings. Carrying nobody with me."

• • •

But because Lawrence Mitchell was Lawrence Mitchell, he did carry others with him. Carlos and the majority of the protestors may have been determined to continue the strike, but several black players decided to follow the star back to the team. The next day, the Conway Tigers boarded the buses for Charleston, for the third game of the season, and when they did, Lawrence and a handful of other returnees were among them. As promised, Chuck Jordan welcomed the returning players into the fold, but with a caveat: They would have to serve a one-game suspension for missing so much practice and game time. That night, against the Middleton High Razorbacks, Lawrence and the others would stand on the sidelines, dressed in their game jerseys but with no helmets or pads. From the waist up, they'd look like Tigers. From the waist down, in their jeans and sneakers, they'd look like civilians. Next week, however, they'd be suited up and fully eligible for the Bell Game against Myrtle Beach.

Eight of Lawrence's teammates followed him across the picket line and onto those buses bound for Charleston, but Coach Jordan declined to provide a list of the returning players to the press, fearing that if the names became public, those players would face increased pressure from the black community to reconsider their decision. As he told the *Sun News*, "I do not want to release their names because I don't want them to be harassed."

According to James Clyburn, one player had already changed his mind about returning to the team. The night before, at Cherry Hill, the player had indicated he was planning to go back to football, but by the next afternoon, he'd reconsidered—apparently, according to Clyburn, after being pressured to do so. "I have direct knowledge [the pressure] is taking place," Clyburn told the newspaper. "What's causing the pressure, I don't know."

From H. H. Singleton's standpoint, these accusations of harassment and pressure were "insulting." He acknowledged that some parents and community members "have told the striking players that the issue of receiving fair treatment is more important than a football season or a college football scholarship," but, he said, "We're not doing any more for them than white families would do for theirs. Black parents have a right to advise their children against what they consider to be exploitation." Whether the player who had changed his mind was "harassed," "pressured," or "advised" is a matter of perspective, but regardless, he didn't make the trip to Charleston. Lawrence Mitchell and several others did, however, and for Tiger fans, that was reason enough to believe the season could somehow be salvaged.

Today, when he's asked about the atmosphere on that bus ride south, about whether there was any animosity among the white players toward the returning black players, Lawrence laughs and says, "I was 6'6", 220 pounds.

There ain't too much they was going to say to me." He laughs again, long and hard. "Naw, I guess everybody was probably happy to have me back. Because I liked to joke around a have a good time. I'm just a team player, man." On those buses and back home in Conway, hopes were high. Surely it was just a matter of time—days, maybe—before all the striking players came back and the team was again the *whole* team.

When the buses pulled up to the stadium at Middleton High, they were met by ten press members and eleven police officers whose ranks were soon bolstered by a four-member mounted unit. Mickey Wilson remembers that the Tigers had been told to expect trouble, and given that the state and national NAACP offices were mobilizing for a march in Conway the following afternoon, it seemed logical that Charleston's black community might also be planning a protest, tonight, right here at the high school. Charleston, after all, had its own history of racial disputes, including an occurrence just three years earlier at the Citadel, the military college located across the Ashley River from Middleton High, in which a black cadet was hazed by a group of white cadets who were dressed like Klansmen. James Clyburn was the state's Human Affairs commissioner in those days, too, so he investigated the Citadel incident, a racial flare-up that sparked months-long outrage in Charleston's black community. Three years later, Clyburn was saying that the tension in Conway was even worse than what he'd seen in Charleston in '86. "I told the governor that this issue in Conway made the Citadel look like a softball game," he said to the *Sun News*. The concern among many was that the arrival of the Tiger football team would rekindle Charleston's anger and frustration all over again.

Chuck Jordan's squad was indeed met by protesters, members of the Charleston County Black Community Development and Rainbow Coalition who were lined up at the front entrance to the stadium, holding signs that read RACISM AT CONWAY HIGH. But there were only six of them, and by all accounts, there was nothing in the demonstration that even approached "trouble." Still, instead of driving directly past the picketers, the Conway bus drivers steered toward a back entrance. In an attempt to make sure the protestors had a chance to be heard, Charleston County Police Chief Jack Sidoran volunteered to direct the buses around front, which would force them to roll past the protest signs, but the demonstrators declined his offer. The Rev. Frank Portee, a Methodist minister who had helped to organize the protest, said, "We did not want to antagonize any spectators from Conway or Middleton." All in all, both the demonstrators and the representatives of the "establishment" described it as a peaceful and orderly protest. Charleston County School Superintendent Robert Burke said, "We wanted a safe situation and still let people have an opportunity to exercise their rights." Chief Sidoran commented, "I think it was very nicely done" and added that the demonstrators were "to be commended for good organization and their non-violent protest."

On the field, with Mickey at QB and most of the team's best players either on strike or under suspension, the offense struggled, and the Tigers lost again, 19–0. Conway gained 106 yards total, and Mickey was responsible for only 30 of those yards. Cleveland Sanders—the black running back who'd been so successful against Summerville—gained 35 yards on fourteen carries, and the longest of the four passes the Tigers completed all night (34 yards) was thrown not by Mickey but by backup quarterback Brian Steele, another one of the "Zebras." A team that had started fall practice with championship hopes was now sitting at 0–3, and in their three losses, they'd been outscored by a combined 95–20. Still, as the clock wound down on the Middleton game, there was reason for optimism. For one, the defense had its best outing of the year, holding the Razorbacks to 169 yards. But more importantly, next week against Myrtle Beach, Lawrence Mitchell and at least seven more of the boycotting players would be fully dressed and eligible.

That night against Middleton, the returning players participated in every team activity except competing in the actual game. They ate the pre-game meal with their teammates. They sat next to their teammates in the locker room and huddled with them on the sideline. And when their teammates came off the field, Lawrence and the returning players were right there to smack them on the shoulder pads.

Before the strike, Mickey Wilson and Lawrence Mitchell had been friends—"good friends," says Lawrence now. In addition to being football players, they were both starters on the basketball team, where Mickey Sr. was Lawrence's coach. "[Mickey] and his father, him and his whole family . . . I always been close to them," Lawrence says. "I mean, we been close for a long time, man. For years."

But once the boycott began, the friendship stalled. "At that point," Mickey says, "there wasn't a lot of talking going on with *me* about anything—from those guys. We just kind of went our separate ways." Mickey went to practice; Lawrence went to meetings at Cherry Hill. And during the school day, when Mickey wasn't in class, he was usually holed up in a coach's office, either Chuck Jordan's or his father's. The insulation was for his protection, Mickey says, to keep him shielded from whatever taunts and jibes might be hurled in the halls, to keep him focused on football instead of on the strike. But even when Mickey and Lawrence did happen upon each other, in the cafeteria at lunchtime, say, tension trumped friendship. To the striking players, Mickey was the guy who'd been handed Carlos's position. To the white Tigers, Lawrence was the team player who'd quit on his team. This ice wasn't going to melt easily, but during the Middleton game, with Mitchell back on the sidelines cheering on Mickey and the rest of the Conway squad, it cracked.

With about eight minutes left in the game, Mickey, who'd been getting throttled by the Razorback defense all night, took a hard hit in his lower back. While he was lying prone on the turf, another Middleton player came in headfirst and walloped Mickey on the buttock. "I took a helmet to my butt," Mickey says now, laughing. "Maybe they cheap-shotted me." His memories of the game aren't entirely clear, but he does remember that this back/buttock combination was the second big lick he took that night. The first was a shot to the head that he says "knocked me silly." This second hit knocked him out of the game. With Mickey on the bench, suffering from a bruised butt and back, Coach Jordan sent in the backup, Brian Steele.

When the game was over, Mickey stood up from the bench and aimed for the handshake lineup at midfield. But shortly after he stepped onto the field of play, his lower back began to spasm. He collapsed face down in the grass. While he twisted in pain, a group of coaches and players, including Lawrence Mitchell, circled him. According to the *Sun News*'s Mel Derrick, who watched these events unfold, Lawrence's eyes were "filled with concern." Mickey Wilson Sr. knelt down next to his son, "tenderly touching him."

Up in the stands, folks who had been exiting down the aisles stopped and pointed. On the field, under the lights, the circle around Mickey grew larger. When it became clear that the quarterback wouldn't be able to get to his feet on his own, Jim Werden, the Middleton coach, called out for a stretcher. But ten seconds, twenty seconds, thirty seconds passed, and no stretcher came.

Lawrence had seen enough. He was tired of waiting. He was tired of foolishness. He was tired of sitting on his ass, hoping the grown folks would take care of things. So he squatted down and slid one arm under Mickey's legs, the other under Mickey's shoulder pads. A wince, a grunt, and the 220-pound defensive end stood up, cradling the much-smaller quarterback in his massive arms. It was the kind of move he'd made a thousand times in the weight room, jacking up a barbell to do bicep curls. But now the strength and athleticism that allowed Lawrence to toss aside offensive tackles like bags of sand were being employed in the service of his friend and teammate. The big-time recruit—the black kid who just three weeks earlier was standing in the bleachers, jeering at the inexperienced quarterback's ineptness—was now carrying the white kid off the field and into the locker room, while a trail of onlookers followed behind.

• • •

The next afternoon, H. H. Singleton and the NAACP staged a protest march through Conway. This was the Saturday after Labor Day, meaning it was the last Saturday of tourist season. In the late morning, families who'd booked a weeklong beach rental for the holiday would be packing up, checking out, and aiming for home. In the early afternoon, vacationers looking to take advantage of the post–Labor Day price drop would be streaming toward the coast. Traffic, outbound and inbound, would inch along U.S. 501, and in Conway—especially around noon, when the flow would be heavy in both directions—Church Street would be crawling with cars. Right then, at the height of the snarl, a quarter-mile stretch of 501, from Racepath to Ninth Avenue, would be blocked off. The NAACP had been granted a permit to march smack down the middle of Church Street, on a Saturday afternoon, at the crescendo of tourist season.

The event was billed as the March Against Intimidation, and just before noon, under a blazing sun, approximately seven hundred protesters gathered along Racepath Avenue and in the Bethel A.M.E. Church parking lot. As a symbol of racial harmony, folks dressed in black and white and volunteers handed out black-and-white-checked ribbons. The protestors held signs that read YE SHALL KNOW WE ARE DETERMINED and DO THE RIGHT THING. They chanted "Say it loud, I'm black and I'm proud!" And they joined hands and sang "We Shall Overcome," bodies swaying in the heat.

Meanwhile, inside the church, H. H. Singleton was meeting with William Gibson, Nelson Rivers, and other state and national NAACP leaders. Earlier that morning they'd held a press conference to announce that the NAACP had filed a lawsuit on behalf of Singleton against the Horry County School District and Superintendent Dawsey. The suit, filed in federal district court the day before, charged that Singleton had been suspended in "retaliation for his exercise of Constitutionally-protected free speech," and it asked for an injunction to reinstate the teacher and bar the school board from further action against him. In an interview with the *Sun News*, Dawsey said that he looked forward to the hearings, which, he predicted, would vindicate him. "I didn't go into this thing as a knee-jerk reaction," he said. "I went in knowing what the circumstances and the facts were."

When the NAACP meeting ended, Singleton and others emerged from the church. Wearing black slacks and a white Cuban shirt, the reverend picked up a bullhorn and addressed the crowd, instructing them on what they should chant as they marched. Then, at about 12:30 p.m., the protestors lined up behind Singleton, Gibson, and Rivers, and together they started walking. The sun poured down on the oak trees and Spanish moss. It baked the fallen pine needles. The marchers wore sunglasses, and they wiped their foreheads with handkerchiefs. "Jordan, do the right thing!" they chanted. "Dawsey, do the right thing!"

The plan called for the protestors to parade for about a half mile each way, from Bethel A.M.E., down Racepath, past Cherry Hill Baptist, and onto Church Street. From there they'd follow Church to Ninth Avenue, where they'd rally in front of the Horry County School District offices. Hank Singleton had tried to talk his father into extending the march an extra mile-and-a-half down Church Street, taking it all the way to Conway High, but, as he says now, "Daddy thought that would be too far." Given the heat and the fact that many of the marchers would be older folks, a walk to the school district offices and back was short enough to be doable but long enough to get the white establishment's attention.

The South Carolina Highway Patrol had already begun diverting U.S. 501 traffic to the side streets and through the neighborhoods, as they would for the two hours it took to complete the march. When the protestors got to Church Street, they found it wide open and empty, except for the more than eighty law enforcement officers (Conway and Horry County Police, State Troopers, and the State Law Enforcement Division, a.k.a. SLED) who lined the sidewalks. If the officers and NAACP were expecting a counterprotest from white community members, it didn't happen. The streets were mostly free of spectators, as many of the white Conwayites who watched the march did so from inside the Waffle House, the Western Sizzlin' Steakhouse, or from one of the other Church Street businesses. At least one white family did take to the sidewalks, moving alongside the marchers, but this family was walking in support of the protest. "I wanted my children to see a march," Janie Johnson told the *Sun News*. "Conway is making history today."

Turning right from Church Street onto Ninth Avenue, the 700 marchers were now a block away from the school district offices, where another 800 to 1,000 protestors, including several white individuals, were gathered around a flatbed truck that had been outfitted with a podium and a P.A. system. With upwards of 1,500 crowd members clapping and chanting along, NAACP officials and community leaders delivered speeches in support of Carlos Hunt and H. H. Singleton. "I thank you for your spirit that shows you are ready to hold out to the end," Cleveland Fladger told the assembled, perhaps as a subtle dig toward Lawrence Mitchell and the other players that had *not* held out. "We are together on this thing, and we will go on!"

Fladger then introduced Carlos Hunt, and with the crowd chanting, "Carlos! Carlos!" Hunt took the podium and made his first public comments since the boycott began. He told the story of the $80 he'd borrowed from Coach Jordan for the class ring, and he included Jordan's maxim about not feeding a dog that bites your hand. This drew a chorus of boos from the crowd, along with shouts of "He's calling you a dog, Carlos!" and "But you're not a dog!"

The support for the Rev. Singleton was just as fervid and vocal, with Nelson Rivers telling the audience, "Today, we've come from all over the state to say, 'Don't mess with our brother.'" As the crowd cheered, he added, "This time they've messed with the *right* one, because we are ready to fight!" Rivers then brought Singleton to the stage and the two men joined hands— high in the air as if in victory. "We not only stand behind you; we stand in front of you," Rivers told Singleton. "And if necessary, we will stand over you!"

The message that seems to have resonated most deeply from that day— with the marchers, with the white community, and with the Conway city leaders and all those law enforcement officers re-routing traffic out on 501— was that this protest was just the beginning. The NAACP pledged to march again next Saturday and every Saturday thereafter until the wrongs that had been done to Hunt and Singleton were righted. Referring to Governor Campbell and Jim Clyburn's efforts to negotiate a resolution, Nelson Rivers told the crowd, "What the Governor is asking for is *quiet*. We don't want quiet; we want justice. Until there is justice, there will be no quiet! We will come to Conway as many times as necessary to bring a halt to the mistreat- ment of our friend and brother. Look at us good, now. At our black and our white. Multiply the number. We're going to be back next Saturday!"

That sentiment was voiced from the audience as well as the dais. "This is just a mini-march; this is just a warm-up," Elouise Davis, a Conway teacher and past President of the Conway branch of the NAACP, told the *Sun News*. "Next Saturday will be the big one." The marchers, now well over 1,000, turned around and walked back to the church, stirring with their steps a feeling of empowerment and determination that swept through Conway's black community.

And that feeling would prove to be more powerful than even the mighty Lawrence Mitchell and his resolve to play football against the wishes of his grandmother, his friends, and his neighbors. By the time the church bells rang the next morning, rumors around town were swirling. The word at the after-service luncheons and at the Sunday dinner tables, on the porches and in front of televisions airing the opening weekend of the NFL season, was that Lawrence had changed his mind a second time. He was quitting the Conway Tigers again, going back to join Carlos and his teammates on the picket line. These rumors were either reason to celebrate or a crushing disappointment, depending on where you stood. One side braced to lose an advantage they thought they'd gained, and the other looked forward to gaining an advantage they thought they'd lost. In between, in the instinctively compassionate act of cradling his friend in his arms, Lawrence Mitchell came closer than anyone else to bridging a racial divide that would only get wider in the months to come.

Coach Jordan heard the rumors, too, and by Monday—the Monday of Bell Game Week—he was expecting the worst but hoping for the best. When Lawrence and three more of the players who'd traveled to Charleston on Friday failed to show up for the 3:30 practice, he once again delayed the start time by a half hour. In the interim, the coach again found himself in a meeting with black community leaders and James Clyburn, back to the negotiating table, as if the Middleton game hadn't happened, as if the sight of Lawrence standing on the sideline in his Conway jersey, cheering for his white teammates, and then carrying the injured Mickey off the field had been some kind Pollyannaish hallucination, invented by naively optimistic Tiger fans or a Hollywood screenwriter desperate for a neat and happy ending.

When Jordan left the meeting, nothing had been resolved. By then he'd had more than his fill of conversations and negotiations, statements and invitations and false hopes. He was ready to concentrate on football, on the big rivalry game that would take place in four days, Lawrence Mitchell or no Lawrence Mitchell. He changed his clothes and headed out to the practice field, where there was no sign of his All-State defensive end. On the way, he told a reporter, "The important thing now is our focus, and our focus has to be that game Friday night against Myrtle Beach."

- 8 -

BE PARANOID

NOW

THAT GAME FRIDAY NIGHT AGAINST MYRTLE BEACH.

How many times have Conway boys uttered those words, to buddies they aimed to drink with, girls they hoped to kiss, sons-a-bitches they were burning to fight?

Hell yeah, son. Check you at that game Friday night against Myrtle Beach.

Hey, darling. Meet me under the bleachers at that game Friday night against Myrtle Beach.

You heard me, punk. See your ass in the parking lot after that game Friday night against Myrtle Beach.

Conway vs. Myrtle Beach. Inland vs. Coast. County Seat vs. Resort Area. Old Town vs. New Town. Like all great feuds—including Clemson vs. Carolina, the college rivalry that dominates the state—the Bell Game is one born in history and geography, plus a dash of the bitterness that might best be called socio-cultural contempt. The pride in one team. The scorn for the other. And neither pride nor scorn emanates solely from community or school. Both seem to run deeper, down to the DNA. Us and Our Kind vs. Them and Theirs.

You hear it in the talk around Horry County:

Know what I hate about Beach people?

Here's the thing with Tiger fans . . .

Look, it's not like everyone on the Beach is a Yankee transplant. There are a few good ones.

Matter of fact, some of my best friends went to Conway High School.

Most of the jabs are friendly, like elbow nudges to the side. But even if it's of the all-in-good-fun variety, the smack talk is indicative of a larger truth. Conway vs. Myrtle Beach isn't just about football. For fans and players, winning or losing the Victory Bell ends up as a kind of shorthand not just for the success of your team but of your *life*. The Bell Game is a bellwether. Lose the game and you're a loser, in the existential sense. Win it and, well, that's why Lawrence Mitchell and so many players from both sides will tell you, "That's what I live for, playing for the Bell."

Chuck Jordan's done more playing and coaching for the Bell than anyone, and if you judge him solely by his record in the Myrtle Beach game, he's not just a winner; he's a daggone vanquisher. A Conway native, Jordan grew up on the south side of town, in a neighborhood called Sugar Hill, which was a mix of black and white families then as it is now. Jordan's father was a plumber, and theirs was a household that, according to the *Sun News*, "encouraged equality of the races." The Jordan home sat on a dirt road, and in that road, the neighborhood kids, black and white, would play pick-up football games in which the wiry-tough Jordan gained a reputation as a scrappy competitor. Later, in high school, his grit won him a spot in the Tiger defensive backfield, where, as Conway High booster Bob Childs told the newspaper, "He'd rack you when nobody else would . . . He wasn't afraid to confront anybody on the field." In the classroom, Jordan was an honor student, just as determined to make good grades as he was to win ballgames. And during the four years he attended Conway High, the Tigers won a heck of a lot of ballgames. Jordan spent 1974, his senior year, as a team captain, and when he graduated in 1975 he did so knowing that over the previous four years the team had gone 34–8–2—with four wins in the Bell Game. Jordan's sweep against the Seahawks was the continuation of a pattern that had been established long before he put on a Tiger uniform. Throughout the '60s and '70s, Conway so thoroughly dominated the rivalry that the Bell Game wasn't much of a game. In the fifteen years from 1961 to 1975, the Tigers lost to the Seahawks only once. By the time Jordan graduated, Conway beating Myrtle Beach had become as predictable as the tides.

After high school, Jordan walked-on to the football team at Presbyterian College, eventually earning a scholarship and a captainship. From there, he moved to Columbia, where he worked as an assistant coach at Richland Northeast High while studying toward a master's degree in administration at the University of South Carolina. With his master's in hand, he advanced to the college ranks, taking a job as an assistant at Presbyterian.

Meanwhile, back home in Conway, Jordan's high school alma mater had descended into a slump. In 1978, after beating Myrtle Beach sixteen of the previous seventeen years, the Tigers lost to the Seahawks. They lost again in '79. That tide, once so predictable, had become a rogue wave. And the damage wasn't limited to the Bell Game; losses were coming in bunches. In '78 the Tigers finished with a record of 1–9. In '79 they went 2–8. Then a string of mediocrity: 7–4, 7–4, 6–5. By the early eighties, Conway was winning again—but not against Myrtle Beach. Headed into the 1983 season, the Tigers had dropped four out of five to the Seahawks. The Conway boys had lost their scrap.

And so in the fall of '83, at the age of twenty-six, Chuck Jordan again found himself on the field for his hometown Tigers, this time as head coach and athletic director. He quickly developed a reputation as a player's coach, demanding but supportive, a guiding mentor who would, as the *Sun News* wrote, "invite team members to his house for supper, give them money for college or to buy suits, and drive kids to post-season football games when they didn't have a way." But he also followed through on the competitiveness and drive he had shown in high school as an undersized defensive back. The kid was a winner—even if he wasn't exactly a kid anymore. Soon, Jordan's winning spirit took hold. In his first year, although the team finished a disappointing 5–5, they beat Myrtle Beach. Jordan now had something to build upon, and build he did. Over the next three years, the Tigers won thirty games, the most successful three-year span in the program's history. The cherry on top of that span? A new streak of four straight wins in the Bell Game. Under their young and tenacious coach, the Tigers were back and literally better than ever. Every Friday night, the Graveyard was shakin'. The stores downtown flew green and gold flags, and the marquees read Go Tigers! Chuck Jordan was arguably the most popular man in town. Conway's favorite son, it seemed, "could walk on the Waccamaw."

Then came 1989.

Still, over the next two decades, Chuck Jordan would build Conway High School into a state powerhouse, and he would become a South Carolina coaching legend. And in all those games Friday night against Myrtle Beach? Back to predictable Tiger domination. Of his first twenty-two Bell Games, Jordan won twenty. Conway fans would joke that the team shouldn't even bother bringing the Victory Bell to the game. Why haul the trophy from the school all the way to the stadium, when we're just going to have to lug it right back? In a boast that was barely an exaggeration, the '88–'89 Conway High yearbook reported that the Tigers "managed to successfully stomp on any meager form of competition" offered by the Seahawks by "step[ping] over, around, and directly on top of the pathetic heads of Seahawk players" and warned that "Myrtle Beach High School might as well erase the image of the bell from their memory." The "rivalry" eventually got so laughable that in 2000 and 2001, the Bell Game wasn't even played. As Mickey Wilson says, "There were a couple of years when he [Chuck Jordan] didn't bother scheduling us because we were so bad, just playing us would hurt their ranking."

Now in his thirtieth year at Conway, Chuck Jordan is again focused on that game Friday night against Myrtle Beach. It's the Wednesday before the Bell Game, and over the phone, he sounds as loose and high-spirited as he has all season. Sure, the team is sitting at a disappointing 2–3, but last Friday, against Marlboro County, Jordan finally saw from his guys the toughness he'd been trying to squeeze out of them since the summer. In that game—coming off three straight losses, including the debacle against the perennially inferior Socastee—the Tigers had every excuse to quit. The stands in the Backyard were maybe a quarter filled, and in the first half Conway was locked in a struggle with a 3A school they'd manhandled 48–14 the year before. Coming out at halftime, the score was tied at 20, but the Tigers quickly found themselves in a 34–20 hole. A fourth straight loss seemed certain, and in the next day's paper, Jordan admitted, "I think we were a little stressed at that point." Then Mykal Moody—the senior, the leader—rushed for one touchdown, threw for another, and with a pair of two-point conversions, Conway took the lead, 36–34. But Marlboro County would score again to go up 40–36.

With less than three minutes to play, Conway faced a fourth down and five from the Marlboro 24-yard line. Rather than kick a long field goal that would still leave the Tigers behind by one point, Jordan decided to go for it. The way he saw it, his team had the home field, the senior quarterback, and the long history of winning on its side. As he'd later say, "The bottom line is that we are Conway." What he doesn't say, but can be inferred, is that over the years Conway hasn't just won a lot, Conway has come to *define* winning. So it's a simple, logical formulation as deductively true as any geometry proof: *1) Conway equals winning. 2) We are Conway. 3) Therefore, we will win.* Like many other teams at the high school and college levels (perhaps most famously Penn State and Marshall), the Tigers have long used the tautological rallying cry, "We are *us!*" But this season, they've added a new element, one that more precisely enumerates their deep tradition. Now, after huddling up and announcing, "We are CONWAY!" they break the huddle with, "We are *TEAM 89!*" Although one may be tempted to read "Team 89" as a tribute to the 1989 squad, the group that Jordan and his staff from that year still cite as having more pride and heart than any they've ever coached, the reality is that "Team 89" signifies that this year's Tigers are the 89th team Conway has fielded since the school began playing football in 1923. Next year's bunch will be Team 90 and so on. Conway's star alumnus Junior Hemingway became familiar with the "Team X" moniker while at the University of Michigan, a school with more wins than any other college program, and he brought the idea south to his high school coach.

Still, as Jordan faced that fourth and five against Marlboro County, he knew that for all of Conway's tradition, talent is what gets you first downs. And in Mykal Moody, the Tigers were certainly blessed with talent. That night, Mykal had already thrown for three touchdowns and rushed for two, but nobody would remember any of it if he didn't convert on this play. So on fourth down, with the game on the line, the senior reared back and fired. And he found freshman Bryan Edwards in the end zone for the touchdown and the win. Jordan's Tigers had halted the losing streak, and maybe, fingers-crossed, built momentum and confidence to carry with them into the Bell Game.

"It's good for a team to win close games," Jordan says now, over the phone. "Because they know they can overcome a struggle." And in the last few years, the Bell Game has been nothing if not a struggle for Conway. In 2007, after dominating the Seahawks for two decades, Jordan's Tigers lost to Myrtle Beach. In 2008, Conway lost again. The next year, Mickey Wilson became the head man for the Seahawks, and in his Bell Game debut, he thumped his old coach. He did it the next year, too. Just like that, the kids from the coast had beaten the inlanders four times in a row. Before this steak, Myrtle Beach had only defeated Jordan twice total. Even in the early '80s, in the years just before Jordan returned to Conway, Myrtle Beach hadn't put together a winning streak longer than two games. "For a long time, Conway dominated," Jordan says. "Now the rivalry is a little more balanced, and that makes for a better game." He's hardly put the period on that sentence before he says, "Don't get me wrong, now. I don't like to lose." And last year, in Moody's junior season, the Tigers broke the losing streak with an upset win at home. All was back to normal in Horry County. Up was up and down was down and Conway was Conway. And if *Conway* means anything, it means cuttin' butt in that game Friday night against Myrtle Beach.

"We celebrate our wins," Mickey Wilson says on the Sunday before the Bell Game, "but we come back on Monday ready to work." His team has reached 4–0, having beaten Carolina Forest two days earlier, the fourth consecutive 4A school Myrtle Beach has taken down to start the season. The Seahawks are the top-ranked 3A squad in South Carolina, not that early-season polls mean much to Mickey. "We're not the best team in the state," he says. "I can tell you that for sure." But the pollsters whose votes determine the rankings say different. Still, on this weekend leading up to the game against the Seahawks' biggest rival, Mickey knows he can't let his players continue to celebrate wins any more than he'd want them moping and sulking after losses. Routine is what keeps you from getting too high or too low. Win or lose, come Monday it's back to work. This is especially true in the lead-up to a rivalry game. You take your guys through the same diligent preparation as always, adhering even more strictly to the football doctrine that has led you here. After all, if you're 4–0 and #1 in the state, whatever you're doing, it's working. So for Mickey, that means more long hours and late nights.

The head coach's office is tucked inside the strength training room and features a large window that looks out to the lifting benches and free weights. Out in the weight room, above the office window hangs a green sign that lists the years of the Seahawks' six state championships. The sign sends a clear message: Myrtle Beach High School is a place where great things are possible if you work hard enough for them. But Mickey's biggest coaching fear is that his players will start to think of the program's past success as a guarantee of future wins. So below the list of championships he's hung a second sign: SUCCESS BREEDS COMPLACENCY. COMPLACENCY BREEDS FAILURE. ONLY THE PARANOID SURVIVE. "We talk about complacency a lot," he says. "That's why I tell them 'Be paranoid.'"

This year the Seahawks have adopted *Be uncommon!* as the team motto, but if there's a fundamental tenet for Mickey's program, it's *Be paranoid!* They often break huddles with "One-two-three. Be paranoid!" And the 2010 state championship rings that Mickey and the upperclassmen wear are inscribed with BE PARANOID! as a permanent reminder of the philosophy that brought them the title. Paranoia might seem at odds with the positive, self-reliant mentality football is supposed to encourage in young men, but to Mickey, paranoia is a healthy by-product of competition. After all, the best way to hold on to what you've earned—a starting position, a Victory Bell, a state championship—is to gird yourself against those gunning to steal it. Being paranoid in football, Mickey tells his players, means constantly looking over your shoulder to see who might be improving faster than you are. It means working harder than the teammate who might otherwise win your job. It means never underestimating (and always outworking) the opponent. It boils down to fighting hard work with harder work.

So the coach takes pride in his offseason conditioning program, which he says is one of the toughest in the state. For the Myrtle Beach team, weekdays in June and July are known as "work days," meaning the players and coaches show up in the weight room at 7:00 a.m. When they walk through the door to begin their intense sessions, they see a whiteboard on which someone has written in bold strokes: *Championships are won by those who embrace hard work and have the discipline to tolerate discomfort.* Mickey models that creed by joining his players on the lifting floor. He's out there, walking from bench to bench, urging each of his guys to push through a few more reps. He's firing them up to try for a team record in one of the four weightlifting categories the coaches track. The bench press and the squat are the marquee events, and this year, Octavius Thomas, O.T., owns them both. The summer is a time of sweat and pain for the players; it's where paranoia is born. And paranoia, Mickey preaches, plus the strength and stamina that paranoia breeds, are why the Seahawks have won those six state championships and four of the last five Bell Games.

Mickey Wilson may hold a winning record against Chuck Jordan, but in coaching, as the old cliché goes, you're only as good as your last game. And in Mickey's last Bell Game, his boys lost to his ex-coach and alma mater. Still, on paper anyway, Myrtle Beach will be the heavy favorite this Friday. They've beaten up on schools from Conway's region for three weeks in a row, including West Florence and South Florence, the two teams that tied for last year's region co-championship above Conway. Two weeks ago, against South Florence, with Myrtle Beach sitting on a 14-point lead midway through the fourth quarter, the ever-paranoid Mickey worked the refs and spurred on his players right up until the final seconds; never mind that that the outcome was already a virtual certainty. In the locker room after the game, Mickey told his team, "They thought they were ready for big-time football." He paused and then completed the thought with comic understatement: "They weren't!" The locker room didn't erupt in jubilation, though; they knew their coach was about to tell them their work was only beginning. And he did, stressing that they still had much improving to do before the following week's game against Carolina Forest High.

Located about halfway between Conway and Myrtle Beach, the Carolina Forest area—a string of developments with ornate entrances and upscale-sounding names—feels suburban, despite the fact that there's no real *urban* section in Horry County. Carolina Forest High opened fifteen years ago, and in that time, both the Tigers and Seahawks have developed a rivalry with the new school. In Conway, some folks point to the creation of Carolina Forest as the primary reason for why Tigers have struggled in recent years. Due to a redrawing of attendance zones, lots of kids who once would have played for Chuck Jordan are now suiting up for the Panthers. Adding fuel to the Myrtle Beach/Carolina Forest rivalry is the fact that Seahawks QB Tyler Keane played for the Panthers as a sophomore, before his family moved into the Myrtle Beach attendance area. High schools aren't technically allowed to recruit football players, but that doesn't stop rumor and speculation. The day before this year's Myrtle Beach/Carolina Forest game, Mickey Wilson explained to the *Sun News* why the Seahawks have had success in attracting players like Tyler: "If a family's moving into our area and they have a football player, they're going to ask 'Hey, where's the better football program at?' They're going to get the response of the Myrtle Beaches and the Conways and that type of thing." The next night, the Seahawks backed up their coach's bravado by beating the Panthers 33–10.

Now, four wins into the season, Mickey's happy but not satisfied. As always, he fears complacency, but this week, he's confident his guys won't lack for motivation. His coaches and players know all too well that the Conway Tigers were the only area team to beat the Seahawks last year. Still, Mickey insists that his team will prepare for Jordan's squad just as they would for any other school on the schedule, which means they'll treat the Bell Game like they treat every game. If you believe the things Mickey says in the heat of July and August, the Conway rivalry is mostly fueled by the fans and the media, not by the coaches and players. The Bell Game isn't a region game, so it's not going to get the Seahawks into (or keep them out of) the 3A playoffs. It has no bearing on the state championship. "In the grand scheme of things," he's been known to say, "it means nothing."

And he's right. But most of what counts as life doesn't happen in the grand scheme; life, and particularly that part of life we pour into sports, is built upon the little day-to-day nothings that add up to everything. On the rare day when we do accomplish a feat that rates in the grand scheme, we try to hold onto it forever, like a firefly in a jar. We commemorate the accomplishment with a token that can never equal what it represents. How do you capture the joy of birth with a birth certificate? Graduation with a diploma? A life with a headstone? And yet we can't clutch the abstract, so we cling to the tangible. Take the Victory Bell trophy. A cheap-looking wooden box with a silver bell sitting on top. Flanking the bell are two player statuettes, and on each side of the box, there's a plate engraved with the final scores going back as far as 1968. The whole thing is maybe a foot-and-a-half high from base to crown. None of it is especially impressive or showy. But on Friday night, the winning team is going to lay claim to that bell, and all the pride and bragging rights that come with it. They'll have their pictures taken with it. They'll watch cheerleaders swoon over it. They'll come away with stories they'll be swapping for decades.

And the losing team will start counting the days until next year.

THEN

The Monday before the '89 Bell Game—the day Lawrence Mitchell walked away from the team a second time—marks the moment when all reasonable hope of ending the boycott and "saving" the season was lost. There would be no compromise. There couldn't be, not with the All-State defensive end back on the picket line and Chuck Jordan holding firm on the quarterback switch. Of course, it only felt like a loss if you *wanted* to save the season. If what you wanted was the larger Conway Movement to keep building—and clearly many blacks in the community, region, and state did, as they planned to stage weekly marches that would dwarf the previous Saturday's protest—then Lawrence's return to the boycott represented an emphatic win.

But why would a player who on Friday appeared so delighted to be back with his team change his mind over the course of one weekend? The *Sun News* floated an answer to that question, and it was an answer that seemed to confirm the suspicions of many whites: Lawrence had been coerced. "Apparently bowing to pressure from the community," read the article, "star lineman Lawrence Mitchell did not come back to the Conway High football team on Monday afternoon." Many folks read "bowing to pressure" as evidence that H. H. Singleton and the NAACP had arm-twisted Lawrence to again walk away.

To this day, whites in Conway grit their teeth over a lot of things Singleton said and did in '89, but his alleged role in pulling Lawrence back to the boycott on the Monday before the Bell Game gets people particularly angry. "Lawrence had returned to the team," they'll say, "but then somebody got to him." They often cite rumors, all unsubstantiated, about a cabal of blacks who harassed, bribed, or outright threatened Lawrence and forced him to reverse course. One story has it that group of black guys showed up at his grandmother's house and told him, in what can only be interpreted as a mafia-style threat, "Lawrence, if you stay with the team, we can't guarantee your safety."

In reality, the somebody who got to him was his grandmother, Gussie Lee Pertell. She was the one who convinced him over the weekend to go back on strike. "Lawrence is trying to do the right thing," she told the *Sun News*, acknowledging that she wanted her grandson to play football—but only if and when *all* the striking players returned. "All of the boys left together," she said, "and I want them all to go back together." Today Lawrence sums up his return to the walkout like this: "My grandmother told me, 'Look, you made a decision, you stick with it.' So I had to go back to the boycott." Most of us find conspiracy theories fascinating, and beyond their scandalous appeal, there's something strangely comforting in the idea of an invisible hand twisting the gears. We've been taught to both yield to and be wary of power structures we can't see and don't fully understand. So we're perhaps compelled to believe that a sudden reversal like Lawrence's—from a man who is glorified for his inner and outer strength—must have been ordered by a band of conspirators rather than suggested by one sweet-hearted grandmother.

With Lawrence back on strike and the two sides more deeply entrenched than ever, people all over Conway, black and white, were beginning to view everyday life through the lens of the boycott and the machinations that caused it and were sparked by it—which led to a climate of suspicion and mistrust, which in turn bred conjecture and fear. To some in the black community, Jordan was no longer just the football coach; he had become a figure of evil. To some in the white community, Singleton had become a kind of boogeyman who grew out of and in turn fueled their worst racial anxieties. And even whites who didn't think of him as an outright threat to social order would say that he was a man whose word couldn't be trusted, that his actions were motivated by his ego, that he was always looking to pick a fight with the white establishment. There were plenty of unconfirmed rumors about Reverend Singleton's real reasons for supporting the boycott, and even now, tales about his supposed ulterior motives are widespread among whites in Conway. But the fact that no one is willing to be quoted in this book as a source of these rumors should give some idea of how much factual basis there is to them. Research and interviews have turned up nothing to suggest that Singleton's motivations were anything other than what he stated at the time of the boycott: wanting to serve as a spokesman and counselor for a group of young men whose cause he supported. But try convincing a lot of white people in Conway of that and you'll find yourself talking to the proverbial brick wall. More than two decades later, the mention of Singleton's name still has the power to generate a visceral reaction that testifies to the kind of effect he had on many Conwayites. A good rule of thumb: If people are still making up stories about you after you've died, then you lived one hell of a life.

The various rumors floating around town may have been unfounded, but they helped foster an atmosphere of uncertainty and anxiety in which both blacks and whites worried that violence might break out at any time. Chuck Jordan says that one day a group of white guys "of questionable character" stopped by his office and volunteered to "get these people off [his] back once and for all." The coach suspects that the visitors had ties to the KKK. Their plan, they told Jordan, was to let a basket of cottonmouths loose in Cherry Hill Baptist while Sunday services were under way. They'd then lock the doors, leaving the churchgoers inside to wrestle with the snakes. Jordan says he threw the knuckleheads out of his office, but not before they'd put a good scare into him. "That's the way the KKK works," he says now. "Once they tell you about it, you're part of it."

The Klan may have been trying to work the back channels in Jordan's office, but approximately five months later, in February 1990, the KKK made a highly visible and public appearance. Several hundred Conwayites lined the streets to watch white-robed and Confederate flag–carrying Klansmen march down Third Avenue and Main Street before stopping at the Horry County Courthouse for a rally. Although it's impossible to know how many of the spectators were Klan-backers and how many were merely curiosity seekers, the *Horry Independent* did report that many of those in attendance "openly supported the Klan's return to Conway" and "didn't mind being interviewed" about their support. Conway resident Larry Graham told the paper, "I think it's high time they come. Singleton has been marching and showing his tail and it's about time white people do the same." Conway's Robert Normandin echoed Graham's sentiment. "I don't understand why when [blacks] march they're standing up for their rights," he said, "but when whites march they're racists." A spectator named Bonnie Todd also felt compelled to stand up for Conway's white residents, asserting that most whites in town were tired of NAACP protests and allegations of racism. "I think they ought to behave themselves," she said, "and let's try to get along." But at the courthouse, SC Grand Dragon Horace King voiced a message that ran violently counter to the goal of Conway's blacks and whites "trying to get along." After advocating for complete segregation of the races, he told any NAACP members that might be lurking in the crowd that he had a message for H. H. Singleton. "The Grand Dragon of South Carolina will no[t] bow down to him," King said. "I'd rather die by his bullet than bow down to him."

There's no way to know if the guys "of questionable character" that paid Jordan a visit in the fall of '89 were with the Klan or not. There's no way to know if they would have actually gone through with their cottonmouths-in-the-church scheme. And five months later, when the Klan finally did crawl out of the woods, there was no way to know if the Grand Dragon, by publicly injecting the idea of gun violence into an already volatile situation, might inspire somebody—white or black—to pick up a pistol and take a shot. Probably not, but then again, maybe so. That's how it felt to live in Conway during the boycott and in the months after. Nothing truly dangerous had happened yet. But it easily could have. And it still might.

That fall Jordan's wife, Pat, began sleeping with a loaded .22 under her pillow, prompted by the nasty phone calls the Jordans were getting at home. Some of the callers were obviously just annoying pranksters, but many made death threats. Mickey Wilson's family was also receiving threatening calls. "You know where I live?" Mickey's dad asked one such caller. "Then get your ass over here, and I'll meet you in the front yard." Mickey's mom adds that during what she remembers as being Bell Game Week, the Wilsons heard a rumor that somebody was planning to shoot Mickey Jr. while he was out on the field. "I was so scared, sitting in the stands," she says. "I was paralyzed with fear. It was a huge crowd, and I was just searching the crowd. I couldn't hardly watch the game, because all I could think of is, my son is gonna be shot." Despite the potential danger, she says she "wanted to keep Mickey Jr. grounded and calm. So we tried to downplay it as much as we could, at home and at school. We said, we're just going to go on with our lives just like we always do—except if it would've been up to me, I'd have pulled him that game that they said there was somebody going to shoot him."

The Singletons also received death threats. At Cherry Hill, both the church and the residence abutted U.S. 501, placing them within easy throwing distance for somebody who might be inclined to chuck a Molotov cocktail through a window. Nobody ever did, but Hank Singleton says the menacing calls had made his mother afraid to answer the phone; he or his father would have to do it. He remembers one time when the phone rang at about 1:00 a.m. and his father answered.

"Nigger, we tired of this shit," the caller said to Rev. Singleton. "We're coming right now to kill you, your wife, and your children."

Singleton hollered, "Well, come on then, if you're coming!" And he slammed the phone down. Then he went to the back of the house and returned with two guns, including his favorite, a Derringer .38 with a pearl handle. He handed the Derringer to Hank and said, "You watch the back of the house, and I'll watch the front of the house. And anything, son, that doesn't look familiar to you, you fire first and ask questions later."

Hank stayed awake for over two hours, until 3:30 or so, sitting by the window, looking out at the backyard and at the parking lot of the church, waiting for somebody strange to intrude onto the property. He was holding the Derringer and, anticipating the inevitable reload, he'd placed extra ammunition on the window side table.

Amid this climate of wariness and worry, people on both sides of the issue would have had every reason to feel that the situation was nearly hopeless, that little could be done to talk sense into those who disagreed. But that didn't mean they weren't trying. Letters to the editor poured into the *Sun News*, breaking into two distinct camps—supporters of Singleton and supporters of Jordan. The Singleton backers focused on the alleged racial motives behind Carlos's removal and on the unfairness of the earth science teacher's suspension. They saw the two occurrences as evidence of a systemic racism that wasn't limited to sports or the school system. Jordan's allies defended the coach's right to play whomever he wanted at whatever position he wanted. They saw the boycott as unwarranted activism and not an authentic response to any real prejudice on the football field, in the schools, or anywhere else in town. As evidenced by these letters, the people of Conway were talking plenty *about* the boycott, but not necessarily *to* one another.

Just over a week before the Bell Game, the *Sun News* published a special editorial section, "Conway in Controversy," that featured opinion pieces written by readers. The resulting submissions to this section—and, similarly, the letters that were sent to the *Horry Independent*, Conway's weekly paper—testify to the racial divide that had been made so evident by the walkout and to the very different fears of folks on each side of that divide. In a letter to the *Sun News*, reader Joyce Jones describes Jordan's actions against Hunt as another in a long string of white abuses of power that had, in her view, eroded many of the gains made by blacks during the civil rights era. She brings up stories of football players at nearby Loris High being "called 'nigger' by one of the white football coaches" and then describes an unidentified school in Conway where 65 percent of the black members of the teaching and professional staff had allegedly fled or been forced out of their jobs over a four-year period, Horry County schools with white principals who had never hired a black teacher, and "whites who maintain that racism does not exist in Horry County." Even worse, according to Jones, were black residents who had been "blindly led by whites" to believe that racism was a thing of the past. Jones then warns of a creeping and insidious racism that had replaced the overt prejudice of the past. Segregated schools, businesses, and drinking fountains may have disappeared, but they had been replaced by something more dangerous: racism that even some blacks had been conditioned to ignore.

The fears expressed by Jones and others were regarded as irrational ranting by many readers who supported Chuck Jordan and John Dawsey. The general sentiment in these letters was that everything that could be done to eradicate racism had already been done. Anyone still speaking out about racism in 1989 was hanging onto just one (admittedly regrettable) part of the past. To complain about racism *was* racism—or, at minimum, these complaints were fueling racial tension rather than abating it. In a letter to the *Horry Independent*, Conway resident Dennis J. Allen wrote, "Conway doesn't have a racial problem, it has an H. H. Singleton problem. It seems he does everything he can to bring publicity to himself. Where there isn't a situation that warrants media attention, he makes one." Allen goes on to describe Singleton as having "the blind support of a lot of good-hearted but unlearned black people," and he characterizes Singleton's cries of racism as "causing tensions to flare between the blacks and whites."

A number of other letters to the two newspapers expressed the same idea—that Singleton wasn't reacting to or fighting against racism, but in fact *was* a racist who was simply "using" the football controversy to generate publicity for the NAACP and for himself. These are essentially the same charges that always seem to be leveled at outspoken black leaders, from Martin Luther King Jr. to Jesse Jackson and Al Sharpton (who'd come to prominence three years earlier, first with the Howard Beach incident and then the Tawana Brawley controversy). A letter by Paul A. Barra describes Singleton's offer to serve as spokesman for the players not only as a "play for notoriety" but as "rabble rousing" that "perverts the energy and idealism of high school students to further his goal of polarizing the races in our communities." Appearing in the paper just one day after John Dawsey suspended Singleton, the letter argues that the teacher's "brand of racism" is intolerable in the schools and that the newspaper's readers should contact local media outlets and demand that Singleton be fired. "If my children were attending Conway Middle School," wrote Barra, "they would not sit for a day in H. H. Singleton's class."

Of course, not all letters, not even those critical of the boycott, took such a one-sided, confrontational approach. Mary E. Moore—the wife of Covel C. Moore, a prominent black minister in Conway—reminds readers that Christ died for everyone's sins, both black and white, and says that if we could all remember that fact, we would "jump out of our skins," there would be "no more racism," and we could "get this thing over with." Moore is black, but her words echo the point of view held by many whites: Can't we just forget this whole race thing? Too often, however, whites take the position that racism is never going to end until *blacks* get over it. *Blacks need to stop grumbling,* this viewpoint suggests. *Stop embracing victimhood. Stop playing the race card.*

There is another group of whites, of course, who understands that blacks can't end racism—just like walls can't end graffiti. And for every white racist, there's another person experiencing white guilt. Still, the white hope for a future beyond race (the "can't we get this thing over with?" position) ends up looking not like a plea for forgiveness exactly, but instead a plea for a kind of forgetfulness. This plea asks us, as a nation and a culture, to be aware of acts of racism from the distant past—but to forget acts of racism from the more recent past and to be effectively blind to racism in the present. As a strategy to end racism, we are asked to ignore its lingering effects. Put into practice, this combination of racial blindness and amnesia leads some whites (and some blacks) driving through a "bad neighborhood" to see people who should blame only themselves for their poverty and their powerlessness. Society hasn't failed them; they have failed themselves. And this failure has come despite equal and sometimes even priority access to schools, jobs, government programs, and community support systems. Whites pleading for this collective ignorance of the cumulative effects of longstanding racism know perfectly well that blacks, statistically speaking, underperform whites in most academic and economic categories (they're not typically so out of touch that they would deny this reality). But for these whites, the fact that each black child is theoretically capable of the same success as a white child allows them to write off the gaps between races as merely examples of differences in talent or motivation.

According to this view, black teenagers who don't read well enough to meet the entrance requirements for Clemson University or the University of South Carolina—the two "flagship" universities in the state—have only themselves to blame, because they likely went to a school where many other children, black and white, did excel in reading. Never mind that the poor achievement of one black teenager who fails to get into Clemson may be close to the norm for thousands of other black teenagers and that this norm is routinely far below the white average. The achievement gap between whites and blacks, according to this view (or, more accurately, non-view) of race, is not really collective, but individual. Yes, the thinking goes, those individual differences may add up to communal disparity, but because our social and educational systems have supposedly achieved racial equality, the real explanation must be individual differences multiplied thousands of times over, not the effect of racial bias or systemic racism. Thus, the persistent belief in a race-free future might be seen not as a genuine hope for racial equality and justice but as the white community's plea to blacks to ignore the obvious disparity between the races or at least not to cite racism and its effects as the cause for that inequality.

Again, to be fair, it's not as if whites who believe in a race-free future are a bunch of covert racists who want blacks to remain in an inferior socioeconomic position. Many of them truly want racial harmony and honestly believe that we can only achieve it by living as if race does not exist. As Mary E. Moore's commentary shows, many blacks also feel this way. Moore begs her fellow Conwayites to leave behind their black and white identities—to figuratively "jump out of [their] skins." "Warmer hearts must dwell inside these skinless bodies we jump out of today," she writes. This is a beautiful sentence and sentiment, but during the boycott, amid all the threats and accusations, too many hearts were anything but warm.

• • •

On the Sunday after the Conway/Middleton game, as rumors were swirling that Lawrence Mitchell would again be quitting the team, Mel Derrick of the *Sun News* wrote a column that expressed a similar hope for a race-free world—or at least for a race-free football team. "White? Black? No, he's just a teammate," read the headline, and in the article, Derrick tells the story of Lawrence carrying Mickey off the field and back to the locker room, citing it as an example of how teammates should treat one another and of the colorblindness we should all strive for. When Mickey tells the story of his injury now, he tells it matter-of-factly, boiling it to the bare bones: "They called for a stretcher, they couldn't find one, and he just grabbed me." From Mickey's perspective, the incident happened quickly, and he doesn't remember any of his teammates or coaches discussing it afterwards. Apparently there was nothing unusual in seeing Lawrence help his friend. Maybe that's because the Tigers already thought of Lawrence as a team guy, a guy who'd never wanted to boycott in the first place. After all, it's not as if Carlos Hunt had helped Mickey off. That would have been talked about. As touching as Lawrence's deed was, it's probably not fair to portray it as a conscious statement by Mitchell on race or on the boycott. Of course, that's exactly the sportswriter's point: The very normalcy of the act showed that racial lines could, in the best of all worlds, dissipate. But in 1989, they hadn't dissipated fully, not in Horry County or anywhere else in America.

And they still haven't. Even now, when you ask white Conwayites what the boycott taught them, some of them will answer, in a phrase often heard around town, "I learned that in 1989, it was more important to be black than to be right." Although this phrase is meant as a jab at black hypocrisy, it also hints at the black unity that was coalescing in the late '80s and early '90s, a unity that was a response to a perceived dismantling of civil rights by the white establishment at all levels, from the football field to the federal government. In remarks that the *Horry Independent* published on the Wednesday of Bell Game Week, Human Affairs Commissioner James Clyburn went beyond his charge of simply investigating the QB position switch and instead tried to contextualize the larger Conway protests, pointing out that they were indicative of frustrations bubbling up with blacks nationally. "I have never seen the lack of hope in the black community that I see in it today," he said. "When you lose hope, there ain't much left." He then drew a straight line between this lack of hope and the economic policies of the Reagan administration, which in Clyburn's view had widened the gap between whites and blacks. "I think that those people who rejoice in what they consider to be the positives of the Reagan legacy," Clyburn said, "they ought to know about these bad racial feelings that the Reagan Administration has left us. He was very successful in turning people against each other," said Clyburn, before adding that Reagan "made greed acceptable. He made self-ishness acceptable."

Clyburn wasn't the only black figure in government blaming Washington for widening America's racial divide. The week before the Middleton game, Supreme Court Justice Thurgood Marshall told a group of federal judges that the Supreme Court, because of rulings made in its most recent term, had "put at risk not only the civil rights of minorities but the civil rights of all citizens." Referring to the era of desegregation that had begun with *Brown v. Board of Education*, the case he had argued and won thirty-five years earlier as chief counsel for the NAACP, Marshall said, "We are back where we started." In 1989, "back where we started" had left South Carolina with a swimming pool in Saluda that wouldn't let black kids swim and a restaurant in North Augusta that wouldn't let black adults eat. It had left America with the Yusef Hawkins shooting in Bensonhurst and the Virginia National Guard's response to the Greekfest protests. And in the coming years, "back where we started" would lead to the Crown Heights riot, the Rodney King riots, and the protests in response to the shooting death of Amadou Diallo.

Back in Conway, Clyburn hadn't yet filed a report on the football boy-cott, but he was clearly concerned about race relations beyond the football field. "When you take all that social impact," he told the *Sun News*, "the emotions in the community and the suspension of a teacher exercising his First Amendment rights who is a chapter president of the NAACP, it's something."

Those two words, *it's something*, mark where Clyburn's view diverged from that of Conway's white majority, most of whom would have said that *nothing* was going on, not really. A coach had made a decision that was well within his rights. Then a whiny kid who wasn't cut out character-wise for the QB position had gone crying to the one person he knew would take his side. And that person was a loudmouth malcontent who saw racism in everything whites did, even in the most innocuous of acts. That agitator then used the quarterback decision as a thin justification for the kind of community-wide movement he'd always wanted to lead. H. H. Singleton became the ringleader behind it all—behind the recent promise of weekly NAACP marches, behind the daily picket lines at the Horry County School District offices, behind calls for the resignation of a winning coach, behind the dismantling of a team that had had the chance to go all the way to the state championship. Like Jesse Jackson and Al Sharpton, H. H. Singleton refused to go along with calls for a race-free future. Instead, he called for a race-aware present, and speaking out in this way made him the very kind of black leader that many whites were suspicious of.

Throughout the first three weeks of the boycott, Carlos Hunt hadn't said much to the media. H. H. Singleton was the spokesman for the players, and he did almost all of the talking. Even at the press conference announcing the walkout, when reporters raised their hands with questions for Hunt, Carlos responded with "no comment" to almost every one. Hank Singleton has kept an amateur-shot video of the event, and if you listen carefully to the Q&A portion, you can hear an unidentified off-screen voice instructing Carlos to say "No comment" immediately after most of the questions. Only when that off-screen voice says, "Answer that" does Carlos actually answer. Very few people in Conway would have had access to this footage, but if they had, it certainly would have stoked fears that the players were puppets being controlled by Singleton and the NAACP. Today in Conway, many whites and even some blacks use terms like "manipulated" and "chess pieces" to describe the boycotting players. Coach Jordan doesn't use those terms exactly, but he often says that the players were good kids who never would have followed through on the boycott without the intervention of Singleton, Cleveland Fladger, and other black leaders. Hunt's silence only served to intensify fears that a small group of instigators—not the black players themselves—were fueling the boycott.

On the Tuesday before the Bell Game, the *Sun News* editors wrote a piece arguing that a solution to the boycott might be found if only Jordan and Hunt would "talk, face to face, issue to issue, man to man." After three weeks of negotiations that had amounted to almost nothing, it seems implausible that the answer was as simple as a discussion between the coach and the player. This plea for direct talks seems to overestimate the human capacity for rational compromise. Even James Clyburn, who said he normally liked to "subscribe to the theory that when people talk to each other, there's a chance of resolution," had by then pretty much abandoned the idea that discussion would end the boycott. "When emotions get intertwined with reason," he said in the paper, "you never know which is going to prevail. Last week, reason seemed to have the upper hand, this week rhetoric seems to have the upper hand."

But the inability to see that the walkout was past the point of no return wasn't the only way in which the editorial failed to capture the reality of the situation. The piece referred to the boycott as a "regionwide, if not nationwide, smudge on Conway's racial reputation." Black readers must have wanted to ask just how pristine that reputation had been before the boycott.

The paper's implicit claim that Conway was blemish-free back in July must have sounded like another whitewashing (pun intended) of history. The editorial then says that the walkout has led to a "now-racial chasm," a claim that seems true except for the word "now." By using the phrase "now-racial" and then mentioning that there had been a "quick deterioration from a football issue to a racial issue," the newspaper was essentially suggesting that the boycott itself had created the "chasm." Blacks might well have countered that the chasm had always existed; whites either couldn't see it or didn't want to.

That Thursday, with both sides' views hardening into competing orthodoxies, the *Sun News* made a controversial move of its own, announcing that the paper would "publish no further letters on the Conway situation" because the opinions and arguments had "become repetitive." Upon reading this announcement, blacks surely felt that their letters were repetitive because the racial situation was repetitive: It never got any better. Whites might have countered that their letters were repetitive because they had yet to convince blacks that racism was a dead issue, that we all had to move on. Even though the *Sun News* was likely just trying to save column inches for other newsworthy items, this decision probably made the events in Conway more susceptible to rumor, promoting the feeling of paranoia on both sides. It was the week Mitchell quit the team a second time. It was the week the NAACP announced subsequent marches that would surely escalate in size. It was the week that Singleton's federal lawsuit against Horry County Schools was assigned to a U.S. District Court magistrate who had the power to issue an immediate but temporary injunction against the suspension. And it was Bell Game Week. All in all, it must have seemed like a curious time for the newspaper to cut off discussion, which may have given all Conway residents—black and white—reason to feel that their voices weren't being heard, that the real decisions were being made behind a curtain of secrecy.

Taught in school to revere Martin Luther King Jr., many whites could support and had perhaps even memorized King's statement from the "I Have a Dream" speech in which he called for a race-neutral, but not necessarily race-free, future. "I have a dream," he said, "that my four little children will one day live in a nation where they will not be judged by the color of their skin, but by the content of their character." But few whites in Conway or anywhere in the United States would have so easily recalled another statement from that same speech, in which Dr. King compares the promises of freedom and justice in the Declaration of Independence and the Constitution to "promissory notes" written to all American citizens. "It is obvious today," King said, "that America has defaulted on this promissory note insofar as her citizens of color are concerned. Instead of honoring this sacred obligation, America has given the Negro people a bad check which has come back marked 'insufficient funds.'"

In 1989, Conway's black community might not have recalled this specific metaphor any more than people in the white community would have, but there's no doubt they would have understood the sentiment. The inferior socio-economic condition of blacks was proof positive to King in 1963 that racism was the limiting and causal factor behind inequality. And twenty-six years later, the Conway Movement showed that blacks remained convinced that their economic situation relative to whites was a product of the enduring though perhaps hidden racial bias of the white majority. Many whites might have said the black community was just being paranoid. Blacks might have responded that for a long time, they hadn't been paranoid enough. Now, Singleton had reminded them to be paranoid again—the kind of paranoia that means girding yourself against those gunning to steal what you've earned. A football position. A teaching job. A voice.

But Singleton and the black community wouldn't be the only ones girding themselves for a fight. Whites in Conway had been taught to be paranoid, too.

- 9 -

PLAYING FOR THE BELL

THEN

TIGER FOOTBALL HAD BEEN AN IMPORTANT SOCIAL ACTIVITY IN CONWAY for decades, but after Chuck Jordan resurrected the program in 1983, fan enthusiasm reached a pitch that bordered on the religious. The team was winning, sure, but more importantly, football became the connective tissue that bound Conway and gave folks a common identity, a shared purpose. The events of 1989 undid some of that unity. These days, many Tiger fans remember the boycott year as the beginning of the end of Conway football's golden age, regardless of the fact that Jordan's teams had some of their most successful seasons in the 1990s and 2000s. In 1989, a sacred rite—Friday night football—was permanently disrupted by "outsiders." More recently, the emergence of Myrtle Beach High School as Horry County's dominant program represents another disruption, an upending of the traditional. In that way, Conway backers are like prototypical Southeastern NASCAR fans who feel betrayed by their sport for its expansion toward foreign car makers, pretty-boy drivers (pretty *girl* drivers, even), and tracks in places like Chicago and Kansas City. The racing itself hasn't changed much; it's still souped-up stock cars making left turns. But it just doesn't feel as Southern as it used to. To good ol' boys it's no longer "our sport." And the empty seats in traditional NASCAR markets like Bristol, Tennessee, and Darlington, South Carolina (sixty miles northwest of Conway), testify to that alienation. Likewise, attendance at the Backyard is also down in recent years, which might hint at a disconnection between Tiger fans and the team that once seemed like the town's common denominator. Then again, the open bleachers might just mean that Chuck's boys aren't winning enough.

Hank Singleton absolutely points to 1989 as the year that Conway's black residents soured on Chuck Jordan and the football program, but some members of Conway's black community extend Hank's reasoning much further, arguing that the Lord Himself is no longer a Tiger fan. They'll suggest, and

140

without a wink, that Jordan's poor treatment of Carlos Hunt sparked God's vengeance and has led to futility everlasting. At a recent NAACP function held at Cherry Hill Baptist, Earl Friday—a student manager for the Tigers in the 1970s, when Jordan played for Conway—put it bluntly: "I'm friends with Chuck," he said. "But Chuck will never win a state championship unless he gets right with God." Phaedra Faulk, the daughter of Rev. Jerry Faulk, who marched in '89 alongside H. H. Singleton, was listening from one row over, nodding her head. "Conway has lost three championship games," she said, "because Coach Jordan is still being judged by God."

The extent of the Lord's interest in the South Carolina 4A state title may be debatable, but the reality of the football schedule is not. In 1989, after Lawrence Mitchell returned to the boycott, the Tigers still had eight regular season games left to play, and no game would be as gratifying to win as the one for the Bell. "That would be the best thing for them," Myrtle Beach coach Doug Shaw (for whom Memorial Stadium is now named) told the *Sun News* the Wednesday before the game, "to beat us as they are right now." And what were the Tigers right then? They were undermanned, no doubt about it. But Chuck Jordan could take some degree of consolation from the fact that the roster finally seemed settled. During the first three weeks of the season, as Mickey says now, "There was a lot of *the black guys are coming back, they're not coming back, they're coming back, they're not coming back.*" But starting with Bell Game Week, it was clear that the striking players would be lost for the year. "Once we got to that point," Mickey says, "it was like, okay, this is our team."

Coach Jordan held on to the hope that his guys would play above their talent level. "We're not going into the game thinking we can't win," he told the newspaper. But Conway's odds of winning were long. Mickey would get the start, but he was still aching with the bruised collarbone and tailbone he'd suffered against Middleton. Even when he'd been healthy, the offense had struggled to put up points, scoring only 20 all year, 14 of which had come during "garbage time" at the end of the Summerville game. How could the Tigers possibly score against a Seahawk team that was 2–0 on two shutouts? Maybe the more realistic goal would be to keep Mickey and everybody else from getting seriously injured. Jordan may have been undefeated in his six matchups against Myrtle Beach, but in a moment of pure coaching honesty, he admitted there was only one way for this year's Tigers to continue the Bell Game winning streak. "Myrtle Beach will have to make some mistakes," he said. "And that's something Doug Shaw coached teams don't do."

For his part, Shaw took pains not to sound as if he was assuming a Myrtle Beach victory. "We have taken the same preparation for Conway we would have if they had all their players," he said. "Conway is not an easy game for us, period." He emphasized that his team couldn't afford to think of the Tigers as anything other than the dominant program in the county, even if this was an unusual year. For all Shaw's niceties, though, the scene was set for what looked to be an epic disaster for Chuck Jordan's squad—a humiliating loss to a team that had taken the Victory Bell home only five times since 1960.

On Friday night, about 4,000 fans packed into Memorial Stadium, and it immediately looked like the blowout everyone was expecting, as the Seahawks got two quick touchdowns. But in the words of the *Horry Independent*, "The Tigers came roaring back" with a five-play scoring drive that covered 70 yards. Then, after Conway intercepted a Myrtle Beach pass, Mickey Wilson took the offense deep into Seahawk territory, completing passes of 14, 10, and 20 yards en route. The drive stalled, and the Tigers were forced to kick a field goal, but headed into halftime, the overmatched visitors had pulled to within four points, 14–10.

Ultimately, the Tigers couldn't pull off the upset, but the final score was a respectable 21–12. Myrtle Beach claimed the Bell for the first time in six years. The consolation prize for Conway was that they'd played their best game of the season. The next day, the *Sun News* wrote: "Many thought Myrtle Beach, the state's fourth-ranked 3A team, would maul Conway . . . [b]ut the Tigers came to town with one thing in mind—winning. And they almost pulled that first victory of the season off." The bruised and undersized Mickey Wilson notched 120 passing yards. Robbie McDonald, the Seahawk QB who was playing with a full roster, threw for only 33.

"You can't ask any more out of a bunch of kids than what ours gave tonight," Jordan said. His Tigers were now 0–4, but for the first time that season, they'd scraped and battled and put up a fight. This was their team. Guys who could go down hard and still get back up. Guys who could forget it and drive on.

NOW

Forty minutes before the present-day Tigers and Seahawks are set to kick off in the Bell Game, the lines to enter Doug Shaw Memorial Stadium are thirty yards long. The mood in these two lines is light despite the midway attraction–grade wait. Handshakes and backslaps abound. Tiger fans say hey to acquaintances who pull for the Seahawks. Myrtle Beach alums laugh along with friends who went to Conway. This camaraderie even among

Reverend H. H. Singleton (center) and Hank Singleton (right). Photo by Charles Slate, courtesy *Sun News*.

Chuck Jordan has coached the
Conway Tigers for more than 30
seasons. Photo by Charles Slate,
courtesy *Sun News*.

Mickey Wilson Jr., head coach
of the Myrtle Beach Seahawks.
Courtesy *Sun News*.

Mickey Wilson in his playing
days at Conway High School.
Courtesy Mickey Wilson.

Lawrence Mitchell signs his letter of intent to play for the University of South Carolina, as his grandmother, Gussie Lee Pertell, looks on. Compliments of *Horry Independent*, Conway, SC.

NAACP members and supporters marching along Church Street, November 1989. Photo by
Charles Slate, courtesy *Sun News*.

Heavy rain streaks the ink on protestor Eula Johnson's sign during the second NAACP March
Against Intimidation. Photo by Charles Slate, courtesy *Sun News*.

Horry County Schools
Superintendent John Dawsey.
Compliments of *Horry
Independent*, Conway, SC.

As soon as H. H. Singleton
was suspended from his teaching duties, the 1989 Conway
football boycott transcended
football. Compliments of *Horry
Independent*, Conway, SC.

Protestors gather at the school district offices during the first NAACP March Against Intimidation. Compliments of *Horry Independent*, Conway, SC.

Myrtle Beach offensive coordinator Wes Streater models Mickey Wilson's football philosophy. Photo by Scott Pleasant.

The Seahawks' giant inflatable helmet. Photo by Eric Hall.

Mickey Wilson and his current staff. Left to right: Mickey Wilson, head coach; Lucas Britt, offensive line; John Sedeska, linebackers and strength; Reggie Alston, defensive backs; Jason Owens, defensive coordinator; Chad Toothman, offensive line; Kevin Colyer, offensive line; Wes Streater, offensive coordinator. Photo by Scott Pleasant.

The Victory Bell. Photo by Joe Oestreich.

Mickey Wilson and the 1989 Conway Tigers drive toward the goal line in the Victory Bell game. They would ultimately score a field goal on this possession to bring the score to 14–10, as close as the game would get. Courtesy Mickey Wilson.

rivals is a reminder that Horry County, although large in geographical size (roughly the square mileage of Rhode Island but with only 27 percent of that state's population), has retained its intimacy, especially among the permanent residents. If you spend enough time on the Grand Strand, you get to a point where it feels like you've met just about everybody. Here at Doug Shaw Stadium, on the night when the county's two traditional powers will meet, the atmosphere feels as much like a family reunion as it does like a football game, down to the fact that the family's two branches are dressed nearly alike, green and gold being the colors of both schools. But remember, nobody fights like family. So don't mistake the pre-game congeniality for a lack of competitiveness. The message sent by these handshakes and back-slaps is *Good to see ya. Best of luck to ya. And we gone kick your ass.*

Inside the stadium, Myrtle Beach fans file into the home stands. Above them, the moon is rising slightly fatter than the crescent on the state flag. Across the field, Conway backers fill the away-team bleachers, which are framed by a postcard sunset, the sky streaked a deep, pumpkin orange. On the green expanse between, the Seahawks and Tigers are going through their warmup drills—Mickey Wilson's squad wearing green Nike jerseys with gold and gray trim and Chuck Jordan's guys dressed in white Russells with gold and green trim. And there's Jordan himself: polo shirt, visor, iPhone strapped to his belt, working with Mykal Moody and the quarterbacks. On the other side of the field, there's Jordan's ex-QB, Mickey Wilson, clapping his hands as he moves from station to station, firing up his guys. Between the two coaches lies 1989 and all of that shared history, but outwardly at least, none of it goes acknowledged. They don't nod to each other or point hello. No knowing smiles or shrugs to suggest *Life's a hell of a thing, ain't it?* On the field, both men are all business, focusing solely on their current teams, not on themselves or on what's long past. They treat each other with the mutual respect of competitors, nothing more or less. Months later, when he's asked if he ever talks with Coach Jordan off the field, Mickey will shake his head and say, "No, not much. I see him some, but we don't talk much. This rivalry has gotten kinda crazy lately." What has happened lately? Mickey doesn't say, but the record book does: Myrtle Beach has won four Bell Games out of the last five. The protégé has beaten up on his mentor.

Warmups complete, both coaches whistle their teams into the locker rooms, tiny cinderblock encampments tucked under the home stands. In the Conway room, Chuck Jordan again extols his team to expect good things to happen, to play hard, and to enjoy the ride. Then he says, "Listen, guys. It won't be easy to break their will. They're tough." And yeah, you get the sense that he means the Seahawk players, who are, after all, undefeated and ranked #1 in the state. But he also seems to be talking specifically about his counterpart in the home locker room. Twenty-plus years ago, Jordan saw firsthand how tough it is to break Mickey's will, and even today, Jordan will say that the younger coach's toughness comes directly from what he endured throughout that '89 season.

For his part, Mickey describes the boycott year as "Some adversity in my life that, I think, made me a better person. Once you go through something like that, it makes you tougher mentally and physically."

Now, Mickey's old coach stands in the middle of the room, surrounded by his current team. He waves them down onto one knee, takes off his visor, and leads them in an Our Father. After the amen, everybody rises and Jordan says, "Remember, guys, we are the Conway Tigers," which can undoubtedly be translated to: *Forget four of the last five years; we have damn near ninety years of tradition on our side. We've been playing football since before their town became a town.* Several student managers are wearing shirts that read CONWAY: WE PLAY BACKYARD FOOTBALL. The sentiment is lost on nobody: Whatever kind of new-fangled ball Mickey and Myrtle Beach are slinging, we'll eat it for lunch.

Then, from deep inside the bunch of bodies, somebody yells, "We are—"
And the answer comes back sixty players strong: "CONWAY!"
"We are—"
"TEAM 89!"

Fifteen minutes before the Seahawks take the field through their giant inflatable helmet, Mickey and his assistants step outside the locker room and into the late-summer twilight. The coaches huddle in the grass, in the green space adjacent to the home bleachers, ostensibly making last-minute preparations but mostly just standing around, taking in the scene. The game plan is set. The work has been done. The important thing right now is to keep everybody loose. With their coaches on the other side of the door, the players crammed in the locker room are left to do whatever it takes to get themselves ready to go. Maybe a senior leader like C.J. Cooper—or, better yet, an injured player like Chocolate Wilson—will rise to give an impassioned speech about laying it all on the line to win back the Bell. Or maybe a thick, meaningful silence will hover over the room, the only sound being the muffled thumping of the marching band in the stands above. As bass drums pulse through the concrete, the players will avoid eye contact and instead let the hypnotic rhythm pull them into a sustained, private meditation on the enormity of the Bell Game.

But that's not what happens. In these precious minutes that could be devoted to rousing speechification—or to visualizing the perfect pass route or mentally running through Coach Wilson's complex play-calling system—the players choose an entirely different option. Seconds after the last coach has left the room, somebody hits *play* on an iPod attached to some external speakers, and instantly these cramped quarters are pumping with the big beat of Ace Hood's remix of Young Jeezy and Lil Wayne's "Ballin." The moment the song begins, many of the black players start to stick-and-move along with the lyrics, liberally spiced with N-words, sexual posturing, and hyper-masculine bragging. Soon a huddle-sized group is rapping and fist-pumping in the middle of the tiny room—a ten-by-twenty-foot rectangle so dense with dressed-out players that a nuclear submariner might get claustrophobic. Two or three of the white guys join their black teammates in the rap circle, but most of the white players just close their eyes and tilt their heads back. The beats appear to bounce off them.

Although many of the white Seahawks surely like rap music (they're probably more likely to listen to Ace Hood or Young Jeezy than the black players are to download a Kenny Chesney song, at any rate), most of them seem to understand that they're not really invited to join their teammates in this pre-game ritual. With so many N-words flying around and so much race-awareness in the room, you've got to believe that even the most dim-witted white guy knows better than to start spitting out rhymes along with the black guys. Because what would he do when the next N-bomb is detonated? Go ahead and say it? Drop out for that line while his black friends re-appropriate the racial slur? So instead of joining in, nearly all of the white guys sit back and stay out of the way. The black players seem perfectly happy to have a few minutes of their own—a song's worth of togetherness that they don't need to feel obligated to share with their white teammates.

In *Remember the Titans*, the film based on the true story of Coach Herman Boone's experience with integrating Alexandria, Virginia's T.C. Williams High School football team in 1971, Denzel Washington's Coach Boone forces the black and white teammates to sit next to each other on the bus, eat with each other during meals, and prepare biographical sketches of each other. About twenty minutes into the movie, the players show they have approached racial harmony when the black and white kids get comfortable lobbing yo-mamma jokes at each other and singing each other's music. During a week of preseason training that is equal parts boot camp and cultural awareness workshop, Boone takes his players on an exhausting pre-dawn run through the woods to a Civil War battlefield where soldiers on both sides died fighting over the very question of whether blacks and whites are equal. In the space of a few movie scenes, the team has been transformed into a model of integration. All the racial tension and bigotry that the players endure from that point forward comes from outside the team. Of course, this newly forged harmony eventually helps the Titans to win an unlikely state championship because, well, that's how movies work. And while it's true that the real-life Titans did win the 1971 Virginia state title, it's doubtful that racial integration was achieved as easily or as quickly as the film suggests. By the end of the season, the on-screen Titans are literally and figuratively dancing together, having learned not just to accept but to appreciate one another.

If the Seahawks' real life locker room scene were a movie, one of the team leaders—perhaps one of the black captains—would walk over to the iPod, hit *pause*, and then give a unifying speech about how we all need to pull together before the big game. And the comic relief at the end of that scene might be the team smart-aleck breaking the tension with something like, "Shee-it, bro'. Them cracker-ass white boys know they my niggas, too."

But there's no such ethnic rapprochement for the Seahawks tonight. None of the players, white or black, would even think of voicing any objection to this cultural cleaving. Nor, to be fair, is there any sense that a racial divide has been widened by the impromptu club scene in the closed locker room. Instead, this temporarily coach-free zone seems like a place where the white guys are simply content to let the black guys be themselves. The self-imposed segregation is no more apparent or troubling to the players than the fact that at school, most of the black kids sit on one side of the lunchroom and most of the white kids sit on the other. Nobody talks about it, and nobody seems to notice anything odd about it, even though here in the Seahawks' locker room, the dancing is done by players on one side of a racial divide that, at times, seems as wide as ever.

That gap is immediately narrowed, though, as soon as the doors open and Mickey Wilson enters. "Okay, hats on!" he says. "Let's go!"

Almost as one, the players snap on their chinstraps and line up to begin the walk through the double doors and down the path to the gate where they enter the inflatable helmet. Occupying a space a small Winnebago could park in, the helmet's square footage is a good bit less than half that of the locker room the players just came from, and yet the entire varsity roster crowds inside, slapping each other on their human-scale helmets. The players' sparkly green headgear has obscured race for the moment, and the members of this team, black and white, are literally as close as they'll ever be.

The players' shouts and howls grow in intensity along with the ominous opening of Metallica's "Enter Sandman," which the stadium P.A. is playing at threshold-of-pain volume. The white players may have opted out of the rap circle in the locker room, but here, the black players are churning along with their white teammates to the sounds of a white band playing what is most definitely white music. And then, just when the hollering has reached a crescendo, a player at the center of the helmet hushes everyone and begins the Cornhusker Prayer. *Dear Lord, in the battles we go through in life* . . . The volume steadily increases until everyone joins in for the last two lines: *CAN'T BE BEAT! WON'T BE BEAT!* And through a chilling wall of fire extinguisher spray, the Myrtle Beach Seahawks sprint onto the field as fireworks light up the sky.

"What's going on out there?" Chuck Jordan yells in the visitors' locker room. "*Fireworks?*" He's standing near the open door, surrounded by his players, everybody jumping and buzzing, cleats clacking on the concrete. "Guys," he says, shaking his head in disgust. "They gotta have fireworks." He looks over at his team, indoctrinated into backyard football, smashmouth football, the Gospel according to Ground Chuck. "They been doing all this talking," he says, "but let me tell you something. As soon as you hit somebody in the mouth, it all goes away." And with that, Jordan leads his Tigers onto the field.

In the minutes before kickoff, the Conway Tiger Pride Marching Band plays "Tiger Rag," the Seahawk student section is on their feet and screaming, and players on both teams appear to be looking over at the Victory Bell sitting behind the Conway bench. The captains head to midfield for the coin toss. For Mykal Moody, Sawyer Jordan, and the other Conway seniors, this is the last chance to play for the Bell, and it would be crushing to leave high school knowing they'd surrendered the trophy. Of course, Tyler Keane, C.J. Cooper, and the Myrtle Beach seniors are just as determined to win the Bell back. In less than three hours, one team will be carrying the trophy into their locker room to celebrate. But that time seems as distant now as the spring drills and summer scrimmages that prepared these players for this very moment. As with all blockbuster games, the forty-eight minutes of playing time will pass both more quickly and more slowly than normal—as if the game is being played in a curious time warp where nifty moves, blistering dashes, and split-second decisions can be recognized for the accelerated events they are, but everything somehow happens in slow motion, too. This perception of football time might explain how coaches and players can remember precise details of a single play from a game that happened years before. As in the seconds before a car crash, the mind and the senses are sharpened to the point where an immense amount of information can be absorbed and then trapped for a lifetime. Ask a former player to describe a key play from a big game and you're likely to be on the receiving end of a five-minute recitation about events that might have lasted only six or seven seconds in "real time." In some games, however, every play seems critical, every possession feels decisive, and every yard matters. Tonight's Bell Game will be like that. An instant classic. One of those matchups that even the third-stringers will remember the details of for years to come.

The Seahawks return the opening kick to their own 40-yard line, and true to Mickey's aggressive offensive scheme, look to score quickly. A first down puts them into Conway territory just a couple of plays later. Mickey then calls for a long pass that appears to be a sure touchdown when receiver Trell Harrell gets well behind the defense. The whole stadium reacts to the sight of Harrell outrunning the Conway secondary and expects to see what Mickey Wilson offenses are known for: ruthless and efficient scoring, the product of a philosophy that says you can't possibly score too many points, especially in the first half. But Tyler Keane overthrows the wide-open Harrell, a rare bad miss for the senior QB. A touchdown had seemed inevitable on this possession, but now Tyler looks tentative. Even his successful passes are low-risk, underneath the defense, not the kind of brash throws he normally fires. The drive stalls at the Conway 20, and the Seahawks attempt a 37-yard field goal, which is blocked by a Tiger who makes it through the line practically untouched.

With that block and subsequent recovery, Conway takes over at their own 40, and the Tigers' balanced passing and rushing attack starts cutting up the Seahawks' defense. Pretty soon, Conway has a first down at the Myrtle Beach 22-yard line—knocking on the door, as they say. But then Myrtle Beach's Kelton Greene intercepts a Mykal Moody pass, a poorly thrown ball flung as the senior quarterback was being flushed out of the pocket. The home crowd doesn't rejoice as much as breathe a collective sigh of relief. Rather than establishing Myrtle Beach's defensive dominance, the interception feels more like a lucky gift. Division I prospects like Moody don't make those mistakes very often.

Myrtle Beach has just been compensated for allowing the blocked field goal, but the scales of football justice don't stay balanced for long. On the very next play, Tyler and freshman running back Brandon Sinclair can't connect on an inside handoff, and the Seahawks fumble the ball back to Conway at the Myrtle Beach 7-yard line. The Seahawk defense returns to the field, their backs against their own end zone. The fumble makes it three possessions and essentially three turnovers in the early going: blocked field goal, interception, fumble. Both teams are off to shaky starts, but the advantage goes to the Conway Tigers, who now have the ball deep in Myrtle Beach territory. Mykal gains five yards on a first-down run, then on two consecutive plays takes the ball straight up the gut of the defense, but both times he's stopped just short of the goal line. For the Tigers, it's fourth and goal from six inches out, and Chuck Jordan is faced with his first big decision of the game.

The coach has a reputation for being conservative, and the conservative play in this situation is to kick the short field goal and put three points on the board. But this year, Jordan hasn't been happy with his spotty kicking game, so perhaps the safer option is to keep the ball in the hands of Mykal Moody, his senior playmaker. Besides, considering how many points Jordan's unusually porous defense has allowed this year (38 per game) and the potency of the Myrtle Beach offense, a field goal probably won't do the Tigers much good. Jordan signals for his offense to stay on the field. They're going for it. Touchdown or bust.

Mykal takes the snap and pushes right up the middle, the offensive and defensive lines locked in what looks like a rugby scrum. As the players wrestle at the goal line, a few of the Seahawks leap in jubilation, thinking they have just stopped Moody on four straight plays. But the line judge positioned on the Conway sideline runs toward the pile with his arms aloft, and the underdog Tigers begin celebrating. With 4:51 to go in the first quarter, the extra point makes it Conway 7, Myrtle Beach 0.

Like all coaches, Mickey hammers home to his players the importance of learning from their mistakes and not dwelling on boneheaded plays. The fumble that gave Conway the ball at the 7-yard line is exactly the kind of situation he hopes will test his players and force them to "handle adversity," one of Mickey's favorite coach-isms, as in "You've got to learn to handle adversity because it's how you respond to that adversity that determines whether you win or not." So far in this game, however, Myrtle Beach is compounding adversity. On the ensuing kickoff, the Seahawks make another costly error when return man Kelton Greene has the ball ripped from his arms. Fresh off their first touchdown, Conway takes over at the Myrtle Beach 30. From there, a nifty double pass play from Sawyer Jordan to Mykal Moody then back to Jordan yields a first down at the 19-yard line. Then, with two minutes left in the quarter, a touch pass from Mykal to Bryan Edwards results in another touchdown. Conway has scored 14 points; Myrtle Beach has tallied three huge mistakes.

With their team behind by two touchdowns, the home stands settle into a numb silence. This is a crowd that has become used to winning often and winning big. But something's not right tonight. Coach Jordan and the Tigers are dominating like they did in so many Bell Games past. Maybe Mickey is crumbling under the weight of the record book, which says Myrtle Beach is supposed to fold in the Bell Game. Maybe the wily ol' coach is reminding the uppity youngster which one of them rules Horry County football. The silence in the Seahawk stands is made more ominous by the fact that across the field, the Conway bleachers are bubbling at full boil. *Of course we're winning. We are Conway. Old Town. Brushing aside New Town like a draft horse swats a stable fly.*

Myrtle Beach's Kelton Greene receives his third kickoff of the quarter and dashes to the 40-yard line—only to have the ball stripped again. A roar goes out from the Conway bleachers. But this time the Seahawks are lucky: the ball flies out of bounds, and Myrtle Beach retains possession. On the Seahawk sideline, Chocolate Wilson, just a few days after getting permission to set aside his post–knee surgery crutches, sprints ten yards to meet Kelton face to face. "Hang onto the football, man!" he yells, shaking his teammate by the shoulders. "Come on!" It's a rare outburst of in-your-face leadership from the injured Chocolate, and even though Kelton's body language shows he's not thrilled to be reprimanded by a fellow player, he's probably fortunate Chocolate got to him before one of Mickey's assistants could.

So the Seahawks keep the ball, and on a third down play that looks like it's going nowhere, Tyler Keane makes a great open-field run to the Conway 38. On the next play, a pass interference penalty gives Myrtle Beach the ball at the Conway 24. Now the Tigers are the ones making the mistakes. A quick screen pass to a wide-open C.J. Cooper, and just like that, Myrtle Beach is on the board. With 58 seconds left in the first quarter, it's Conway 14, Myrtle Beach 7. Seahawk fans breathe easy now that their team is back in the game.

Buoyed by the change in momentum, the Seahawk marching band starts up a sultry version of James Brown's already sultry "Pass the Peas," a dirty funk arrangement that the Myrtle Beach band likely borrowed from the Marching 101, the band from South Carolina State, a historically black university in Orangeburg. As the music slinks along, the cheerleaders work their way through relatively chaste choreography, but in the stands, a few girls join in with moves that hint at what golf junketeers might see in one of the many gentlemen's clubs located within a few miles of the stadium. This combination of barely controlled violence and thinly veiled sexual imagery is partly what makes football, even at the high school level, so popular. Like so many things Americans love, football is typically presented as a mixture of danger and sexuality. A live game—especially a televised game—is like a Michael Bay movie: Quick jumps from scene to scene build a world that moves fast but always in predictable directions. And every so often, the audience is treated to an image of a nubile, all-American girl to remind them that the players on the field, the young men risking their very lives for our entertainment, will be rewarded with the attention of the ladies. In football and all gladiatorial sports, the fans can watch, but the heroes—from Spartacus to Joe Namath on down—get the girls.

The Tigers start the next drive on their own 20, and before the Myrtle Beach crowd has finished celebrating their team's score, Conway running back Tyreke Phillips takes the a handoff around the right side, jukes a couple of tacklers, and continues untouched until he is forced out of bounds at the Myrtle Beach 5, after a gain of 75 yards. The Seahawks are again faced with the job of keeping Moody and the Tigers out of the end zone on first and goal. After three QB-keepers and a change of direction at the end of the first quarter, the Tigers are looking at fourth down and goal from the 1-yard line. Once again, Chuck Jordan has the choice of taking the relatively sure three points or gambling for a touchdown, and once again the veteran coach rolls the dice.

All eyes are on Mykal Moody, but this time, he's not lined up behind center. Instead, he's flanked out on the right side at receiver, and it's Phillips—the back who ran the ball 75 yards to the 5—who takes the direct snap. Perhaps expecting a quick screen to Moody or a power run up the middle, the defense doesn't react quickly enough when Phillips takes the ball around to the left, and he runs in for an easy touchdown. The extra point makes the score 21–7, and the game again looks all right and proper for Conway. Chuck Jordan's defenses don't typically give up a 14-point lead. Then again, Chuck Jordan's usually not the kind of coach who passes up easy field goals to risk going for it on fourth down. He seems to know something in those venerable coaching bones: This game won't be won by playing it safe or holding to convention. He also knows that in their first game of the year, against Irmo, the Seahawks were down by 15 in the third quarter and still wound up winning, so this Myrtle Beach team is nowhere near out of it.

Mickey Wilson knows that, too. As his players walk off the field after giving up the score, he smacks a few of them on the helmet and says, "That's okay" and "Just keep fighting." Unlike his gruffer counterpart across the field, Mickey isn't much of a screamer when his players make knuckleheaded mistakes or find themselves in tough situations. He tells them to embrace the challenge as an opportunity to grow and improve. In other words: handle adversity.

Two touchdowns behind, the Seahawks now find themselves shoulder-pads deep in adversity. But a quick drive down the field—featuring a conversion on third and 22 and aided by a defensive holding penalty on third and goal from the 9—results in a C.J. Cooper touchdown. Conway 21, Myrtle Beach 14. Then, after the Tigers fumble the kickoff return, it takes Tyler Keane only five plays and ninety-odd seconds to move his team 62 yards for another touchdown. Tigers 21, Seahawks 21. In the span of five game minutes, Mickey's squad has gone from fourteen down to all tied up. Adversity handled, and then some. Two minutes later, after a weak punt by Conway gives the Seahawks a short field, Tyler hits Trell Harrell on a 52-yard touchdown pass that makes the score Myrtle Beach 28, Conway 21 with just over four minutes left until halftime. Before the teams break for the intermission, they each find the end zone again. Halftime score: Seahawks 35, Tigers 28. Folks, we got ourselves a barnburner.

"That's big-time football!" Mickey Wilson says to his team, gathered in the tight pocket of their locker room. "I love it!" Then he quiets his players and says, "We gave them fourteen points out there. Just *gave* them those points." He doesn't list the mistakes, but as he looks around, he pauses long enough to let everybody recall the fumbles, missed tackles, and blown coverages that put them two touchdowns behind at two separate points during the half. Mickey can't stomach botches like this from a team he's sure is better than their inland rivals. "You know we are in way better shape than they are," he says, but unlike his other halftime speeches this season, Mickey doesn't guarantee victory based on the superior conditioning of his team. Instead, he tells them they've got to quit making mistakes if they want to walk out with the Victory Bell. "You got twenty-four minutes to bring the Bell back to Myrtle Beach," he says. "Now bow your neck and fight like heck!"

The Seahawks spend the remainder of the break drinking Gatorade and cooling off in the grassy area outside the locker room. Mickey and his coaches talk second-half strategy behind a pickup truck parked inside the stadium gates. A few fans and parents descend from the stands to walk among the team and offer encouragement. The players give nearly imperceptible facial tics in return. Locked in the tunnel vision of game day, they respond overtly only to their coaches and to each other. Even the cheerleaders who wander by to say hi and wish the players good luck are brushed off with a don't-bother-me-now nod that comes off as more businesslike than unfriendly. On any given school day, these same boys might sprint down the hallway to be at the right classroom door to intercept a pretty girl, but for the three hours of game time, they seem immune to the goodwill of girls, parents, fans, and friends. And with tonight's job only halfway done, focused detachment is exactly what Mickey wants from them.

Meanwhile, instead of squeezing his fifty-plus guys into the tiny visitors' locker room, Chuck Jordan has led them to a sandy spot in the far southwest corner of the stadium, where an ambulance and an Horry County Schools activity bus are parked, next to a utility shed and under a grove of longleaf pines. Unlike in the locker room, there's space to spread out here, away from the bleachers and the bands. A few players stand at the hurricane fence; a few sit on the tailgate of the ambulance; a few sit on the ground, leaning against the shed. It's dark back here, out from under the stadium lights, and relatively cool. The ocean breeze blows through the trees, shaking the pine needles. No comfy chairs. No training tables.

After meeting with his assistants on the other side of the activity bus, Jordan asks his players to gather around. He's standing by the driver's door of the ambulance; his Tigers are all down on one knee, arranged between him and the fence. "I want forty-eight minutes of football," he says. "You've given me twenty-four." He looks out at his players, sweat beading on their faces, knees pressing into the sandy ground. "Now give me twenty-four dag-gum more."

Third-quarter scoring begins when the Tigers recover a muffed punt return and run the ball in for a touchdown that ties the game at 35. It's yet another mistake that, by Mickey's points-given-away count, means the Seahawks have now handed the Tigers three charity touchdowns. On the next Myrtle Beach drive, after leading his team deep into Conway territory, Tyler Keane throws another interception. A visibly upset Mickey Wilson paces the sideline with more intensity than he's shown all year. But the Seahawks force Conway to punt, and shortly after Mickey's offense returns to the field, Tyler tosses another touchdown pass on a play that was set up by a 50-yard run by freshman running back Brandon Sinclair. Myrtle Beach 42, Conway 35.

Already, Tyler Keane has connected on six touchdown passes to three different receivers. A few plays later, when Mykal Moody hits Malcolm Green on a 70-yard touchdown bomb to tie the score at 42, five different players have scored for the Tigers. With just over three minutes to go in the third quarter, Conway and Myrtle Beach have combined for 84 points, and before the quarter ends, the teams will each score yet another touchdown. To describe this Bell Game as a shootout is to do an injustice to ordinary football shootouts and probably to some actual guns-and-ammo shootouts, too. A better metaphor might be the powerfully shifting winds of the hurricanes that periodically slam the Carolina coast.

The clock flips to the fourth quarter, and the scoreboard reads Myrtle Beach 49, Conway 49. Players on both sides hold four fingers aloft to signify that the final twelve minutes belong to them. The cliché says that in a game like this, it's a shame either team has to lose. The greater shame, however, would be if a game like this were to end in a tie. Fortunately, the South Carolina High School League long ago adopted an overtime system. There will be a winner tonight, and there will be a loser. In a culture that tries, in so many ways, to remove the sting of failure from childhood, a culture that has taken to handing out trophies to every kid who participates, tonight's brutal demonstration on how you can work hard, deserve success, but still end up losing is perhaps one of the rare lessons in "handling adversity" we allow for young people. Football players, like all high school athletes, always face the pain of losing, but rarely is that pain as agonizing as it will be tonight for one of these teams.

After so much back and forth scoring in the first three quarters, fans on both sides surely expect more of the same in the final twelve minutes, but through most of the fourth quarter, the score remains 49–49. Then, with just under four minutes to play, Tyler Keane hits Malik Waring on a 12-yard scoring pass to lift Myrtle Beach to a 56–49 advantage. It's Keane's eighth touchdown pass of the night (tying both the school record and the state record) on 520 passing yards (a school record). The only problem for the Seahawks is that with three minutes and change to go in the game, they've left Mykal and the Tigers a whole lot of time to operate.

Conway takes the ball at their own 20-yard line, down 56–49 with 3:31 to play. Eighty yards and eight points separate the Tigers from the Victory Bell. Chuck Jordan's squad is only one week removed from a come-from-behind win against Marlboro County, so they're already a confident bunch, and Mykal, as he has all night, makes covering 80 yards against the top 3A team in the state look as easy as ice cream. With a combination of short passes and QB-keepers, the Tigers push down the field, and in two minutes of game time, they find themselves at the Seahawk 13-yard line. The clock reads just over a minute left in regulation. The fans in the Conway bleachers lean forward as if they might be able to nudge their team the final few yards. The Myrtle Beach faithful clench their seats, willing their boys to somehow hang on. But so far tonight, for every punch thrown by one team, there's been a counterpunch thrown by the other. Now, with a 13-yard run around the left side, Mykal lands that answering punch, scoring the touchdown that brings his team to within one point. Tiger fans cheer like mad. Seahawk fans shake their heads at the seeming inevitability of the score. It's been that kind of night.

Myrtle Beach 56, Conway 55. The clock reads 1:12. All that's left is for the Tigers to nail the extra point and then hang on until overtime. But with no hesitation, without calling a timeout to mull it over, Jordan leaves his offense on the field. He's going for two; he's playing for the win. To his quarterback, he makes a go-get-'em fist. Expect good things to happen.

Mykal quickly lines up in the shotgun formation. The two-point attempt catches the Seahawk defense off guard, and they scramble into position. A reporter on the Myrtle Beach sideline says, "Holy shit! He's going for it," and the stadium is hushed in a shocked silence as the crowd suddenly realizes that Jordan—product of the old-school, a by-the-book conservative—is gambling for the third time tonight, this time with the Bell on the line. It's an eye-blink decision, as many choices in football are, made in the quick turnaround between plays. Fans can take all the time they want to question a coach's call, but that coach usually has only a few seconds to make it.

The shotgun snap to Moody is too low, and it hits the ground. But the state-of-the-art FieldTurf gives the ball a forgiving bounce, and the Tiger quarterback catches it cleanly on the short hop. Surely he will keep the ball himself as he did on the first all-or-nothing possession tonight, a play that resulted in his finding a seam and crossing the goal line. But no. Mykal takes one step forward, then sets his feet. He looks over the line into the end zone where his tight end Nathaniel Nesbitt is open . . . wide open . . . too open. Mykal floats the ball over the outstretched arms of the defensive line, and the ball comes in high—but not too high, *perfect*, in fact—to Nesbitt. The tight end reaches up, and for a nanosecond, he appears to have the football secured in both hands. But as he tries to haul down the pass . . . the win . . . the Bell . . .

He drops it. The football falls to the turf.

If Dallas Cowboy Jackie Smith, who famously muffed what would have been a game-tying touchdown in Super Bowl XIII, was in that instant "the sickest man in America," according to Verne Lundquist who did play-by-play on the game, then right now Nathaniel Nesbitt, bless his heart, is the sickest teenager in Horry County.

A few kneel-downs later, the Seahawks and Tigers line up for the post-game handshakes, and as soon as the Myrtle Beach players finish their "good game" grunts, Octavius Thomas sprints to the Conway bench, grabs the Victory Bell, and races back toward his teammates, trophy held high. Fans in the home bleachers give the Seahawks a standing ovation. And while many in those bleachers are too young to remember the day in 1989 when in this very stadium Myrtle Beach ended a six-year losing streak and took the Bell from a depleted Conway squad, there are at least two men on the field who remember that moment vividly.

The handshake between Chuck Jordan and Mickey Wilson goes quickly. No reminiscing, no warm embrace, no meaningful nod. A clasp of the hands and the two men separate, but before they do, Mickey leans in and says something to his old coach.

When asked about it later, Mickey says, "I told him, 'That was a great call.'"

And when prodded about Coach Jordan's reaction?

"Nothing," says Mickey. "He just walked off the field."

- 10 -

THE COMING STORM

NOW

"I WANT Y'ALL TO LISTEN UP," MICKEY WILSON SAYS TO HIS PLAYERS AND coaches, all of them squeezed into the home team locker room. He smiles, his teeth as straight and white as new bowling pins. Then he thwacks his championship ring against the Victory Bell, making a sound they ain't never heard in Conway.

The Seahawks smack fives and pound fists. They're 5–0. They're the #1 3A team in the state. And, having just beaten their biggest rival, they're the undisputed champs of Horry County football.

But Mickey hushes them with his palms and says, "You haven't won *anything* yet." The five wins that his guys have racked up so far have been more or less an extended preseason. Now comes the slate of five region games—the conference matchups that determine who gets into the state championship playoffs and where those teams will be seeded. Standing there in front of a squad that tonight answered every punch Conway threw, Mickey is proud of how his team has handled adversity. Still, he worries that amid all the high-fiving and fist-pounding, their competitive edge will go dull. They'll stop being paranoid. The good news is that the Seahawks haven't lost a region game in four years, not since this year's seniors were in the eighth grade. That's also the bad news. Winning twenty straight region games and four region championships in five years can make the region title seem like a birthright. The Victory Bell has barely stopped ringing, and Mickey is already worried that the Seahawks have become accustomed to the kind of success that breeds complacency.

So now, before he opens the doors and lets his kids go celebrate the win with their families, friends, and girlfriends, he tells them about a text message he recently sent to Everett. Just Everett. No last name. Meaning, as every Seahawk knows, Everett Golson, the ex–Myrtle Beach quarterback who is now off at Notre Dame. Some of the current players lined up alongside

Everett two years earlier when he led the Seahawks to their second state championship in three seasons, but even those too young to have shared the field with the star QB listen hard whenever his name is mentioned. Everett is playing major college ball. He's the dream made real.

In this, his redshirt freshman year for the Fighting Irish, Golson has been competing against junior Tommy Rees for the starting job. When asked before the season if he thought his ex-quarterback could win the position, Mickey said, "I think he could win the Heisman." At the time, it just sounded like a proud coach's boast because freshman QBs (even redshirt freshmen) rarely start for big-time college programs. But now, after leading the resurgent Irish to a win against Michigan State that has brought the team to 3–0 and has them closing in on the AP top ten, Golson seems to have beaten out Rees as the starter. The battle wasn't easy or assured, Mickey reminds his players. Even though the season is young, the quarterback has already suffered setbacks—like in Notre Dame's second game, against Purdue, when Everett was benched in favor of Rees after getting banged up and losing a costly fumble. But Golson worked hard enough in the intervening week of practice to be named the starter for the next game, the one against Michigan State. The victory over the Spartans was the Irish's first win against a top-ten opponent in seven years, and for Mickey Wilson, Everett's chin-up response to being benched was an object lesson in the importance of handling adversity. After the game, the coach sent Everett a text that read, *Now you have to handle success.*

To the current Seahawks the message is clear: Beating Conway to stay undefeated is a worthy accomplishment, but bringing home the Bell tonight doesn't guarantee a win next week. Neither does the happy fact that Myrtle Beach hasn't lost a region game since George W. Bush was sitting in the Oval Office. At this point, even though they are 5–0, the Seahawks haven't taken a single step toward winning the region title or toward their ultimate goal, which is to raise the state championship trophy. So now's the time to handle success. And handling success means respecting the journey. It means understanding exactly how far you have to go—knowing that trouble is always out there waiting, gathering strength.

The Seahawks' run at the region and state championships begins a week later, against Wilson High School at Florence Memorial Stadium—a place not exactly known for luxury. The parking lot is unpaved; the home and away stands are bare concrete; and if there's a locker room for the visiting team, Mickey decides not to use it. Back home at the beach, the Seahawks dress in their football-only field house and play on NFL-grade synthetic turf, but here, they'll get taped and dressed in the unmown field behind the bleachers and they'll play on grass that's already badly worn. When the Seahawks' bus unloads at the stadium a little less than two hours before kickoff, Mickey looks around, shakes his head and says, "We're very fortunate to play where we play. When you come to a place like this, it's kinda tough."

After the team has finished dressing in the scrubby field, Mr. Byrd gathers the players under the visitors' stands for the pre-game prayer. As he talks, dance music bumps through the stadium speakers and gnats swarm everybody's line of vision. About a minute into his attempt at inspiration, he suddenly pauses. The players are much more focused on swatting the gnats and pulling the sand spurs from their socks than on listening to their team minister. "Okay," he says, "There are a lot of distractions, I know." And in what seems to be an ad-lib moment, Mr. Byrd asks, "What do gnats and sand spurs have in common?" Hearing no response, he answers his own question: "Gnats will aggravate the hound dog out of you. Sand spurs will aggravate the hound dog out of you." He brushes away a squadron of buzzing bugs. "This team tonight is like gnats and sand spurs. They might just aggravate the hound dog out of you, too, if you let 'em—if you lose focus."

After running through a David vs. Goliath analogy ("You're a lot more like Goliath than David. They will be like David if you let 'em"), Mr. Byrd closes by offering a moment of silent prayer "for all these young boys who stepped up and became men last week." He seems to be asking God to ensure that the Seahawks—who matured in football years by virtue of beating Conway in such a dramatic game—won't backslide into boyhood tonight against Wilson High, a team they should easily beat. *What we need now*, he might be praying, *is for this team to learn how to handle success*. Of course, there isn't any actual silence during this silent prayer because the gnats are dive-bombing everyone's ears and the players are smashing gnat after gnat against their faces, making *whap* sounds that work in syncopation with the dance soundtrack that is still thumping through the P.A. system.

"This is perfect," Mickey says after the moment of "silence" has passed. "Music playing, gnats everywhere. If you can focus through that, you can stay focused tonight." In his pre-game speech, he tells his team they have ten steps left to take in order to win the state championship: five region games and five rounds in the 3A state playoffs. "Tonight," he tells his guys, "is the first step!" And it's a successful one. The final tally is Myrtle Beach 54, Wilson 21.

A week earlier, in the locker room after the Bell Game, Mickey used Everett Golson as a source of inspiration, but in tonight's post-game speech, delivered on the sand-spurred field behind the bleachers, he doesn't mention his former QB. Perhaps that's because in Everett's next start, against the Michigan Wolverines—played just one day after the Victory Bell game—the ex-Seahawk went a disappointing three for eight for 30 yards with two interceptions before being replaced yet again by Tommy Rees. The Irish won, but Golson's position on the depth chart was growing ever precarious.

Standing on that scraggly field, Mickey doesn't know that Everett will win back the starting job. He doesn't know that by season's end Everett will lead the Irish to the BCS championship game against Alabama. He doesn't know that after losing the national title to the Crimson Tide, Everett will be suspended by Notre Dame for next year's fall semester—causing him to miss the entire 2013 football season—for an unspecified academic violation. What Mickey does know, as he addresses a Seahawk team that has now risen to 6–0 and expects those wins to keep on coming, is something he has seen a lot of players learn the hard way: Handling success ain't easy.

The Seahawks' next matchup, against Socastee High School, has all the makings of a trap game: confident favorite vs. surprisingly talented underdog. Socastee comes into Doug Shaw Stadium unranked in the state, despite a record of 6–0. One of those wins, of course, came against Conway, a team the Braves hadn't beaten since 1998, which is one year longer than the last time Socastee beat Myrtle Beach, in 1999. The Seahawks may be riding a twelve-game winning streak against the Braves, but as kickoff approaches, Mickey and his coaches understand that they aren't facing a predictably inferior Socastee squad. Not only are they expecting a tough game from the Braves, they're looking forward to it. Another chance for the Seahawks' success to be put to the test.

For the Myrtle Beach players, however, a twelve-year winning streak is practically forever, so despite their coaches' warnings to stay focused, Socastee might as well be a Pee Wee League team. When the Seahawks take the field to "The Champ Is Here," they do so with a little extra swagger. What they don't know is that this week—by order of Socastee's athletic director, former Coastal Carolina University head coach David Bennett—the Braves practiced for two hours with "The Champ Is Here" blaring from the stadium speakers. So now Socastee has started to think of Myrtle Beach's walk-on mix as their own hype music, and as the ball is set for kickoff, the Braves match the Seahawks swagger for swagger.

Still, when Tyler Keane connects with Ray Ray Pointer for an 18-yard touchdown pass on the first drive of the game, the muted reaction from the home stands suggests that Seahawk fans have already chalked up the victory. Myrtle Beach's long-held superiority in the region appears doubly

safe when Socastee fails to move the ball past the 30 on their first possession and is forced into a punting down. The expectation of an inevitable
win becomes even stronger when a bad snap prevents the Braves from getting the punt off and the Seahawks take over at the Socastee 15. A few plays
later, on fourth and goal from the 16, Mickey reluctantly sends in his kicker,
Max Huggins, who booms it straight and true, and for a moment the score
appears to be State Heavyweight Myrtle Beach 10, Horry County Tomato
Can Socastee 0. But a flag against the Braves for roughing the kicker leaves
Mickey with a tough call: keep the three points or take the penalty and a
first down at the 9-yard line. It's actually not that hard a decision for Mickey.
High-powered offenses are fueled by big play touchdowns, not piddly field
goals. So the coach sends Tyler and the offense back on to the field, a move
that runs counter to the old adage that says *never take points off the board.*
And wouldn't you know it, there's a reason why an adage becomes an adage,
because just like that Keane makes one lousy throw and *bam*—Socastee defensive back Matt Chatfield intercepts the pass and returns the ball 98 yards
to the end zone, leveling the score at 7–7. Speaking later of his choice to give
back the points and go for the touchdown, Mickey says, "I hate kicking field
goals. I have always been the type that would go for it. I've always been of a
mindset to attack. First and goal at the nine? I'll take that every time." It's a
decision firmly within Mickey's offensive philosophy, but one that's awfully
hard not to second-guess after the score goes from 10–0 to 7–7 over the
span of two plays.

The pick-six stuns the Seahawk fans, and an uncomfortable silence
hangs over the home bleachers like wet Spanish moss. As the game continues, all the breaks seem to go Socastee's way. All the close calls go against
Myrtle Beach. Mickey's guys just can't get anything going on offense. Tyler
looks oddly tentative as he throws another interception, then another, then
another and another—five total. On the sidelines, the quarterback is standing all by himself, a boy on an island. His teammates are shaking their heads
in disbelief. One defensive player flops on the bench and says to nobody in
particular, "We losing to Socastee? *Socastee?*" Then he buries his head in a
towel.

When the clock finally winds down to zero, the scoreboard reads So-
castee 27, Myrtle Beach 17. The suddenly dazed and humbled Goliaths of
Region VII have been felled by a David they underestimated. The Socastee
Braves are the new undisputed champs of Horry County football.

Gathering his players in the locker room after their first region loss in
four years, Mickey says, "The best thing in the world just happened." The
loss won't keep them from winning a state championship, he says. It just

shows the coaches what the team needs to work on in order to get better. Then he raises his voice to a decibel level he hasn't hit all year. "And if you don't believe that, clean out your gotdang locker!" Losing, he says, should bring a team together, and good teams see losses as opportunities to improve, not as disappointments. "If I hear any talk about *it was his fault* or *his fault* or *the quarterback could have played better* or *the defense should have done this or that*," he says, "I'll clean your locker out so gotdang fast."

And it's no idle threat. One kid, a senior who during the game said to another player, "I can't believe we're losing to Socastee. This is embarrassing. I don't even want to be associated with this team," has already been locked out of the locker room. He and another complainer will later be dismissed from the team.

Message: When adversity comes, don't just handle it. Handle it together.

The next day in the *Sun News*, Mickey echoes the "forget it and drive on" motto of his former coach, saying, "They [Socastee] deserved to win that ball game. We're going to take this as a lesson and learn from it. We're going to drive on."

And the Seahawks do drive on from the unexpected loss to Socastee, notching relatively easy wins over St. James, Georgetown, and North Myrtle Beach to end the regular season with a 9–1 overall record, 4–1 in the region. Socastee, however, runs their slate undefeated, so the Region VII title belongs to the Braves, and they'll get the higher seed in the state playoff bracket. Socastee came in to Doug Shaw Stadium and proved to be a much stronger foe than expected, but it's not like the Seahawks had no prior warning about the opponent they were about to face. The Braves had already scored more points against Carolina Forest than Myrtle Beach had, and their defense had limited Conway to only two touchdowns—the same Conway team that put up 55 against the Seahawks. The danger signs were there, but the players, the fans, and maybe even the coaches didn't take those signs as seriously as they should have.

Success, after all, breeds complacency.

And complacency breeds failure.

Or, as Mr. Byrd points out in a later pre-game speech, "Pride goeth before destruction. And a haughty spirit before a fall" (Proverbs 16:18).

THEN

The Atlantic hurricane season runs from early June to late November, meaning that hurricane season and football season overlap. Along the

South Carolina coast, hurricanes are a potential threat every summer and fall, but they don't happen every year. The state might go a decade or more without a storm coming ashore at hurricane strength. And the longer the interval between hurricanes, the more coastal residents tend to let down their guards. Like Californians whose pulses barely quicken for anything less than six on the Richter Scale, many South Carolinians default to a seen-it-all-before attitude when named storms start charging westward from Africa over the Atlantic: *Aww, it's just a Category 1. That ain't nothing.* Most of these storms never make landfall—not as hurricanes and not in the Palmetto State—and on the rare occasions they do, the results are rarely as bad as predicted by NOAA and the television weather people. In 1989 Grand Strand residents hadn't seen a truly large hurricane since Gracie in '59 and, before that, Hazel in '54. During the three essentially hurricane-free decades leading up to '89, widespread development occurred along the Carolina coast. On the Grand Strand, many of the low-slung mom-and-pop hotels had been torn down and replaced with towering resorts, and the population of Horry County more than doubled, growing from 68,247 in the 1960 census to 144,053 thirty years later. In his book *Hurricane Destruction in South Carolina*, local historian Tom Rubillo describes the years from 1961 to 1988 as "the dullest on record in South Carolina as far as hurricanes are concerned," but adds, "this same period of time is significant nonetheless, for it corresponds with a surge in building of new housing and resorts of various types along South Carolina's coast." Three decades without a major storm had left the Myrtle Beach area swelling with residents and tourists, many of whom regarded the coastline solely as an economic engine or the site of a dream home—not as a potentially treacherous border zone where the sea smacks the land.

All those beachfront hotels and sand-swept condos—born of bravado.

The day after the '89 Bell Game, the rain came. It was Saturday, the afternoon of the NAACP's second March Against Intimidation. The week before, during the first march, H. H. Singleton, Nelson Rivers, and other local and national NAACP leaders had pledged to walk every Saturday until the earth science teacher was reinstated, and they'd promised that the crowds would grow larger as the weeks progressed. As Elouise Davis, past president of the Conway NAACP, had said, this second march would be "the big one." A potent storm of protest was already escalating, as evidenced by a sharp increase in the membership numbers of both the local and the state NAACP. In the Conway area alone, some three to five hundred new recruits had joined the organization since the boycott began. And at around noon on that Saturday, September 16, approximately 2,500 protestors, including many of these new NAACP members, were gathering in the Bethel A.M.E. Church lot—a thousand more marchers than the week before. They carried signs that read TELL DAWSEY THE 50'S & 60'S ARE PAST and RENEW SINGLETON'S CONTRACT TODAY! And as they had the Saturday before, many of them dressed in black and white as a symbol of racial unity. Chanting "Do the Right Thing!" they walked toward U.S. 501, which was again closed to traffic. Then lightning flashed and rain fell. At the front of the pack, H. H. Singleton turned to Nelson Rivers and said, "Rivers, what we gonna do?"

"Let's put the umbrellas down," Rivers said, "and keep on marching." Twenty-three years later, at the Homegoing Ceremony for H. H. Singleton, he'd add, "And the enemy was amazed that the folk would not stop marching even in the rain."

Indeed, rather than sending people scattering back to the church, the storm only seemed to enliven and unify the protestors. The walk continued straight down Church Street toward the Horry County School District offices. As thunder cracked and the rain poured, the ink on the protestors' signs ran in streaks and their black-and-white clothes clung wet and heavy to their bodies. According to the *Sun News*, "the crowd seemed electrified."

Sitting in the parking lot of the school board offices was a flatbed truck, and once again, a series of speakers took the makeshift stage. "We welcome you back to Conway again," Singleton said to the mass of people standing in the lot. "The reason you are back here is that the racists have not heard us, but we are here to tell them that never again will racism and bigoted acts be the order of the day."

Encapsulating the mood of the marchers, who were fired up despite the rough weather, Rivers said, "We will walk in rain and snow because we will not go back to the bad old days." Then he promised daily pickets in front of the school district offices beginning Monday, and he talked of expanding the protests beyond Conway to Myrtle Beach. He told the crowd, "we will come preach at the beach because we want justice." With Conway business owners—mostly white, of course—already complaining that the first march had cut off access to Church Street's shops and stores, this threat to do the same in Myrtle Beach, the epicenter of tourism in the region, must have rung like a warning bell.

The second march was evidence that the Conway Movement was not only growing in numbers, it was growing in political influence. State Senator Kay Patterson of Columbia, the chair of the South Carolina Black Caucus, spoke to the crowd, telling those assembled, "I came here today because I heard there was a quarterback who said 'I ain't going to go back.'" Patterson's

appearance marked the first time that a statewide leader not directly affiliated with the NAACP was willing to stand up and say that racism was
the root cause of the problems in Conway. As the storm continued, Senator
Patterson said from the stage, "We want justice to roll down like the water."

The next morning, coverage of the second March Against Intimidation was
pushed to Section D of the Sunday paper, perhaps to make room for a front-
page story that warned of a different kind of storm: "Caribbean Braces for
Hugo Fury," read the headline. This was the first mention in the *Sun News*
of the tropical cyclone that had formed a week earlier when a group of
thunderstorms blew west off the coast of Africa and over the course of four
days grew in strength from tropical depression to tropical storm to hurricane. Forecasters were warning that Hugo might be "the most powerful
hurricane to hit the [Caribbean] region since Hurricane David in 1979." For
Grand Strand residents, though, a comparison to David wasn't necessarily
a reason to head out and buy batteries and bottled water. As deadly as that
storm had been as it tore through the Dominican Republic, by the time it
hit South Carolina, it was no longer at hurricane strength. "[David] dumped
a lot of rain," writes Rubillo, the South Carolina hurricane historian, "but no
lives were lost [in South Carolina] and damage was comparatively minor."
As they shook open their newspapers that Sunday morning, most Horry
County residents surely figured Hugo, at worst, would be as "comparatively
minor" as David, and even more likely, it would fizzle out long before reaching the eastern seaboard, as Hurricane Gabrielle—the most recent named
storm of the '89 season, the "G" storm—had done less than a week before.

The next day, Monday, September 18, Hugo slammed into Puerto Rico
and then angled west-northwest toward the Bahamas. In its wake, the hurricane's 140-mile-per-hour winds had left Puerto Rico, the Virgin Islands,
and the other Leeward Islands with at least twenty-eight dead and tens of
thousands homeless. This news surely got the attention of Horry County
residents, but it still wouldn't have caused many folks to evacuate or even
take precautions. After all, San Juan, Puerto Rico, is about 1,300 miles from
Myrtle Beach, and the paths of storms like Hugo are notoriously difficult to
forecast. The day before, a meteorologist at the National Hurricane Center
had told the AP it was "too early to tell if the storm will even hit the United
States." That kind of cautious reserve would have been enough to keep most
folks from raiding their local Food Lions and Ace Hardwares for peanut
butter and plywood. And more drastic steps like moving valuables to the
relative high ground of the attic and taking time off work to head inland
to a hotel or to a relative's house would have seemed not only unnecessary

but costly and time consuming. South Carolinians had learned that when it came to hurricanes that were still over a thousand miles offshore, there was no need to panic.

On that Monday, the day Hugo clobbered Puerto Rico, NAACP protesters formed a picket line in front of the Horry County School District offices. Marching silently back and forth on the sidewalk, they arrived in three shifts of approximately twenty picketers each, with the first arriving at 7:30 a.m. and the last taking over at 3:30 p.m. Protest organizer Cleveland Fladger wore one sign that read WE ARE DISCIPLINED, DETERMINED, DEDICATED—NAACP and held another that proclaimed LOVE ONE ANOTHER. A TOWN (AND A FOOTBALL TEAM) DIVIDED CANNOT STAND. Others raised signs asking for H. H. Singleton's return or pleading for Carlos Hunt to get another chance to play quarterback. The group planned to picket every day for the next two weeks if their demands were not met.

Two days later, on Wednesday, the Horry County school board held their first monthly meeting since Singleton's suspension. As was typical, the meeting began with a public forum, but at this particular forum, the crowd was much larger than normal. Approximately 350 people attended the opening session, including over two hundred members of the black community, many of whom wore T-shirts that read NAACP FIRED UP AND READY TO GO! on the front and DO THE RIGHT THING on the back. As twenty-five law enforcement officers stood post in and around the building, four community members got up and spoke before the board, two speaking in favor of the action taken by John Dawsey and the school administration and two, including Cleveland Fladger, speaking in support of Carlos Hunt and H. H. Singleton. Those speaking for Hunt and Singleton were applauded by the black majority in the crowd; those speaking in support of Dawsey were booed and jeered. At one point, Fladger, according to the *Sun News*, "stood up to quiet the audience when [a white resident] said blacks have become less educated since desegregation [and that] the NAACP leadership had substituted a social Gospel for the law of God."

After the public forum, the board members met privately in a closed session, during which they agreed to investigate the question of whether Chuck Jordan acted unfairly in his dealings with Carlos Hunt. However, they indicated that their decision would likely come after the football season had ended. Even if they were to decide that Jordan had acted inappropriately, by that time it would be too late for Carlos to return to the field. The board also agreed to grant a request by Carlos's mother, Kathy Thomas, for a grievance hearing, but they voted to wait to conduct the hearing until after

Singleton's lawsuit against the district was decided. Given the pace of most lawsuits, it appeared that Ms. Thomas's complaint wouldn't be dealt with anytime soon.

Nearly a month after the boycott began, the school board had finally agreed to take up the issue, but in the opinion of one board member, Republican James Dunn, they had already waited too long. In an article that ran in the paper the morning of the meeting, Dunn pointed out that other local and state officials, including Mayor Long and Governor Campbell, had at least attempted to bring some sort of resolution to the issue, while the school board had remained silent and inactive. "The mayor is offering suggestions and setting up a committee. The governor is involved. And what's the board doing? Not a thing," Dunn said. "Where is our leadership?" Later, he added, "We've been told to be quiet on this [by school district attorney Bruce Davis] while Dawsey continues to go ahead and bungle everything he does." The superintendent, for his part, indicated that he had been working toward a resolution since the boycott began, adding that "[t]he board knows very little about what's going on."

To many blacks in Conway, the school board's delay in responding to the crisis looked like more of the same old, same old. More of the same tendency by whites to dismiss or trivialize blacks' issues. More of the white establishment's desire to put off actions that might address blacks' concerns. Whether the Hunt position switch and the Singleton suspension had been racially motivated or not, the board's reticence only helped ensure that race relations in Conway would get worse before they got better. The resulting anger and mistrust on both sides could potentially take years to repair, if they could be repaired at all.

Meanwhile, it had become clear that Hurricane Hugo was going to strike the United States. The question was where. On Tuesday, the *Sun News* reported that South Carolina municipalities and emergency agencies were "getting ready for the worst." But meteorologists and hurricane forecasters hadn't yet pinpointed the unlucky states and cities. One scenario called for landfall anywhere between northern Florida and southern North Carolina; another had Hugo stalling and then drifting up toward the mid-Atlantic and the Northeast. Still, as Paul Knight, a meteorologist with the Weather Communications Group at Penn State University, warned, it didn't seem likely that Hugo would "turn out to sea" as Gabrielle had recently done. The consensus among experts was this: Although Hugo's track couldn't be predicted with confidence until Wednesday or Thursday, the storm would absolutely make landfall somewhere on the East Coast.

During this week of uncertainty and trepidation in Horry County, the exact paths of both Hurricane Hugo and the Conway Movement may have been unknown, but anyone could see that these twin storms were showing no signs of slackening. What seems clear now, though, is that, as powerful as Hugo was, it was destined to dissipate long before the racial tensions welling up in Conway would. In their passage across the Atlantic, hurricanes gather strength as they travel over warm waters and cloud after cloud is sucked into the storm's spiraling arms. The heat energy of the summer is amassed into a collective force that only weakens when the storm meets land or drifts into the colder waters of the North Atlantic. Every hurricane is short-lived, soon to be starved of the thermal fuel that powers it. The Conway Movement, however, was fueled by a resentment that ran long and deep and was unlikely to simply blow over.

Members of Conway's black community had vivid memories and first-hand experiences with racial inequality and bigotry. They had suffered a lingering history of economic and social injustice, even if many whites would have scoffed at blacks' claims of persecution. When the boycott started, a common reaction among Conway's white community was, *Where did THIS come from?* Whenever racial tension flares up seemingly out of nowhere, there is always an incident like the Carlos Hunt switch that sets in motion a series of events that leads to a larger conflict. The conventional wisdom goes like this: The X event on Y date was the spark that ignited a tinderbox/powder keg/other easily combustible metaphor for the kind of racial discord that, in another cliché, simmers under the surface of any seemingly harmonious place. This tinderbox-up-in-flames analogy suggests that when the underlying conditions are right, a single incident will spark a wildfire of racial discontent.

But the truth is, conditions in America are nearly always right for a racial conflict—in city after city, town after town, in the North, South, East, and West. Moreover, a spark—the kind of incident that could potentially set off a racial conflict—happens somewhere every day. In practically every jail and prison, black inmates are serving time in disproportionate numbers to whites. In many schools, white and black students live mostly separate social lives. At many colleges and universities, even those institutions that are working hard to address the achievement gap between whites and blacks, odds are if you're a black person working on the campus, you wear the uniform of the grounds crew or the custodial staff, not the robes and tams of the faculty. And perhaps one of the most disturbing but rarely questioned aspects of the racial divide is that the terms *black church* and *white church* aren't just common usage, but are accurate descriptions of the congregations that gather inside those churches. In an environment with this degree of racial separatism and inequality, it's remarkable that news-making events like Bensonhurst, Virginia Beach, and, three years later, the Rodney King riots in Los Angeles, aren't more common. And considering how seemingly mundane the Conway spark was (a football coach naming one player as the starter over another), the salient question probably isn't *How did this happen?* but *Why doesn't this happen more often?*

Every year forecasters attempt to predict how active the hurricane season will be. These predictions are based on an immense amount of data, and they're spit out by supercomputers running sophisticated weather modeling software, but they are often flat wrong. Experts can't say exactly when or where these storms will form or how many will make landfall. The best they can do is state the odds of a certain number of hurricanes forming before the end of the season. Even with the conditions well known, even with satellites tracking cloud formations and a flotilla of buoys reporting data on air and water temperatures and ocean currents, the best meteorologists can do is make an educated guess. As in the Atlantic, where summer and fall always hold the potential for devastating hurricanes, America is a place where racial flare-ups always seem just one inciting incident away.

By Wednesday, projections from forecasters had Hugo making landfall on Thursday evening or Friday morning, likely on the coast of Georgia or South Carolina. Myrtle Beach officials began urging those living in low-lying areas to evacuate. The next day, the news got worse for South Carolina residents: Projections showed that Hugo would probably hit just north of Charleston, at just about high tide. The *Sun News* announced that the storm would be South Carolina's worst since Hurricane Gracie in 1959. This news finally shook Grand Strand residents of out of the slumber of complacency. Folks taped and boarded windows. Guests were evacuated from hotels. Governor Campbell ordered a mandatory evacuation for beach areas, and evacuees filled shelters. U.S. 501 was lined with vehicles headed inland and upstate. On the rear window of one evacuating car, someone had painted: HUGO-DIS-WAY WEGO-DAT-WAY!

Minutes after midnight on Friday, September 22, Hugo came ashore at Sullivan's Island—a few miles north of Charleston and about ninety miles south of Myrtle Beach—as a Category 4 hurricane with sustained winds of 138 mph and a ten- to twenty-foot storm surge. By 8:00 a.m., it had left South Carolina entirely and was weakening to a tropical storm as it blew into western North Carolina. But in between, during those eight early morning hours, Hugo did catastrophic damage throughout the Palmetto

State. The storm killed at least eighteen people. It caused over three billion dollars in insured losses, and with many homes uninsured, the total dollar amount came much closer to four or five billion. The American Red Cross estimated that approximately 5,400 homes were destroyed, and the state highway department reported that almost 18,000 miles of roads were damaged or covered with debris. In the coastal areas of Horry, Georgetown, and Charleston Counties, nearly 6,000 structures were wrecked or ruined. And all across the state, electricity, water, and sewer services were interrupted.

Along the Grand Strand, hotels flooded, palm trees were down, and piers were washed away. In Garden City, a beach community on the South Strand, the front row of oceanfront properties was reduced to pilings. Horry County Administrator M. L. Love "estimated 85-90 percent of the single family homes along [the] Garden City strip on the ocean front were destroyed and 95 percent of Garden City's tax base was gone." The *Sun News* was forced to print Saturday's paper at a plant in Columbia, using *The State* newspaper's printing presses. And yet, unlike Sullivan's Island and Isle of Palms, the areas immediately north of Charleston that were hit hardest by Hugo, many spots on the Grand Strand came through the storm just fine, with "very little indication a hurricane had passed by except for a few signs bent or knocked down and a few downed trees."

Protected to some degree by its inland location, Conway was spared the worst damage, but all over town roads were strewn with power lines and broken tree limbs. People in Conway counted themselves as lucky, but only because they knew that the damage elsewhere on the coast had been so much more severe. In all, twenty-two South Carolina counties would be declared disaster areas, and Hugo would become the costliest hurricane in American history—until three years later when Andrew tore through South Florida.

Wind and water. All that damage—caused by wind and water, both of which are almost always pleasantly calm on the Grand Strand. The twenty-five post-Hugo years have been marked by another spike in population growth and property development along the South Carolina coast. The very economy of this area, after all, is based on the relative safety of the ocean and the winds that drive the waves ashore. But the same elements that are usually placid and perhaps even seem under our control, can, if a certain set of factors come together, bring about the kind of destruction not seen in a generation. And while there hasn't been a hurricane or a racial conflict in Horry County since 1989 that matches the twin storms of that year, the fact is that the conditions are still right for both.

DRIVING ON

NOW

FIDO. IT'S THE MANTRA THAT HAS STEERED CHUCK JORDAN THROUGH heartbreaking losses and heroic wins. It has helped him move beyond seasons that ended with near misses in championship games and a year like 1989, where the highest drama took place off the field—from the protests to the press coverage to the hurricane. For Jordan's current Tigers, several days have passed since the crushing defeat in the Bell Game, and although the coach has by necessity driven on, it's clear that he hasn't entirely forgotten that 56–55 final score or his call to go for two points and the win rather than play for overtime.

Turns out the decision to go for two wasn't as split-second as it appeared to those watching from the stands. He'd actually made up his mind eighty yards earlier, after the Myrtle Beach touchdown that had given the Seahawks a 56–49 lead. As soon as Mykal and the Conway offense took the ball at their own 20, down 7 with just over three minutes left, Jordan said to his offensive coordinator, Charles Divine, "Get me a play ready. If we score, we're going for the win." The Tigers scored, Divine dialed up the play, Mykal handled the low snap, and from there everything went right except the one thing that mattered: The tight end couldn't pull down the pass.

When asked what Mickey Wilson said to him during the post-game handshakes, Jordan says his ex-quarterback told him, "That was a great call. You got me." "But we *didn't* get him," Jordan says. He exhales audibly. "The kid just dropped it." If there was any temptation among the Tiger players to blame the loss on the tight end, Nathaniel Nesbitt, the coach stifled it in the locker room after the game, demanding that nobody single out that particular drop. "Any one play could have made the difference," he said then, over the sounds of sixty sniffling youngsters.

Now, headed into the first game of region ball, he's much more concerned about his defense than he is about Moody and the talented offense which, despite the loss, still racked up half-a-hundred against the #1 3A team in the state. "You put up fifty-five points," Jordan says, laughing, "you think that ought to be enough to beat anybody—even the USC Gamecocks." The struggling defense, he says, has been the story of the season. His team is 2–4 largely because his D is yielding an average of 41 points per game. The man who runs the defensive unit for Jordan is Kelly Andreucci, who, as most football fans in Conway know, is Mickey Wilson's brother-in-law. Jordan isn't blaming Andreucci for the loss to Myrtle Beach any more than he's blaming Nesbitt, but still, he's obviously frustrated by the opposing teams' lofty point totals. Even in the Tigers' last win, against Marlboro County, Andreucci's unit gave up 40. "We lived on the edge in that game," Jordan says. Then his mind travels forward to the Bell Game and the 56 points his defense allowed. "And when you live on the edge, you die on the edge."

The start of region ball, however, brings with it the promise of new life. Whereas most coaches preach the importance of focusing solely on the next opponent, of "taking it one game at a time," Jordan will admit that he's "always practicing for the twelfth game," by which he means the first game of the state championship playoffs. Back in the '80s, when the Tigers competed in the Big 16, every team in that class made the playoffs, regardless of their record. Today, the Tigers play in 4A, Class II, which features a playoff bracket determined by region standings and then seeded via a complex points system that includes quality wins, region wins, and strength of schedule. Of the five teams in Conway's region, only three will survive into the postseason. The Tigers might no longer have the luxury of playoff assurance, but they do have history on their side: Conway has qualified for the postseason every year since 2000. The previous season, in 1999, Jordan's guys didn't make the tournament despite finishing with a solid record (8–3 on the year, 5–2 in the region). At 2–4, this year's squad has already lost more games than that 1999 team did, so among Tiger fans, there's genuine reason for concern. But still, now that the offense appears to be humming, if Jordan and Andreucci can get the defense righted in the region, they have a good chance of making it to the head coach's coveted twelfth game. Conway may have suffered a bitter loss to Myrtle Beach, but their two primary team goals, the region championship and the state championship, are still out there to be won. "I don't know if we're good enough to turn it around," Jordan tells the *Sun News*. "We're going to find out."

That Friday, the Tigers bus up to Florence Memorial Stadium to take on the 5–1 West Florence Knights, the defending region champs whose only loss this season came against Myrtle Beach. In the first half, Andreucci experiments with untested blitzes and alignments, and during key plays, he juggles personnel, sending Malcolm Green, Bryan Edwards, and a few other starters from the offense in to play defense. Suddenly the Tiger D is playing with a newfound toughness, and at the half, Conway has held the Knights to a respectable 14 points. Mykal and the rest of the offense, however, have been shut out, so the Tigers find themselves down by two touchdowns. In the locker room, Jordan, by his own admission, "chews the offense's butt."

Were there any doubts about the virtues of an ol' fashioned butt-chewing, the kids from Conway put them to rest in the second half when Mykal and the offense catch fire. The senior quarterback throws for three touchdowns, runs for two, and amasses 414 yards of total offense as he leads the Tigers to 35 second-half points. Just as impressively, the defense holds West Florence scoreless after halftime, limiting them to two measly first downs. Conway takes its first region game 35–14.

"That's the best half of football we've played all season," Jordan says afterwards, adding, "West Florence is the best team we've seen since Northwestern." It doesn't take a photographic memory to recall that Myrtle Beach is one of the teams Conway has played since Northwestern, so Jordan's praise for the Knights is also a jab against Mickey Wilson and the Seahawks. For the Conway Tigers, a loss to Myrtle Beach functions just like the bell that sits atop the relinquished trophy: It resonates long after the initial hit.

But with this win against the defending region champs, the Tigers have a good start on the new life they're looking for. Oddly, though, region ball will have to wait a week, as Conway, due to a quirk in the schedule, is next slated to play one last non-region game, against 1–6 West Ashley, a 4A school from the Charleston area. Even though West Ashley's record is much worse than Conway's, and even though a win against the out-of-towners won't count in the region standings, this week feels important. First of all, this is Conway's homecoming game. But moreover, it's a chance for Jordan and his guys to prove to their fans and to themselves that last week's potent offense and dogged defense weren't isolated phenomena, to prove that the Tigers are finally playing up to their talent level.

You couldn't script a better homecoming than the scene in the Backyard on this Friday night. The autumn air smells like wet grass and Bojangles chicken and biscuits. The band wails "Tiger Rag," and the cheerleaders chant *We are the mighty, mighty Tigers.* On the hill beyond the north end zone, teenagers huddle and flirt. In the grassy area next to the visiting bleachers, elementary-aged boys play touch football. When the homecoming queen is announced, the stadium rings with girl-squeals of delight and awe. And, best of all, in front of the largest and most jubilant crowd of the season,

Conway explodes for 56 points and a win. Mykal Moody—who days earlier found out he'd been named to the Shrine Bowl of the Carolinas, an annual all-star game in which top players from South Carolina compete against all-stars from North Carolina—accounts for six touchdowns, running for two and throwing for four, including three to Malcolm Green, who also was selected for the Shrine Bowl. The senior quarterback eventually leaves the game with a stubborn thigh bruise that has been bothering him for a few weeks, but the Tigers build a 56–19 lead, and then cruise to a 56–45 win. With Mykal and Malcolm rolling, the defense much improved, and the win/loss record squared at 4–4, the homecoming crowd leaves the Backyard with biscuits in their bellies and smiles on their faces.

If the sudden turnaround seems too perfect to endure, that's because it is. From the beginning, this year has been marked by ups and downs and backs and forths, so going into the next region game against 6–2 South Florence, Conway fans might be understandably worried that the boomerang of close calls and heartbreak will inevitably come arcing back. After trailing 15–7 at the half, Conway grinds on to tie the score at 22 early in the fourth quarter. The teams trade late touchdowns, and the game heads into overtime tied at 29. With Mykal having already thrown for two touchdowns (both to Malcolm) and run for two more, the Tigers are a confident bunch heading to overtime. Even after South Florence scores a touchdown on their first extra period possession to go up 36–29, Conway has every reason to believe that the momentum they've built over the last two games will hold. When the Tigers get their shot in overtime, they promptly take the ball down to the 10, and on third and goal from the 4, the red-hot Mykal throws a perfect fade to the back of the end zone for Bryan Edwards, who leaps and catches it—out of bounds. It's a close call, but there's no instant replay in high school football and no time to complain because the play clock is running. Fourth down. Last shot. Mykal keeps the ball, slides to the left, sees a crease, cuts back, and dives for the goal line. He appears to push the ball across the plane of the goal—and video replays will indicate that he *did* push the ball across it—but the line judge signals no. Six inches short. Game over. The Conway side erupts in protest, but the referees are already running off the field. The Tigers fall to 1–1 in the region, 4–5 on the year. It's been that kind of season. Up, down. Back, forth. Or, as Jordan puts it when asked to comment about the two controversial calls that ended the game, "That's just the way the daggum ball bounces, baby."

The next week, at home against Sumter in the second-to-last game of the regular season, the daggum ball keeps bouncing that same sour way.

It's senior night for Team 89, the last time Mykal Moody, Malcolm Green, Sawyer Jordan, and the sixteen other seniors will ever play at Conway High School—unless somehow the Tigers are fortunate enough to pull off a miracle finish, win the region title, and host a home playoff game. On Conway's first possession, the offense goes three and out, with Mykal limping back to the huddle after each play, clearly hobbled by that slow-healing thigh bruise. When the senior QB staggers off the field on fourth down, Jordan says to him, "Mike, you're out." Then the coach turns to his backup, sophomore Ethan Smith, and says, "Ethan, you're in." Mykal takes off his helmet, dons his red Shrine Game baseball cap, and on what might be his last night in the Backyard, watches his team fall behind 24–7 before halftime. Down by 17 at home, Conway seems certain to slide to 1–2 in the region. So much talent and experience—two Shrine Bowlers, nineteen seniors, coming off an 8–4 season—and yet their chances of even making the playoffs seem as long as the Atlantic is wide. Sometimes a football season feels like a blues song. Maybe Team 89, like the squad from the year its name echoes, was born under a bad sign. All bad luck and trouble.

In the second half, the blues get a shade bluer when the lanky Ethan Smith, who had looked impressive in leading the team back to within 10, 24–14, goes down with a broken collarbone, the same injury Mykal suffered back in the spring. With Moody limping on the sideline and Smith wincing on the bench, sitting next to his worried mother and being attended to by the training staff, Jordan calls for the third string quarterback, his son Sawyer, "Sawdawg," who immediately comes in a tosses a bomb to Malcolm that gets the Tigers into scoring position. A few plays later, the board reads 24–21, and Conway—playing with a 5'10", 162-lb. coach's son at QB—has seized the momentum. Down, up.

And up and up and up. Behind the gutsy play of Sawyer Jordan and 185 rushing yards from senior Jaquail Crosland, the Tigers score 27 unanswered points in the second half to win 34–24. It's a near reflection of the game that kicked off region ball three weeks ago, against West Florence, when the defense turned stingy and the offense outscored the opponent 35–0 in the second half, but this time Conway did it two quarterbacks down. "I guess ol' Sawdawg had to get it done," Coach Jordan says after the game, without a smile, so cool and dispassionate you'd never guess he's talking about a kid whose diapers he changed.

Thirty football minutes ago, Conway's playoff chances were nearly nil. Now, the Tigers are 2–1 in the region and in a tie for second place with the team they just beat. With one game left to play, against the Carolina Forest Panthers, the worst the Tigers can do is finish third in the region, meaning that they're guaranteed a playoff spot. But even more improbable is this: Next week, if West Florence beats South Florence, and if Conway beats Carolina Forest—and they absolutely *should* beat Carolina Forest, a squad that is currently languishing at 1–9 on the season and 0–3 in the region, a squad that has only defeated Conway one time in the school's entire history—then Team 89, for all this season's ups and downs and backs and forths, will take home the region championship and the high tournament seeding that comes with it. The ball just bounced back the other way, baby.

THEN

Hugo was a hurricane-sized pause button. During the frantic buildup, landfall, and aftermath of the storm, much of what had constituted daily life along the Grand Strand that autumn—including the football season and the Conway Movement—was temporarily set aside while residents tended to more immediate concerns, like sorting through the wet remnants of beach houses, boat docks, and fishing piers. Even for the lucky folks who suffered minimal damage, there was still cleanup to be done: downed limbs to chainsaw and shingles to replace. Supporters of H. H. Singleton had picketed in front of the school district offices until the day before Hugo struck; then they'd temporarily suspended the protest, promising to continue after the storm passed. The Conway Tigers were supposed to have kicked off against the Georgetown Bulldogs approximately nineteen hours after the hurricane made land, but the game, like all high school football contests in Horry County that weekend, had been postponed. Conway and Georgetown would meet at the end of the season, after what would have been the final game of region ball. Looking back on the hurricane now, Chuck Jordan says that, storm damage aside, "Hugo was a blessing in disguise," because after the second NAACP march, with the picketing under way and the legal battles on the horizon, the city of Conway "was about to explode." The storm, he says, calmed everything down for a minute.

But it was a short minute. By Tuesday, four days after the hurricane, Singleton's supporters had already reconstituted their protest at the school district offices. Hugo hit exactly one month after the boycotting players walked off the football team, and during that tumultuous month the Conway Movement had grown from one disgruntled player challenging a coach's personnel decision to a statewide racial cause célèbre. The issues involved in the ongoing dispute had snowballed from Carlos Hunt's position switch, to the suitability of black quarterbacks generally, to the fairness or unfairness of Singleton's suspension, to all the disparities—economic, social, and political—between blacks and whites in Conway, Horry County, and the entire state of South Carolina. Hugo may have forced a temporary halt, but after the streets were cleared of debris, the movement quickly regained momentum.

Still, October began with an apparent blow to Singleton's cause—or at least a blow to one tenet upon which the Conway Movement was built. A week after Hugo struck, Human Affairs Commissioner James Clyburn mailed a letter to the school board "and other community members" (who were not named in news coverage of the letter) documenting the initial findings of his investigation into the Carlos Hunt position switch and the subsequent boycott. In his comments, Clyburn stated plainly that racism was not a factor in Coach Jordan's decision to move Hunt to defensive back. As evidence, the commissioner cited four points: 1. Jordan's tape recording of his meeting with H. H. and Hank Singleton on which, according to Clyburn, the reverend "absolved Jordan of racial intentions more than once." 2. That Jordan had started a black quarterback during three of his six years at Conway High. 3. That Jordan told Carlos he had been switched to defensive back not only to "strengthen the team," but also because the player would see an "individual benefit" in that two colleges (Newberry and Presbyterian) were scouting him as a defensive back or wide receiver. 4. That a number of striking players told Clyburn and his staff that Jordan had never "shown favoritism to white ballplayers over black ballplayers." One of the boycotting players apparently went so far as to say that "Jordan was his best friend."

The commissioner's findings may have exonerated Chuck Jordan of racism, but they did not amount to categorical support of the coach or his actions. Clyburn suggested that Jordan's decision to move Hunt might have been inappropriate in that it was—in the view of the commissioner and his staff—at least partly a result of the personal dispute between the coach and the player (over the $80 loan for the class ring) rather than a move based solely on the quarterback's performance on the field. Clyburn noted that he agreed with an acquaintance who'd recently suggested that Jordan had let "his personal quarrels with Hunt effect [sic] his moral decision." In the letter that documented the findings, the commissioner admitted that the coach may have been guilty of "punishing rather than disciplining Hunt," but he also pointed out that "personal quarrels are not necessarily racial incidents."

Two weeks earlier, an editorial in the *Horry Independent* had also vindicated Jordan—but for precisely the opposite reason. In the paper's view, Jordan did not have a personal squabble with Hunt. This view centered on the fact that the $80 Jordan had loaned Carlos for the ring had come not from his own pocket but from the $200 discretionary fund provided to the coach by the Conway Booster Club. The newspaper questioned the "wisdom of such a fund," but argued that once Carlos had failed to make payments on his debt, Jordan was justified in suspending him from the basketball team (a suspension which some believe led to Hunt's position switch on the football team). If the money had come from Jordan personally, the editorial suggested, then suspending Hunt would have been out of line because the loan would have been a private matter between two individuals and the suspension would have represented an unfair attempt to punish the player for reasons that had nothing to with sports. However, because the money had come from the Booster Club fund, the paper argued that Jordan essentially had no choice but to suspend Carlos. The coach not only owed it to the Boosters to protect their money, he owed it to the player to teach him about personal responsibility. And as the editorial pointed out, in the past Jordan had disciplined other (unnamed) athletes who had failed to repay similar loans, so fair was fair.

Perhaps the most telling sentence in the editorial, though, is this one: "From the beginning, we have found it difficult to believe Chuck Jordan is a racist." Many folks in Conway would have taken this position—*Jordan is not a racist*—as a given, just as the paper's editors had. And once you assume that fact, then the logic of the editorial's argument becomes no more questionable than the commutative property of addition, which states $A + B = B + A$. In his math classroom, Jordan had probably explained the commutative property to his students hundreds of times over the years, and its immutable and incontrovertible truth had served as the foundation for most of the algebraic principles he would teach. In declaring Jordan definitively vindicated, the newspaper's commutative logic went like this: *Student owes money + student isn't paying back money = student isn't paying back money + student owes money*. And the sum of both sides of the formula added up to *Coach is justified in suspending student*. But regardless of what order you state the equation in, it doesn't account for the complicating variables of human emotion, like frustration or pride or even best intentions. It doesn't account for a community-wide history of racial prejudice or for an isolated personal quarrel. Math problems often begin with a given, like "Let us assume that the train's rate of speed over the 500-mile trip is a constant 75 miles per hour." The trouble with such assumptions, though, is that they don't hold up in the real world, where a train can never maintain a constant speed and where confounding variables are nearly always present. Assuming that such complicating factors don't exist—especially those sentiments and prejudices that make us all so complex and flawed—may simplify and regularize the world, but it leads to an inaccurate model of the world.

One additional complication with regard to the question of Jordan's alleged racism or lack thereof came down to semantics. H. H. Singleton and Cleveland Fladger, by their own admission, had never actually called Jordan a racist. In a letter to the *Horry Independent* signed by both leaders, they stated very clearly, "This protest has never accused Mr. Jordan of being a racist." Still, they stated equally as clearly that Jordan's decision to move Carlos away from the QB position *was* racist. In that very same letter, they wrote, "This protest imputes the above action [moving Carlos from the QB position] by Coach Jordan as being racially motivated." The point, according to Singleton and Fladger, is that it is possible for a person who is not a racist to *act* in a way that is racist. Or, as the Reverend Covel Moore would later argue at the Horry County school board's hearing to decide if Singleton should be fired, "You don't have to be prejudiced to do a prejudiced act. Whether you're stepping on my foot intentionally, you're still stepping on my foot."

This view of racism takes the responsibility away from the individual and makes the entire culture culpable. The question for the two black leaders was not whether Jordan thought *I need a white quarterback*, but whether he was, consciously or unconsciously, privileging the white QB over the black one based on preconceived notions about race and about the skill set necessary to play the position. It wouldn't take an overt racist to do that; all it would take is a person who had spent a lifetime inundated with images of white quarterbacking superiority—which is to say practically everyone, even most blacks. "The question must be asked," wrote Singleton and Fladger, "Would Mr. Jordan have acted similarly had Carlos been white." They were essentially countering Clyburn's four points of evidence with *yes, Jordan is not a racist, but he is still capable of doing something that* is *racist. Replacing Carlos with Mickey was a racist action by a non-racist person.* Many Americans would have been (and still would be) uncomfortable with this subtle distinction, because it's easier to simply label a person as racist or not racist without acknowledging that, in reality, humans rarely fit into such neat, binary opposites.

Of course, the story of the boycott is usually told in neat, binary terms that don't always conform to reality. Every newspaper article and lunchtime conversation about the events of 1989 seems to rely on distinct, opposing categories like "the white community" and "the black community" in order to capture the prevailing atmosphere in Conway at the time. And admittedly, so does this book. But the truth is, while there were two predominant points of view and those two camps did break largely along racial lines, there were exceptions. There were blacks who saw Singleton as an egotistical blowhard just as there were whites who felt that blacks had been treated unfairly on the football team, in the schools, and in Conway generally. There were whites who supported Jordan but not Dawsey and the school district, and there were blacks and whites who couldn't have cared less about Hunt's status on the team, but backed Singleton in his fight for reinstatement. The range of opinions and reactions to the boycott and to Singleton's firing is much more complex than a simple white-vs.-black model can capture, as is perhaps best illustrated by Clyburn's findings and the reactions to those findings.

While the commissioner found no evidence of racism on Jordan's part, he couldn't say the same for the school system. "I have made it very clear from the beginning that this agency has found race to play a part in some recent decisions by the Horry [Conway] County School District," the commissioner wrote. He did not mention Dawsey's suspension of Singleton specifically; he'd indicated earlier that the Singleton case was best left to the legal system. Instead, he cited two previous Conway incidents in which his investigators had found race to be a factor. Still, it's hard not to hear at least a gesture toward Singleton's suspension in the statement about race playing a part in some of the school district's "recent decisions."

One month after Clyburn's letter was published, the commissioner would give a ninety-minute briefing about the Conway football boycott to the South Carolina Human Affairs board, and in that briefing he would again deny that Jordan's decision was racially motivated. "It's just as far from being race as anything you have ever seen," he told the board members. "You can stay down there [in Conway] from now until next year, and you will not find race involved in this football incident." A month to reflect on what he had learned in his investigation seemed to have strengthened Commissioner Clyburn's conviction that racism was not to blame for Hunt's losing the starting quarterback spot. And today, almost twenty-five years later, when now-Congressman Clyburn is asked to comment on the issue, he maintains that view. "It was a coach's decision," he says, "pure and simple."

In denying that race was a factor, Clyburn risked not only alienating Singleton, Fladger, and black community leaders, but also being seen by blacks statewide as little more than a puppet of Governor Carroll Campbell and the white establishment. The seed for this perspective was perhaps planted two weeks before Clyburn's initial findings were published, when newspapers reported that some of South Carolina's black leaders were accusing Governor Campbell of being "too quiet" in fighting racism. As head of the

Human Affairs Commission, Clyburn led the very department responsible for investigating racial incidents, and he refused to echo other black leaders' criticism of Campbell. "I think he's played a proper role," the commissioner said of the governor. Clyburn had recently been vocal in criticizing the Reagan administration for exacerbating racism, but the fact that the commissioner refused to take the same stance against Carroll Campbell—a man who had once led protests against school busing and had joined in on the 1988 Bush presidential campaign's dubious-at-best, racist-at-worst criticisms of the Democratic nominee, Massachusetts governor Michael Dukakis, for furloughing convicted murderer Willie Horton—caused some blacks to write off Clyburn as a man willing to side against his own people if doing so helped him maintain his political position. Singleton called Clyburn's report on the football boycott "totally irrelevant and insulting," and Fladger called Clyburn "a disgrace to the black people of Conway." In a written response to Clyburn's findings published two weeks later, Singleton and Fladger made even stronger criticisms of the commissioner's report, calling it a "salient hoax" that had been perpetrated by Clyburn and others to "'cover up' acts of overt racism" and to "avert a possible racial confrontation that would deface Conway and Myrtle Beach and thereby exposing [*sic*] the state's number one tourist attraction to financial risk." For Singleton and Fladger, collusion with the white establishment seemed to be the only logical explanation for the commissioner's findings. From their perspective, Clyburn was playing for the other team.

The perception within the black community of a betrayal by the commissioner might have been strengthened when school board member Terry Hucks said of Clyburn's report, "It was good to hear that perspective from a black individual." While many whites might have read Hucks's remark as a hopeful statement about a black man being able to evaluate a racial issue neutrally and objectively, some blacks would surely have seen it as the white establishment saying *We like Jim Clyburn because he's not uppity. He knows his place. He's one of the good ones.*

Again, in his findings Clyburn didn't address the school district's suspension of Singleton; but it seems evident that the commissioner disagreed with Dawsey's decision and felt that the courts would likely overturn it. If Clyburn indeed sided with Singleton on the suspension issue, then why would Singleton and Fladger have attacked the commissioner so strongly and so publicly? A possible explanation might be found in the first of Clyburn's four points of evidence, the tape recording on which Singleton allegedly absolved Chuck Jordan of "racial intentions." By now, the Conway Movement had transcended the question of who should play quarterback, but even so, what would it mean to the larger cause if H. H. Singleton—who at the press conference announcing the boycott had accused Jordan of a "callous and racial intolerance that seems to have bordered on racial bigotry"—had later admitted to Jordan personally that he didn't think the coach's "intentions" (which is to say, motivations) were racist? Would Singleton himself be vindicating Jordan on both sides of the semantic distinction the reverend had made between being a racist and acting like a racist? Or on the other hand, would Singleton, by admitting that he didn't question Jordan's intentions, be strengthening his argument that although the coach was not a racist, he nonetheless had committed a racist act?

Regardless of Singleton's characterization of Jordan and regardless of Jordan's intentions in replacing Hunt at QB, the school board and the federal court system would soon be ruling on whether or not Dawsey's suspension of the earth science teacher had been justified. And while Singleton waited for his case to be adjudicated, he certainly would benefit from the symbolic and emotional support of those rallying around him *and* around Carlos— as well as from the considerable legal and practical support offered by the NAACP. Singleton was locked in a legal battle against a school district that was standing firmly behind Jordan and the football team, so regardless of what the reverend said on that tape, he would have been unlikely to agree with Clyburn that it amounted to him "absolving" the coach of anything.

Just as the Conway Movement had entrenched its position and could therefore not yield or make concessions, so too had Coach Jordan and his supporters. Despite a record of 0–4 heading into region ball, the coach couldn't very well make a 180-degree turn and start begging the boycotting players to come back. He'd already made all of the gestures toward reconciliation he was willing to make, and his supporters were absolutely wedded to the concept of a coach's incontrovertible right—his duty, even—to determine who plays where. No explanation or justification was necessary. In fact, coaches are often praised for ignoring the opinions of others (the media, the fans, and other "outsiders") and applauded for standing firm when they make tough and unpopular decisions.

Many of the people—white and black—who will tell you that Jordan is absolutely not a racist and that he had sound football reasons for moving Hunt to defense, will still admit that he is nothing if not stubborn. And stubbornness, of course, is also a trait for which coaches are admired. So when folks talk about Jordan's brand of stubbornness, they almost always smile as they do it. Many of them will then argue that a more uncooperative brand of stubbornness existed among H. H. Singleton and his supporters. The coach, they'll say, was the reasonable one. After all, it was Jordan who kept delaying the start time of practices to give the striking players a chance to show up; it was Jordan who extended the invitation to the boycotters before the Middleton game; and it was Jordan who welcomed Lawrence Mitchell and several others strikers back for that game, even if Mitchell would later decide to walk away a second time. And it was Jordan who, during negotiations with Carlos Hunt's mother, Kathy Thomas, had been so willing to compromise, he allegedly offered to speak to Carlos personally to assure the player that he would try to use him at QB. Reports indicated, however, that Thomas rejected the settlement because Jordan refused to put that part of the deal in writing.

Like many aspects of the Conway boycott story, this offer from Jordan to Carlos's mother can't easily be verified or refuted. And even if the coach had ultimately welcomed Hunt back to the team and told him that he would "try" to use him at quarterback, there's no guarantee that Carlos would have ever played a down behind center. There's no way of even knowing if Jordan was sincere in his offer to "try." Whatever deals were or were not on the table, we know one thing for sure: The boycotting players never returned to the field that season. In their absence and in the wake of Hugo, the mostly white Tigers drove on as best they could.

There's never a good time for a Category 4 hurricane to make landfall, but for Coach Jordan's team, the postponement of the Georgetown game looked like a stroke of luck in a season in which luck was in short supply. The Tigers were coming off a surprisingly close 21–12 loss to Myrtle Beach in the Bell Game, but the depleted and inexperienced squad had been beaten up for four straight weeks. "The layoff allowed us to nurse some injuries," Jordan said during the week after Hugo, "and fundamentally we've been improving just about every day." Who knew? If they kept getting better each week, it might not be too late to pull off a couple of wins and salvage a respectable season.

With Georgetown now moved to the end of the November, Conway's first post-hurricane game was against the South Florence Bruins in the opening of region ball for both teams. But if the Tigers went up against South Florence thinking an extra week of rest would make them competitive, they didn't think so for long. On the first play from scrimmage, Bruins running back Reggie Richardson took the ball 75 yards for a touchdown, and South Florence went on to win 35–0, outgaining Conway 307 yards to

56. Coach Jordan was left with the smudgiest of silver linings: "They [the Tigers] went out there and gave us everything they had," he said, "and you can't ask them to do more than that."

The next Friday, Conway lost to Dillon 29–0 in a game where Mickey Wilson threw an interception that ended the Tigers' only scoring threat, the defense surrendered two easy touchdowns in less than four minutes, and the punt team gave up a safety when a long snap sailed over the kicker's head and out of the end zone. It was now clear that any momentum the Tigers had built in the Bell Game wasn't enough to carry them past Hugo and into region ball. The two most recent defeats were more lopsided and hopeless than the four losses before the storm. At 0–6 and with no hope of Lawrence, Carlos, and the rest of the boycotters returning to the field, the Tigers were in the middle of a disastrous season that, headed into the homecoming game against Marlboro County, had the distinct potential to get worse.

More than any other game, homecoming week, as the name implies, is supposed to be a time of literal and figurative togetherness. Folks who have moved away come back to remember the old days and reconnect with people they might not have seen since last homecoming. Folks who still live in town buy a ticket and show up at the stadium, even if the team is having a down year. For one week, for one game, everyone with a connection to the school makes a grand show of support and unity. In a small town like Conway, the homecoming game itself is only the most celebrated ritual in a program of events that form a pastiche of archetypal Americana: fireworks displays, parades down Main Street, hay rides and bonfires, dances and pep rallies. The twin messages of homecoming are *we like it here* and *we're in this together.*

So perhaps it's ironic—but not necessarily surprising—that vandals chose homecoming week to deface Conway High. When teachers and students showed up for classes the Thursday before the Marlboro County game, they found graffiti outside on the front wall of the school, reading CONWAY IS STUPID, FIGHT THE POWER, PUBLIC ENEMY, CHUCK JORDAN, and HONKEYS, along with what the *Sun News* would only describe as "profane words." Paint had also been flung onto a van used by the school's athletic department. Before the day was over, the graffiti had been removed by custodians, but the impression of aggressiveness left by this vandalism couldn't be washed away as easily.

The defacement of the building must have been on Principal Tommy Lewis's mind when he and other administrators made the call to change the location and start time of the next day's homecoming pep rally. Traditionally, the rally had been held at the end of the school day in the gymnasium, but "in an effort not to create a situation where verbal or physical interchanges could occur," it was moved six miles off campus to the Graveyard, where it would begin just a half hour before kickoff. Asked about the students' reaction to the postponement of the pep rally, Principal Lewis said, "They don't like it, but they understand it." Some students acted on that dislike by skipping their sixth-period classes in protest. Eleven were suspended for three days.

The fall semester at Conway High was remarkable not for such incidents but instead for what everyone now remembers as a surprisingly calm and ordinary atmosphere. Ask anybody who studied or taught there in 1989, and they will inevitably say something like "the students saw the boycott as a community thing that didn't involve them" or "the kids just didn't talk about it." Nobody remembers (and there were no reports of) fistfights between white and black students or classes disrupted by racially charged shouting matches. Instead, those who were there then will say now: "It's a wonder there wasn't more trouble." Principal Lewis wasn't simply putting a good face on the situation when after the graffiti incident he told the *Horry Independent*, "The behavior of 99 percent of our students has been exactly what we expect. We're very proud of them and our faculty." If a racial storm was circling Conway, then, even with the vandalism and the pep rally protest, the high school itself was the eerily calm eye.

What might have forestalled open conflict among the students at Conway High? Beyond the Renaissance Program—which Larry Biddle, an assistant principal in '89, largely credits for the stability of the school during the boycott—many kids had, no doubt, been warned by their parents to just go about their regular business and let the adults settle things. All over town, parents were surely coaching their children: *Keep your head down and don't talk about that mess, okay?* Still, Mickey Wilson and most anybody else who was a student at the time will admit that the halls were humming with a palpable tension, even if it never broke into violence. The students may have learned to live with the racial friction, but they couldn't ignore it completely. Even after they got used to it, it was still there, like the smell of the school cafeteria or the squeak of sneakers on a vinyl hallway floor.

The relative calm might also have held in part because the football team's performance was so historically awful. With the winless Tigers not a threat to make a deep playoff run, the on-field action would have seemed too hopeless for anyone to spend much time worrying about. There was no question that the loss of the black players had hurt the team, and *hurt* isn't even the right word. The '89 Tigers *weren't* the Tigers, really. The team didn't represent the racial makeup of the town; it didn't represent the makeup of the student body; and it didn't reflect the winning history of Conway football, especially the history that had been forged during the Chuck Jordan era. If the depleted team had mounted a few wins, it's possible that some of the white students would have vented their frustration against striking black kids: *We would have been even better if not for this bullshit boycott.* But without the black players, the team was so undermanned it wasn't just hurt, it was neutered.

The football team's fate was clear. Loss upon loss upon loss. The open question was H. H. Singleton's suspension—an issue that would soon be taken up by the school board and the court system. Conway High students would have recognized the Singleton case and the attending debate over free speech as important, but most of them probably wouldn't have felt passionate enough about these matters to throw a punch over them. Like teenagers everywhere, Conway High kids were focused primarily on the world contained within the walls of their own school, and thus, it's not that surprising that one of the few visible signs of trouble that fall wasn't a racial conflict at all, but a muted outcry from students who'd been cheated out of a chance to leave class early for a pep rally.

Conway dropped the 1989 homecoming game to Marlboro County 42–0. The *Sun News* described the contest as simply "a beating." Mickey passed for a fairly respectable 88 yards, but the Tiger offense netted only 73 yards because Conway's running attack *lost* 15. The next week, the Tigers were shut out by Hartsville 20–0 in a game the *Sun News* didn't even cover and the *Horry Independent* struggled to find a positive in. The defense may have forced six turnovers and played an "inspired game," but more than two months into a disastrous season, Tiger fans had to be getting tired of backhanded compliments like, "Despite being behind, the Conway players and coaches remained very enthusiastic throughout the game." *Forget the enthusiasm. How about a daggone "W" for a change?*

Now with a record of 0–8, Coach Jordan's team had been bested by a cumulative score of 249–32, and in four straight games they'd failed to put up a single point. The Ground Chuck offense had run into a wall. Although the Tigers had gained 163 yards on the ground against Summerville in week two, they wouldn't go over a hundred yards rushing in a game for the rest of the year. In most weeks, the Tigers' rushing total would be less than 50 yards, and in two matchups they'd total negative yardage (minus 15 against Marlboro County and negative 7 against Socastee). With the ground game shut down, Conway found much of their limited success throwing the ball, but "success" would be an egregious misrepresentation of what was happening on the field. Mickey Wilson had yet to throw a touchdown pass, and the Tigers had become so insignificant that the *Sun News* didn't run articles or even print box scores for two Conway games that October. When the local papers did publish post-game reports, the headlines read "No Joy in Conway," "South Florence Runs Roughshod Over Conway," and, a week later when Jordan's squad dropped to 0–9 with a 28–0 loss to West Florence, "Knights Pound Tigers." It was Conway's fifth straight shutout. In four games that month, they'd been outscored 119–0. Still, for Tiger fans, the West Florence game did provide a glimpse of hope for the future, as Mickey threw for 172 yards on fifteen of twenty attempts. Speaking of his young QB's performance that night, Coach Jordan said, "The ole boy's been catching a lot of heat, and I thought he played a great game. That's the best game we've had at quarterback."

There were now two contests left in the regular season, an away game against Socastee and the home finale against Georgetown. After that, it would be on to the playoffs. As a Big 16 school, Conway was guaranteed a spot in the tournament, but as bad as they'd been getting pummeled—even by smaller schools, schools that hadn't beaten the Tigers in years—they had no shot of advancing, especially since their putrid record would place them on the bracket as a bottom seed, doomed to be dismantled in the first round by one of the top teams. We all love underdog stories, but against a powerhouse like Northwestern or Greenwood—the Muhammad Alis of the Big 16—Conway wasn't going to suddenly morph into Leon Spinks and pull off the upset. No, in the playoffs the Tigers would be more like a rawboned peanut vendor plucked from the upper deck and dropped into the ring for the inevitable annihilation.

So if Coach Jordan's guys were to have any chance of getting a win in 1989, it would have to be against either Socastee or Georgetown. The good news was that the Braves and the Bulldogs were both about as bad as the Tigers were. Going into their game against Conway, Socastee was 1–8. By the time they faced Conway, Georgetown was 1–9, and their only win had come against Socastee. Despite having not scored a point in over a month, Jordan's guys went into the last two regular season games optimistic that they could pull off a shocker.

On the first Friday in November, the 0–9 Tigers lined up against the 1–8 Braves. And the Tigers played well. The Conway defense kept the Socastee offense out of the end zone, and they held the Braves to minus 7 yards passing. The Tiger offense had a comparatively good game, too, with Mickey

Wilson throwing for 138 yards and completing fifteen of twenty-two passes. Conway was forced to punt only three times all night, suggesting that, yes, Mickey and his offensive unit had been able to build on the slow but steady progress they'd made over the previous four weeks. However—and it's a big *however*—Socastee blocked two of those three punts. And the Braves returned both of those blocks for touchdowns. Final score: Socastee 14, Conway 0. The Tigers were shut out for the sixth straight time, and they fell to 0–10 with one regular season game left to play, against Georgetown in the matchup that had been rescheduled because of Hugo. If they were going to post a win, this was their last realistic shot.

- 12 -

ADVERSITY

NOW

THE GOAL FOR MICKEY WILSON'S SEAHAWKS, THIS AND EVERY SEASON, IS TO survive four playoff rounds in November for the chance to play one game in December: the 3A state championship. The location of the title game alternates on a yearly basis between Clemson University and the University of South Carolina. This year's championships will be played at Clemson's Memorial Stadium, a venue best known for the hill that rises behind the east end zone, and for the rock—Howard's Rock, named for former coach Frank Howard—that sits atop that hill. Before every home game, the Clemson Tigers take the field by first touching the rock and then running down the hill, a ritual that Brent Musberger, the television play-by-play announcer, has called "the most exciting 25 seconds in college football." Reverence for such traditions might seem like a grand absurdity, but to anyone who cares about football in South Carolina, the hill up in Clemson is sacred ground. Even if you're a fan of Clemson's fiercest rival, the USC Gamecocks, you still recognize the hill's significance, though you may hate what it represents. Every high school player in the state wants a chance to play in Memorial Stadium, but you only earn that chance by winning your way into the championship game. Tonight, in the second round of the playoffs, Myrtle Beach's path to Clemson runs though Hanahan High School.

Ninety minutes before kickoff, as the visiting Seahawks file out of their two buses, the temperature is cool but pleasant. Windbreaker weather. But closer to kickoff, when the crowd starts to arrive at Wiley Knight Stadium, the temperature has dropped to the mid-40s, which for folks from the Low Country is downright cold. Behind the home bleachers stands a mythically large oak tree whose branches are draped with Spanish moss that hangs nearly to the ground. Seen from the visiting side, the tree, which is easily a hundred years old, suggests permanence and stability. But it's the Seahawks who come into tonight's game with tradition, history, and six state championships on their side. Like Myrtle Beach, the Hanahan Hawks hold a record this season of 10–1, but not all 10–1 records are created equal. This is Hanahan's first year at the 3A level, having moved up this season after twenty-eight years in class 2A. And they fattened their record with a bunch of early wins over 2A schools. They even played a 1A team. Myrtle Beach, on the other hand, has beaten five 4A teams this year. Four of those five play in Conway's region, so even though the Seahawks finished second in their own 3A region (because they lost to Socastee), they are essentially the champions of the 4A division that Conway belongs to (because they are 4–0 against teams from that region).

Bottom line: Tonight feels like a sure win for Myrtle Beach.

And why wouldn't it be? The Seahawks are rolling. They closed out the regular season by destroying rival North Myrtle Beach 55–0. Last week, in the opening round of the playoffs, they pounded Manning 43–14. Mickey Wilson's team hasn't lost since the Socastee game in week seven. So here at Hanahan, road game or not, the Seahawks are the heavy favorite—so heavy, in fact, that the players are already looking ahead to the next two rounds of the playoffs. Coaches may preach the importance of never overlooking an opponent, but tonight, the Myrtle Beach players can't stop talking about how badly they want a rematch with Socastee. It just so happens that if both teams keep winning, the brackets will bring the Seahawks and the Braves together in the 3A semi-final game—also known as the Lower State Final— the matchup that determines which school from the southern half of the state will play the Upper State Final winner for the title in Clemson.

As they run through pre-game warmups, the Seahawks are teeming with confidence. They're the better team, from the better region, with the stronger schedule and the more illustrious history. And if that weren't enough to put an extra bounce in the Seahawks' steps, tonight Myrtle Beach will have Chocolate Wilson back on the field. After sitting out the entire regular season while recovering from knee surgery, the highly recruited senior DB finally got medical clearance to play last week, but in that game he wasn't exactly tested by a Manning offense that had trouble passing the ball. Still, he showed he could backpedal and make cuts, and his return has everyone believing the Seahawks have a legitimate shot at another title run. Chocolate is a kid who charms you into believing the hype. When asked if he feels good about tonight's game, he flashes a smile and says, "Yes, sir. We should take this one no problem. These guys were in 2A last year." Then he shoots a playful wink. Good-looking and instantly likeable, Chocolate is as sweet as his nickname, and it's easy to imagine he came by the moniker more for his smooth manner than for his skin color.

Soon after kickoff, Myrtle Beach scores on a touchdown pass from Tyler to C.J., and it looks like Chocolate's confidence is warranted. But then the offense sinks into a funk. The Seahawks don't score again in the first half, and at the break they trail 14–7. Instead of filing into the locker room, the coaches lead the players on a short walk to Hanahan's baseball field.

Mickey quiets his team with a raised hand. "Okay. Hats off," he says. He pauses to get everyone's attention, his eyes moving from one player to the next. "They're better than I thought they were," he finally says. "You're in a dog fight." He doesn't tell them the score is zero-zero, and he doesn't remind them that they have trained harder than every other team in the state. Instead, he says, "You look like a boxer that got popped once and got stunned." The good news, he stresses to his guys, is that if they listen to their coaches and play hard, they'll be able to get up off the mat. "This is fun," he says. "I want you to go have fun out there."

But he doesn't smile, and none of the Seahawks behave like this is play-time. As Bruce Springsteen's "Glory Days" blares over the stadium P.A., the words sound a warning to the Myrtle Beach squad, a powerhouse team that has earned its confidence but lost its paranoia: *Glory days, well, they'll pass you by*, sings Bruce, *in the wink of a young girl's eye.*

The players break into their position groups, and with his defensive backs gathered in a meeting along the first base line, assistant coach Reggie Alston rants about coverage mistakes in the first half. "C'mon," he tells them. "This is a freakin' 2A team!" In that circle stands Chocolate, who nods vigorously in agreement with the coach and slaps his teammates on the back as if to say *we got this.* The Seahawks are too good to lose this early in the playoffs. No way are they going home yet. Not this year. Not this team. Not with seniors like Sean Michael Orcutt and Octavius Thomas. Not with Tyler and C.J. out there hooking up for touchdowns. When the second half goes the way it's supposed to, nobody will remember that Myrtle Beach trailed by a touchdown while "Glory Days" served as a soundtrack.

On the second play of the second half, Hanahan's Anthony Smalls chucks a bomb in Chocolate's direction. The pass is underthrown, a wobbly flyer from a quarterback who doesn't have enough arm to hit a receiver who has outrun the coverage. It's the kind of ball a big-time recruit like Chocolate should eat for dessert, but he's rusty, he's out of position, and nobody's backing him up on the play. The ball lands in the receiver's hands. Chocolate lunges desperately to make a touchdown-saving tackle, but he falls just short, and suddenly the Seahawks are down 21–7. Minutes later they give up another score, and the board reads 27–7. In order for Myrtle Beach to advance to the next round, they'll need their biggest comeback of the year.

The teams trade quick TDs to make it 34–14, and with time running out on the third quarter, the deficit remains 20. On their next possession, the Seahawks find themselves facing fourth and 13 from their own 17-yard line. Clearly a punting down. But desperate times, desperate measures. Mickey decides to go for it—knowing that if his team fails, they'll give Hanahan the ball within easy striking distance, close enough to put the game out of reach. In the stands, heads turn to the scoreboard as if to ask, *On fourth and thirteen? In his own territory? In the third quarter?* On the sideline, somebody asks a TV reporter, "Is Mickey really going for it here?" and the reporter shrugs as if to say *I'm just as stumped as you are.* Even for a coach whose offensive philosophy is attack-attack-attack, this call looks more like prayer than strategy.

But it works.

Tyler connects with fellow senior Ray Ray Pointer for a first down, energizing the Seahawks and the Myrtle Beach fans who have travelled a hundred miles to be here on this cold night. Suddenly, the offense has caught fire. A few plays later, a touchdown brings the score to 34–20. And then, early in the fourth quarter, another Seahawk TD makes it 34–26. Blocked extra-point kicks after each of these scores have kept the tally from being a more manageable 34–28, but 8 points down in the fourth quarter is still a winnable game. A touchdown and a two-point conversion would give Myrtle Beach its comeback. One more touchdown. Just one more.

That touchdown never comes. With the clock counting down on their season—and for Tyler, C.J., Chocolate, and all the other Myrtle Beach seniors, their high school *careers*—the players on the sideline look toward the scoreboard and let out sighs of exasperation. Fog rises from their mouths and dissipates into a pitch-black sky. One kid drops to all fours and begins pounding the ground with his fists. Another grabs him from behind by the collar and screams, "Get up! Get your ass up!" Losing is bad enough; loserlike behavior is worse.

After a dazed walk through the handshake lineup, the Seahawks mope back to the baseball field that served as their halftime locker room. Now secluded behind the outfield fence, their barely suppressed sniffles escalate to open sobs. Some fall to their knees; some look up as if to ask God Himself how he could have allowed this to happen. A tearful Chocolate Wilson embraces one of his assistant coaches and says, "I just love this team so much." Tyler wipes his eyes and waves his teammates away. He's not ready to talk to anyone just yet. Offensive coordinator Wes Streater surveys the crying players and says, "This is hard. This is so hard."

After giving the kids a few minutes to compose themselves, Mickey pulls them together. "I can't tell you how proud I am of you," he says. "Seniors, I can't say enough about your character. All you guys are champions. Don't let anybody tell you different."

The Seahawks have finished the season 10–2. They spent much of the year at the top of the state rankings. But they didn't win their region, and they didn't make it up to Clemson. It will take some time before they feel anything but shocked, disappointed, or angry.

Mickey raises his hand for silence. "I know this stings, guys," he says, "but this will pass. One day, you'll be my age—40 with a couple kids at home—and you'll look back and say, 'I never loved anything as much as I did high school football.'" He pauses for the briefest of moments, and in that pause, he must be thinking back to his own playing days, to his own teammates and the adversity they handled together. "You guys will love each other," he says, "for the rest of your lives."

After a few more minutes to let the tears subside, the team boards the buses for the ride back to the beach. The only thing left to do this season is the tedious task of collecting the players' equipment. Of course, that same gear will be handed back out soon enough, because football season never really ends; it just takes a short timeout.

Before the playoffs can begin for Chuck Jordan's current Tigers, they've got one more piece of perfunctory business to take care of: getting past the anemic Carolina Forest Panthers. It's the first Friday in November, and here in Big Cat Stadium the night sky is clear and a light wind blows the cleansing smell of loblolly pines across the Carolina Forest High School campus. The pine smell seems to bring with it the promise of a fresh start for Conway. Mykal, Malcolm, Sawyer, and the rest of the Tigers have fought through 10 games in a season that has to this point been underwhelming: a 5–5 record, a bitter loss to Myrtle Beach, a slow-healing thigh bruise that has left Moody limping. But despite all that, they somehow find themselves on the verge of a region championship. A Conway win combined with a South Florence loss will net the Tigers the Region VI title and ensure them a high seed in the playoffs and the favorable first-round matchup that comes with it. And then, if they can finally sustain a little momentum, who knows? As Chuck Jordan has said this week, "We're a good 5–5 team. In the playoffs we're gonna get somebody that's gonna look over at us and expect to see a patsy."

But first, the game tonight against the 1–9 Panthers. Jordan's challenge is to convince his players not to see a patsy when they look over at the

Carolina Forest sideline. The coach knows the contest won't be a cakewalk. Mykal—who this week was named a finalist for South Carolina's Mr. Football award, which recognizes the top player in the state—won't be able to play because he's still hobbled by that thigh bruise. And second-stringer Ethan Smith has the broken collarbone, so he's wearing street clothes. The Tigers are down to QB number three, Sawyer Jordan. Ol' Sawdawg got it done last week in the big come-from-behind win against Sumter, but it's no easy trick replacing a Mr. Football finalist, and last week's comeback, exciting as it was, doesn't guarantee anything against the Panthers. "These guys want to win the game more than you do," Jordan has been telling his team this week in practice. "This will make their season." He's been trying to get his players to understand that a victory tonight will make *Conway*'s season. Win and they could be champions. Lose and they'll limp into the playoffs with a 5–6 record and a perilously low tournament seeding.

Come kickoff time, it's obvious that the Tiger fans appreciate the stakes. Attendance at the Backyard may have been light this season, but here at Big Cat Stadium, there are at least as many spectators dressed in green and gold as there are wearing the Carolina Forest black and cardinal. The Conway Tiger Pride Marching Band is in especially spirited form, too, running through "Tiger Rag" with a little more breath in the horns and pop on the drums. The Tiger football team, however, starts the game sluggishly. Headed into the second quarter, the teams are mired in a scoreless tie, and on the sideline, Mykal, despite a visible limp, is pacing like an expectant father in a maternity ward hallway. He's all nervous energy—with nowhere to put it.

"Is it killing you not to be out there?" a reporter asks him.

"*Killing* me," he says, and he walks back toward the bench, where he's just as impotent as the ball boy, the drum major, or the reporter whose question he just answered.

With 9:44 to play before halftime, Carolina Forest takes a 7–0 lead on a 20-yard pass play to tight end Ryan Yurachek. That score and a subsequent Panther fumble seem to snap the Tigers from their funk, and a few minutes later, Sawyer has the offense rolling on a drive that results in a touchdown run by Jaquail Crosland, the back who rushed for 185 yards last week. The game is tied at 7–7. Then, with just over a minute left in the second quarter, Sawyer connects on a swing pass to Malcolm, who bobs and weaves down to the 1-yard line. First and goal Tigers. If Conway can score here—and they have four plays in which to do it—they'll have seized the momentum heading into the half. Coach Jordan sends in the versatile Crosland to take the direct snap out of the wildcat formation—but the running back fumbles the ball. The Panthers recover. Momentum lost. As the teams head into the lockers, the game remains tied.

Chuck Jordan has two sons: Cannon, the older of the two, and Sawyer, the younger. Cannon and Sawyer: weapon and tradesman. And tonight, in this grind of a game, Sawyer is playing up to his workmanlike name. He's quarterbacking, punting, and returning punts. When Crosland comes in to run the wildcat, Sawyer lines up at receiver. But guts and hard work don't always add up to points on the board, and through most of the third quarter, the game stays locked at 7. Then with five minutes left in the third, the Panthers score to go up 14–7. As in the first half, the fact of falling behind to a prohibitive underdog seems to have quickened Tiger blood. After intercepting a Carolina Forest pass, Conway ties the game at 14 on a 5-yard run by Crosland. With the score tied, however, the Tigers again lose their sense of urgency, and they find it nearly impossible to move the ball. Conway came into tonight averaging 35 points per game. Carolina Forest averages a mere 18. The Tigers and Panthers are like the hare and the tortoise—but in this case the hare only kicks it into gear when he's looking at the tortoise's backside.

With the clock winding down on the fourth quarter, the teams are still tied at 14. But then, perhaps sensing that time is running out on their season, the Tigers finally come alive. Sawyer goes back to work, leading Conway on what has the feel of a winning drive. With a minute left, the third-stringer has brought his team to the Panther thirty, and on the sideline, Mykal pumps his fist in Sawyer's direction, as if the Mr. Football finalist can shake some game-saving magic from his hands and pump it across the field to his understudy. Sawyer takes the shotgun snap and tosses toward tight end Kahmil Cooper, but the ball floats just enough to give the Panther defense time to close the gap on the Tiger tight end. Sawyer's pass is intercepted. The game will be decided in overtime. Meanwhile, sixty miles inland, West Florence has beaten South Florence 33–10. If Conway can find a way to win, they'll be region champs.

Under the alternating possession overtime system, both teams will have a chance to play offense. If one team has broken the tie after the first round, the game is over; if not, the game moves to a second round of offensive possessions. The Panthers get the ball first, and quickly find the end zone on a quarterback keeper to go up 21–14. The Tigers once again find themselves losing, and once again, being behind seems to ignite them. With yet another Jaquail Crosland rushing TD, his third of the game, Conway ties the score at 21. In the second overtime, the Tigers start with the ball and go with the hot hand, Crosland, who on third and goal appears to be slipping toward the end zone. But the hole collapses, and he's taken down at the 3-yard line. Conway is forced to kick a field goal, a 20-yarder that sails though the uprights, and now the Tigers are sitting on their first lead of the night, 24–21. If Chuck Jordan's defense can hold the Panthers scoreless on this possession, it's game over.

But it hasn't been that kind of season for Conway. All year, it seems, crucial defensive stops have been as rare as rubies. And sure enough, on second and goal from the nine, Panther QB Will Brunson finds Kyle Belack in the back of the end zone. Belack makes a highlight-reel catch, gets one foot in bounds, and the Panthers beat the Tigers for the second time in school history. The Region VI championship goes to West Florence. At 5–6 on the year and 2–2 in the region, Conway ends the regular season in a three-way tie for second place. While the Panthers celebrate in the end zone, the Tigers walk off the field in humiliation, their butts thoroughly cut.

When the playoff brackets are released the next day, the implications of the loss to Carolina Forest become brutally clear. Had they completed the once seemingly assured task of beating the Panthers, the Tigers would have entered the postseason as a fourth seed, hosting a home game against an eleventh-seed team. Instead, Conway is seeded sixteenth in a sixteen-team tournament, forced to play on the road against the defending state champion Goose Creek Gators, who are riding a twenty-five-game winning streak and are the top-ranked 4A team in South Carolina and #11 nationally. "Part of the key in a 4A playoff schedule is getting good matchups early," Jordan says, knowing that his team has drawn the toughest matchup possible.

To make matters worse for the Tigers, it looks doubtful that Mykal Moody's thigh bruise will have healed enough by Friday to allow him to play. And Jordan would much rather sit his star quarterback than risk further injury that could jeopardize Mykal's college career. "He could have played [against Carolina Forest]," the coach tells the *Sun News*, "but I'm never going to compromise a kid for a football game." All week, Jordan insists that Moody's status is day-to-day, but come Friday night, the coach makes the safe, long-term decision. In what could be his final game as a Conway Tiger, Mykal will watch from the bench.

Sawyer gets the start, and it quickly turns into a game both Jordans would just as soon forget. Goose Creek jumps out to a 27–0 lead and cruises to a 48–7 win. The Gators amass 450 yards rushing, with four separate players going over 100. In the fourth quarter, Goose Creek rests their starters, emptying the bench to give the second and third stringers a chance to see playoff action. Sawyer throws three interceptions and spends much of the game dusting himself off after being sacked. The Gator defense gives him such a beating that during the post-game handshakes, Goose Creek coach Chuck Reedy tells Chuck Jordan, "Coach, your son's the toughest kid I've ever seen." Jordan will later compare Sawyer's outing against Goose Creek to the night in 1989 when Mickey Wilson was so pummeled by Middleton that he had to be carried off the field by Lawrence Mitchell.

It's a two-hour drive up the coast back to Conway, and the buses pull into the high school at about midnight. Everybody's tired and disappointed, but there's one final task to complete. Coach Jordan and his staff collect the players' jerseys and pants and get the sweaty uniforms into the wash. On Monday afternoon, the players and coaches gather for one last time so that the kids can turn in the helmets, pads, and other gear—the final, semi-ceremonial indication that for Team 89 the season is over.

Except it's not.

The next day, Tuesday, the pendulum of this back-and-forth year comes swinging back toward the good (or at least the bizarre) when South Carolina High School League Associate Commissioner Dru Nix announces that Goose Creek has been disqualified from the playoffs for using an ineligible player in the win over Conway. Jordan's squad will be awarded a 1–0 victory by virtue of forfeit, and the Tigers, despite the 48–7 punishing the Gators gave them, will move on to play the Bluffton Bobcats on Friday night. A spokeswoman for the Berkeley County School District, the district that contains Goose Creek High, says that the school self-reported to the SCHSL a student transcript error which revealed a violation of league guidelines. The district has appealed the decision, and league officials have agreed to consider the appeal in a hearing scheduled for the following day.

For Chuck Jordan, a victory that takes place around a conference table instead of on a football field is a hollow one, especially given how thoroughly the Gators dominated his team. So when Jerome Singleton, the commissioner of the SCHSL, calls the coach to let him know that Conway is back in the playoffs, Jordan says, "Jerome, we don't deserve to be there. You need to leave Goose Creek in there."

"They don't have a choice," the commissioner says. "You're in, and you can either forfeit or play."

Jordan has been around long enough to know what a competitive playoff team looks like, and his team, as the Goose Creek loss made clear, isn't one. Still, if the powers on high are going to give his guys another shot, he's going to take it. "We'll play," he tells the commissioner. And that Tuesday after-noon, one day after collecting the gear, Chuck Jordan and his staff call the team together to pass the helmets and pads right back out. For the Tigers, it's the ultimate Hail Mary play, a later-than-last-second comeback. Or as Jordan says, "It's like one of those Christmas presents under the tree that you're not sure whose it is. But you *hope* it's yours."

At the hearing the following day, the SCHSL denies Goose Creek's appeal. The league also denies a request from the school district for reinstatement under the league's "mercy rule," in which the school essentially says, *Okay, we blew it. We admit it. Now please go easy on us.* The two denials seem to make it official: Goose Creek is out, Conway is in. The specific nature of the viola-tion isn't disclosed to the public, other than to indicate that against Conway the Gators played a kid that shouldn't have been allowed on the field because he had already used up his four years of eligibility. Although the student's name is never released, word soon gets out that the ineligible player wasn't a starter, and he certainly hadn't given Goose Creek a competitive advantage. In fact, he was a bench-warmer, a "special needs" student who only got into the game for a few downs during the fourth quarter, long after the result had been decided, and only then because Coach Reedy wanted to give the kid a chance to play, even if it was just for a minute or two.

"I'm good friends with Chuck Reedy and I hate it for him," Jordan says on the afternoon before the Goose Creek appeal is denied. "They're a good football team, and I would like to see them defend their state title." Still, Jordan is not going to deny his seniors one more chance to put on the green and gold, and besides, the verdict is out of his hands. "With that door open for us, we're going to walk through it," he says. "We want to make the most of it." And on Friday night, when the Tigers walk through that door, it's looking more and more possible that Mykal will be healthy enough to walk with them. "He's not 100 percent, but his 75 percent is better than a lot of people," Jordan says of Moody. "We anticipate that he will [play]." The back-from-the-brink Tigers spend Wednesday and Thursday practicing for an away game against the 11–1 Bluffton Bobcats.

After learning about Goose Creek's suspension, Jordan may have initially felt like Chuck Reedy's Gators were much more deserving of a chance to keep playing than he and his Tigers were. But Jordan's an almost patho-logically optimistic football coach, one who always expects to win, so after preparing for two days, his attitude changes; his competitive nature kicks in. No longer is he thinking that this Tiger team isn't playoff worthy. Now he's looking at Bluffton on film, thinking, *we're gone get these guys.*

Meanwhile, ninety miles to the south, the Berkeley County School District files an injunction with the Ninth District Circuit Court of South Carolina, asking for a temporary restraining order that would allow Goose Creek to move forward in the playoffs until the SCHSL can hold open hearings on the issue. Attorneys for the school district argue that they need more time to present their argument for the team's reinstatement, which boils down to the claim that the ineligible player—who had only seen the field on seventeen downs all year—isn't ineligible, because, as a "special needs" student, he should be subject to federal disability rules that would grant him an extra season of playing time. The case is complicated, which is exactly the school district's point. They need more time to sort it out, and since, according to the SCHSL constitution, the state playoffs can't be paused or delayed, the district's lawyers are asking the circuit court judge to allow the Gators to play on Friday until a new hearing can take place the following week. Judge Roger Young indicates that he'll render a decision on Friday, and for the second time in Chuck Jordan's coaching career, the end of a Conway Tiger football season is linked to action that will be taking place not on the gridiron, but in a courtroom.

On Friday morning, the Tigers arrive at school fully anticipating that shortly after lunch they'll be boarding the buses for the four-hour trip south to Bluffton. But they also understand that the judge is expected to issue a ruling at any time, a ruling that might end their season once and for all. In the halls of Conway High and all over Horry and Berkeley counties, folks are staring at their smartphones, trying to get the latest news by following the Twitter feed of a Charleston *Post and Courier* reporter. By noon, there's still no announcement. Jordan knows that in order to make it to Bluffton in time for warmups and kickoff, the team has to leave by 1:30, but the last thing he wants is to set out on the road, get the bad news, and then have to turn the buses around, so he's prepared to push the departure to the last possible minute.

It doesn't come to that. At about 12:30, just before Jordan's assistants start loading gear onto the buses, Judge Young announces his decision: He has granted the restraining order. Goose Creek will host Bluffton tonight.

Down in Bluffton, the Bobcats, who thought they'd be playing a home game against the Tigers, now scramble to prepare for the bus ride to Goose Creek. The judge's ruling states that the SCHSL must reconvene to review the case by 5:00 p.m. on Monday. By that time, Goose Creek will have beaten Bluffton 35–25. In the Monday hearing, the SCHSL league will again rule against Goose Creek, meaning that Bluffton, despite their loss, will move on in the playoffs to play Northwestern, the team that blew out Conway 55–19 in the second game of the season.

Here in Conway, upon hearing the news of the restraining order, Chuck Jordan is torn. He's disappointed that his guys won't get to play tonight, but also knows that they didn't really earn the chance in the first place. Now, for the second time in a week, he and his coaches are forced to collect the pads and equipment. But Jordan doesn't send his players home just yet. They showed up that morning expecting to play a game, so the coach is going to let them play one. After leaving the field house, instead of walking back toward the parking lot, Jordan leads his guys into the stadium, down the hill, and onto the field. Nobody's wearing pads or helmets; those have been stowed until May, when spring practice for Team 90 will start. But in their Tiger jerseys and athletic shorts, Mykal, Malcolm, Sawyer, and the rest of the seniors take the field one last time. The coaches roll out a couple of balls, and the kids arrange themselves into groups and start playing. It's a seven-on-seven game, just like the "passing league" scrimmages played in June and July. No contact, no referees. No score, even. There's no crowd. No cheerleaders. No band. No Bojangles truck.

This isn't the bright lights of the 4A state playoffs; this is backyard football.

THEN

Ever since Chuck Jordan came home to Conway, November had been a month when lunch-counter conversations centered on playoff football and the Tigers' chances for that long-awaited first state championship. But in November of '89, the biggest contest in town was set to happen in a courtroom. On the first Friday of the month, a few hours before the Tigers would lose to Socastee 14–0 on two blocked punts, the school district announced that the board would finally hold a hearing to decide if H. H. Singleton should be fired—as Superintendent Dawsey had recommended back in August. Singleton's attorney, Armand Derfner, had filed a temporary restraining order to delay the hearing until after Singleton's suit against the district was settled in federal court, but by the end of business that Friday, the federal magistrate had not granted the order, so come Monday, the hearing would go forward.

On Monday morning, in a room normally used for traffic court, the board opened four days of testimony relating to Singleton's suspension. If the members voted to uphold Dawsey's recommendation, the earth science teacher, who had been on paid leave since the beginning of the semester, would be fired. A crowd of about seventy supporters on both sides of the issue filled every seat in the courtroom, with many members of the black community wearing NAACP: FIRED UP AND READY TO GO T-shirts. Unable to find open seats, more people stood outside in the hallway, and board chairman Henry Marlowe ordered that the doors be propped open so those standing in the halls could hear. The proceedings would run like a court trial, with each side making statements, providing evidence, and calling witnesses to testify. The school board would act as the jury.

On the first day, two witnesses took the stand, Conway High principal Tommy Lewis and Chuck Jordan, whose testimony lasted for most of that day's session. The coach described a team that had been ravaged by an unnecessary boycott that Reverend Singleton—not the players themselves—had instigated and sustained. As evidence, Jordan mentioned that Lawrence Mitchell had once told him, "I don't know if the Rev's going to let us go or not." And he related what Carlos Hunt had told him months earlier: "But coach, you've got to understand, the NAACP can't come out of this looking bad." Singleton was the man whose job was on the line, but Jordan's credibility and reputation were unofficially at stake as well, so he spent the good part of four hours justifying his original decision to move Carlos to defense. The Tigers may have gone 8–4 the previous season with Hunt at QB, he said, but they could have won more if Carlos had had a better attitude. The 1988 team had been a serious contender for the state title, but they lost in the first round of the playoffs, and according to Jordan, Carlos was partially to blame. The coach described Hunt as a problem player—the kind of guy who would work hard one day, but sulk and whine all through the next practice. Worse, he said, Carlos had a problem following orders and would often change plays at the line of scrimmage. The coach admitted that Carlos had scored a touchdown on one such audible, but he also cited two other freelance decisions by his ex-quarterback that had failed—and had possibly even caused the Tigers to lose.

Jordan testified about the harassing phone calls and death threats he'd been receiving. He'd had to get his phone tapped, he said, and his home was under police surveillance. He mentioned that his players had been intimidated at school, and he spoke about Conway High students who had suddenly stopped looking him in the eye or even responding when he addressed them. He lamented the fact that junior varsity football had been eliminated because he'd needed to move players from that team up to the varsity level. He spoke of his disgust when the boycotters had shown up en masse at the first game and cheered for the opposition. And he said that one of his biggest disappointments was that seniors like Lawrence Mitchell had missed their final opportunity to impress college scouts. Even non-striking seniors had paid a price, he said, giving an example of a place kicker who had had very few opportunities to kick field goals because the Tiger offense so rarely got into scoring position. Asked by school district attorney Bruce Davis if the boycott had affected the team, Jordan replied, "Well, we're 0 and 10. You read between the lines. We ain't worth a crap."

After Jordan was excused, Derfner, Singleton's attorney, reminded the board that although the coach's testimony was "powerful and poignant," the football boycott was not on trial. Neither was the plight of the team. This proceeding was about Singleton's job and his right to free speech. Derfner's point is both clear and compelling. On the stand, Jordan had delivered a detailed narrative of a team and a coach that were struggling through a painful season, but as moving as the story was, how was it relevant to the question of Singleton's employment? Singleton had been suspended for causing a "disruption to the educational process," a disruption so severe it had allegedly prevented him from being an effective teacher. He hadn't been suspended for crippling the football team or for being a thorn in the coach's side. Still, Bruce Davis and the school district clearly wanted to prove that Singleton had done and been both. In coercing the players to boycott and in accusing Coach Jordan of racist behavior, Davis argued, Singleton had caused a wave of havoc that had surged from the football field to the class-room, one that warranted termination of his employment.

On Tuesday, in an effort to determine if Singleton had indeed been re-sponsible for the boycott, the board subpoenaed Lawrence Mitchell. The Monday after the Middleton game, Lawrence had followed the wishes of his grandmother and gone back on strike, but by now, ten games into the sea-son, he'd become very vocal about how much he regretted leaving the team. In the week before the subpoena was issued, Mitchell gave two interviews to the *Sun News* in which he said that striking for the entire season wasn't his choice. "I wish now that I'd played football," he told the paper. "I think everybody involved in the [boycott] wishes they'd played." He admitted that he didn't think anything good had come out of the strike, and he stressed that Chuck Jordan was a good person who had never wronged him. "To me," Lawrence said, "the boycott is over. I just want to play ball." With only one game left in the football season, playing ball meant suiting up for the Conway High basketball team, which had begun practice the week before. The head coach of the basketball team, of course, was Mickey Wilson Sr. "We're delighted to have Lawrence with us," Wilson said. "He's a leader, a team player, a hard worker."

Lawrence was at basketball practice when he was served the subpoena, and he came directly from the gym to the courtroom, still wearing his shorts and basketball shoes. On the stand, when he was asked if he had told reporters that he regretted the strike and wished he had played his senior season, he replied yes, he had said those things. Then board member Frankie Blanton posed the important question to Lawrence: Were you advised to boycott the football team by Reverend Singleton?

In the courtroom, Armand Derfner was holding his breath—not because he thought that his client had coerced the players into boycotting but because he was worried that if even one witness *said* that Singleton had convinced the kids to boycott, then his case would collapse. Singleton would be fired. And Derfner was certain that the conservative federal judges who would later hear the case on appeal would agree: If Singleton had encouraged students to boycott, then he had abused his position as a teacher and the firing would be justified—free speech or no free speech.

Now, by answering Blanton's question, Lawrence Mitchell might provide the testimony that swung the case either way. "It weren't Reverend Singleton," Lawrence said. "It was just the players, just people in the church. They decided on, you know, what they was going to do."

"That's the question we want to get answered," Blanton said.

Asked that same question today, Lawrence says Singleton played a bigger role in launching the boycott than the player claimed when he answered Blanton's question in 1989. Maybe back then, Lawrence wasn't comfortable naming Singleton as an instigator—not on the stand, not in that crowded room. Maybe his recollections have shifted in the years since the walkout. Or maybe Reverend Singleton simply floated the boycott as one possible option among many. Maybe the idea wasn't Singleton's at all. Regardless, during the hearing, Lawrence was unwilling to cite Singleton as the disruptive force.

To demonstrate that the earth science teacher had interfered with the educational process, Bruce Davis called Gil Stefanides, the principal at Conway Middle, to testify about the sixty-one parents who had requested that their children not be compelled to take Singleton's class. He spoke of an increase in disciplinary problems at the school, and he related the story of a black mother who had told him that her son had been misbehaving "because he had been going to those nightly meetings at Cherry Hill Baptist Church, [where] they are told to question everything that happens at school." Principal Lewis painted a similar picture of daily life in his hallways.

But even if Singleton had been a catalyst for these sorts of problems, wasn't he, in his role as NAACP chapter president and spokesman for the striking players, protected by the principles of free speech, so long as his protests didn't take up school time or use school resources? Wouldn't his advice to the players be just as protected as if he had led an after-school political meeting? Principal Stefanides testified that on two occasions, boycotting players had come to Conway Middle to speak with Singleton, thus disturbing him during work time. However, when six of the parents who had asked that their kids be pulled from Singleton's classes spoke before the board, none of them had any specific complaints about his behavior in the classroom.

Much of the disruption at Conway Middle School, of course, could be blamed on the parents who were complaining about Singleton. Or on the upheaval caused by the suspension itself. After all, Superintendent Dawsey admitted at the hearing that he knew "all hell was going to break loose" if he suspended Singleton, but he said, "I decided I was willing to bear any burden or pay any price to see that this man did not teach any children in Horry County." On the third day of the hearing, while being cross-examined by Derfner, Dawsey added to his *bear any burden, pay any price* assertion this clarification: ". . . if it meant giving my life to do that, that was a commitment I made, sir." Asked today if he would change anything about how he handled the Singleton suspension, Dawsey steadfastly says no and insists that the record shows he was "a good superintendent after all."

Davis argued that Singleton's accusations of racism against Coach Jordan had made it "impossible for [Singleton] to function effectively as a teacher" and that "[t]hey could not have school at Conway as long as Rev. Singleton was present there." In retrospect at least, this argument seems fairly exaggerated. It's dubious that Singleton's presence had made it "impossible" to operate the school. And even if, as Principal Stefanides stated, Conway Middle did suffer more behavioral problems than normal that fall, the fact is Singleton had been suspended during the first week of the semester. How could his presence be blamed for the increase in disciplinary issues if he wasn't even there?

At the press conference announcing the boycott, Singleton had given no indication that the players were planning to cut classes or misbehave or violate the school's dress code or in any way disrupt the school day itself. So whatever Singleton's role in initiating the strike, the result was a group of kids who'd merely decided to stop playing football, nothing more or less. Conway High enrolled approximately 1,900 students in 1989. If half of those were boys, that would put the male student population at around 950. A varsity football team suits up fifty to sixty players, meaning there were about 900 Conway boys that fall who also were not playing football. The thirty or so black players who walked off the team were making a choice that the vast majority of their peers had already made. And how can choosing not to play a sport be considered a disruption to the learning environment?

Coaches often remind their players that being a member of a school-sponsored team is a privilege, not a right. No one is entitled to a spot on the roster, much less required to play. This view of athletics as an earned honor is central to Jordan's insistence that coaches must have autonomy in deciding who plays and where they play. A teacher, by contrast, doesn't get nearly the same autonomy. Jordan couldn't refuse a student a seat in his algebra classroom on the grounds that he or she wasn't particularly gifted at math or had a less-than-ideal attitude toward the subject. The student has a right to be in that class, and the teacher has a legal and professional obligation to provide everyone an equal opportunity to learn. But coaches aren't required to give everyone an equal chance to play sports. Some kids are superior athletes, and those are the ones coaches put on the field.

Without stating it openly, Jordan and his supporters had drawn a clear line of distinction between the school's responsibility to and relationship with students participating in the classroom versus on the playing field. After all, Jordan hadn't gone to the principal and asked that Carlos Hunt be suspended from school for not repaying the ring loan; Principal Lewis would have laughed him out of the office for doing so. But it had seemed perfectly within his rights as the athletic director to suspend Carlos from the basketball team. The distinction between the right to an education and the privilege of playing sports is sacrosanct, as it should be.

But if we agree on this separation between academics and athletics, it seems untenable to assert that a challenge to the leadership of the athletic program could represent a disruption to the educational environment—or at least a disruption so severe that it that would make education "impossible." Claiming that Singleton had forfeited his role as an educator by involving himself in the boycott makes no more logical sense than claiming a teacher had unfairly disrupted the athletic program by failing a student in a class, thus rendering him or her academically ineligible for sports. In his roles as teacher, coach, and athletic director, Jordan had no doubt seen the athlete-becomes-academically-ineligible scenario play out any number of times, and he would have been expected to uphold the integrity of the educational program at the expense of the athletic program because, as coaches often tell their players, academics comes first. This hierarchy between athletics and academics is so well understood and universally accepted that violating the primacy of academics is considered one of the most dishonorable things a coach can do.

That said, it could be that in Conway in 1989, Tiger football was held so sacred that messing with the team was, in fact, a disruption to the learning environment. Perhaps beyond the question of whether Singleton constituted a disruptive force in the school, the board members were actually ruling on whether the town should tolerate a man who had challenged and potentially altered a hallowed component of the local culture.

Whatever the "real" reasons for suspending Singleton—and it seems likely that there were multiple motivations for doing so—the school district surely knew it was in for a fight on First Amendment grounds. As bedrock as football is to a small Southern town like Conway, the right of free speech is even more fundamental, and most Americans would accept this premise, at least in theory. But in practice, supporting free speech gets trickier for many people when the speech runs counter to the predominant values of the culture in which it takes place. During John Dawsey's testimony, the superintendent said that in his opinion, if a man "is drawing his salary from you and works for you, he owes to you some loyalty." *Loyalty* is the same word that Jordan used months before, in the meeting with H. H. and Hank Singleton, when he was discussing Carlos Hunt's unwillingness to go along with the position switch. In that meeting Jordan insisted that loyalty meant accepting "the decisions the bossman makes [even if it] isn't always the best decision in the world." Dawsey seems to have been insisting that the earth science teacher was at minimum guilty of disloyal speech, which is to say speech that ran counter to the values of the school system (i.e., the bossman). But disloyal speech is still protected speech, and in his closing statements, Armand Derfner argued that "The speech that needs protection the most is the speech we hate to hear the most."

Bruce Davis conceded that employees do have the right to speak against their bosses, but he insisted, "The Constitution and free speech don't protect the right to lie." This point hinged on whether Singleton had been sincere in his belief that Jordan's decision to move Carlos Hunt had been racially motivated. Davis claimed that at the press conference announcing the boycott, when Singleton alleged that Coach Jordan had made a racist decision in moving Carlos from quarterback to defensive back, the reverend had spoken with a "loathing for the truth." Singleton's allegation against Jordan had been, in Davis's words, "so lacking in responsibility and judgment and honesty as to reflect a clear unfitness for teaching."

Of course, *racism* and *racist* are words that are slippery and difficult to define, so it would be nearly impossible to prove that Singleton had said something untrue at the press conference. Instead, Davis tried to show that Singleton himself didn't believe that Jordan was a racist. Therefore, accusing

Jordan of racism wouldn't just be baseless, it would be a lie of conscience and a lie in actuality. And since teachers are supposed to be beacons of truth, liars can't be effective teachers. Ergo, the suspension was justified and Singleton should be fired.

To prove his point, Davis played the tape Jordan had made of his meeting with H. H. and Hank Singleton during which the reverend repeatedly said that he wasn't calling Jordan a racist. Davis argued that this audio recording was proof that Singleton didn't believe Jordan was a racist; therefore, if Singleton attributed racial motivations to the coach's decision, then that would be a lie. Armand Derfner countered that there is a difference between saying "You are *not* a racist" and "I'm not *calling* you a racist," a hair-splittingly clever rebuttal, especially considering that Singleton, as a minister and teacher, made his living primarily by talking. Crafting arguments and defining terms were two of the key skills in both of his professions.

Board chairman Marlowe said he chose the small traffic court space because he wanted to limit the chances of a disruption, but with nearly three months of conflict now reaching a climax and people on opposing sides seated so closely together, tensions were bound to boil over. Chuck Jordan managed his stress level by chewing tobacco while listening to testimony, but others weren't as successful at reining in their emotions. Recent Conway graduate Jeff Sherman, who is black, cussed on the stand as he was being questioned by Bruce Davis, and he offered a none-too-playful shadow-boxing swipe toward Davis's shoulder on his way back to his seat. Carlos Hunt's mother shook her head so vigorously during Jordan's testimony that Davis paused in his questioning to ask her to stop the "terribly distracting" gestures. Later, after changing seats to get out of Davis's line of sight, she rose to her feet and called out to Jordan, "You sitting there lying," which forced Marlowe to bang his gavel and ask for order in the courtroom. All during the week of testimony, people on opposite sides of the issue mumbled insults until finally, after hearing a few too many stage-whispered jabs, Marlowe warned the crowd "We will not tolerate harassment" and threatened to have anyone who disrupted the proceedings removed.

Jordan says that during one break in the proceedings, he opened the door to the restroom to find Cleveland Fladger standing at a urinal. Jordan walked up to the next urinal and stood beside his former coach, a man he had once sweated and bled for but who was now lined up on the opposing side. "You know this isn't right," Jordan said.

"I know," Fladger said, according to Jordan. The older man zipped and flushed. "But we're gonna get you anyway."

Despite the tension, no actual violence broke out and no one was arrested. Like two school kids taunting each other but never throwing a punch, both sides seemed to realize they had a lot to lose if they ever went beyond posturing and name calling. One reason for the relative restraint probably rested in the fact that the white majority possessed almost all the power in Conway. Whites held sway in the city government, in the school system, and in that packed courtroom, where an all-white school board would be deciding Singleton's fate. To continue the schoolyard analogy, everyone knows that somebody is going to get blamed for any altercation that causes people to gather round and yell "Fight! Fight!" Even if no punches are thrown, somebody is going to be punished, and this somebody will serve as the example for others who might be foolish enough to attempt the same thing. Would H. H. Singleton be that somebody?

No matter how the school board ruled, the case was likely far from over, because Singleton's suit was still pending in federal court. Even if Singleton for some reason decided to drop his suit, Fred Sumpter, a Human Affairs Commission board member, vowed to seek an official probe into the Horry County School District's actions against the earth science teacher. "If they do [fire Singleton]," he said, "Human Affairs will be back." Which meant, of course, that Jim Clyburn would be back. Sumpter was aware that many members of the black community had felt betrayed by Clyburn for finding no evidence of racism in the football matter, and he defended the commissioner by drawing a line of distinction—as Clyburn himself had—between Jordan's decision to move Carlos Hunt and Dawsey's decision to suspend Singleton. "I was satisfied with Clyburn's findings in the Conway case," Sumpter said, by which he meant the Conway *football* case. Anyone from the black community accusing Clyburn of being a tool of the establishment had it all wrong, according to Sumpter, because "Jim is no Uncle Tom."

The last day of testimony, Friday, was devoted primarily to parents of striking players, all of whom defended Singleton and maintained that he had merely counseled the kids and served as their spokesman. Harvey Dixon, father of Terrance Dixon, said the players had approached the minister for guidance because he was the only person they knew to turn to. Whites, he said, have any number of community leaders, but for blacks in Conway, Singleton was pretty much the one and only. "If I had a problem," said Dixon, "that's who I'd go to." Other parents testifying on Singleton's behalf spoke of the meeting at Cherry Hill during which the vote to boycott was taken. That meeting, they said, was mostly spent asking the players questions, and at no time did Singleton advise them to quit the team, much less coerce them.

On that final day of the hearing, Reverend Covel Moore, a retired Horry County biology teacher, made the point that racism is a problem that transcends the school system and the football team. "We seem to have institutionalized racism here," he said, "and it hasn't just started." Armand Derfner, in his closing statement, echoed this sentiment that Singleton had not, as some in the white community were suggesting, caused an increase in tension between whites and blacks. All he had done was bring to light what already existed. "To say that the boycott or Reverend Singleton created a racial division," Derfner argued, "is a little bit like saying a thermometer created a fever."

At 5:15 p.m. on that Friday, the school board began their deliberations. The board was legally entitled to ten days to rule on the matter, but with member Dorothy "Charlie" Chandler scheduled for surgery on the following Monday, it appeared likely they would render a decision that evening or the following afternoon. Their two choices sat in stark contrast. Side with Superintendent Dawsey and Singleton would be fired, a move that would certainly lead to a battle in federal court on First Amendment issues. Go against the superintendent's recommendation, and not only would Singleton be back in the classroom, but the boycott and the larger Conway Movement would get something like an official endorsement from the very power center the protesters were challenging.

After two and a half hours of deliberations that afternoon, the board failed to reach a decision. The members decided to suspend talks for the night and reconvene the following afternoon. They walked out of their chambers at 7:45 p.m., plenty of time to drive to the Graveyard and catch most of the last home football game of the year, against Georgetown, the contest that had been postponed because of Hurricane Hugo.

TOTAL AND COMPLETE VICTORY

THEN

"ALL RIGHT, BOYS," CHUCK JORDAN SAID FOR THE LAST TIME THAT 1989 season, "the lights are on."

The Conway buses rolled by the Jiffy Shop, and there they were, the lights, glowing high over the Graveyard in the November night. Nearly three months had passed since the first trip the Tigers had made from the high school to the stadium. During that time, so much had changed—and so little. Back in early August, this had been a squad with a whole season to look forward to, a team ranked #3 in the state, a full roster of kids, black and white, all with championship dreams. Even after the boycott began, essentially dashing those dreams, there was still an almost palpable electricity on the night of that first game, a buzz that had been generated by uncertainty about what might happen on and off the field. Would a last-minute miracle end the strike? If not, could the white kids pull off a win against a lousy Hillcrest team? How would the protest play out in the stands? Would a sneering remark spark a melee?

On that night—the night when these buses had stopped at the red light in front of Cherry Hill Baptist, where the boycotting black players lined up to watch their white teammates parade past—police were everywhere. Reporters were everywhere. Spectators were sardined into the bleachers. Tonight, however, as the Tigers walked off the buses and began warming up for the last game of the regular season, nobody was paying much attention—at least not compared to that first game. No extra cops. No throng of reporters. A light crowd in the stands. The buzz was long gone. There was still a football game to be played, of course. And there was still a mass meeting happening at Cherry Hill. Reverend Singleton was still suspended; Carlos, Lawrence, and the others were still on strike; and the black community was still fired up and ready to go. But on this final Friday night at the Graveyard, uncertainty had been replaced by an inescapable truth: The boycott had turned a championship-caliber team into a squad of hapless losers.

Still, the football gods and Mother Nature—in the form of a Category 4 hurricane—had conspired to make tonight's contest a fair fight, the hapless against the hapless. The Georgetown Bulldogs, despite being led by former Buffalo Bills and Denver Broncos coach Lou Saban, had racked up only one win on the year. They averaged a meager 7.5 points per game. Chuck Jordan's team hadn't scored a point since September, having been shut out for six straight weeks. And in their last outing they'd lost 14–0 on those two blocked punts that were returned for touchdowns. Ten games into the season, the depleted Tigers couldn't even kick the dang ball away without fear of the line collapsing, an opposing player busting through and getting a hand on the punt, and one of his teammates scooping up the ball and taking it in the opposite direction. Punting is supposed to be the prudent option, the triumph of safe over sorry. But for the Tigers, the punt play had become a high-wire act.

With just over a minute left in the first quarter and his Tigers backed up in their own territory, Chuck Jordan took a deep breath and sent in punter Russell Johnson and the rest of the kicking team. And sure enough, a Georgetown player, Germaine Manning, slipped into the backfield and swatted Johnson's punt to the turf. Manning's teammate Aaron Cobb recovered the ball in the end zone, and after missing the extra point, the Bulldogs took an early 6–0 lead. Up in the stands, Tiger fans could only shake their heads at the futility. If there was a more humiliating way to surrender a touchdown than via a blocked punt, the football gods had yet to invent it.

The score remained 6–0 thorough most of the second quarter, and then, with under three minutes until halftime, Coach Saban sent in the Bulldog punt team. Say one thing for the football gods: They must have a sense of humor, if not justice, because suddenly it was a Conway player, Briggs Dickerson, who found a clear path to the punter. Dickerson reached out and blocked the kick, which defensive back Michael Timbes picked up and returned 24 yards for a Tiger touchdown. "I just looked down," Timbes says now, "and the ball happened to be right there." Chuck Jordan's squad had finally caught a break. Conway fans looked up at the scoreboard and saw a number other than zero for the first time since the Bell Game, back when "Hugo" might still have referred to the author of *Les Misérables* and *The Hunchback of Notre Dame*. Tiger kicker Tim Waldron came in to boot the extra point, and hot damn, for the first time all season, Jordan's boys were winning.

Conway's 7–6 lead held through the third quarter and halfway through the fourth. Then, with just 6:50 of game time standing between the Tigers and their first victory, they faced a fourth down from their own 27. If there ever was a punting down, this was it, and Jordan again sent in Russell Johnson and the kicking team. It's easy to imagine that along the sidelines and in the stands, folks were crossing their fingers and sending silent prayers up to the heavens. The Tigers were back on the high wire, this time with the game on the line.

Johnson signaled for the snap, and the ball came in low, too low to field cleanly. Faced with no other option, he simply fell on it. The refs blew their whistles and waived the play dead. Georgetown ball. The good news for the Tigers was that the punt hadn't been blocked. The bad news was that the Bulldogs were now taking over at the Conway 17-yard line. But Michael Timbes and the rest of the Tiger defense stiffened. After three downs, the Bulldogs had not only failed to advance the ball, they'd lost a yard, sliding back to the 18. So on fourth down, with just over five minutes left in the game, they lined up for a 35-yard field goal. If the ball sailed through the uprights, Conway would almost surely finish the year 0–11. If it missed, the Tigers would likely win. And winning a game—even if it was the only game that season, even if it came against a school that had also won only once—would be a well-deserved reward for players who'd stuck together even as the team and the town cracked apart.

The two sides lined up. The snap, the hold, the kick. The ball sailed toward the goalposts, but it fell short and to the right. Conway held on to win 7–6.

Tiger fans stormed the field, joining the players and coaches in celebration in the end zone. With everything the Conway team had endured that season, it would be hard to blame them for feeling that they were entitled to this moment. That the good guys had finally merited an achievement worthy of the character they'd shown. That it was destiny.

"It was worth the whole kit and caboodle," Mickey Wilson told reporters. As the season had ground on, they'd already ceased to be simply a group of guys who wore Tiger uniforms; they'd become a team. Now they were more than that. Now, at last, they were a *winning* team.

"We finally whipped somebody," Jordan said, smiling. "I feel about as good right now as I have in quite a while." He was as proud of his guys as he'd been at any time in his career. "This win means as much to our kids and our community [as] any game we've ever played."

Robert Anderson would later write in the *Horry Independent* that the win "was all it took to wipe away a season of anguish," that it made "everything right with the world, if only for one night." Sports fans want so desperately to believe that what happens on the field has a larger meaning, that it has the power to "make everything right." This search for meaning might be why so many people will toss the front page of the paper with a grunt of disgust but spend half an hour devouring the sports section. Day after day, the hard news confirms our suspicions that the world is in constant, unfixable turmoil. Finding meaning on the front page may be next to impossible—finding the type of meaning that feels right and just, anyway—but every now and then, the sports section delivers. The kid whose mom died of cancer goes on to win a championship in her honor. The small-town underdogs triumph over the big-city bullies. The boycott-addled squad finally gets a win. Never mind that the zero-sum arithmetic of sports means that, year after year, the number of winners is exactly equal to the number of losers. Never mind that with thousands of teams playing all the time, some team is bound to have a miracle win nearly every day. Never mind that in every game both teams have essentially the same motivations and the same cosmic right to a victory. These kinds of stories feel good because they make so much emotional sense, if not rational sense. They satisfy a deep human need to find order within chaos.

As the victory celebration continued on the field at the Graveyard, the Tiger players, coaches, and fans were treated with one brief chance to feel that everything in Conway was back to normal. For a few minutes, they could forget the boycott, the losses, the hurricane, the Singleton case, and the fact the race relations remained as strained as ever. As Michael Timbes, the player that scored the winning touchdown, says now, "It felt like old times."

To everybody who'd stormed the field, it wouldn't matter one whit that a week later, the sixteenth-seeded Tigers would be drilled 42–3 in the first round of the playoffs by the top-seeded Spring Valley Vikings, bringing Conway's 1989 season to a fittingly inglorious end. The real end to the season, the one that everybody associated with the team remembers, happened right there in the end zone, where Jim Kester, a man from Columbia who'd been following the story of the '89 Tigers in the newspaper, was passing out bumper stickers that he'd spent $300 of his own money to print up. They read CHUCK JORDAN—COACH OF THE YEAR.

A group of Conway players lifted their coach onto their shoulders, and they carried him from the end zone out toward the midfield stripe. The crowd erupted in cheers. But Jordan felt uneasy about so much adulation being focused on him; he'd always thought it was more appropriate to deflect the praise toward the kids. *They* had won the game. So he quickly slipped down off the shoulder pads and back onto the field, where he sought out one of those kids, running back Cleveland Sanders, a black player who'd

stuck with the team, a so-called Zebra. At that moment, Sanders also happened to be looking for Jordan. "Coach," Sanders said, smiling like a kid on
Christmas, "we finally got one."

"Yeah, we did," Jordan said. "You did great."

"No," Sanders said. "*We* did great."

The coach put his arm around the player and together they walked off
the field in victory.

With the win against Georgetown, it felt like old times on the football field.
From the black community's point of view, it felt like old times off the field,
too. And that was the trouble. Prejudice and intolerance were rampant, just
as they'd always been. The white establishment seemed to be ignoring black
concerns, just as it always had. But there was hope, faint as it was, that the
school board would nudge Conway into *new* times by voting to reinstate
H. H. Singleton to his teaching post. Given that the prevailing sentiments
of the black and white communities were in direct opposition, the board
members found themselves in a pickle. As reporter Rebecca James put it
in the *Sun News*, if the board upheld Dawsey's recommendation to fire the
earth science teacher, "many [would] be upset and outraged. If the board
reinstate[d] him, many [would] be upset and outraged." Board member
Richard Jordan (no relation to Coach Jordan) admitted that the Singleton
case had put him in "the most difficult position I have ever been in, in my
life." A few days later he added, "I don't see any winners in this case. It's a
pure lose situation."

Rev. Singleton sure didn't see the situation as pure-lose, though. He and
his supporters absolutely stood to score a win—but it would be a victory
many in the white community weren't prepared to accept. Some whites, despite their insistence that they were not opposed to Singleton because of his
race, still had trouble turning a blind eye to how Singleton *looked.* Cindy
Dexter, a white Conway Middle School parent, admitted, "Mr. Singleton
scares me to look at him. He's a big man, and my daughter's small. He looks
like he might be mean." Others indicated that they would move their children to a private school if the earth science teacher were reinstated—even if
their kids were not enrolled in Singleton's class. A white parent named Larry
Causey predicted that if Singleton was allowed to return to the classroom,
"it would take more police officers than they have in Conway" to handle the
angry crowd of white protestors.

On the Saturday after the Georgetown game, the school board returned
to the district offices to resume deliberations. Whichever way the board voted, some members of the black community felt that the hearings themselves

had been worthwhile, because they had provided an occasion for whites to be told—in some cases for the first time—what conditions in Conway looked like from the black perspective. "I think it was a total surprise to the white community that blacks are standing up," Rev. Covel Moore said. And at least one school board member, Frankie Blanton, conceded that he'd "learned a great deal that [he] didn't know existed."

After meeting for three hours—and with eighty black community members lining the halls, waiting for the verdict—chairman Henry Marlowe emerged and announced that the board had again failed to reach a decision. He said the members would reconvene at a later date, and although South Carolina law required them to render a verdict within ten days of the conclusion of the hearings, Marlowe gave no indication of when he and his colleagues might take up the issue again. Singleton's supporters walked outside and arranged themselves in a circle, where they sang "We Shall Overcome." Then Rev. Jerry Faulk led them in prayer. "As we wait," Faulk said, "we ask that you, oh God, look upon the hearts of these board members."

The following Thursday, Marlowe announced that the board would resume deliberations on Saturday—the same day that the NAACP would be staging a march though Myrtle Beach, the third major protest since the birth of the Conway Movement but the first to extend beyond the city limits. "Preach at the Beach," the NAACP was calling the rally, and from their standpoint, the board's decision to meet on the afternoon when a thousand or more of Singleton's supporters would be marching seemed suspicious at best. "I don't want to speculate on why the school board decided to reconvene on the day of the march," Nelson Rivers said, "but they have to realize that there are more than one or two black people in Horry County. We will have someone there."

The march would begin at noon and run right through the touristic heart of South Carolina. An hour later and fifteen miles inland, the board meeting would commence, and this time, rather than gathering at the school district offices, the members had agreed to convene at Conway High School. Whether or not the location change was a symbolic gesture—and what the new location indicated about how the vote might go—was anybody's guess.

At noon that Saturday, 1,200 marchers took to the Myrtle Beach streets. With H. H. Singleton leading the way—flanked by the director of the South Carolina State Law Enforcement Division and at least thirteen more officers and state troopers—the protestors paraded east on 21st Avenue, straight toward the ocean and the resort hotels that lined it. The Conway Movement may have begun in an effort to counter perceived injustice on the football field and in the school system, but William Gibson asserted that "since we have been in the area, we have noticed other inadequacies." He pointed to the limited role of blacks in management positions in Myrtle Beach's crucial hospitality industry. "Blacks," he said, "are seen mostly as maids, janitors, and maintenance workers."

Myrtle Beach Chamber of Commerce chairman Grant Kuhn responded by arguing that the NAACP's claims about a lack of minorities in management were overblown, and he cited as evidence his own hotel, where half of the supervisors were black. "The [business] community might not be taking a proactive stance," he said, "but they are not neglecting it." Horry County blacks, however, had begun to see "not taking a proactive stance" on racial equality and "neglecting it" as two sides of the same coin.

Wearing a black T-shirt that read PREACH AT THE BEACH 1989, Singleton led the protestors in spirited chants of "Do the right thing!" and "Fired up! Ready to go!" The fact that the reverend was marching meant that he wouldn't be at Conway High to hear the results of the vote, but nothing he could say to the board now would make a difference anyway. He could do more good here on the coast, walking in solidarity with his supporters, than he could at the school, sitting passively while the board did whatever they were going to do. Joining Singleton at the front of the pack were Nelson Rivers, William Gibson, and, for the first time, Benjamin Hooks, the executive director of the NAACP, who told those assembled, "If I'm ashamed of anything, I'm ashamed it took me so long to get here. If they can get Rev. Singleton, they can get me and you."

As the procession made its way down Ocean Boulevard, through a canyon of high-rise resorts, 1,200 voices reverberated off the hotel walls. On the upper floors of those hotel towers, high above the street, black maids gathered on balconies, where they waved to the passing congregation. They were dressed in their housekeeping uniforms, carrying cleaning products and bath towels. When Singleton cried out, the maids answered back, towels hurricaning over their heads. "Fired up!" they shouted down to the marchers. "Ready to go!"

Meanwhile, at Conway High, the Horry County School Board had gathered in executive session. Two hours later, they adjourned the private meeting and reassembled in the school's mini-auditorium, in front of a crowd of about forty. The board had now deliberated in closed sessions for a total of nearly eight hours, so the members likely knew what their decision would be. Before the official vote took place, however, Republican Richard Heath offered a motion that would reinstate Singleton to the school system, but not allow him back in the classroom. It failed by a 5–2 margin, with only Heath and fellow Republican James Dunn in favor. And with that motion defeated, it now seemed clear that the board had decided to fire the earth science teacher. In a last-ditch attempt to save Singleton's job—or, given the near certainty of the result of the vote, a desire to add a note of commentary to the official record—Heath argued that his fellow members should reinstate Singleton because his suspension hadn't stemmed from his behavior in the classroom or for violating any specific policy. Besides, Heath noted, the case was ultimately going to be adjudicated in U.S. District Court, and "How do you think any court in the land will decide," he asked his colleagues, "when confronted with a question of a black man in Conway, SC, speaking out about a black football boycott for racial reasons?"

The vote came up 5–1 in favor of firing Singleton. When the result was final, it was met, according to the *Horry Independent*, "with a thin-lipped silence by the largely black crowd." Heath represented the lone dissenting vote. James Dunn abstained, as he had promised he would, because he felt that Superintendent Dawsey and attorney Bruce Davis had prejudiced the board against Singleton in an earlier session.

Five votes to one. Nelson Rivers called it a "declaration of war."

When Preach at the Beach broke up at 3:00 p.m., many of the marchers hoped to make it back to Conway so they could be present at the school when the vote was taken, but by the time they crossed the Waccamaw River, the meeting was over and the decision had been announced. So they headed for Cherry Hill Baptist, and by 4:00 p.m. more than a hundred people were sitting in the pews.

H. H. Singleton was obviously disappointed by the board's action, but he was confident that he'd win his civil suit against the school district. "I'm glad that this board does not have the final decision," he said, "and I'm looking forward to our day in court."

But that day in court was still many months away, and even Singleton's confidence couldn't suppress the outrage that was evident in Cherry Hill Baptist that afternoon. "I suspect," Rivers said, "that some people will have to work overtime to calm the tension and anger that's going to be experienced in the black community."

That anger jelled into an immediate response from Horry County blacks. On the Monday following the vote, over 1,000 black community members (including many black teachers who were now openly concerned about their own job security) gathered at Cherry Hill, where they voted to remove their children from school in protest of Singleton's firing. Over the next two days, in schools throughout Horry County, hundreds of black kids were signed out of classes by their parents. Many of the protesting students spent that Tuesday and Wednesday—the two days before Thanksgiving—at the church, in a study hall of sorts. They worked on homework while their parents drafted a letter petitioning the school system not to rehire Superintendent Dawsey when his contract came up for renewal in a few weeks. Singleton had been fired for disrupting the educational process, but ironically, even Conway High School principal Tommy Lewis admitted that the current protest—parents pulling their kids from school—was the first significant disturbance of the fall semester. "It's disruptive," he said, "when you have to interrupt the teacher three or four times to pick up a student."

Over the holiday weekend, the NAACP held yet another March Against Intimidation in Conway, and at the end of that two-mile walk that again boasted over 1,000 protestors, Singleton announced that the black parents had voted to send their children back to school on Monday. The kids did return to classes after Thanksgiving break, but with their attendance came a new protest, a "lunch-out," during which students brought meals from home rather than buying food from school cafeterias. As with the previous week's planned absences, the lunch-out was orchestrated specifically to send a message—an economic one this time—to Superintendent Dawsey and the school board. "Whites pressured the superintendent and he responded," Singleton said, referring to the Conway Middle School parents who had complained to Dawsey back on the first day of school. "Now black parents are showing their own with displeasure with him."

In the days after the vote to fire Singleton, some of the board members publicly defended their decisions. Richard Jordan indicated that many of the issues in the case were too complicated to work through on his own, and he admitted that he had relied on Dawsey and Bruce Davis for assurances that the school system had followed federal and state law in suspending Singleton. As for the issue of free speech, he said, "I don't know whether it was protected speech or not. I know the school board attorney and John Dawsey say it wasn't, and even if it was, the disturbance in the school system would outweigh the benefits of the protection of freedom of speech." Why putting an end to the supposed disturbance was more important than protecting free speech, Jordan didn't explain. Taking a view similar to Jordan's, board member Dorothy Chandler said, "I just think the overwhelming factor to me was the damage done to the students." She didn't explain, though, how the alleged damage amounted to anything that could be described as "overwhelming" or why it was a more important concern than Singleton's

Constitutionally guaranteed rights. Board member Terry Hucks suggested there were elements to the case that the general public didn't know. He didn't offer specifics, but he did say, "You don't know until you see the whole story." After four days of detailed public testimony and over two months of newspaper and television coverage, what exactly did people outside the board not know? What hidden facts could have informed the board's decision?

During the week before Thanksgiving, after learning about the student walkout in response to Singleton's firing, Hucks expressed what had been a standard opinion among local whites during the boycott season. "I don't agree with parents using their children as pawns in a game," he said, "and that's what they tend to be doing is using their children for political reasons, and I totally and adamantly oppose that." This view holds that Singleton and the black community had unfairly "used" a group of "children" who ultimately paid too large a price for whatever point had been made by the boycott. In fact, if you ask many members of Conway's white community today, they'll say that the walkout *didn't* succeed in making a point, that it was a theatrical exercise staged for the sole purpose of feeding one man's ego. They'll tell you that in drawing attention to himself, Singleton sacrificed the best interests of the players and caused a lot of needless agitation. But even if this view of the activist and minister as a self-serving troublemaker is correct, the explanations for his firing don't hold up to logic, common sense, or the perspective afforded by two decades' worth of hindsight. After the school board had made its decision, the question for the U.S. District Court to adjudicate was: Did the firing hold up to the letter of the law?

Not: *Is H. H. Singleton an advocate or an agitator?*

Not: *Is Carlos Hunt a victim or a whiner?*

Not: *Is Coach Jordan fair-minded or is he prejudiced?*

Not: *Was the football boycott justified?*

But simply: *Was Singleton legally fired?*

As individual board members defended their ruling, others, black and white, were quick to condemn it. James Clyburn—whom Singleton, Fladger, and Gibson argued had betrayed his own people by finding in his report that Chuck Jordan's decision to move Carlos was not based on racist motives—criticized the vote as "unwise, untimely, and legally tenuous." He admitted for the first time that he saw Dawsey's original decision to suspend Singleton "the same way." The commissioner clearly felt that Singleton had a good chance of winning his civil case against the school system, and he argued that in the interim, the board would have been smart to enact Richard

Heath's proposal of allowing Singleton to stay in a non-classroom job. "I thought the board owed it to the community down there," Clyburn said, "even if they thought their legal position was correct."

On the Tuesday after Singleton was fired, the *Sun News* ran an editorial that strongly opposed the decision, calling it "the wrong message at the wrong time to the wrong people." In the column, the paper's editorial board detailed three reasons for why the verdict was unsound. The first was the Constitutional argument. "The message the board sends to teachers and other school employees," the writers claimed, "has a chilling effect on their free speech, their free expression and their free assembly." The second was a matter of image. "The picture that emerges of Horry County is that of pre-integration, Old South times." The third was that the decision was an "affront to the black community." Blacks, the writers argued, "have a perspective that has been ignored by the board's vote, further alienating [them] and fueling their beliefs that the white community is dedicated to crush[ing] black resistance." The editorial ended by framing the impending legal battle in terms as clear-cut as H. H. Singleton himself might have, as a contrast between old thinking and free speech, between the actions taken by the school system and the rights guaranteed in the Constitution. The federal courts, the paper said, "will determine whether the board or the First Amendment should prevail."

As folks flipped their calendars to the last month of 1989, things went back to something like normal at Conway High. The Tiger basketball team, led by Lawrence Mitchell and Mickey Wilson, jumped out to a 3–0 record by winning the North-South Basketball Classic, a tournament in which Lawrence was named the MVP. A few days later, Lawrence shocked the college football recruiting world by declining scholarships from powerhouse programs and instead electing to attend the University of South Carolina, where he hoped to play football and basketball. Mickey Wilson, despite his turbulent year behind center, was one of four Tigers named to the Class 4A, All-Region V team, as selected by the head coaches of the schools in the conference. Mickey finished the year having completed 79 of 171 passes for 821 yards, and although those numbers may seem fairly pedestrian and not quite up to all-star snuff, Chuck Jordan defended his quarterback against charges that he might have received the sympathy vote from opposing coaches. "These kind of statistics are great for someone on a 1–11 team," Jordan said. "He's probably the best leader I've ever had at quarterback."

Carlos Hunt, who in his junior season had been an ace shooting guard, did not join Lawrence and Mickey on the basketball court that winter. He'd been suspended from the team—but not for anything to do with the football boycott. According to coach Mickey Wilson Sr., Carlos had been dismissed for not participating in the required preseason workouts. Interestingly, neither H. H. Singleton nor the NAACP had accused Wilson Sr., the father of the point guard, of acting unfairly toward Carlos in levying the suspension. Maybe this was because Carlos no longer wanted to play basketball anyway, or maybe, with a courtroom battle on the horizon and countywide issues of inequity to address, the Conway Movement was now focusing on concerns that were more consequential than whether or not one kid suited up for a high school squad. The original controversy of Carlos's position switch had led to greater awareness, William Gibson said, of a range of inequalities between the races in Horry County. He compared the football boycott to a "runny nose on patient who has a major virus and possibly pneumonia."

Now that he was officially fired, Singleton was suddenly without a source of steady income. Before, when he'd been merely suspended, he'd been drawing his teacher's salary, but upon the board's decision, those paychecks stopped coming. The silver lining was that while his advocacy on behalf of the players had cost Singleton his job, it had also made him a much-in-demand public speaker, and NAACP branches statewide began hiring him for paid engagements. The football strike and the school board decision were over, and the attendance boycott and lunch-out both only lasted a few days, but the activism on the part of Singleton, Rivers, Gibson, and the NAACP continued. Early in December, Conway voters rejected an issue that Singleton had worked to put on the ballot, one that would have mandated that city council members be elected by a system of single-member districts rather than by the existing, at-large system that had resulted in five of the six council members being white in a city that was forty percent black. After the measure was voted down, Singleton and the NAACP promised to sue the city of Conway unless single-member districting was put into place.

A week later, three hundred people, most of them black, filled the Conway High mini-auditorium to standing-room capacity, as they waited to hear if the Horry County school board would vote to extend Superintendent Dawsey's contract. Despite a petition signed by at least a thousand community members demanding that the superintendent not be reinstated, and despite a *Sun News* editorial that called for Dawsey to retire, the board voted 5–2 (the two dissenters were Heath and Dunn) to extend his contract for another two years. The crowd booed, and the auditorium was peppered with angry voices. Michael Dixon, a black parent in attendance, said, "The board needs to stop thinking of white parents as constituents and black parents as a pressure group." On the heels of Dawsey's extension, the NAACP announced a new strategy, "Black Dollar Days," wherein blacks would shop using only Susan B. Anthony coins and two-dollar bills so that merchants would get a tangible picture of just how economically substantive black Conwayites were.

Four months had passed since Carlos Hunt had approached H. H. Singleton with the story of the dog and the ring, sparking the boycott, the suspension, and the Conway Movement. In that time, Conway's black community had met and marched and made speeches and written letters and formed picket lines and held protest signs—and what had it amounted to? From the black perspective, the white establishment still couldn't (or wouldn't) hear their cries for justice and fairness. A few task forces and biracial committees had been formed, but how much stock could be placed in those gestures when Dawsey was still holding on to his job while Singleton was still fighting for his?

That December, the University of Houston's Andre Ware won the Heisman Trophy, becoming the first-ever black quarterback to do so and thus offering evidence that the conventional wisdom about black QBs was changing. But off the field, in Conway and elsewhere, the protests would continue. The fight would continue. It would have to—because despite the many assertions from whites that racism, though regrettable, was ancient history, as 1989 wound down Conway's black community got another cruel reminder of just how endemic bigotry remained in South Carolina, when the sheriff of Richland County—the county that includes Columbia, the capital—allegedly told a reporter for *The State* newspaper that the best way to handle crime at one local shopping mall was to "keep the niggers out."

The national NAACP would eventually shift its attention to other race-related incidents, and the early 1990s would be marked most notably by the Crown Heights riots and the Rodney King riots. Closer to Conway, the NAACP's South Carolina Conference would begin to galvanize around an effort to remove the Confederate flag from the statehouse, a protest that in 2000 resulted in the compromise of moving the flag from atop the dome of the Capitol to a Confederate monument that sat on the statehouse grounds.

But before all that would happen, Reverend Singleton would finally have his day in federal court.

School board member Richard Heath and others had predicted that Horry County Schools would lose the case in the courtroom. These predictions turned out to be correct. On April 1, 1991, almost two years after the spring drills in which Coach Jordan switched Carlos Hunt to defensive back, Federal Judge Clyde H. Hamilton issued a forty-five-page decision in favor of H. H. Singleton.

Hank Singleton remembers being home with his parents on the day they got the good news. The phone rang, and on the other end was Armand Derfner, his father's attorney. Reverend Singleton hung up and gave his wife a bear hug. Then he turned to Hank, and said with a sly grin and a long, pointed finger, "Rein*state*ment, boy."

The judge's decision boiled down to two arguments that, in retrospect, seem like obvious objections to Singleton's firing. First, the judge said, Singleton was not the person who had caused a disruption at Conway Middle School. The real disruption had been caused by the white parents who had demanded that their children be pulled from his classes. If they hadn't brought their concerns to Principal Stefanides, it's likely the school day would have gone ahead normally. Second, when he made the remarks that had allegedly disturbed the educational process, Singleton had been acting as the head of the Conway NAACP. As such, his speech was protected by the First Amendment and not subject to punishment by the school system.

Three months later, on July 12, the two parties in the lawsuit reached an agreement that put Singleton back in his teaching position at Conway Middle and awarded him $61,953—two years' worth of back pay plus interest—and $62,000 in legal fees and court costs. And while some members of the black community expressed disappointment that Singleton hadn't been awarded punitive damages, Hank Singleton points out that his father hadn't sued for punitive damages. H. H. Singleton didn't want an exorbitant civil settlement that would have drained the coffers of the school system. He wanted the salary he'd lost, and he wanted his job back.

In mid-August, the earth science teacher was preparing to return to the classroom, gathering his rocks and artifacts, tweaking his lesson plans. There were rumblings that a few white parents were planning to protest Singleton's reinstatement, and Conway Middle had received calls from parents who threatened to remove their children from the school, but there were no indications that the opening of the semester would be marked by significant disturbances. "In 1989, we were not prepared for the disruption," Principal Stefanides said. "We had not understood how polarized the community had become. We have all matured since then."

Two Saturdays before the first day of classes, the NAACP staged another march on that well-trodden route down Church Street, from Cherry Hill Baptist to the Horry County School District offices. But this wasn't a March Against Intimidation; this was a celebration. Two hundred people joined in the festivities, carrying placards and chanting "We did overcome!" and "H.H. will teach!" At the front of the procession, flanked by Nelson Rivers and William Gibson, walked H. H. Singleton. "The Lion of the Conway Movement," as Rivers would call him twenty-one years later at his Homegoing Ceremony, again wore a black and white NAACP T-shirt. This one wasn't printed with FIRED UP AND READY TO GO, however. Instead it read: TOTAL AND COMPLETE VICTORY! In a speech at the district offices, Singleton spelled out the totality and completeness of the win. "There is victory economically," he said. "There is victory legally. There is victory constitutionally with reference to legal and civil rights."

But even as they cheered and celebrated, Singleton and his supporters knew that this victory, despite its significance, wasn't really total or complete. In the drive for justice and equality, there would be many more causes to take up. There would be more conflict to endure. There would be more losses to overcome.

"We have crossed the river," Nelson Rivers told those assembled, "but we still have the ocean to go."

EPILOGUE

TWENTY-FIVE YEARS LATER, THE BOYCOTT REMAINS A SUBJECT THAT PEO-
ple in Conway often speak about in whispers. Local whites get especially
tongue-tied when the subject of 1989 comes up, presumably because they
don't want to risk sounding racist. They'll often tell you that they weren't
supporting a white kid over a black kid; they were supporting the coach's
prerogative to choose who plays where. H. H. Singleton, they'll say, thought
he was doing right, but he should have stuck with leading Cherry Hill Baptist and the NAACP instead of trying to run the football team. Similarly,
there are blacks in Conway who still don't much like Chuck Jordan. They
won't come right out and say he was racist, but they will say that he didn't
treat Carlos fairly, that he didn't give the kid a chance.

Lots of people, black and white, mostly just don't want to stir up all that
trouble again. *Let it die*, they'll say. *The past is the past.* But as long as there
are folks in town who still remember that year—and Conwayites tend to
stay close to home long after high school graduation—stories of the boycott
will endure.

When Coach Jordan talks about the '89 season, he says it helped him
achieve "a peace that surpasses understanding" and believes that he was able
to endure that year because God gave him a level of patience that "wasn't
natural." He'll sometimes repeat a story of an exchange that happened in the
early 1990s, a few years after the boycott. One afternoon, when the school
day was over, he looked out his office window toward the parking lot, and he
saw a black teenager standing next to her car. The hood was propped open
and she was staring down at the engine. Jordan walked outside and asked if
he could help. She said she couldn't get the car started.

"Hang on a minute," he said. And he pulled his truck around, and then
took out a set of jumper cables.

A little while later the girl turned her key, and the car started. "Thanks,"
she said, "Mister . . . sorry, what's your name?"

"Coach Jordan," he said.

Suddenly, according to the coach, she looked scared, like she'd seen a ghost.

"Is something wrong?" he asked her.

"I was brought up thinking you were the devil," she said.

As he tells the story, it's clear that he's still nursing wounds from '89. It's also clear that he doesn't want to linger in the past. He's driven on. He's had no choice. After all, there's always a new season to prepare for.

Hank Singleton admits that some black community members will still ask him, "Why'd you have to go and do Chuck Jordan like that?" But he says that he runs into many more people around the state, around the country even, who recall the boycott and the larger movement it sparked as "a magical time."

To the members of Conway's black community who were "grown folks" (to use Lawrence Mitchell's words) back in '89, the boycotting players were and remain heroic figures, boys who made tremendous individual sacrifices for the greater good. But the striking players themselves seem to almost universally regret the boycott—not just Lawrence Mitchell but every other player interviewed for this book. None of the players we spoke with thinks that Chuck Jordan had racist motivations for moving Carlos, and every one we spoke with states unequivocally that if he could do the '89 season all over, he would have played football. Every striking player we spoke with confirms that, to his knowledge, just about all the boycotters, even the ones we couldn't reach, feel the same way. And really, who can blame them for their regret? Yes, race relations are better now in Conway, in America, and on the nation's football fields than they were in 1989. These days, when the boycotting players—now in their early forties, of course—read the paper or tune in to the news, they no longer hear stories about whites-only swimming pools or restaurants. When they watch football, they see black quarterbacks all the time. But they also read about how schools are often essentially as segregated today as they were decades ago, even if that segregation is unofficial. And they hear the racist comments made by former NBA franchise owner Donald Sterling that echo those made by Jimmy "The Greek" and Al Campanis. And they see images of Trayvon Martin, the unarmed black teenager who was shot in Florida. And Michael Brown, who was shot by a police officer in Ferguson, Missouri. Surely they ask themselves: Was the boycott worth it? What has changed?

And what about Carlos Hunt, the player at the eye of the storm? How does he feel today? The answer to that question is not definitive because Carlos was unwilling to participate in this project. When we asked Lawrence Mitchell if he still stays in touch with Carlos (who we're told now works for a school system in Florida), Lawrence said, "Me and Carlos are always going to be friends. We've known each other for a long time, and we still talk, but, like I say, you know, I guess he just didn't make good decisions, man."

When asked if he thinks Carlos regrets the boycott, Lawrence said, "I know he do. Any kid, you know, who's playing sports all [his] life don't play [his] senior year, man, yes, he's regretting it. That's something that's going to stick to him to his grave, man. I mean, it's sticking to me. I'm still going through it."

When Lawrence Mitchell's name is mentioned today in Conway, folks inevitably have three responses, almost always in this order: 1. They'll tell you how great an athlete he was. 2. They'll tell you what a good guy he is. 3. They'll ask if he's staying out of trouble. The body language accompanying this last question is often a downcast glance and a slow shake of the head.

As an athlete, Lawrence is most often compared to two players: Lawrence Taylor (the NFL Hall of Famer) and Jadeveon Clowney (the former University of South Carolina defensive end who recently became a number one NFL draft pick). Like others who still call Lawrence the best athlete they've ever seen, Mickey Wilson talks wistfully about Mitchell's physical strength and athletic prowess. "I mean, this joker was huge," he says, laughing.

Mickey then relates a story he heard about one of Lawrence's first practices as a South Carolina Gamecock, a tale he originally heard from Chris Rumph, a recruiter from the University of Alabama who'd come to Myrtle Beach to scout Chocolate Wilson. After chatting for a while, Mickey and Rumph soon realized that they had both played with Lawrence, Mickey at Conway High and Rumph at USC.

"Oh my God. Do *I* know Lawrence *Mitchell*?'" Rumph said, before launching into an anecdote about Lawrence's jaw-dropping ability on the field. Mickey retells the story in a combination of his own words and Rumph's:

> *The very first full-contact practice that they had at the University of South Carolina with Lawrence . . . , they had a back by the name of . . . Brandon Bennett, I think, was his name. He was a good back, played in the NFL. And Lawrence was the outside linebacker. . . . They ran a toss sweep to the other side of the field, and they said Lawrence took off and ran Brandon Bennett down from [behind . . .], grabbed him by the back of the shoulder pads, they said, and went shoonk and just threw him out of bounds like he was a little rag doll. And they said the next day in the paper—and I think I've still got this somewhere—it said something like "Superman has arrived at USC."*

Lawrence ended up being academically ineligible his freshman season, so by the time he finally saw action on the field for the Gamecocks, the sophomore hadn't played in a live game since his junior year of high school. On the opening kickoff of his first game in two years, he tore cartilage in his left knee and the debilitating injury forced him to sit out the whole season. Chuck Jordan blames the injury partially on bad luck and partially on the boycott, which, the coach says, got Lawrence out of game shape and out of academic shape. From there, Lawrence's college career was plagued by physical, academic, and legal trouble, including a misdemeanor charge for credit card fraud after he and several other USC players allegedly used a credit card illegally to make a number of telephone calls.

Many folks in Conway remember Lawrence more for the fact that he never lived up to his Superman-like potential than for his role in the boycott, and they'll cite his struggles as one of the saddest parts of the whole 1989 story. "Unfortunately," says Mickey, "his road that he had to travel down was not a good one." And here Mickey seems to be speaking specifically about the road that steered Lawrence toward run-ins with the law.

"I check on that Reuben Long site sometimes," Chuck Jordan says, referring to the website that lists people who have been arrested and held at Horry County's J. Reuben Long Detention Center, "and I see Lawrence's name in there way too often." Indeed, a search for "Lawrence Mitchell" on the prison's webpage turns up two recent arrests for petty crimes.

When the authors of this book spoke with Lawrence on one occasion, he was working construction by day and tending bar at night. But a few days later, he'd apparently quit the bartending job after getting into an argument with his boss. A co-worker at the bar, a woman named Mary, told us, "Lawrence is such a nice guy. If you've got a problem with him, you've got to check yourself." She was obviously taking Lawrence's side in whatever argument he'd had with management. "Lawrence Mitchell is a man," she said. "You don't talk to him like he's a boy. He's a man."

Ask folks in Conway about Carlos Hunt, and people generally break into two camps. Whites remember him as a whiny kid who didn't understand what it meant to be part of a team. Among many blacks, though, he's a kind of folk hero—a brave teenager who showed maturity beyond his years by speaking truth to power. It'd be going too far to call him a messianic figure, but there are people in town who admire his self-sacrifice and think of him as leading the boycott not just to get his position back, but also out of a desire to improve playing conditions for every player who came after him.

• • •

Why do so many people still have such strong feelings about a conflict that ended with the main combatants in pretty much the same places as where they started—Singleton teaching, Jordan coaching, and Dawsey superintending? From a legal standpoint, the issues in *Singleton v. Horry County Schools* aren't all that noteworthy. It's certainly not one of those cases that every law student will be forced to grapple with if they want to appreciate the nuances of the First Amendment or understand the fine points of employment law. The federal courtroom "battle" that ultimately decided the case wasn't very dramatic in and of itself, either. Unlike a landmark verdict as in *Brown v. Board of Education*, the judge's decision has had no significant, lasting effect on how the courts or society now view race issues. And again, many of the players who boycotted will tell you now that the strike achieved little more than costing them a year on the field.

Why is it, then, that the events of '89 still resonate in Horry County and beyond? The answer can be expressed in one word: football. Had Carlos been a pitcher moved from the starting rotation to the outfield or a point guard moved to shooting guard on the hardwood, it's likely the public outcry would have been muted. Football—especially in the South—isn't just another sport that young people play. A football game is part tribal ceremony, part passage into manhood, and part battleground on which we decide which school or town is greater than another. In a very real sense, football is who we are, or at least who we want to be. Ask anybody why they wear a cap with a college logo on it or put a high school bumper sticker on their car, and if they answer honestly, most of them will say *because that's my team*, and they're probably not talking about the volleyball squad or the cross-country runners or what happens in the classroom.

Considering everything that football represents—and more specifically what the position of quarterback represents—the rapid escalation in '89 from a coach's decision to a racial movement isn't entirely surprising. Nor is the opposition to that movement. By questioning the coach who served as leader of the troops who put their very lives on the line to bring glory to the school and the town, Singleton and the boycotting players had challenged more than Chuck Jordan's authority. Their act of civil disobedience threatened many Conwayites at a much more personal level. When the boycotters refused to play the sacred game of football, they and their spokesman were seen not as thoughtful citizens of a free country who felt strongly enough to sacrifice for their cause. They were seen as disloyal—as traitors, even.

At the press conference announcing the boycott, Singleton enumerated the reasons for the players' decision, but to a lot of people in Conway, he might as well have said *defection*. He could just as easily have been announcing that the players were going AWOL, because to many Tiger fans, their decision to quit over a benched black quarterback was just as ridiculous and disloyal as if army troops had refused to storm Utah Beach on D-Day because General Eisenhower hadn't promoted enough Italians or Irish to officer positions. Sure, anybody can see that ethnic fairness is an important issue, but not more important than beating the Germans. Or the Seahawks. Make your political or social point in the off-season, *but not now, gotdangit! We got a game to play!*

If you haven't lived in a football-centric culture, you might reasonably question how the sport could ever attain such importance. But it can, and it does. For many people, football isn't just a significant part of who they are; it *is* who they are. Every football Friday night, in stadiums all over America, the bleachers are peppered with former high school players who, to one degree or another, define themselves by their ongoing relationship with the game. Some of these ex-players are now purely spectators, content to grab a dog and cheer for the local team, even if they grew up and went to school in a town hundreds of miles away. Some are alums, keeping tabs on the old alma mater, cutting checks to the booster club and memorizing stats from the box score. Some are fathers of current players, watching their sons live out the next generation's glory days. Regardless of their current stake in the game, the fact that these ex-players once blocked and tackled will always form a crucial part of their identities. The percentage of the identity that has sprung from the gridiron varies from man to man, of course. Some have compartmentalized their time on the team, filing it under *Something Fun I Used to Do*. Some have brought the lessons and dictums from their playing days forward and have incorporated them into their adult worldview ("Forget It and Drive On," "Handle Adversity"). And some seem unable to let go of their playing days, period. Their football success has become a supernova that outshines everything else they ever do. We mock these guys for their too-long stories and their too-small varsity jackets. We write TV sitcoms around them to the point where "lunkheaded ex–football star" has become a recognizable archetype. (Think of Al Bundy on *Married with Children* and Hank Hill and his buddies on *King of the Hill*.) It could be said that most coaches are just returning to the scene of their greatest past glory, too—including Mickey Wilson and pretty much every member of his staff except defensive backs coach Reggie Alston, who had an impressive college career at the University of Utah and then had some workouts with the Atlanta Falcons of the NFL. But high school football coaches are lucky. They've figured out how not to graduate from the game they love.

After the unexpected playoff defeat at Hanahan, the 2012 Myrtle Beach Seahawks gathered on the baseball field behind the stadium to mourn a loss. But they weren't just mourning a loss in that one game, a defeat that marked the end of their season and of their championship hopes. They were mourning the loss of Tyler Keane, C.J. Cooper, Chocolate Wilson, Sean Michael Orcutt, Octavius Thomas, and the fourteen other seniors who, in the second it took for the clock to count down from 0:01 to 0:00, had become *former* high school players.

A whole year later, in the fall of 2013, with their alma mater again competing in the 3A playoffs, many of those graduated ex-players make a return to Doug Shaw Stadium, where they stand on the Seahawk sideline—now in street clothes, as spectators. They've framed their high school diplomas. They're now almost a semester deep into their first year of college. They no longer need to be here at the stadium. Except that they *need* to be here. Because tonight is the Lower State Finals. If the Myrtle Beach Seahawks can beat Marlboro County, they'll be off to the state championship game, which this year will be played at the University of South Carolina, in Williams-Brice Stadium, home of the Gamecocks.

It's the last Friday in November, the day after Thanksgiving, and standing here on the sidelines are Chocolate Wilson and Sean Michael Orcutt. They're lined up right alongside their ex-teammates, cheering for them to reach a level of success that eluded these ex-players in their own senior year. Tyler Keane couldn't make it tonight because his current college team, the nearby Coastal Carolina Chanticleers, is preparing for an NCAA playoff game. But he's come to just about every home game this year, including the first-round playoff game played at Doug Shaw a few weeks ago. And look, here's C.J. Cooper—dreadlocks flowing, smile beaming—and here's Everett Golson, who back in January started for Notre Dame in the BCS National Championship game. Perhaps Mickey was right a year earlier, on that baseball field at Hanahan High, when he told his players they'd never love anything as much as they love high school football. Asked tonight if they enjoy playing in college as much as they did high school, Chocolate, Sean Michael, and C.J. all say no—with a wince that suggests they hate to admit as much. Asked if they'd like to be out there on the field tonight with this year's Seahawks, they all smile and nod yes.

With the graduation of these three players and so many other seniors from the year before, the team playing tonight began the season with much lower expectations than last year's squad. The Seahawks had simply lost too much talent to be competitive. This would be a rebuilding year, and at the beginning of the season, the Seahawks played like a team under construction, starting with a woeful record of 1–3 heading into the Bell Game against Conway. The seniors from the year before must have felt mixed emotions as they followed their former team: disappointed that these Seahawks were struggling, but relieved to know that their absence had been felt, that they weren't easily replaced. Then, Mickey's squad crushed Chuck Jordan's Tigers 41–7 and that win seemed to boost them in the right direction.

Conway High went on to finish the season 2–9, Jordan's worst record since 1989, and this did nothing to silence the fans who had already been calling for his retirement, which further emphasizes that even a coach as revered as Jordan (revered to a great extent specifically because of the unwavering tenacity he displayed in 1989), still has to win ballgames. The Cult of Jordanism can only survive so many losing seasons before the prophets of doom come calling for the proverbial coaching head. The heat on Jordan got so hot that in November the president-elect of the Conway Solid Gold Booster Club, local attorney L. Cole Smith—father of Tiger quarterback Ethan Smith, Mykal Moody's backup the previous year—wrote a letter to the editor of the *Horry Independent* calling for Jordan's resignation. But despite the poor record and the increasing criticism, at season's end, Chuck Jordan was still sitting the same office he'd been occupying for thirty-one years.

Meanwhile, after beating Jordan's squad in the Bell Game, Mickey's Seahawks won four of five contests in the region to enter the playoffs at 6–4. Not nearly as strong a record as the year before, but unlike the year before, this Myrtle Beach team—perhaps because they weren't good enough or experienced enough not to—stayed paranoid. They won their first three playoff games to set up this contest tonight: the Lower State Final.

If the current Seahawks win, then the recently graduated players will again have to tackle mixed emotions; but this time it will be the pride and pain of watching their younger former teammates celebrate a trip to the state championship game, an accomplishment that last year's Seahawks had assumed was their destiny. Tyler and C.J. may have been the shining example of senior leadership last year, but if this year's team hopes to reach the championship game, they'll have to do it with two sophomores—*sophomores*—leading the way: quarterback Drayton Arnold and running back Brandon Sinclair. And tonight, the current, sophomore-led Seahawks do win. In front of a packed set of home stands and all those former players, Myrtle Beach dominates Marlboro County, 20–6. They have earned a trip to Columbia to play Daniel High School for the 3A state championship. The fireworks explode in the November sky, and the former players chant along with the current players: "We goin' to da 'ship! We goin' to da 'ship!"

One week from tonight, these young Seahawks will bus up to the USC campus for "da 'ship." They'll practice in the shadow of the 80,000-seat Williams-Brice Stadium on a scrubby field that, somewhat disappointingly, pales compared to their home turf. But then, a half-hour before kickoff, they'll emerge from the players' tunnel onto the pristine expanse of the stadium field. As they go through their pre-game warmups in this mammoth venue, they'll sneak glimpses at the upper deck, at the banners commemorating the Gamecocks' 1969 ACC championship and their 2010 SEC East Division title.

At halftime, with the score tied 7–7, they'll come off the field via the same route the USC Gamecocks always take at the intermission. They'll pass under the awning structure that prevents overly enthusiastic or angry fans from raining high fives or half-full cups of Jack and Coke down on the players, and then they'll push through the glass doors that open onto a carpeted hallway that leads to the Gamecocks' locker room. As they walk down this hall, the players will fall silent. Then, standing in front of the locker room doors, they'll stare with the gape-mouthed wonder of pilgrims completing the journey to Mecca, before someone finally pushes the doors open and they file into the room. Once inside, they'll read the memos and schedules that are still pinned to the bulletin boards, stand in front of oversized changing stalls that have the Gamecock logo etched into each locker, and sneak a few peeks into the USC players' lounge with its big-screen TVs, leather recliners, pool table, and juice bar. Naturally, they'll wonder what it would be like to play at this level, in the mighty Southeastern Conference, college football's premier league. *This is the dream,* the surroundings will seem to say. *And it could all be yours.* But for nearly all of these players, odds are that this will be their last visit to a big-time NCAA Division I locker room. After they graduate, they'll be off to college or the working world, their playing days over except for intramural flag football or the occasional alumni reunion game.

Before they leave the lockers to go back on the field, Mickey Wilson will tell them, "You play hard in the second half—give me two more quarters in your life—and you'll be state champions today." And the Seahawks *will* be state champions, winning 24–21 on a field goal by Sean Huggins with one second left on the clock. And Mickey will bring another state championship trophy back to Myrtle Beach High School, his second state title in five years as Seahawk head coach.

But tonight, here in Doug Shaw Stadium, at the Lower State Finals, nobody knows that yet. Nobody knows that these players will soon be sized for championship rings, that the stadium will need to be outfitted with a new state championship banner, that the 2013 team will take its place in Seahawk history next to squads from 1980, 1981, 1983, 1984, 2008, and 2010. All anybody knows tonight is that this lineup is doing what last year's team couldn't do. This team is going to da 'ship. As Mr. Byrd often says, "Once a Seahawk, always a Seahawk." So for Chocolate, C.J., and Sean Michael—and for every player that has ever suited up for Myrtle Beach—tonight's win is a reason to cheer. But that doesn't mean it's easy to watch a younger kid who's wearing your jersey number celebrate an achievement you missed out on.

While the current team is whooping it up in the locker room—half listening as Mickey tells them to enjoy the win tonight but be ready to come back to work on Monday to start preparing for the championship game—parents, girlfriends, and reporters linger on the field, waiting for a chance to talk with the players. And a few minutes later, when the locker room doors open and the smiling Seahawks spill out, Chocolate, C.J., and Sean Michael are already gone.

AUTHORS' NOTE

ON A SUNNY SATURDAY IN MARCH 2013, THE TWO OF US—SCOTT AND JOE—
showed up at Cherry Hill Missionary Baptist for an open house hosted by
the Conway branch of the NAACP. The Cherry Hill building that sits on
the corner of Church and Racepath today isn't the same one that the Rev.
H. H. Singleton presided over in 1989. The church was rebuilt in 2001, and
the new building, which is set back further from the street, has a sleek and
modern look. As we made our way through the doors that afternoon, we
were struck by how bright and airy the new building is. Because this was a
Saturday open house as opposed to a Sunday service, the church was maybe
a quarter filled, and instead of dresses, the women wore blouses and skirts.
The men wore polos and slacks. Most of the people were black. Some—the
two of us and a few others—were white. Newcomers signed in and shook
hands and introduced themselves, and everyone nodded approvingly at the
buffet tables that lined the back wall, piled high with ham and deviled eggs,
macaroni and cheese, and casserole after delicious-looking casserole.

But before lunch began, there were prayers and announcements, and
there were updates on the various causes the branch had taken up (advocating on behalf of tenants who had grievances with landlords and on behalf
of parents who felt pressured by the school system to place their children
in the "special needs" program, to cite two examples). Toward the end of the
official remarks, the proceedings moved to an open segment where visitors
could ask questions or make statements. At that point, the two of us announced that we were working on a book about the 1989 Conway football
boycott, and we said we'd be grateful if people would be willing to share
with us what they remembered from that year. After we made our pitch to
the gathering, some attendees seemed enthusiastic about the prospect of a
book about the boycott, and a few were happy to share their stories right
then and there. But most in the church that day seemed to eye us a little sus-
piciously. We had each come with a stack of business cards to pass around,
and we walked out to the parking lot with most of those cards still in our
hands.

Still, as we drove away, we talked about how well the afternoon had gone. We'd suspected, of course, that the idea of two white guys writing a book with a significant racial component would be met with understandable skepticism—and perhaps even outright hostility. We hoped that people in Conway, black and white, wouldn't see us as trying to profit unfairly from experiences that weren't ours. But we worried that the black community might see this book as a small-scale example of the kind of exploitation of blacks by whites that our nation has witnessed for centuries. And we worried that the white community might see the events of '89 as a story we could never fully understand because we hadn't been there. When we started this project, we'd both lived in Conway for a number of years; but we're not from here, which might, in some people's minds, mean that we can't ever be *of* here, either. As writers, our only option was to jump in and tell the truth as we saw it, though perhaps, in Emily Dickinson's famous phrase, to *tell it slant*. But *truth* is hard to find and even harder to define, so how would we know when we were telling it? In a narrative with as many characters, settings, and events as this one, would we ever know that we had gotten every detail correct? We had to accept that we wouldn't know for sure.

However, when it comes to our way of telling the story—our *slant*—we can say pretty definitely what we had in mind. We wanted to tell a football story set in a time of racial discord rather than a story about a protest movement that happened to have been started by a football incident. The differences between those two approaches are obvious and can be seen throughout the book. Was ours the best angle for the story? We'll leave that for others to decide.

About a week after the open house at Cherry Hill, at the invitation of current chapter president Abdullah Mustafa, we visited an NAACP meeting, again with the purpose of letting attendees know about the book project. Inside a local community hall, we sat with the officers of the organization at a long, rectangular table while they conducted chapter business. For over an hour, the officers talked about paying for phone bills and maintaining call lists before Abdullah introduced us to the group. Again, we got a friendly but lukewarm response: some nodding heads and a few people saying things like "sounds like a good book." Just when it seemed that the meeting would move on to the next agenda item, one woman, who was black, stood up and asked us, "How do you plan to handle your biases?" In asking her question, she didn't seem hostile in the least. She didn't quite seem skeptical, either. She was perhaps more curious than anything else: How *do* you plan to handle your biases? She seemed to be empathizing with us, while acknowledging the difficulty all of us face every day trying to transcend our prejudices and preconceived notions.

The assembled group waited through a few beats of silence as we tried in vain to formulate a simple answer to a complex question. "Well," Joe finally said, "I guess the first step is to admit we have them."

And we do have biases, of course, but like most people, our biases are so ingrained that it can be difficult to recognize them. Scott is a forty-something white male Tennessean. Joe is a forty-something white male Ohioan. Surely those facts influence how we see the boycott. So does the fact that we both work on a university campus. So does the fact that we're diehard football fans (college mostly—Scott roots for Auburn, Joe for Ohio State). And the fact that in our CD collections you'll find *Super Hits* by George Jones and *Fear of a Black Planet* by Public Enemy. But how would those biases affect us as writers? We didn't know then, and we don't really know now—more than two years after beginning research on the book.

When we tell people in Conway that we're writing about the boycott, they'll often ask us, "Who do you think was right, Jordan or Singleton?" We understand why they are curious to hear our response, but as with the issue of handling biases, our answer to the "who was right" question is somewhat unsatisfying. If *right* means "being honest and trying to do what's best," then we think Jordan and Singleton were both right. If *right* means "morally good," then we still think both men were right. There's no evidence whatsoever that Chuck Jordan is a racist, and there's lots of evidence to indicate he had sound football reasons for moving Carlos to defense. On the other hand, H. H. Singleton had good reason to believe that Carlos was a victim of the kind of subtle, systemic racism that is harder to defeat than overt racism. And given the many examples of violent, hateful, overt racism that blacks in Horry County and America have suffered (and continue to suffer), who could blame him for taking up Carlos's cause so vocally? The point is, everybody—from Chuck Jordan and H. H. Singleton to John Dawsey and the school board members, to Lawrence Mitchell and Carlos Hunt—was trying to do right. But *right* is just as slippery as *truth*.

In the Spike Lee film that was released two months before the boycott, there's a scene where Da Mayor, the old neighborhood drunk played by Ossie Davis, calls Mookie, the pizza deliverer played by Lee, over to the brownstone stairs where the older man has been watching the comings and goings of his Brooklyn street. "Doctor," Da Mayor says to Mookie, seemingly apropos of nothing, "always do the right thing."

"That's it?" Mookie asks, anxious to finish his deliveries.

"That's it," Da Mayor says.

We've tried to do the right thing in writing this book. To us that means recording these events as truthfully as we know how.

ACKNOWLEDGMENTS

The authors would like to express their deepest gratitude to the following people and organizations for making this project possible:

Chuck Jordan and Mickey Wilson Jr. for the access and insight.

Hank Singleton III for generously sharing memories of his father and of Conway circa 1989.

Mary Battle for her thorough and thoughtful master's thesis on race relations in Conway during the boycott.

Megan Fahey for hours spent staring at microfilm, Maddie Johnson for hours spent staring at the bibliography and notes, and Jenifer Butler for hours proofreading and working on the index.

The *Myrtle Beach Sun News* (especially Rebecca James, Mel Derrick, Yolanda Jones, Joseph Serwach, Mark Johnson, Charles Slate, and Carolyn Callison Murray) and the *Horry Independent* (especially Kathy Ropp and Robert Anderson) for telling the story first and for reminding us of the irreplaceable value of local journalism.

Dave Moniz, Bryan Burwell, Hank Hersch, and the other members of the state and national media who reported on the '89 football boycott.

Lawrence Mitchell, Leon Grissett, Hunter Spivey, Michael Timbes, Cleveland Sanders, Michael Pickett, Edward Smalls, Scott Thompson, Nate Thompson, Craig Dunlap, Corey Dunlap, and all the 1989 Conway Tiger football players and coaching staff.

Armand Derfner, Congressman James Clyburn, John Dawsey, Mickey Wilson Sr., Mona Wilson, Phaedra Faulk, Earl Friday, Larry Biddle, Preston

McKever-Floyd, Arne Flaten, Margene Willis, Wardell Brantley, the staff of the Conway Branch of the Horry County Memorial Library, the Conway Branch of the NAACP (especially Abdullah Mustafa and Winifred Anderson), and the staff of the Avery Research Center at the College of Charleston (especially Daron Calhoun and Elizabeth Wilkins).

The 2012 and 2013 Myrtle Beach Seahawks coaches, players, and staff, including: John Cahill, Nona Kerr, Wes Streater, Jason Owens, Reggie Alston, Kevin Colyer, John Sedeska, Brad Poston, Tim Christy, Matt Moss, Doug Carr, Eugene Everhart, James "Bubba" Lewis, Jonathan Boggs, Andrea Sulewski, Bill Hosford, Pastor Ronny Byrd, Tyler Keane, C.J. Cooper, Sean Michael Orcutt, Octavius Thomas, Griffin Wright, C.J. Robinson, D'Andre "Chocolate" Wilson, Kelton Greene, Max Huggins, Sean Huggins, Renard Pointer, Cordell Brown, Hunter Floyd, Heath Gray, Markyl Grissett, Drayton Arnold, Brandon Sinclair, Graham Vaughn, and Drew "Chip" Cook.

The 2012 Conway Tigers coaches, players, and staff, including: Matt Vanadore, Kelly Andreucci, Charles Divine, Steve Hall, Steve Parsley, Carlton Terry, Reid Murdock, Cedric McKnight, Stephen Burris, Bob Vosbrinck, Gabe Moreland, Kyle Cavalini, Stacey Baynham, Sawyer Jordan, Mykal Moody, Malcolm Green, Tyreke Phillips, Jaquail Crosland, Kahmil Cooper, and Nathaniel Nesbitt.

Special thanks to Craig Gill, Anne Stascavage, Will Rigby, and the staff at the University Press of Mississippi and to John Rudolph at Dystel & Goderich Literary Management.

Additionally, Scott Pleasant would like to thank Nelljean Rice, Brianne Parker, Kelly Gerald, Ditty Nicolaides, Bobby Swanay, Cynthia Port, Robert Alfonso, James and Louise Pleasant, Gary and Carroll Pleasant, Cheryl Clearwater, Regina Ammon, Dan Ennis, Aliyyah Willis, Joe Cannon, and Denise Paster. Special thanks to Rose for suggesting the topic for the book. Special "you're welcome" to Rose for not asking her to proofread the manuscript.

Joe Oestreich would like to thank his colleagues at Coastal Carolina University (especially Dan Albergotti, Jason Ockert, and Cara Blue Adams), the Ohio State University MFA Program in Creative Writing (especially Lee Martin, Lee K. Abbott, Michelle Herman, and Erin McGraw), Will Allison, Kyle Minor, Jason Skipper, Richard Oestreich, Mary Anne Oestreich, Jill

Keasel, and his family and friends. Special thanks to Kate, Beckett, and Eleanor for all their love and support. This book would not have been completed without a generous grant and scholarly reassignment time from Coastal Carolina University.

NOTES

—In a crowded post-game locker room . . . silence his rejoicing players—

During the 2012 and 2013 seasons, Scott Pleasant was allowed access to the Myrtle Beach Seahawks by Coach Mickey Wilson. During that same period, Joe Oestreich was given access to the Conway Tigers by Coach Chuck Jordan. Unless specified otherwise, all firsthand accounts throughout the book of games, practices, meetings, and other team activities during the 2012 and 2013 seasons come from the authors' notes taken as they spent time with the teams they followed. Also: Here and throughout the book "Mickey Wilson" and "Mickey" refer to Mickey Wilson Jr. When referring to Mickey Wilson Sr. the authors use the "Sr." suffix.

CHAPTER 1. GRAVEYARD/BACKYARD

—The black Baptist minister . . . in the Conway High School auditorium—

In this chapter and throughout the book, descriptions of the Rev. Singleton's Homegoing Ceremony on January 5, 2013, come from the authors' notes taken after attending the ceremony, the program for the ceremony, and the DVD of the ceremony listed below:

Homegoing Celebration in Loving Memory of the Late H.H. Singleton II, directed by Wardell Brantley, January 5, 2013 (Conway, SC: As-One Media and Rejoice Christian Network, 2013), DVD.

—Later, during preseason practice . . . toward their spokesman, H. H. Singleton.—

Hank Hersch, "Choosing Sides," *Sports Illustrated*, November 27, 1989, 42–43.

—When Barack Obama tells the story . . . chanting it from within the crowd—

"The Story of 'Fired up! Ready to go!' Obama for America 2012," YouTube video, 4:31, posted by BarackObamadotcom, April 4, 2012, http://www.youtube.com/watch?v=QhWDFgRfi1Q.

—Chuck Jordan's office sits . . . from the auditorium.—

Unless otherwise noted, material in the remainder of this chapter comes from the following source:

Chuck Jordan, interviewed by both authors, Conway, South Carolina, December 5, 2012.

—Jordan commiserated with John McKissick . . . 600 career wins.—

Chris Dearing, "Summerville's John McKissick Is the Winningest Football Coach at Any Level," *The State* (Columbia, SC), October 26, 2012, http://www.thestate.com/2012/10/28/2498176/summervilles-john-mckissick-is.html.

—Lawrence Mitchell—the stud-recruit . . . many more big-time colleges—

Mark Johnson, "No Foolin'—Tigs' Mitchell Is For Real," *Myrtle Beach Sun News*, August 13, 1989, B1.

—went to H. H. Singleton for guidance—

Hank Singleton III, interviewed by Joe Oestreich, Conway, South Carolina, March 2, 2013.

—Shortly thereafter, the players . . . the boycott was on—

From a DVD of the Rev. H. H. Singleton's press conference announcing the boycott on August 22, 1989.

—One month from now, Golson . . . against Alabama.—

Notre Dame would lose the championship game, and after the season, Golson would be suspended from school for an unspecified academic issue. He would return to play for the Irish in 2014.

"Golson Accepts Suspension," *ESPN.com*, May 28, 2013, accessed May 7, 2014, http://espn.go.com/college-football/story/_/id/9313557/everett-golson-banned-notre-dame-fighting-irish-poor-academic-judgment.

CHAPTER 2. BITING THE HAND

—Add the Tigers' championship-game expectations . . . for a combined 3,009 yards.—

Rich Chrampanis, "Conway's Moody Picks Up SEC Offer," *CarolinaLive.com*, last modified March 2, 2012, accessed May 7, 2014, http://www.carolinalive.com/sports/story.aspx?id=726127#.U2OX54VJW2w.

—Junior Hemingway, a wide receiver who . . . Sugar Bowl win against Virginia Tech.—

"Junior Hemingway Bio," *GoBlue.com*, accessed May 7, 2014, http://www.mgoblue.com/sports/m-footbl/mtt/hemingway_junioroo.html.

—Perhaps most impressively . . . seventh round of the NFL draft.—

"2012 NFL Draft Results and Analysis," *ESPN NFL DraftTracker*, accessed May 7, 2014, http://insider.espn.go.com/nfl/draft/rounds/_/round/7/year/2012.

—Fourteen million people a year visit the Myrtle Beach area.—

"Myrtle Beach Area History: History and Local Folklore," *VisitMyrtleBeach.com*, accessed May 7, 2014, http://www.visitmyrtlebeach.com/about/history/.

— . . . a town of 18,688 that's every bit as charming as Church Street is charmless.—

United States Census Bureau, "State and County Quick Facts—Conway (city), South Carolina," last modified March 27, 2014, accessed May 7, 2014, http://quickfacts.census.gov/qfd/states/45/4516405.html.

—Conway's most salient feature . . . Turpentine, Tobacco, and Tourism—

Charles Joyner, foreword to *Horry County, South Carolina: 1730-1993*, by Catherine H. Lewis (Columbia: University of South Carolina Press, 1998), ix–xiv.

—Jordan has always taken pride . . . back in 1989—

Dave Moniz, "Reconciliation Under Way in Conway Football Spat," *Spartanburg Herald-Journal*, September 9, 1989, C2.

—The '88-'89 Conway High School yearbook . . . Mickey, the white point guard.—

"Stepping Up to New Heights" in *Stepping Stones to Excellence: Conway High School Mirror 1989*, Susan Timmons and Sarah Young, eds. (Conway, SC: Conway High School, 1989), 249.

—Led by the legendary John McKissick . . . '83, '84, and '86—

Jason Gilmer, "Winning Traditions," *GoUpstate.com*, last modified November 30, 2005, accessed May 7, 2014, http://www.goupstate.com/article/20051130/NEWS/511300353.

—Conway had played Summerville . . . start of spring practice—

"Conway High School—1980–1989 Football Results," *South Carolina Football: History of South Carolina High School Football*, accessed May 7, 2014, http://www.scfootballhistory .com/School/Decade/80.aspx?schoolid=177.

—Of the 22 players . . . both football and basketball—

Mark Johnson, "No Foolin'—Tigs' Mitchell Is For Real," *Myrtle Beach Sun News*, August, 13, 1989, B1.

—Chuck Jordan has called Lawrence "the best athlete I've ever coached."—

Chuck Jordan, interviewed by both authors, Conway, South Carolina, December 5, 2012.

—The defensive end could run a half-mile in just over two minutes—

Hank Hersch, "Choosing Sides," *Sports Illustrated*, November 27, 1989, 46.

— . . . at the Five-Star Basketball Camp . . . Patrick Ewing, and Isiah Thomas—

Mark Johnson, "No Foolin'—Tigs' Mitchell Is For Real," *Myrtle Beach Sun News*, August, 13, 1989. B1.

—But football was Lawrence's first love . . . at any position—

Mel Derrick, "Mitchell Called Third Best in U.S.," *Myrtle Beach Sun News*, August 15, 1989, B1.

— In 1988 he completed 37 of 92 passes—

Mel Derrick, "Conway's Jordan Wants to Do the Right Thing," *Myrtle Beach Sun News*, August 23, 1989, B4.

—But the 605 yards on those 37 completions . . . starting quarterback, pro or college.—

"Joe Montana—Career Stats," *NFL.com*, accessed May 7, 2014, http://www.nfl.com/ player/joemontana/2502166/careerstats.

—Hunt averaged less than six carries per game—

Mel Derrick, "Conway's Jordan Wants to Do the Right Thing," *Myrtle Beach Sun News*, August 23, 1989, B4.

—In 1989, 42 percent of Conway's 9,819 citizens were black—

United States Census Bureau, "1990 Census of Population and Housing Public Law 94-171 Data (Official)," accessed May 7, 2014, http://censtats.census.gov/pl94/pl94.shtml.

—any black Tiger fan in 1989 . . . black quarterbacks.—

Hank Singleton III, interviewed by Joe Oestreich, Conway, South Carolina, March 2, 2013.

—first time in sixty years . . . "caught the devil"—

Armand Derfner Collection, "Transcript of Jordan Testimony at Singleton School Board Hearing," Avery Research Center for African American History and Culture, College of Charleston. Box 127, Folder 1.

—"nigger lover"—

Bryan Burwell, "Small-Town Football Feud Sparks Full-scale Racial Rift," *Detroit News*, October 15, 1989, C17.

—**Going into the 1989 season . . . six seasons as coach**—

Hank Hersch, "Choosing Sides," *Sports Illustrated*, November 27, 1989, 42.

—**In order to commemorate . . . and the letters *QB*.**—

Hank Hersch, "Choosing Sides," *Sports Illustrated*, November 27, 1989, 42.

—**Carlos's anticipation . . . "the betterment of the team."**—

Hank Hersch, "Choosing Sides," *Sports Illustrated*, November 27, 1989, 42.

—**A few weeks earlier . . . the quarterback decision."**—

Armand Derfner Collection, "Transcript of Jordan Testimony at Singleton School Board Hearing," Avery Research Center for African American History and Culture, College of Charleston. Box 127, Folder 1.

—**"When you take a QB and move him . . . (as a defensive back and wide receiver)."**—

Mark Johnson, "Wanted: Experience; Contact Conway," *Myrtle Beach Sun News*, August 13, 1989, B8.

—**Carlos was initially disappointed . . . "Happy as a lark"**—

Armand Derfner Collection, "Transcript of Jordan Testimony at Singleton School Board Hearing," Avery Research Center for African American History and Culture, College of Charleston. Box 127, Folder 1.

—**As Lawrence Mitchell would later tell *Sports Illustrated* . . . all that important."**—

Hank Hersch, "Choosing Sides," *Sports Illustrated*, November 27, 1989, 46.

—**Back in November . . . use at his discretion.**—

Hank Hersch, "Choosing Sides," *Sports Illustrated*, November 27, 1989, 43.

—**He kept the money in a filing cabinet . . . "teach kids about life."**—

Rebecca James, "Booster Club Loan Fund Unusual in Area Schools," *Myrtle Beach Sun News*, September 15, 1989, A1.

—**So after Carlos missed a few payments . . . *you stop feeding the dog.***—

Joseph J. Serwach and Yolanda Jones, "Former Conway QB Tells His Story," *Myrtle Beach Sun News*, September 11, 1989, A1.

— **Jordan reinstated Carlos . . . reclaimed his ring.**—

Armand Derfner Collection, "Transcript of Jordan Testimony at Singleton School Board Hearing," Avery Research Center for African American History and Culture, College of Charleston. Box 127, Folder 1.

— **. . . his backcourt mate . . . 25 yards the previous year as his backup**—

Mel Derrick, "Conway's Jordan Wants to Do the Right Thing," *Myrtle Beach Sun News*, August 23, 1989, B4.

—**Mickey Wilson says now . . . without much complaint.**—

Mickey Wilson Jr., interviewed by both authors, Conway, South Carolina, November 21, 2012.

—**But Carlos's seeming acquiescence . . . per Jordan's team rules.**—

Armand Derfner Collection, "Transcript of Jordan Testimony at Singleton School Board Hearing," Avery Research Center for African American History and Culture, College of Charleston. Box 127, Folder 1.

CHAPTER 3. RACEPATH

—The Seahawks play their games . . . college and pro teams have adopted.—

"Doug Shaw Memorial Stadium," *Myrtle Beach Local Government Page*, accessed May 17, 2014, http://www.cityofmyrtlebeach.com/dougshaw.html.

—Before the railroad came through . . . to distinguish it from Conway, the Old Town.—

Catherine Lewis, *Horry County, South Carolina 1730–1993* (Columbia: University of South Carolina Press, 1998), 74–75.

—Some newspaper articles pointed out the rarity of a freshman starting over a senior—

Ian Guerin, August 23, 2007 (4:20 p.m.), "The Freshman Phenom Will Start," *Prep Talk: Inside High School Sports Blog*, accessed March 11, 2014, http://thesunnews.typepad.com/preptalk/2007/08/the-freshman-ph.html.

—Mickey says now . . . an eighth grader."—

Mickey Wilson Jr., interviewed by both authors, Conway, South Carolina, November 21, 2012.

—Last season, with Golson off at Notre Dame . . . with C.J. completing 19 and Tyler 24—

Here and throughout the book, statistics for the Myrtle Beach Seahawks have been gathered from the team's website:

Myrtle Beach Football (on *HomeTeamsOnline.com*), accessed May 8, 2014, http://www.hometeamsonline.com/teams/?u=MYRTLEBEACHFOOTBALLCOM&s=football&t=c.

—"He's just such a great athlete . . . at the next level."—

These quotations are taken from an interview with Mickey Wilson Jr. conducted by Mark Haggard of the WPDE television station in Myrtle Beach, South Carolina. The interview can be found online in a video that accompanies this news article:

Rich Chrampanis, "MB to Use One QB, Carvers Bay Has D1 Prospect," *CarolinaLive.com*, last modified July 3, 2012, accessed May 7, 2014, http://www.carolinalive.com/sports/story.aspx?id=772427#.U2OuqIVJW2w.

—"Oh, yeah . . . why we're asking this of him."—

Mickey Wilson Jr., interviewed by Scott Pleasant, Myrtle Beach, South Carolina, May 21, 2012.

—Carlos Hunt spent the summer . . . team needed him on defense.—

Hank Hersch, "Choosing Sides," *Sports Illustrated*, November 27, 1989, 43.

—"You've got a choice . . . or you don't have to play." —

Armand Derfner Collection, "Transcript of Jordan Testimony at Singleton School Board Hearing," Avery Research Center for African American History and Culture, College of Charleston. Box 127, Folder 1.

—That's when the calls started coming in . . . "Have you heard about Carlos?"—

Hank Singleton III, interviewed by Joe Oestreich, Conway, South Carolina, March 2, 2013.

—Among other causes . . . upper-management opportunities for African Americans—

From the program for H. H. Singleton's Homegoing Ceremony.

—The varsity and junior-varsity . . . racially biased in their selections.—

Lesia J. Shannon, "NAACP: Principal Bowed to Whites in Squad Additions," *Myrtle Beach Sun News*, May 8, 1987, A7.

—Possibly in response to these complaints . . . "only added additional persons."—

Lesia J. Shannon, "NAACP: Principal Bowed to Whites in Squad Additions," *Myrtle Beach Sun News*, May 8, 1987, A7.

—Black students, parents, and teachers . . . resolve the problem."

Lesia Shannon and Denise Barbree, "Conway Racial Dispute Escalates into Student Protests," *Myrtle Beach Sun News*, May 13, 1987, A1 and A4.

—Two years later, Darryl Stanley . . . you should stick with it."

Andre Christopher, "Former Players Back Jordan," *Myrtle Beach Sun News*, August 27, 1989, B1.

—"It's got nothing to do with us . . . football is not here because of the cheerleaders."—

Scott Thompson, interviewed by both authors, Conway, South Carolina, January 9, 2014.

—Six days after Singleton's press conference . . . fourteen white girls and two black girls.—

Lesia J. Shannon, "School Officials Agree to Trim Conway JV Cheerleader Spots," *Myrtle Beach Sun News*, May 14, 1987, A1 and A6.

—"In the letter, Dawsey warned . . . for your dismissal."—

Armand Derfner Collection, "May 25, 1987 Letter from Dawsey to Singleton," Avery Research Center for African American History and Culture, College of Charleston. Box 129, Folder 1.

—". . . if this same or similar situation . . . equality for all people."—

Armand Derfner Collection, "June 29, 1987 Letter from Singleton to Dawsey," Avery Research Center for African American History and Culture, College of Charleston. Box 129, Folder 1.

—"Any black person with a sense of history had heard that [justification] before."—

The above quotation and the narrative that is told in the remainder of this section of the chapter come primarily from the interview listed below, but it is substantially corroborated by information in other sources.

Hank Singleton III, interviewed by Joe Oestreich, Conway, South Carolina, March 2, 2013.

—. . . the two men met for the first time . . . in the coach's office.—

This accounting of this meeting has been distilled from the thirty-four-page transcript of Jordan's tape recording. The quotations are accurate but have not in every case been positioned in chronological order. For the complete transcript, see the following source:

Armand Derfner Collection, "Transcript of Recorded Conversation," Avery Research Center for African American History and Culture, College of Charleston. Box 126, Folder 2.

—Back in 1989 . . . the North Myrtle Beach Chiefs—

"Friday's Football Jamboree Will Bring Out the Area's Best," *Myrtle Beach Sun News*, August 15, 1989, B1.

—In the days leading up to Jamboree . . . but in the state.—

Mark Johnson, "No Foolin'—Tigs' Mitchell Is For Real," *Myrtle Beach Sun News*, August 13, 1989, B1.

—. . . the third-ranked 4A school in South Carolina—

I. J. Rosenberg, "A Change at QB Tears Town Apart—Black-White Switch Spurs Boycott, Rally," *Atlanta Journal-Constitution*, September 2, 1989, E7.

—**The junior was sacked several times . . . end zone on the next offensive play.**—

"Teams Tune Up in Football Jamboree," *Myrtle Beach Sun News*, August 19, 1989, B5.

—**Adrian attended the jamboree . . . would have agreed.**—

Yolanda Jones, "Football Jamboree Annual Family Event," *Myrtle Beach Sun News*, August 19, 1989, A1.

—**Seemingly unaware of any trouble . . . "just fun and games."**—

Mel Derrick, "A Reunion of Football Pals," *Myrtle Beach Sun News*, August 20, 1989, B1.

—**That Sunday, the Singletons again met with the black Tigers. . . .**—

Information and quotations relating to the meeting in this paragraph and in the next four paragraphs come from the interview listed below, but material from the interview has been substantially corroborated by printed sources and other interviews:

Hank Singleton III, interviewed by Joe Oestreich, Conway, South Carolina, March 2, 2013.

—**The next day at 3:30 . . . let's practice football."**—

Armand Derfner Collection, "Transcript of Jordan Testimony at Singleton School Board Hearing," Avery Research Center for African American History and Culture, College of Charleston. Box 127, Folder 2.

—**". . . you're going to play on my terms."**—

Hank Hersch, "Choosing Sides," *Sports Illustrated*, November 27, 1989, 44.

—**. . . Jordan was feeling good . . . "tonight at the church."**—

Armand Derfner Collection, "Transcript of Jordan Testimony at Singleton School Board Hearing," Avery Research Center for African American History and Culture, College of Charleston. Box 127, Folder 2.

—**That evening the black cohort . . . "Fired up! Ready to go!"**—

Hank Hersch, "Choosing Sides," *Sports Illustrated*, November 27, 1989, 44.

—**"At that moment . . . any longer than a week."**—

Hank Singleton III, interviewed by Joe Oestreich, Conway, South Carolina, March 2, 2013.

—**A grainy DVD transfer of a videotape of the event . . .**—

The DVD of the press conference was provided by Hank Singleton III. The descriptions of and quotations from the press conference in this paragraph and in the next seven paragraphs are taken from this DVD.

—**arrogatedly**—

The dictionary definition for the root word *arrogate* does not seem to fit the context of Singleton's speech. Thus, his use of *arrogatedly* here may be a malapropism for "arrogantly" or simply a mispronunciation. Or it could be that the Rev. Singleton was using the word in a sense that the authors of this book have not considered.

—**A few days after the Redskins' Super Bowl win . . . so successful on the field.**—

Judy Mann, "Putting Racism to Rest," *Washington Post*, February 3, 1988, D3.

—**According to Snyder . . . fired him immediately**—

Clarence Page, "Thanks for Being Honest, Jimmy 'The Greek'—Too Honest," *Chicago Tribune*, January 20, 1988, accessed May 27, 2014, http://articles.chicagotribune .com/1988-01-20/news/8803230751_1_thighs-black-professional-sports.

—**In a post-season retrospective . . . also big and strong."**—

John Papanek, "The Odyssey of Little Homer," *Sports Illustrated*, December 28, 1981, accessed March 12, 2014, http://sportsillustrated.cnn.com/vault/article/magazine/MAG 1125121/index.htm.

—Chuck Jordan admits that Mickey Wilson ... "You have to go with your gut."—

Chuck Jordan, interviewed by both authors, Conway, South Carolina, March 14, 2012.

—... led the JV team to 9–1 record...—

Armand Derfner Collection, "Transcript of Jordan Testimony at Singleton School Board Hearing," Avery Research Center for African American History and Culture, College of Charleston. Box 127, Folder 1.

—The day after the boycott began ... "an outstanding athlete, no question."—

Mel Derrick, "Conway's Jordan Wants to Do the Right Thing," *Myrtle Beach Sun News*, August 23, 1989, B4.

CHAPTER 4. WEEK ZERO

—Conway's population has nearly doubled ... so has the population of the county—

This calculation was arrived at by comparing official 1990 census data to official census estimates for 2012. The data is available online at the following locations:

United States Census Bureau, "1990 Census of Population and Housing Public Law 94-171 Data (Official)," accessed May 8, 2014, http://censtats.census.gov/pl94/pl94.shtml.

United States Census Bureau, "State and County Quick Facts," accessed May 8, 2014, http://quickfacts.census.gov/qfd/states/45/45051.html. (Horry County, 2012) http://quickfacts.census.gov/qfd/states/45/4516405.html. (Conway, 2012)

—Or maybe it's because ... it was the thing to do.—

Hank Singleton III, interviewed by Joe Oestreich, Conway, South Carolina, March 2, 2013.

—Over the last three years ... the Tigers won a combined thirty-three—

"Conway High School," *South Carolina High School Football History Page*, accessed May 8, 2014, http://www.scfootballhistory.com/School/TeamHome.aspx?SchoolID=177.

—"I think the people in this community ... want to see me do the right thing."—

Mel Derrick, "Conway's Jordan Wants to Do the Right Thing," *Myrtle Beach Sun News*, August 23, 1989, B1.

—The thirty-six black players ... automatic dismissal from the team—

Mel Derrick, "Conway's Jordan Wants to Do the Right Thing," *Myrtle Beach Sun News*, August 23, 1989, B1.

—Hillcrest was perhaps the weakest ... longest active run of futility in the state.

"Hillcrest-Dalzell: Games from 1980-1989," *South Carolina High School Football History Page*, accessed May 8, 2014, http://www.scfootballhistory.com/School/Decade/80.aspx?schoolid=235.

—"If we have to ... we'll get fired up and go after them."—

Mel Derrick, "Conway's Jordan Wants to Do the Right Thing," *Myrtle Beach Sun News*, August 23, 1989, B1.

—Looking back on it now ... cave in to their demands.—

Chuck Jordan, interviewed by both authors, Conway, South Carolina, March 14, 2012.

—On Wednesday, though, Jordan had reason to hope . . .—

Information and quotations about the players' meeting with Coach Jordan and Conway's football practice on August 23, 1989, in this paragraph and in the next three paragraphs come from the sources listed below:

Armand Derfner Collection, "Sequence of Events as Recorded by Chuck Jordan," Avery Research Center for African American History and Culture, College of Charleston. Box 127, Folder 6.

Armand Derfner Collection, "Transcript of Jordan Testimony at Singleton School Board Hearing," Avery Research Center for African American History and Culture, College of Charleston. Box 127, Folder 2.

Mel Derrick, "'No Comment' Is Rule for Conway Players," *Myrtle Beach Sun News*, August 24, 1989, B1 and B5.

—"Sure they want to play football . . . But they don't want to play football at all costs."—

Rebecca James, "Conway Football Boycott Continues," *Myrtle Beach Sun News*, August 24, 1989, A8.

—On Thursday, there again seemed reason to hope . . .—

Information, quotations, and dialogue relating to the meetings and the practice session in the remainder of this section of the chapter come from the following sources:

Armand Derfner Collection, "Transcript of Jordan Testimony at Singleton School Board Hearing," Avery Research Center for African American History and Culture, College of Charleston. Box 127, Folder 2.

Armand Derfner Collection, "Sequence of Events as Recorded by Chuck Jordan," Avery Research Center for African American History and Culture, College of Charleston. Box 127, Folder 6.

Hank Hersch, "Choosing Sides," *Sports Illustrated*, November 27, 1989, 46.

Mel Derrick, "Another Day of Hopes and Heartbreak for Conway Team," *Myrtle Beach Sun News*, August 25, 1989, B1 and B5.

—He'd begun fall practice . . . we're going to be successful."—

Mel Derrick, "Another Day of Hopes and Heartbreak for Conway Team," *Myrtle Beach Sun News*, August 25, 1989, B1 and B5.

—Mark Johnson, the *Sun News* sportswriter . . . first game in two years."—

Mark Johnson, "Prep Football," *Myrtle Beach Sun News*, August 24, 1989, B1.

—That evening, Jordan loaded his players . . .—

Information and quotations in this paragraph come from the source listed below:

Scott Thompson, interviewed by both authors, Conway, South Carolina, January 9, 2014.

—But first, in order to get from Thorny's . . .—

Information and quotations in this paragraph come from the following sources:

Hank Singleton III, interviewed by Joe Oestreich, Conway, South Carolina, March 2, 2013.

Mickey Wilson Jr., interviewed by both authors, Conway, South Carolina, November 21, 2012.

—After the team passed by, Carlos, Lawrence, and the rest . . .—

Unless otherwise noted, information and quotations relating to what happened on the evening of August 25, 1989, at Cherry Hill Baptist Church and at the Conway vs.

Dalzell-Hillcrest football game in this paragraph and in the next three paragraphs come from the following four sources:

Chrysti Edge and Yolanda Jones, "Striking Tigers Watch Team Lose," *Myrtle Beach Sun News*, August 26, 1989, A1 and A5.

Hank Singleton III, interviewed by Joe Oestreich, Conway, South Carolina, March 2, 2013.

I. J. Rosenberg, "A Change at QB Tears Town Apart—Black-White Switch Spurs Boycott, Rally," *Atlanta Journal-Constitution*, September 2, 1989, E7.

Robert Anderson, "It's Been a Rough Week for the Conway Tigers," *Horry Independent*, August 30, 1989, A8.

—Inspired by the 1917 silent parade . . . minority set-asides—

John M. Broder, "Thousands Stage Silent March on Capitol: Civil Rights Gathering Protests Recent Supreme Court Decisions," *LosAngelesTimes.com*, August 27, 1989, accessed May 8, 2014, http://articles.latimes.com/1989-08-27/news/mn-1753_1_supreme-court-decisions.

—Hillcrest scored on a 22-yard touchdown . . . Hillcrest 20, Conway 0.—

Mark Johnson, "Hillcrest Outmans Tigers 34-6: Boycott Drains Conway Team," *Myrtle Beach Sun News*, August 26, 1989, B3.

—The louder the striking players chanted . . .—

Information and quotations about the Dalzell-Hillcrest game in this paragraph and in the next two paragraphs come from the following sources:

Chrysti Edge and Yolanda Jones, "Striking Tigers Watch Team Lose," *Myrtle Beach Sun News*, August 26, 1989, A1 and A5.

Hank Hersch, "Choosing Sides," *Sports Illustrated*, November 27, 1989, 44.

Hank Singleton III, interviewed by Joe Oestreich, Conway, South Carolina, March 2, 2013.

—Reminded now of the black Tigers . . . about the whole boycott."—

Mickey Wilson Jr., interviewed by both authors, Conway, South Carolina, November 21, 2012.

—During the halftime intermission . . . goaded into a fight.—

Hank Singleton III, interviewed by Joe Oestreich, Conway, South Carolina, March 2, 2013.

—When the clock finally hit 0:00 . . . "And that's the same way I feel," the coach said.—

Mark Johnson, "Hillcrest Outmans Tigers 34-6," *Myrtle Beach Sun News*, August 26, 1989, B1 and B3.

—They were outgained . . . after the game had been settled.—

Mark Johnson, "Hillcrest Outmans Tigers 34-6," *Myrtle Beach Sun News*, August 26, 1989, B1 and B3.

"You know, we got beat, of course . . . That was definitely tough."—

Mickey Wilson Jr., interviewed by both authors, Conway, South Carolina, November 21, 2012.

—The Cherry Hill group . . . "Niggers go home!"—

Nick Ravo, "Marchers and Brooklyn Youths Trade Racial Jeers," *NewYorkTimes.com*, August 27, 1989, accessed May 8, 2014, http://www.nytimes.com/1989/08/27/nyregion/marchers-and-brooklyn-youths-trade-racial-jeers.html.

—They wouldn't have known, but perhaps could have predicted . . .—

Information about the incidents at Virginia Beach in this paragraph comes from the following two sources:

Roy M. Campbell, "Why Virginia Beach Happened," *Philadelphia Inquirer*, September 10, 1989, accessed May 8, 2014, http://articles.philly.com/1989-09-10/news/26100185_1_greekfest-black-youths-disturbance.

Aaron Applegate, "The Painful Legacy of 1989's Greekfest Endures," *PilotOnline.com*, September 8, 2009, accessed May 8, 2014, http://hamptonroads.com/2009/09/painful-legacy-1989s-greekfest-endures.

CHAPTER 5. WORK TOGETHER, WALK TOGETHER

—Last week against Georgetown . . . second half with the big lead.—

"Week 0 Georgetown 25 Conway 42," YouTube video, 2:57, posted by WPDE NewsChannel 15, August 17, 2012, http://www.youtube.com/watch?v=meLGMnmmYYA.

—Late in the second quarter, the Tigers had a chance . . .—

Details from this game in this paragraph and in the next paragraph are taken from the following source:

Ian Guerin, "Northwestern Drubs Conway 55-19," *Heraldonline.com*, August 25, 1989, accessed March 12, 2014, http://www.heraldonline.com/2012/08/25/4213231/northwestern-drubs-conway-55-19.html.

—stride—

While the word "strife" would seem to make more sense in this context than "stride" (and would provide a rhyme with "life"), most versions of this prayer found online—like the one chanted by the Myrtle Beach Seahawks—use the word "stride" instead.

—"I have a son in jeopardy . . . there is going to be fuel for a fire."—

Mel Derrick, "Rational Thinking Needed Quickly," *Myrtle Beach Sun News*, August 27, 1989, B1.

—During the week . . . was discussed—

Rebecca James, "Activist Teacher Avoids Reprimand," *Myrtle Beach Sun News*, August 26, 1989, A1 and 10.

—"unprofessional and inappropriate behavior"—

Armand Derfner Collection, "May 25, 1987 Letter from Dawsey to Singleton," Avery Research Center for African American History and Culture, College of Charleston. Box 129, Folder 1.

—announced that the district . . . problem to be dealt with."—

Rebecca James, "Activist Teacher Avoids Reprimand," *Myrtle Beach Sun News*, August 26, 1989, A1 and A10.

—The first day of school . . . bring in police if necessary to quell violence—

Joseph J. Serwach, "Conway Strike Looms Over First Day of School," *Myrtle Beach Sun News*, August 28, 1989, A1.

—Principal Tommy Lewis said . . . the school day "boring."—

Rebecca James, "Conway Coach Cuts Boycotting Players," *Myrtle Beach Sun News*, August 29, 1989, A5.

—**Looking back now . . . peaceful beginning to the school year.**—

Larry Biddle, interviewed by both authors, Conway, South Carolina, May 6, 2014.

—**The "Renaissance Program," . . . "than he used to."**—

The special wraparound cover of the January 1989 issue of *Life* was sponsored by Jostens—the company best known for selling class rings and cap-and-gown sets. The sponsored material congratulated Conway High School on being recognized by the President's Commission on Education for its innovative work with students.

"The Day the President's Commission on Education Came to Conway, South Carolina," *Life*, January 1989, n.p. (wraparound cover).

—**A group of white parents . . . "no matter what color."**—

Rebecca James and Ettie Newlands, "Parents Seeking Boycott of Singleton's Classes," *Myrtle Beach Sun News*, August 29, 1989, A1 and A5.

—**Although Singleton stressed . . . other than earth science**—

Rebecca James, "District Suspends Singleton: Boycott Organizer Calls Act Unfounded," *Myrtle Beach Sun News*, August 30, 1989, A10.

—**Snyder's firing by CBS . . . breaking baseball's color barrier**—

Transcripts of Campanis's remarks are available in many places on the Internet, but a transcript can't accurately capture the exchange between Campanis and Koppel. A YouTube video of the incident can be found at the following link:

"Al Campanis Racist Remarks on *Nightline* (April 6, 1987)," YouTube video, 2:13, posted by Dingo Ate My Baby!, January 18, 2011, http://www.youtube.com/watch?v=O4XUbENGaiY.

—**"Until last week . . . many whites do not."**—

Rebecca James and Sammy Fretwell, "Boycott Shows Tension," *Myrtle Beach Sun News*, August 27, 1989, A1.

—**Ike Long, the white Mayor of Conway . . . something that's just not there."**—

Rebecca James and Sammy Fretwell, "Boycott Shows Tension," *Myrtle Beach Sun News*, August 27, 1989, A6.

—**The day the boycott began . . . I think it's outsiders behind this."**—

Mel Derrick, "Conway's Jordan Wants to Do the Right Thing," *Myrtle Beach Sun News*, August 23, 1989, B1.

—**Former Conway City Councilman . . . but then it leaks out."**—

Rebecca James and Sammy Fretwell, "Boycott Shows Tension," *Myrtle Beach Sun News*, August 27, 1989, A6.

—**Earlier that summer of 1989 . . . refusal to serve blacks.**—

"Campbell's Racism Policies Called Too Quiet," *Myrtle Beach Sun News*, September 18, 1989, A1.

Bruce Salter, the seventy-five-year-old owner . . . "[t]hey came to harass me."—

Jeff Kunerth, "Small-town Bar Runs into Some Big-time Trouble," *Orlando Sentinel*, October 8, 1989, accessed May 8, 2014. http://articles.orlandosentinel.com/1989-10-08/news/8910082910_1_salter-buffalo-room-naacp.

—**Once again, the coach found himself . . . back to square one."**—

Rebecca James, "Conway Coach Cuts Boycotting Players," *Myrtle Beach Sun News*, August 29, 1989, A1 and A5.

—**When practice started . . . the core of his team, were gone.**—

Mel Derrick, "Jordan Looks to Summerville," *Myrtle Beach Sun News*, August 29, 1989, B1 and B3.

—**After practice, in front of a crowd of reporters and fans, Jordan read his statement.**—
Chuck Jordan, "Jordan's Statement," *Myrtle Beach Sun News*, August 29, 1989, B1.

—**The *Sun News*'s Mel Derrick . . . what his team would look like.**—
Mel Derrick, "Jordan Looks to Summerville," *Myrtle Beach Sun News*, August 29, 1989, B1.

—**The following morning, Tuesday, H. H. Singleton . . .**—
The description of Singleton's suspension by John Dawsey in the remainder of this chapter is based on material from the following four sources:

Armand Derfner Collection, "Transcript of November 7, 1989 John Dawsey Testimony," Avery Research Center for African American History and Culture, College of Charleston. Box 127, Folder 8.

Burwell, Bryan, "Small-Town Football Feud Sparks Full-scale Racial Rift," *Detroit News*, October 15, 1989, C1.

Gil Stefanides, telephone interview by Joe Oestreich, November 21, 2014.

Hank Singleton III, interviewed by Joe Oestreich, Conway, South Carolina, March 2, 2013.

CHAPTER 6. FROM THE SAME SPOON

—**"In high school football" . . . "After all, I'm the one who taught 'em."**—
Chuck Jordan, telephone interview by Joe Oestreich, September 5, 2012.

—**As Rich Chrampanis . . . fooled by that 1 and 2 record,"**—
"Week 2 Rock Hill 34 Conway 13," YouTube video, 1:20, posted by WPDE NewsChannel 15, August 31, 2012, http://www.youtube.com/watch?v=IG_cFohEvG4.

—**"Kids are going to emulate . . . thinking about the *next* game."**—
Chuck Jordan, telephone interviewed by Joe Oestreich, September 5, 2012.

—**News of H. H. Singleton's suspension spread quickly through the black community . . .**—
Information and quotations about the reaction to the Rev. Singleton's suspension in this paragraph and in the next three paragraphs come from the interview listed below:
Hank Singleton III, interviewed by Joe Oestreich, Conway, South Carolina, March 2, 2013.

—**Reporters weren't allowed . . . approximately seven hundred people**—
Chrysti Edge, "Blacks Gather to Protest Singleton Suspension," *Myrtle Beach Sun News*, August 30, 1989, A1.

—**Hank cites a figure more like 1,300 . . . "It was on."**—
Hank Singleton III, interviewed by Joe Oestreich, Conway, South Carolina, March 2, 2013.

—**One attendee at the Cherry Hill meeting that night was . . .**—
Dr. McKever-Floyd's comments and recollections in this paragraph and in the next two paragraphs come from the interview listed below:
Preston McKever-Floyd, interviewed by both authors, Conway, South Carolina, July 24, 2013.

—During the meeting . . . *speak up for themselves*—

Hank Singleton III, interviewed by Joe Oestreich, Conway, South Carolina, March 2, 2013.

—In a statement . . . "put this uppity colored boy in his place."—

Rebecca James, Ron Morrison, and Sammy Fretwell, "Conway Mayor Forms Committee to Look at Race Relations," *Myrtle Beach Sun News*, September 2, 1989, A14.

—Former Conway councilman Cleveland Fladger . . . get him like that."—

Rebecca James, "District Suspends Singleton: Boycott Organizer Calls Act Unfounded," *Myrtle Beach Sun News*, August 30, 1989, A1.

—Herman Watson, president . . . Conway's in for the fight of its life."—

Chrysti Edge, "Blacks Gather to Protest Singleton Suspension," *Myrtle Beach Sun News*, August 30, 1989, A10.

—The next two mornings . . . H. H. Singleton be reinstated—

Rebecca James, "Civil Rights Activists Organize, Orchestrate to Make Their Point," *Myrtle Beach Sun News*, September 1, 1989, A10.

—Noting that the teacher's suspension . . . responsible reason to do either."—

Rebecca James, "Conway Blacks Denied Petition: Schools Chief Refuses Football Coach's Removal," *Myrtle Beach Sun News*, August 31, 1989, A1 and A11.

—In response, the protestors . . . his position as superintendent.—

Rebecca James, Ron Morrison, and Sammy Fretwell, "Conway Mayor Forms Committee to Look at Race Relations," *Myrtle Beach Sun News*, September 2, 1989, A14.

—"It's been hell . . . It's ugly."—

I. J. Rosenberg, "A Change at QB Tears Town Apart—Black-White Switch Spurs Boycott, Rally," *Atlanta Journal-Constitution*, September 2, 1989, E7.

—After moving so many . . . the varsity squad—

Chuck Jordan, interviewed by both authors, Conway, South Carolina, April 22, 2014.

—Before kickoff, Jordan told his team . . . to play well.—

Monty Cook, "Conway Falls 42-14," *Myrtle Beach Sun News*, September 2, 1989, B4.

—On the heels . . . rally at Cherry Hill Baptist.—

Rebecca James, "Conway Game Quiet; Boycott Spreads to Band," *Myrtle Beach Sun News*, September 2, 1989, A1 and A14.

—. . . twelfth consecutive day . . .—

Hank Singleton III, interviewed by Joe Oestreich, Conway, South Carolina, March 2, 2013.

—As the Cherry Hill crowd was meeting . . . to cheer on the overmatched Tigers.—

Rebecca James, "Conway Game Quiet; Boycott Spreads to Band," *Myrtle Beach Sun News*, September 2, 1989, A1.

—By halftime, the score was Summerville 35, Conway 0.—

Monty Cook, "Conway Falls 42-14," *Myrtle Beach Sun News*, September 2, 1989, B1.

—Down to merely twenty members . . . Conway crowd cheered that, too.—

Rebecca James, "Conway Game Quiet; Boycott Spreads to Band," *Myrtle Beach Sun News*, September 2, 1989, A14.

—Mickey Wilson completed only five of twelve passes for 56 yards that night . . .—

Information and quotations relating to the Summerville game in this paragraph and in the next paragraph come from the following source:

Monty Cook, "Conway Falls 42-14," *Myrtle Beach Sun News*, September 2, 1989, B1 and B4.

—Sanders says now that his loyalty to the team was rewarded . . .—

Cleveland Sanders, interviewed by both authors, Conway, South Carolina, May 18, 2014.

In 1989 Conway was a place . . . almost its own religion."—

Joseph J. Serwach, "Conway Strike Looms Over First Day of School," *Myrtle Beach Sun News*, August 28, 1989, A1.

—As Summerville's John McKissick said . . . That's all there is to it."—

Mel Derrick, "In Conway, Both Sides Need to Erase the Line," *Myrtle Beach Sun News*, September 3, 1989, B10.

—Randy Beverly, who played . . . that's absurd."—

"What People Are Saying," *Myrtle Beach Sun News*, August 28, 1989, A5.

—"I moved Hunt because . . . I win with defense."—

I. J. Rosenberg, "A Change at QB Tears Town Apart—Black-White Switch Spurs Boycott, Rally," *Atlanta Journal-Constitution*, September 2, 1989, E7.

—And many of Jordan's former players . . . only about winning, never race.—

Andre Christopher, "Former Players Back Jordan," *Myrtle Beach Sun News*, August 27, 1989, B1.

—John Avant, an African American . . . Chuck's credibility as a coach."—

Joseph J. Serwach, "Conway Strike Looms Over First Day of School," *Myrtle Beach Sun News*, August 28, 1989, A5.

—Dawsey described the meeting . . . compete on the field.—

Rebecca James, "No Progress Made in Conway Dispute," *Myrtle Beach Sun News*, September 1, 1989, A1 and A9.

—As an example . . . we gave him a chance."—

Sammy Fretwell, "Jordan: Not Used to Boos," *Myrtle Beach Sun News*, September 3, 1989, A1.

—Jimmy Sherman . . . Rev. Singleton's hand."

Jimmy Sherman, "Justice Should Prevail" (letter to the editor), *Myrtle Beach Sun News*, August 31, 1989, A13.

—George Latimer . . . blame the black community" for the boycott—

George Latimer Jr., "Newspaper Is Racist" (letter to the editor), *Myrtle Beach Sun News*, August 31, 1989, A13.

—On the Friday of the Summerville game, Mayor Ike Long . . .—

Unless otherwise noted, information and quotations on the committee formed by Mayor Long in this paragraph and in the next paragraph come from the following source:

Rebecca James, Ron Morrison, and Sammy Fretwell, "Conway Mayor Forms Committee to Look at Race Relations," *Myrtle Beach Sun News*, September 2, 1989, A1 and A14.

—Six days earlier, Mayor Long had said . . . that's just not there."—

Rebecca James and Sammy Fretwell, "Boycott Shows Tension," *Myrtle Beach Sun News*, August 27, 1989, A6.

—A hundred and thirty miles west . . . "in the situation."—

Rebecca James, "S.C. Human Affairs Chief Investigates Dispute," *Myrtle Beach Sun News*, September 8, 1989, A1 and A6.

—who in 1993 . . . Democrat in the House—

"Biography—Assistant Democratic Leader," *Assistant Democratic Leader James E. Clyburn* accessed August 22, 2014 http://assistantdemocraticleader.house.gov/index.cfm?p=Biography.

—had already sent . . . to investigate the allegations of racism—

Rebecca James, "S.C. Human Affairs Chief Investigates Dispute," *Myrtle Beach Sun News*, September 8, 1989, A1 and A6.

—That weekend . . . chanted "Fight the Power."—

D. W. Page (the Associated Press), "NAACP Faults Va. Beach Actions," *Myrtle Beach Sun News*, September 5, 1989, A1.

—Given that tourism . . . overwhelming tourism leader—

Dave Moniz, "Struggling Against Racism's Shadow, Conway Still Trying to Heal Wounds of '89," *State* (Columbia, SC), August 18, 1990, A1.

—The commissioner's first decision . . . old-fashioned give-and-take.—

Rebecca James, "S.C. Human Affairs Chief Investigates Dispute," *Myrtle Beach Sun News*, September 8, 1989, A6.

—That evening . . . return to the team.—

Details of this call come from the following two sources:

Chuck Jordan, interviewed by both authors, Conway, South Carolina, March 14, 2012.

Armand Derfner Collection, "Sequence of Events as Recorded by Chuck Jordan," Avery Research Center for African American History and Culture, College of Charleston. Box 127, Folder 6.

—The coach refused to sign . . . *including that of quarterback.*—

Rebecca James and Yolanda Jones, "Conway Coach Asks Blacks to Rejoin Team," *Myrtle Beach Sun News*, September 8, 1989, A6.

—Jordan insisted that the statement not single out any specific player—

Information and quotations relating to the writing of the statement inviting the players to return come from the following two sources:

Rebecca James and Yolanda Jones, "Conway Coach Asks Blacks to Rejoin Team," *Myrtle Beach Sun News*, September 8, 1989, A1 and A6.

Dave Moniz, "Some Who Boycotted Team Return," *State* (Columbia, SC), September 9, 1989, A1.

—Striking player Michael Pickett . . . anything about that."—

Michael Pickett, interviewed by Scott Pleasant, Conway, South Carolina, May 5, 2014.

—Moreover, they'd scheduled . . . busloads with them.—

"NAACP March," *Myrtle Beach Sun News*, September 8, 1989, A1.

—On the Thursday . . . another meeting at Cherry Hill,—

Information and quotations relating to this meeting and Mitchell's announcement come from the following four sources:

Hank Hersch, "Choosing Sides," *Sports Illustrated*, November 27, 1989, 46.

Lawrence Mitchell, telephone interviewed by both authors, October 15, 2013.

Michael Pickett, interviewed by Scott Pleasant, Conway, South Carolina, May 5, 2014.

Yolanda Jones and Sammy Fretwell, "Some Blacks Rejoin Conway Team," *Myrtle Beach Sun News*, September 9, 1989, A1 and A5.

CHAPTER 7. SHAKEN UP

—According to a 2006 report by the Centers for Disease Control . . .—
Information about sports injuries in this paragraph and in the next paragraph comes from the CDC report listed below:
Centers for Disease Control, "Morbidity and Mortality Weekly Report," *CDC.gov*, last modified September 29, 2006, accessed May 9, 2014, http://www.cdc.gov/mmwr/preview/ mmwrhtml/mm5538a1.htm.
—The trainers shone penlights . . . president of the United States?—
Andrea Sulewski (head trainer for the Myrtle Beach Seahawks), interviewed by Scott Pleasant, Myrtle Beach, South Carolina, August 3, 2013.
—The verdict this time . . . would be "mild concussion"—
"Myrtle Beach 33, Irmo 27," YouTube video, 2:20, posted by WPDE NewsChannel 15, August 25, 2012, http://www.youtube.com/watch?v=-X8aYFBCZ-U.
—In the week following tonight's game . . . the debilitating injury it had appeared to be.—
Mickey Wilson Jr., interviewed by Scott Pleasant, September 7, 2012.
—A month from now . . . shock of losing a brother.—
Associated Press, "Ronald Rouse, 18, Dies During Game," *ESPN.com*, October 6, 2012, http://espn.go.com/high-school/football/story/_/id/8468314/high-school-lineman-south -carolina-collapses-tackle-dies.
—Lawrence Mitchell had already been tempted to break the strike.—
References in this chapter to Lawrence Mitchell's recollections and thoughts about the 1989 season, including his experiences at the Middleton game on September 8, come from the following source:
Lawrence Mitchell, telephone interview by both authors, October 15, 2013.
—Earlier that year, a recruiter . . . kid could play on Sundays right now."—
Mickey Wilson Sr., interviewed by both authors, Conway, South Carolina, October 23, 2013.
—After all, as James Clyburn mentioned . . . the one everyone listens to."—
Rebecca James, "Star Player Returns to Boycott," *Myrtle Beach Sun News*, September 12, 1989, A1.
—As he told *Sports Illustrated* . . . you've already proved yours."—
Hank Hersch, "Choosing Sides," *Sports Illustrated*, November 27, 1989, 46.
—when he walked out of the church . . . 'Don't go back.'"—
Hank Hersch, "Choosing Sides," *Sports Illustrated*, November 27, 1989, 46.
—But because Lawrence Mitchell was Lawrence Mitchell, he did carry others with him.—
Information and quotations from 1989 relating to Lawrence Mitchell's brief return to the team for the Middleton game come from these two sources:

Armand Derfner Collection, "Sequence of Events as Recorded by Chuck Jordan," Avery Research Center for African American History and Culture, College of Charleston. Box 127, Folder 6.

Yolanda Jones and Sammy Fretwell, "Some Blacks Rejoin Conway Team," *Myrtle Beach Sun News*, September 9, 1989, A1 and A5.

—**When the buses pulled up . . . a four-member mounted unit.**—

Chrysti Edge, "Charleston Blacks Picket Conway's Football Squad," *Myrtle Beach Sun News*, September 9, 1989, A1.

—**Mickey Wilson remembers that the Tigers had been told to expect trouble**—

References in this chapter to Mickey Wilson Jr.'s recollections and thoughts about the 1989 season, including his experiences at the Middleton game on September 8, come from the following source:

Mickey Wilson Jr., interviewed by both authors, Conway, South Carolina, November 21, 2012.

—**James Clyburn was the state's . . . he said to the *Sun News*.**—

Sammy Fretwell, "Conway Racial Dispute Described as One of Worst in S.C. History," *Myrtle Beach Sun News*, September 9, 1989, A5.

—**Chuck Jordan's squad was indeed . . . their non-violent protest."**—

Chrysti Edge, "Charleston Blacks Picket Conway's Football Squad," *Myrtle Beach Sun News*, September 9, 1989, A1 and A5.

—**On the field, with Mickey at QB . . .**—

Information about the Middleton game on September 8, 1989, in this paragraph and in the next paragraph comes from the following source:

Mel Derrick, "Conway Loses Again, But Gains Six Suspended Players," *Myrtle Beach Sun News*, September 9, 1989, B1 and B4.

—**Before the strike, Mickey Wilson . . . close for a long time, man. For years."**—

Lawrence Mitchell, telephone interview by both authors, October 15, 2013.

—**But once the boycott began, the friendship stalled. . . .**—

Unless otherwise noted, information and quotations in this paragraph and in the next paragraph come from the following source:

Mickey Wilson Jr., interviewed by both authors, November 21, 2012.

—**With Mickey on the bench . . . Coach Jordan sent in the backup, Brian Steele.**—

Mel Derrick, "Conway Loses Again, But Gains Six Suspended Players," *Myrtle Beach Sun News*, September 9, 1989, B4.

—**When the game was over, Mickey stood up from the bench . . .**—

The story of Lawrence Mitchell carrying Mickey off the field that is told in this paragraph and in the next two paragraphs is taken primarily from the article listed below, but it is substantially corroborated by other print sources and interviews conducted by the authors.

Mel Derrick, "White? Black? Now, He's Just a Teammate," *Myrtle Beach Sun News*, September 10, 1989, B1.

—**The next afternoon . . . would be completely blocked off.**—

"Today's NAACP March," *Myrtle Beach Sun News*, September 9, 1989, A1.

—The NAACP had been granted . . . the crescendo of tourist season.—

"NAACP March," *Myrtle Beach Sun News*, September 8, 1989, A1.

—The event was billed . . . bodies swaying in the heat.—

Yolanda Jones, "NAACP Pledges Weekly Marches," *Myrtle Beach Sun News*, September 10, 1989, A1 and A8.

—Meanwhile, inside the church . . . circumstances and the facts were."—

Yolanda Jones, "NAACP Files Lawsuit to Bar Action Against Singleton," *Myrtle Beach Sun News*, September 10, 1989, A1.

—When the NAACP meeting ended, Singleton and others emerged . . .—

Information and quotations about the NAACP march on September 9, 1989, in this paragraph and in the next eight paragraphs come from the following sources:

Hank Singleton III, interviewed by Joe Oestreich, Conway, South Carolina, March 2, 2013.

Joseph J. Serwach and Yolanda Jones, "Former Conway QB Tells His Story," *Myrtle Beach Sun News*, September 11, 1989, A1.

Kathy Ropp, "Blacks Continue Boycott, Protests: Hundreds Parade in Conway," *Horry Independent*, September 13, 1989, A1 and A14.

"Today's NAACP March," *Myrtle Beach Sun News*, September 9, 1989, A1.

Yolanda Jones, "NAACP Pledges Weekly Marches," *Myrtle Beach Sun News*, September 10, 1989, A1 and A8.

—Coach Jordan heard the rumors . . . but hoping for the best.—

Information and quotations about Lawrence Mitchell's decision to return to the team in this paragraph and in the next paragraph come from the following source:

Rebecca James, "Star Player Returns to Boycott," *Myrtle Beach Sun News*, September 12, 1989, A5.

CHAPTER 8. BE PARANOID

—Win it and, well . . . playing for the Bell."—

Lawrence Mitchell, telephone interview by both authors, October 15, 2013.

—A Conway native, Jordan grew up on the south side of town . . .—

Unless otherwise noted information relating to Coach Jordan's biography in this paragraph and in the next three paragraphs come from the two sources listed below, but the information has been corroborated by the authors' interview with Coach Jordan on April 22, 2014:

Sammy Fretwell, "Jordan: Not Used to Boos," *Myrtle Beach Sun News*, September 3, 1989, A1 and A6.

Hank Hersch, "Choosing Sides," *Sports Illustrated*, November 27, 1989, 63.

—when he graduated in 1975 . . . four wins in the Bell Game—

"Conway High School Football Results—1970–1979," *South Carolina High School Football History Page*, accessed May 10, 2014, http://www.scfootballhistory.com/School/Decade/70.aspx?schoolid=177.

—Throughout the '60s and '70s . . . lost to the Seahawks only once—

Data compiled from the following two sources:

"Conway High School Football Results—1960–1969," *South Carolina High School Football History Page*, accessed May 10, 2014, http://www.scfootballhistory.com/School/Decade/60.aspx?schoolid=177.

"Conway High School Football Results—1970–1979," *South Carolina High School Football History Page*, accessed May 10, 2014, http://www.scfootballhistory.com/School/Decade/70.aspx?schoolid=177.

—Meanwhile, back home . . . dropped four out of five to the Seahawks.—

Data compiled from the following two sources:

"Conway High School Football Results—1970–1979," *South Carolina High School Football History Page*, accessed May 10, 2014, http://www.scfootballhistory.com/School/Decade/70.aspx?schoolid=177.

"Conway High School Football Results—1980–1989," *South Carolina High School Football History Page*, accessed May 10, 2014, http://www.scfootballhistory.com/School/Decade/80.aspx?schoolid=177.

—Soon Jordan's winning spirit took hold . . . four straight wins in the Bell Game.—

"Conway High School Football Results—1980–1989," *South Carolina High School Football History Page*, accessed May 10, 2014, http://www.scfootballhistory.com/School/Decade/80.aspx?schoolid=177.

—Conway's favorite son, it seemed, "could walk on the Waccamaw."—

Sammy Fretwell, "Jordan: Not Used to Hearing Boos," *Myrtle Beach Sun News*, September 3, 1989, A1.

—Of his first twenty-two Bell Games, Jordan won twenty.—

Data compiled from the following sources:

"Conway High School Football Results—1980–1989," *South Carolina High School Football History Page*, accessed May 10, 2014, http://www.scfootballhistory.com/School/Decade/80.aspx?schoolid=177.

"Conway High School Football Results—1990–1999," *South Carolina High School Football History Page*, accessed May 10, 2014, http://www.scfootballhistory.com/School/Decade/90.aspx?schoolid=177.

"Conway High School Football Results—2000–2009," *South Carolina High School Football History Page*, accessed May 10, 2014, http://www.scfootballhistory.com/School/Decade/00.aspx?schoolid=177.

—In a boast . . . "bell from their memory."—

"Stepping Over the Competition . . . The Tradition Continues," in *Stepping Stones to Excellence: Conway High School Mirror 1989*, Susan Timmons and Sarah Young, eds. (Conway, SC: Conway High School, 1989), 24.

—The "rivalry" eventually got so laughable . . . hurt their ranking."—

Mickey Wilson Jr., interviewed by Scott Pleasant, Myrtle Beach, South Carolina, August 3, 2013.

—a 3A school they'd manhandled 48–14 the year before—

"Conway High School Football Results—2010–Present," *South Carolina High School Football History Page*, accessed May 27, 2014, http://www.scfootballhistory.com/School/Decade/10.aspx?schoolid=177

—A fourth straight loss . . . we were a little stressed at that point."—

Ryan Elswick, "Conway Wins Shootout with Marlboro County," *Myrtle Beach Sun News*, September 14, 2012, accessed May 10, 2014, http://www.myrtlebeachonline.com/2012/09/14/3059767/conway-wins-shootout-with-marlboro.html.

—As he'd later say, "The bottom line is that we are Conway."—

Ryan Elswick, "Conway Wins Shootout with Marlboro County," *Myrtle Beach Sun News*, September 14, 2012, accessed May 10, 2014, http://www.myrtlebeachonline.com/2012/09/14/3059767/conway-wins-shootout-with-marlboro.html.

—But this season, they've added . . . his hometown and his old coach.—

Chuck Jordan, telephone interview by Joe Oestreich, October 10, 2012.

—"It's good for a team to . . . overcome a struggle."—

Chuck Jordan, telephone interviewed by Joe Oestreich, September 19, 2012.

—And in the last few years . . . winning streak longer than two games.—

Information compiled from the following sources:

"Conway High School—Football Results 2010–Present," *South Carolina High School Football History Page*, accessed May 27, 2014, http://www.scfootballhistory.com/School/Decade/10.aspx?schoolid=177.

"Conway High School—Football Results 2000–2009," *South Carolina High School Football History Page*, accessed May 27, 2014, http://www.scfootballhistory.com/School/Decade/00.aspx?schoolid=177.

"Conway High School—Football Results 1990–1999," *South Carolina High School Football History Page*, accessed May 27, 2014, http://www.scfootballhistory.com/School/Decade/90.aspx?schoolid=177.

"Conway High School—Football Results 1980–1989," *South Carolina High School Football History Page*, accessed May 27, 2014, http://www.scfootballhistory.com/School/Decade/80.aspx?schoolid=177.

—"For a long time, Conway dominated . . . I don't like to lose."—

Chuck Jordan, telephone interviewed by Joe Oestreich, September 19, 2012.

—"We celebrate our wins . . . I can tell you that for sure."—

Mickey Wilson Jr., interviewed by Scott Pleasant, Conway, South Carolina, September 16, 2012.

—"We talk about complacency . . . I tell them 'Be paranoid.'"—

Mickey Wilson Jr., interviewed by Scott Pleasant, Myrtle Beach, South Carolina, July 10, 2013.

—Carolina Forest High opened fifteen years ago—

"About Us," *Carolina Forest High School*, accessed May 27, 2014, http://cfh.horrycountyschools.net/pages/Carolina_Forest_High_School/About_Us.

—Adding fuel to the . . . that type of thing."—

Ian Guerin, "Myrtle Beach's Keane Makes Return to Carolina Forest on Friday," *Myrtle Beach Sun News*, September 13, 2012, accessed May 27, 2014, http://www.myrtlebeachonline.com/2012/09/13/3057067/myrtle-beachs-keane-makes-return.html.

—"In the grand scheme of things . . . it means nothing."—

Mickey Wilson Jr., interviewed by Scott Pleasant, Myrtle Beach, South Carolina, August 3, 2013.

—The Monday before the '89 Bell Game . . . the season was lost.—

Information and quotations about Lawrence Mitchell's return to the team in this paragraph and in the next paragraph are taken from the following source:

Rebecca James, "Star Player Returns to Boycott," *Myrtle Beach Sun News*, September 12, 1989, A1 and A5.

—**"Lawrence is trying to do the right thing . . . go back together."**—

Rebecca James, "Star's Return to Boycott Explained," *Myrtle Beach Sun News*, September 14, 1989, A1.

—**"My grandmother told me . . . go back to the boycott."**—

Lawrence Mitchell, telephone interview by both authors, October 15, 2013.

—**Chuck Jordan says that . . . you're *part* of it."**—

Chuck Jordan, interviewed by both authors, Conway, South Carolina, March 14, 2012.

—**in February 1990, the KKK made a highly visible and public appearance.**—

Information and quotations about the February 1990 Klan march in this paragraph are taken from the following source:

Robert Anderson, "Crowd Claps As KKK Goes to Courthouse," *Horry Independent*, February 7, 1990, A1.

—**That fall, Jordan's wife, Pat . . . made death threats.**—

Hank Hersch, "Choosing Sides," *Sports Illustrated*, November 27, 1989, 63.

—**Mickey Wilson's family . . . meet you in the front yard."**—

Mickey Wilson Sr., interviewed by both authors, Conway, South Carolina, October 23, 2013.

—**"I was so scared . . . somebody going to shoot him."**—

Mona Wilson, interviewed by both authors, Conway, South Carolina, October 23, 2013.

—**Hank Singleton says the menacing calls . . .**—

This accounting of the fearful atmosphere at Cherry Hill and story of the threatening phone call come from the following source:

Hank Singleton III, interviewed by Joe Oestreich, Conway, South Carolina, March 2, 2013.

—**Just over a week before . . . opinion pieces written by readers**—

"Conway in Controversy," *Myrtle Beach Sun News*, September 7, 1989, A8.

—**reader Joyce Jones . . . conditioned to ignore.**—

Joyce Jones, "Racist Acts, Many In, Out of Schools," *Myrtle Beach Sun News*, September 7, 1989, A8.

—**In a letter to the *Horry Independent* . . . between the blacks and whites."**—

Dennis J. Allen, "Singleton Is Problem," *Horry Independent*, September 13, 1989, A2.

—**A letter by Paul A. Barra . . . sit for a day in H.H. Singleton's class."**—

Paul A. Barra, letter to the editor, *Horry Independent*, August 30, 1989, A2.

—**Mary E. Moore . . . "get this thing over with."**—

Mary E. Moore, "Out of Skins; Less Racism," *Myrtle Beach Sun News*, September 7, 1989, A8.

—**"Warmer hearts must dwell inside . . . she writes.**—

Mary E. Moore, "Out of Skins; Less Racism," *Myrtle Beach Sun News*, September 7, 1989, A8.

—**Mel Derrick of the *Sun News* . . . back to the locker room**—

Mel Derrick, "White? Black? Now, He's Just a Teammate," *Myrtle Beach Sun News*, September 10, 1989, B1.

—**When Mickey tells the story . . . he just grabbed me."**—

Mickey Wilson Jr., interviewed by both authors, Conway, South Carolina, November 21, 2012.

—**In remarks that the *Horry Independent* . . . made selfishness acceptable."**—

Kathy Ropp, "Clyburn Traces Racial Problems to Reagan Era," *Horry Independent*, September 13, 1989, A5.

—**The week before the Middleton game . . . "We are back where we started."**—

Linda Greenhouse, "Justice Criticizes U.S. Court's Civil Rights Rulings," written for the *New York Times*, reprinted in *Myrtle Beach Sun News*, September 9, 1989, A1 and A5.

—**"When you take all that . . . it's something."**—

Sammy Fretwell, "Conway Racial Dispute Described as One of Worst in S.C. History," *Myrtle Beach Sun News*, September 9, 1989, A5.

—**Throughout the first three weeks of the boycott . . .**—

From a non-commercial DVD of the press conference privately owned and loaned to the authors by Hank Singleton III.

—**On the Tuesday before the Bell Game . . . man to man."**—

"Coach and Player: They Need to Talk," *Myrtle Beach Sun News*, September 12, 1989, A8.

—**Even James Clyburn . . . rhetoric seems to have the upper hand."**—

Rebecca James, "Star Player Returns to Boycott," *Myrtle Beach Sun News*, September 12, 1989, A5.

—**The piece referred to the boycott . . . "now-racial chasm."**—

"Coach and Player: They Need to Talk," *Myrtle Beach Sun News*, September 12, 1989, A8.

—**the *Sun News* made a controversial move . . . "become repetitive."**—

"Letter to Readers," *Myrtle Beach Sun News*, September 14, 1989, A15.

—**It was the week that . . . injunction against the suspension.**—

Rebecca James, "Singleton Suspension Case Assigned to Judge," *Myrtle Beach Sun News*, September 13, 1989, A1 and A9.

—**"I have a dream . . . content of their character."**—

Martin Luther King Jr., "I Have a Dream" (transcript), August 28, 1963, accessed May 10, 2014, http://www.archives.gov/press/exhibits/dream-speech.pdf.

—**"It is obvious today . . . come back marked 'insufficient funds.'"**—

Martin Luther King Jr., "I Have a Dream" (transcript), August 28, 1963, accessed May 10, 2014, http://www.archives.gov/press/exhibits/dream-speech.pdf.

CHAPTER 9. PLAYING FOR THE BELL

—**Hank Singleton absolutely points to 1989 . . .**—

Hank Singleton III, interviewed by Joe Oestreich, Conway, South Carolina, March 2, 2013.

—**At a recent NAACP function . . . he gets right with God."**—

Earl Friday, interviewed by both authors, Conway, South Carolina, March 16, 2013.

—Phaedra Faulk . . . still being judged by God."—

Phaedra Faulk, interviewed by both authors, Conway, South Carolina, March 16, 2013.

—"That would be the best thing . . . to beat us as they are right now."—

Mark Johnson, "Seahawks Hope to Hear a Bell Friday Night," *Myrtle Beach Sun News*, September 14, 1989, B1.

—"There was a lot of . . . this is our team."—

Mickey Wilson Jr., interviewed by both authors, Conway, South Carolina, November 21, 2012.

—Coach Jordan held on to the hope . . .—

The two coaches' pre-game comments and other information relating to the 1989 Bell Game in this paragraph and in the next paragraph come from the following source:

Mark Johnson, "Seahawks Hope to Hear a Bell Friday Night," *Myrtle Beach Sun News*, September 14, 1989, B1 and B5.

—a team that had taken the Victory Bell home only five times since 1960—

Compiled from Myrtle Beach and Conway game records since 1960 at the website listed below:

South Carolina High School Football History Page, accessed May 27, 2014, http://www .scfootballhistory.com.

—On Friday night, about 4,000 fans packed into Memorial Stadium, . . .—

Accounts of and quotations relating to the 1989 Bell Game in this paragraph and in the next three paragraphs come from the two following sources:

Mark Johnson, "Seahawks Dump Testy Tigers," *Myrtle Beach Sun News*, September 16, 1989, B1 and B4.

Guy Dozier, "Tigers Pull Up Short Against Archrival MB," *Horry Independent*, September 20, 1989, A8.

—aching with the bruised . . . he'd suffered in the Middleton game.—

Mel Derrick, "Conway Loses Again, But Gains Six Suspended Players," *Myrtle Beach Sun News*, September 9, 1989, B4.

—roughly the square mileage of Rhode Island—

United States Census Bureau, "State and County Quick Facts—Horry (county), South Carolina," last modified March 27, 2014, accessed May 20, 2014, http://quickfacts.census .gov/qfd/states/45/45051.html.

—Months later, when he's asked . . . gotten kinda crazy lately."—

Mickey Wilson Jr., interviewed by both authors, Conway, South Carolina, August 3, 2013.

—Myrtle Beach has won four Bell Games out of the last five.—

"Conway High School—Football Results 2010–Present," *South Carolina High School Football History Page*, accessed May 27, 2014, http://www.scfootballhistory.com/School/ Decade/10.aspx?schoolid=177.

"Conway High School—Football Results 2000–2009," *South Carolina High School Football History Page*, accessed May 27, 2014, http://www.scfootballhistory.com/School/ Decade/00.aspx?schoolid=177.

—Twenty-plus years ago . . . throughout that '89 season.—

Chuck Jordan, interviewed by both authors, Conway, South Carolina, March 14, 2012.

—For his part, Mickey describes . . . tougher mentally and physically."—

Mickey Wilson Jr., interviewed by both authors, Conway, South Carolina. November 21, 2012.

—In *Remember the Titans* . . . appreciate one another.—

Remember the Titans, directed by Boaz Yakin (2006: Walt Disney Pictures, in association with Jerry Bruckheimer Films, Buena Vista Home Entertainment, 2006), DVD.

—tying both the school record—

"Myrtle Beach Seahawks Records and Achievements," *Myrtle Beach Football* (on *Hometeamsonline.com*), accessed May 10, 2014, http://www.hometeamsonline.com/teams/default.asp?u=MYRTLEBEACHFOOTBALLCOM&t=c&s=football&p=records.

—the state record—

"Palmetto's Finest Record Book: Football," *South Carolina High School League*, accessed May 12, 2014, http://www.schsl.org/2012/PFfb.pdf.

(Note: While the state record for touchdown passes in a game is eight, as the .pdf at the link above states, Tyler Keane's name is not listed as one of the record holders. In a brief interview on May 11, 2014, Mickey Wilson explained that Tyler's name is missing from that list because no one from Myrtle Beach had yet submitted his name and proof of the accomplishment to the South Carolina High School League, as is required for certification of all state sports records.)

—520 passing yards (a school record)—

"Myrtle Beach Seahawks Records and Achievements," *Myrtle Beach Football* (on *Hometeamsonline.com*), accessed May 10, 2014, http://www.hometeamsonline.com/teams/default.asp?u=MYRTLEBEACHFOOTBALLCOM&t=c&s=football&p=records.

—If Dallas Cowboy Jackie Smith . . . play-by-play on the game—

"Super Bowl XIII: Dallas Cowboys' Jackie Smith's Key Drop Helps Steelers Win," *NYDailyNews.com*, December 29, 2013, http://www.nydailynews.com/sports/football/super-bowl-xiii-sickest-man-america-article-1.1561166#ixzz2y9HzdWal.

—When asked about it later . . . "He just walked off the field."—

Mickey Wilson Jr., interviewed by Scott Pleasant, Conway, South Carolina, September 23, 2012.

CHAPTER 10. THE COMING STORM

—"I think he could win the Heisman."—

Mickey Wilson Jr., interviewed by both authors, Myrtle Beach, South Carolina, May 21, 2012.

—But now, after leading the resurgent Irish . . . losing a costly fumble.—

"Tommy Rees Comes Off Bench to Engineer Notre Dame's Winning Drive," *ESPN.com*, September 8, 2012, http://espn.go.com/ncf/recap?gameId=322520087.

—But Golson worked hard enough . . . top ten opponent in seven years,—

"No. 20 Notre Dame Beats No. 10 Michigan State 20–3," *SportsIllustrated.CNN*.com, accessed 7 April 2014, http://sportsillustrated.cnn.com/football/ncaa/gameflash/2012/09/15/49664/.

—"We're very fortunate to play where we play."—

Mickey Wilson Jr., interviewed by Scott Pleasant, Florence, South Carolina, September 28, 2012.

—**Perhaps that's because . . . growing ever precarious.**—

Brian Hamilton, "Kelly: Notre Dame Offense, QB Must Improve," *Chicago Tribune*, September 23, 2012, http://articles.chicagotribune.com/2012-09-23/sports/chi-kelly-notre -dame-offense-qb-golson-must-improve-20120923_1_qb-golson-notre-dame-offense -everett-golson.

—**. . . Everett will be suspended by Notre Dame . . . unspecified academic violation.**—

Lamond Pope, "Suspended Irish QB Everett Golson admits cheating on test," *Chicago Sun-Times*, October 29, 2013, accessed September 8, 2014, http://www.suntimes.com/ sports/colleges/23420462-419/suspended-irish-qb-everett-golson-admits-cheating-on -test.html#.VA9XFl4mUdt

—**What they don't know . . . blaring from the stadium speakers.**—

Ian Guerin, "Socastee Knocks Off Rival Myrtle Beach," *Myrtle Beach Sun News*, October 5, 2012, accessed April 7, 2014, http://www.myrtlebeachonline.com/2012/10/05/3099524/ socastee-knocks-off-rival-myrtle.html#storylink=cpy.

—**"I hate kicking field goals . . . I'll take that every time."**—

Mickey Wilson Jr., interviewed by Scott Pleasant, Conway, South Carolina, October 7, 2012.

—**The next day in the Sun News . . . We're going to drive on . . .**—

Ian Guerin, "Socastee Knocks Off Rival Myrtle Beach," *Myrtle Beach Sun News*, October 5, 2012, accessed April 7, 2014, http://www.myrtlebeachonline.com/2012/10/05/3099524/ socastee-knocks-off-rival-myrtle.html#storylink=cpy.

—**In 1989 Grand Strand residents . . . Hazel in '54.**—

Tom Rubillo, *Hurricane Destruction in South Carolina: Hell and High Water* (Charleston, SC: History Press, 2006), 112–15.

—**. . . the population of Horry County more than doubled**—

1990 U.S. Census Data.

—**In his book, *Hurricane Destruction in South Carolina* . . . along South Carolina's coast**—

Tom Rubillo, *Hurricane Destruction in South Carolina: Hell and High Water* (Charleston, SC: History Press, 2006), 115.

—**It was Saturday, the afternoon of the NAACP's second March Against Intimidation.**—

Accounts and quotations from this second NAACP march are taken from a privately owned DVD of the Singleton Homegoing ceremony kindly loaned to the authors by Hank Singleton III, and from the following source:

Yolanda Jones, "NAACP Pledges Weekly Marches," *Myrtle Beach Sun News*, September 10, 1989, A1 and A8.

—**a sharp increase in the membership numbers**—

Yolanda Jones, "NAACP Boosts Membership, and S.C. Disputes Are Helping," *Myrtle Beach Sun News,* September 14, A1 and A9.

—**With Conway business owners . . . Church Street's shops and stores**—

Sammy Fretwell, "Marchers May Have Cut Business Access," *Myrtle Beach Sun News*, September 12, 1989, A1 and A5.

—The second march was evidence . . . justice to roll down like the water."—

Yolanda Jones, "1000 More Join NAACP's Weekly March," *Myrtle Beach Sun News*, September 17, 1989, D3.

—"Caribbean Braces for Hugo Fury," . . . Hurricane David in 1979—

Robert Glass, "Caribbean Braces for Hugo Fury," *Myrtle Beach Sun News*, September 17, 1989, A1.

—As deadly as that storm had been . . . damage was comparatively minor—

Tom Rubillo, *Hurricane Destruction in South Carolina: Hell and High Water* (Charleston, SC: History Press, 2006), 115.

—Hurricane Gabrielle—the most recent named storm . . . less than a week before—

Ron Morrison, "Strand Takes Precautions Against Hugo," *Myrtle Beach Sun News*, September 19, 1989, A1.

—The next day, Monday, September 18 . . . tens of thousands homeless.—

"The Life of Hurricane Hugo," in *Hurricane Hugo and the Grand Strand*, Cynthia J. Struby, ed. (Myrtle Beach: Sun Publishing, 1989), 7.

—The day before, a meteorologist . . . the storm will even hit the United States."—

Robert Glass, "Hugo Pummels U.S. Virgin Islands: Storm Expected to Hit Puerto Rico Today," *Myrtle Beach Sun News*, September 18, 1989, A1.

—On that Monday . . . if their demands were not met—

Rebecca James, "Protesters Picket School-District Offices," *Myrtle Beach Sun News*, September 19, 1989, A8.

—Two days later . . . social Gospel for the law of God—

Rebecca James, "School Board to Review Coach's Actions," *Myrtle Beach Sun News*, September 21, 1989, A8.

—After the public forum . . . lawsuit against the district was decided—

Rebecca James, "School Board to Review Coach's Actions," *Myrtle Beach Sun News*, September 21, 1989, A8.

—Nearly a month after the boycott began . . . very little about what is going on—

Rebecca James, "School Board Keeping Low Profile on Racism Issue," *Myrtle Beach Sun News*, September 20, 1989, C6.

—Meanwhile . . . somewhere on the East Coast—

Ron Morrison, "Strand Takes Precautions Against Hugo," *Myrtle Beach Sun News*, September 19, 1989, A1.

—By Wednesday, projections from forecasters . . . Georgia or South Carolina—

"Hugo Aiming for U.S. Coast," *Myrtle Beach Sun News*, September 20, 1989, A1.

—Myrtle Beach officials began urging those living in low-lying areas to evacuate—

Lesia J. Shannon and Lisa Greene, "Evacuation Urged for Some Areas," *Myrtle Beach Sun News*, September 21, 1989, A1.

—The next day, the news got worse . . . Hurricane Gracie in 1959—

Chrysti Edge, "Strand Braces for Fury of Storm," *Myrtle Beach Sun News*, September 22, 1989, A1.

—Folks taped and boarded windows . . . HUGO-DIS-WAY WEGO-DAT-WAY!—

Sammy Fretwell and David Hill, "Grand Strand Scurries to Protect Itself from Disaster," *Myrtle Beach Sun News*, September 22, 1989, A1.

—Minutes after midnight . . . sewer services were interrupted—

"The Life of Hurricane Hugo," in *Hurricane Hugo and the Grand Strand*, Cynthia J. Struby, ed. (Myrtle Beach: Sun Publishing, 1989), 7.

—Along the Grand Strand . . . a few downed trees—

"Hugo Trashes Grand Strand," *Myrtle Beach Sun News*, September 23, 1989, A1.

—In all, twenty-two South Carolina counties would be declared disaster areas—

"The Life of Hurricane Hugo," in *Hurricane Hugo and the Grand Strand*, Cynthia J. Struby, ed. (Myrtle Beach: Sun Publishing, 1989), 7.

—Hugo would become the costliest hurricane . . . Andrew tore through South Florida—

"The 30 Costliest Hurricanes," *WeatherUnderground*, 2014, accessed April 2, 2014, http://www.wunderground.com/hurricane/damage.asp.

CHAPTER 11. DRIVING ON

—For Jordan's current Tigers, several days have passed since the crushing defeat . . .—

Coach Jordan's comments on the 2012 Bell Game in this paragraph and in the next four paragraphs come from the following source:

Chuck Jordan, telephone interviewed by Joe Oestreich, October 10, 2012.

—Conway has qualified for the postseason . . . 5–2 in the region).—

"Conway High School—Football Results 2010–Present," *South Carolina High School Football History Page*, accessed May 27, 2014, http://www.scfootballhistory.com/School/Decade/10.aspx?schoolid=177.

"Conway High School—Football Results 2000–2009," *South Carolina High School Football History Page*, accessed May 27, 2014, http://www.scfootballhistory.com/School/Decade/00.aspx?schoolid=177.

"Conway High School—Football Results 1990–1999," *South Carolina High School Football History Page*, accessed May 27, 2014, http://www.scfootballhistory.com/School/Decade/90.aspx?schoolid=177.

—"I don't know if we're good enough . . . We're going to find out."—

Ian Guerin, "Conway Football Entering Pivotal Stretch," *Myrtle Beach Sun News*, October 1, 2012, accessed April 8, 2014, http://www.myrtlebeachonline.com/2012/10/01/3091889/prep-notebook-conway-football.html.

—In the locker room, Jordan, by his own admission, "chews the offense's butt."—

Chuck Jordan, telephone interview by Joe Oestreich, October 10, 2012.

—Were there any doubts . . . Conway takes its first region game 35–14.—

Accounts of the 2012 Conway–W. Florence game are taken from the two following sources:

Robert Anderson, "Huge Second-half Comeback Gives CHS Tigers Region Win," *Horry Independent*, October 11, 2012, A7.

"Week 7 Conway 35 Conway 42," YouTube video, 2:13, posted by WPDE NewsChannel 15, October 5, 2012, http://www.youtube.com/watch?v=LkIrX2isXbo.

—"That's the best half of football . . . we've seen since Northwestern."—

Chuck Jordan, telephone interview by Joe Oestreich, October 10, 2012.

—He appears to push . . . judge signals no.—

"Week 9 Conway 29 South Florence 36," YouTube video, 6:11, posted by WPDE NewsChannel 15, October 19, 2012, http://www.youtube.com/watch?v=qdfhV2HPNS0.

—Or, as Jordan puts it . . . the daggum ball bounces, baby."—

Chuck Jordan, telephone interview by Joe Oestreich, October 31, 2012.

—Behind the gutsy play of Sawyer Jordan . . . second half to win 34–24.—

Ian Guerin, "Conway Rallies to Knock Off Sumter," *Myrtle Beach Sun News*, October 26, 2012, accessed May 27, 2014, http://www.myrtlebeachonline.com/2012/10/26/3137455/conway-rallies-back-to-knock-off.html.

—"I guess ol' Sawdawg . . . a kid whose diapers he changed.—

"Week 10 Sumter 24 Conway 34," YouTube video, 3:40, posted by WPDE NewsChannel 15, August 17, 2012, October 26, 2012, http://www.youtube.com/watch?v=kZh-nUYu0y4.

—But even more improbable . . . seeding that comes with it.—

Ian Guerin, "Prep Notebook: Carolina Forest Looks to Play Spoiler Against Conway," *Myrtle Beach Sun News*, October 29, 2012, accessed May 27, 2014, http://www.myrtlebeachonline.com/2012/10/29/3142165/prep-notebook-carolina-forest.html.

—Supporters of H. H. Singleton picketed . . . the storm had passed.—

Joseph J. Serwach, "Conway Marchers Resume Picket," *Myrtle Beach Sun News*, September 27, 1989, C1.

—Looking back on the hurricane now . . . about to explode."—

Chuck Jordan, interviewed by both authors, Conway, South Carolina, March 14, 2012.

—But it was a short minute . . . at the school district offices.—

Joseph J. Serwach, "Conway Marchers Resume Picket," *Myrtle Beach Sun News*, September 27, 1989, C1.

—A week after Hugo struck . . . move Hunt to defensive back.—

Rebecca James, "Clyburn Finds No Evidence of Racism," *Myrtle Beach Sun News*, October 3, 1989, C1 and C7.

—As evidence, he cited . . . Jordan was his best friend."—

Information about and quotations from Clyburn's letter in the remainder of this paragraph and the next paragraph are taken from the following source:

James Clyburn, "Clyburn Gives Report on Conway," *Horry Independent*, October 4, 1989, A2.

—Two weeks earlier, an editorial in the *Horry Independent* . . .—

Information about and quotations from the editorial in this paragraph and in the next paragraph come from the following source:

"Chuck Jordan Fully Vindicated," *Horry Independent*, September 20, 1989, A2.

—One additional complication . . . being racially motivated."—

H. H. Singleton and Cleveland Fladger, "Singleton, Fladger Write: The Boycott Shall Continue," *Horry Independent*, October 25, 1989, A2.

—Or, as the Reverend Covel Moore . . . still stepping on my foot."—

Rebecca James, "Board to Decide Singleton's Fate Today," *Myrtle Beach Sun News*, November 11, 1989, A13.

—"The question must be asked . . . had Carlos been white."—

H. H. Singleton and Cleveland Fladger, "Singleton, Fladger Write: The Boycott Shall Continue," *Horry Independent*, October 25, 1989, A2.

—"I have made it very clear ... the commissioner wrote.—

James Clyburn, "Clyburn Gives Report on Conway," *Horry Independent*, October 4, 1989, A2.

—He did not mention ... best left to the legal system.—

Rebecca James, "Clyburn Finds No Evidence of Racism," *Myrtle Beach Sun News*, October 3, 1989, C7.

—One month after Clyburn's letter ... involved in this football incident."—

Bobby Bryant, "Conway Inquiry Finds No Racism," *Myrtle Beach Sun News*, November 4, 1989, A1.

Sports Illustrated rendered this quotation somewhat differently. According to *SI*, Clyburn said that Jordan's decision to move Carlos Hunt was "as far from racism as anything I've been involved in."

—And today, almost twenty-five years later ... pure and simple."—

James Clyburn, telephone interview by Joe Oestreich, August 2, 2012.

—The seed for this perspective ... the commissioner said of the governor.—

"Campbell's Racism Policies Called Too Quiet," *Myrtle Beach Sun News*, September 18, 1989, A1.

—Clyburn had recently ... for exacerbating racism—

Kathy Ropp, "Clyburn Traces Racial Problems to Reagan Era," *Horry Independent*, September 13, 1989, A5.

—refused to take the same stance against Carroll Campbell—

"Campbell's Racism Policies Called Too Quiet," *Myrtle Beach Sun News*, September 18, 1989, A1 and A5.

—Singleton called Clyburn's report ... black people of Conway."—

Rebecca James, "Clyburn Finds No Evidence of Racism," *Myrtle Beach Sun News*, October 3, 1989, C1.

—In a written response ... logical explanation for the commissioner's findings.—

H. H. Singleton and Cleveland Fladger, "Singleton, Fladger Write: The Boycott Shall Continue," *Horry Independent*, October 25, 1989, A2.

—The perception within the black community ... from a black individual."—

Rebecca James, "Clyburn Finds No Evidence of Racism," *Myrtle Beach Sun News*, October 3, 1989, C7.

—And it was Jordan who ... part of the deal in writing.—

Rebecca James, "Clyburn Finds No Evidence of Racism," *Myrtle Beach Sun News*, October 3, 1989, C1.

—There's never a good time ... luck was in short supply.—

Chuck Jordan, interviewed by both authors, Conway, South Carolina, March 14, 2012.

—"The layoff allowed us ... improving just about every day."—

"High School Teams Get Back on the Ball Tonight," *Myrtle Beach Sun News*, September 29, 1989, B1.

—With Georgetown now moved ... ask them to do more than that."—

Gary Long, "South Florence Runs Roughshod Over Conway," *Myrtle Beach Sun News*, September 30, 1989, B1.

—The next Friday, Conway lost . . . out of the end zone.—

Guy Dozier, "Tigers Fall to Dillon," *Horry Independent*, October 11, 1989, A8.

—So perhaps it's ironic . . . washed away as easily.—

Bob Kudelka, "Vandals Write on Conway High Walls," *Myrtle Beach Sun News*, Oct 14, 1989, C2.

—The defacement of the building must have been on Principal Tommy Lewis's mind—

Information about and quotations related to acts of vandalism at Conway High in this paragraph and in the next paragraph come from the following source:

Robert Anderson, "Resolution to Boycott Stalemated: Graffiti Sprayed at CHS," *Horry Independent*, October 18, 1989, A1.

—Beyond the Renaissance Program . . . during the boycott—

Larry Biddle, interviewed by both authors, Conway, South Carolina, May 6, 2014.

—Still, Mickey Wilson and most anybody . . . never broke into violence.—

Mickey Wilson Jr., interviewed by both authors, Conway, South Carolina, November 21, 2014.

—Conway dropped the 1989 . . . attack *lost* fifteen.—

Gary Long, "No Joy in Conway as Tigers are Shut Out," *Myrtle Beach Sun News*, October 14, 1989, B5.

—The next week, . . . enthusiastic throughout the game."—

Mark Johnson, "Tigers Fall to Hartsville," *Horry Independent*, October 25, 1989, A8.

—Now with a record of 0–8, Coach Jordan's team had been bested—

The statistics in this paragraph and throughout the remainder of the chapter were compiled from game reports published in the *Horry Independent* and the *Myrtle Beach Sun News* during the 1989 season.

—When the local papers did publish . . . "Knights Pound Tigers."—

These headlines are taken from the following three sources:

Gary Long, "No Joy in Conway as Tigers are Shut Out," *Myrtle Beach Sun News*, October 14, 1989, B5.

Gary Long, "South Florence Runs Roughshod Over Conway," *Myrtle Beach Sun News*, September 30, 1989, B1.

Guy Dozier, "Knights Pound Tigers," *Horry Independent*, November 1, 1989, A8.

—Speaking of his young QB's . . . best game we've had at quarterback."—

"Knights Zap Conway; Aynor Blanks GSF," *Myrtle Beach Sun News*, October 28 1989, B5.

—On the first Friday in November, . . . completing fifteen of twenty-two passes.—

Guy Dozier, "Two Blocked Punts Give Socastee Win Over Tigers," *Horry Independent*, November 8, 1989. A9.

—Conway was forced to punt . . . Socastee 14, Conway 0.—

Gregg Holshouser, "Blocks Give Braves Boost Over Conway," *Myrtle Beach Sun News*, November 4, 1989, B1.

CHAPTER 12. ADVERSITY

—This year's championships . . . 25 seconds in college football."—

"Death Valley," *ClemsonTigers.com*, accessed May 11, 2014, http://www.clemsontigers.com/ViewArticle.dbml?ATCLID=205504983.

—**Like Myrtle Beach . . . twenty-eight years in class 2A.**—

Blondin, Alan, "Myrtle Beach's Rally Falls Short Against Hanahan," *Myrtle Beach Sun News*, November 9, 2012, accessed May 11, 2014, http://www.myrtlebeachonline .com/2012/11/09/3162191/myrtle-beachs-rally-falls-short.html.

—**And they fattened their record . . . over 2A schools.**—

"Hanahan High School: Games from 2010–2013," *South Carolina High School Football History Page*, accessed May 11, 2014, http://www.scfootballhistory.com/School/TeamList .aspx.

Hanahan played four 2A teams (Timberland, Bishop England, Edisto, and Hampton) as well as one 1A team (Military Magnet). They won four of these games—losing only to Timberland.

—**When asked if he feels good . . . These guys were in 2A last year."**—

D'Andre "Chocolate" Wilson, interviewed by Scott Pleasant, Hanahan, South Carolina, November 9, 2012.

—**As Chuck Jordan has said . . . expect to see a patsy."**—

Chuck Jordan, telephone interview by Joe Oestreich, October 31, 2012.

—**"These guys want to win the game . . . This will make their season."**—

Chuck Jordan, telephone interview by Joe Oestreich, October 31, 2012.

—**When the playoff brackets are released the next day . . .**—

Information about and quotations relating to Conway's matchup with Goose Creek in this paragraph and in the next paragraph come from the following source:

Ian Guerin, "Conway Draws National Powerhouse Goose Creek in First Round of Playoffs," *Myrtle Beach Sun News*, November 3, 2012, accessed May 11, 2014, http:// www.myrtlebeachonline.com/2012/11/03/3151359/conway-draws-national-powerhouse .html#storylink=cpy.

—**The Gator defense gives him . . . carried off the field by Lawrence Mitchell.**—

Chuck Jordan, interviewed by both authors, Conway South Carolina, April 22, 2014.

—**The next day, Tuesday . . . ineligible player in the win over Conway.**—

Lawrence Conneff, "Goose Creek Removed from Playoffs; Bobcats Wait to Learn Opponent," *BlufftonToday.com*, November 13, 2013, accessed April 28, 2014, http://www .blufftontoday.com/bluffton-news/2012-11-13/goose-creek-removed-playoffs-blufftons -next-opponent-be-determined#.U1ktqoVJW2w.

—**Jordan's squad will be awarded . . . Bluffton Bobcats on Friday night.**—

Ian Guerin, "SCHSL Upholds Goose Creek Ruling; Conway Back in State Playoffs," *Myrtle Beach Sun News*, November 14, 2012, accessed April 28, 2014, http://www.myrtle beachonline.com/2012/11/14/3170304/schsl-upholds-goose-creek-ruling.html.

—**A spokeswoman for the Berkeley . . . scheduled for the following day.**—

"Berkeley Schools: 'Error in Transcript' Led to Goose Creek DQ," *ABCNews4.com*, November 13, 2012, accessed April 28, 2014, http://www.abcnews4.com/story/20084671/ defending-champs-goose-creek-high-dqd-from-football-playoffs.

—**For Chuck Jordan, a victory that takes place around a conference table . . .**—

Information and quotations relating to Coach Jordan's exchanges with the SCHSL commissioner in this paragraph and in the next two paragraphs come from the following source:

Chuck Jordan, interviewed by both authors, Conway South Carolina, December 5, 2012.

—**And that Tuesday afternoon . . . helmets and pads right back out.**—

Ian Guerin, "SCHSL Upholds Goose Creek Ruling; Conway Back in State Playoffs," *Myrtle Beach Sun News*, November 14, 2012, accessed May 11, 2014, http://www.myrtle beachonline.com/2012/11/14/3170304/schsl-upholds-goose-creek-ruling.html.

—**Or as Jordan says . . . you *hope* it's yours."**—

Chuck Jordan, interviewed by both authors, Conway South Carolina, December 5, 2012.

—**At the hearing the following day . . . Conway is in.**—

Rich Chrampanis, "Goose Creek Appeal Denied, Conway Officially Back in Post-season," *CarolinaLive.com*, November 14, 2012, accessed April 28, 2014, http://www.caroli nalive.com/sports/story.aspx?id=825539#.U1kr20VJW2w.

—**Although the student's name . . . just for a minute or two.**—

Bob Cook, "For Goose Creek High, Advancing in the South Carolina Football Playoffs Means Winning in Court and on the Field," *Forbes.com*, November 16, 2012, accessed April 28, 2014, http://www.forbes.com/sites/bobcook/2012/11/16/for-goose-creek-high-advanc ing-in-the-south-carolina-football-playoffs-means-winning-in-court-and-on-the-field/.

—**"I'm good friends with Chuck Reedy . . . against the 11–1 Bluffton Bobcats.**—

Ian Guerin, "SCHSL Upholds Goose Creek Ruling; Conway Back in State Playoffs," *Myrtle Beach Sun News*, November 14, 2012, accessed May 11, 2014, http://www.myrtle beachonline.com/2012/11/14/3170304/schsl-upholds-goose-creek-ruling.html.

—**After learning about Goose Creek's suspension . . . *we're gone get these guys.***—

Chuck Jordan, interviewed by both authors, Conway South Carolina, December 5, 2012.

—**Meanwhile, ninety miles to the south . . . open hearings on the issue.**—

Phillip Bowman, "Goose Creek Gives Up Fight," *Charleston Post and Courier*, November 21, 2012, accessed April 28, 2014, http://www.postandcourier.com/article/20121121/PC20/121129908/goose-creek-gives-up-fight&source=RSS.

—**Attorneys for the school district argue . . . extra season of playing time.**—

Bob Cook, "For Goose Creek High, Advancing in the South Carolina Football Playoffs Means Winning in Court and on the Field," *Forbes.com*, November 16, 2012, accessed April 28, 2014, http://www.forbes.com/sites/bobcook/2012/11/16/for-goose-creek-high-advanc ing-in-the-south-carolina-football-playoffs-means-winning-in-court-and-on-the-field/.

—**The case is complicated . . . not on the gridiron, but in a courtroom.**—

Ian Guerin, "Conway's Season Over Regardless of Goose Creek's Fate," *Myrtle Beach Sun News*, November 16, 2012, accessed April 28, 2014, http://www.myrtlebeachonline.com/2012/11/16/3173942/judge-knocks-conway-out-of-playoff.html.

—**It doesn't come to that . . . prepare for the bus ride to Goose Creek.**—

Information in this paragraph about the judge's ruling and the immediate aftermath comes from the following three sources:

Chuck Jordan, interviewed by both authors, Conway, South Carolina, December 5, 2012.

Ian Guerin, "Conway's Season Over Regardless of Goose Creek's Fate," *Myrtle Beach Sun News*, November 16, 2012, accessed April 28, 2014, http://www.myrtlebeachonline.com/2012/11/16/3173942/judge-knocks-conway-out-of-playoff.html.

Lawrence Conneff, "Goose Creek Removed from Playoffs; Bobcats Wait to Learn Opponent," *BlufftonToday.com*, November 13, 2013, accessed April 28, 2014, http://www

.blufftontoday.com/bluffton-news/2012-11-13/goose-creek-removed-playoffs-blufftons
-next-opponent-be-determined#.U1ktqoVJW2w.

—**Here in Conway, upon hearing the news of the restraining order, . . .**—

Information in this paragraph about Coach Jordan and his team's reaction to the judge's
ruling in the Goose Creek case comes from the following two sources:

Chuck Jordan, interviewed by both authors, Conway, South Carolina, December 5, 2012.

Chuck Jordan, interviewed by both authors, Conway, South Carolina, April 22, 2014.

—**On the first Friday of the month . . . the hearing would go forward.**—

Rebecca James, "Singleton's Fate to Wait Until Monday," *Myrtle Beach Sun News*,
November 4, 1989, A1.

—**On Monday morning . . . those standing in the halls could hear.**—

Kathy Ropp, "District Attacks Singleton," *Horry Independent*, November 8, 1989, A1 and
A14.

—**The proceedings would run . . . school board would act as the jury.**—

Rebecca James, "Coach Testifies at Teacher's Suspension Hearing," *Myrtle Beach Sun
News*, November 7, 1989, C3.

—**The coach described a team that had been ravaged . . .**—

Information and quotations from Chuck Jordan's testimony come from the following
three sources:

Armand Derfner Collection, "Transcript of Jordan Testimony at Singleton School
Board Hearing," Avery Research Center for African American History and Culture, College
of Charleston. Box 127, Folders 1 and 2.

Kathy Ropp, "District Attacks Singleton," *Horry Independent*, November 8, 1989, A1 and
A 14.

Kathy Ropp, "Jordan Explains Causes for Replacing Hunt," *Horry Independent*,
November 15, 1989, A1 and A2.

—**After Jordan was excused . . . right to free speech.**—

Rebecca James, "Coach Testifies at Teacher's Suspension Hearing," *Myrtle Beach Sun
News*, November 7, 1989, C1 and C3.

—**Still, Bruce Davis and the school district . . . termination of his employment.**—

Armand Derfner Collection, "Transcript of Bruce Davis's Opening Statement," Avery
Research Center for African American History and Culture, College of Charleston. Box 127,
Folder 1.

—**On Tuesday, in an effort to determine . . .**—

Information and quotations in this paragraph relating to Lawrence Mitchell's thoughts
on the boycott come from the two following sources:

Mel Derrick, "Conway's Mitchell Set for Basketball," *Myrtle Beach Sun News*, November
2, 1989, B1.

Mel Derrick, "If Mitchell Could Only Turn Back the Clock," *Myrtle Beach Sun News*,
November 5, 1989, B1 and B4.

—**Lawrence was at basketball practice . . .**—

Information and quotations relating to Lawrence Mitchell's testimony come from the
following two sources:

Armand Derfner Collection, "Transcript of Lawrence Mitchell Testimony at Singleton School Board Hearing," Avery Research Center for African American History and Culture, College of Charleston. Box 127, Folder 8.

Kathy Ropp, "District Attacks Singleton," *Horry Independent*, November 8, 1989, A1 and A14.

—**In the courtroom, Armand Derfner was holding his breath . . .—**

Information in this paragraph regarding Armand Derfner's state of mind during the week of school board hearings comes from the following source:

Armand Derfner, telephone interview by both authors, May 13, 2014.

—**Asked that same question today . . . answered Blanton's question in 1989.—**

Lawrence Mitchell, telephone interview by both authors, October 15, 2013.

—**Or maybe Reverend Singleton . . . one possible option among many.—**

Hank Singleton III, interviewed by Joe Oestreich, Conway, South Carolina, March 2, 2013.

—**To demonstrate that the earth science teacher had interfered . . .—**

Unless otherwise noted, information about and quotations from or relating to the hearings in this paragraph and in the next two paragraphs come from the following source:

Kathy Ropp, "District Attacks Singleton," *Horry Independent*, November 8, 1989, A1 and A14.

—**". . . if it meant giving my life to do that, that was a commitment I made, sir."—**

Armand Derfner Collection, "Transcript of John Dawsey Testimony at Singleton School Board Hearing," Avery Research Center for African American History and Culture, College of Charleston. Box 126, Folder 3.

—**Asked today if he would change . . . "a good superintendent after all."—**

John Dawsey, telephone interview by both authors, July 26, 2013.

—**Davis argued . . . Rev. Singleton was present there."—**

Rebecca James, "Board to Decide Singleton's Fate Today," *Myrtle Beach Sun News*, November 11, 1989, A1.

—**". . . is drawing his salary from you and works for you, he owes to you some loyalty."—**

Armand Derfner Collection, "Transcript of John Dawsey Testimony at Singleton School Board Hearing," Avery Research Center for African American History and Culture, College of Charleston. Box 127, Folder 8.

—**". . . the decisions the bossman makes . . ."—**

Armand Derfner Collection, "Transcript of Recorded Conversation," Avery Research Center for African American History and Culture, College of Charleston. Box 126, Folder 2.

—**But disloyal speech is still . . . speech we hate to hear the most."—**

Rebecca James, "Board to Decide Singleton's Fate Today," *Myrtle Beach Sun News*, November 11, 1989, A1.

—**Bruce Davis conceded . . . clear unfitness for teaching."—**

Kathy Ropp, "District Attacks Singleton," *Horry Independent*, November 8, 1989. A14.

—**To prove his point . . . "I'm not *calling* you a racist,"—**

Kathy Ropp, "District Attacks Singleton," *Horry Independent*, November 8, 1989. A14.

—**Board chairman Marlowe said . . . disrupted the proceedings removed.—**

Rebecca James, "Singleton Hearing Brings Out Best, Worst in Folks," *Myrtle Beach Sun News*, November 12, 1989, A6.

—Jordan says that during one break in the proceedings . . .—

The story of this exchange between Jordan and Fladger comes from the following source:

Chuck Jordan, interviewed by both authors, Conway, South Carolina, March 14, 2012.

—Even if Singleton for some reason . . . "Jim is no Uncle Tom."—

Yolanda Jones, "Singleton Suspension Targeted: Human Affairs Official Seeks Probe Regardless of Decision," *Myrtle Beach Sun News*, November 9, 1989, C1.

—The last day of testimony, Friday, was devoted primarily to parents . . .—

Information about and quotations relating to the school board hearings in this paragraph and in the next paragraph come from the following source:

Rebecca James, "Board to Decide Singleton's Fate Today," *Myrtle Beach Sun News*, November 11, 1989, A13.

—At 5:15 p.m. on that Friday, the school board began their deliberations.—

Rebecca James, "Board to Decide Singleton's Fate Today," *Myrtle Beach Sun News*, November 11, 1989, A1.

—The board was legally entitled . . . that evening or the following afternoon.—

Rebecca James, "Singleton's Fate Could Be Decided Today," *Myrtle Beach Sun News*, November 10, 1989, A1.

—After two and a half hours . . . reconvene the following afternoon.—

Rebecca James, "Board to Decide Singleton's Fate Today," *Myrtle Beach Sun News*, November 11, 1989, A1.

CHAPTER 13. TOTAL AND COMPLETE VICTORY

—And there was still a mass meeting happening at Cherry Hill.—

Hank Hersch, "Choosing Sides," *Sports Illustrated*, November 27, 1989, 63.

—They averaged a meager 7.5 points per game.—

"Georgetown High School—1980–1989 Football Results," *South Carolina High School Football History Page*, accessed May 22, 2014, http://www.scfootballhistory.com/School/Decade/80.aspx?schoolid=216.

—With just over a minute left in the first quarter . . .—

Unless otherwise noted, information about and quotations relating to the Conway vs. Georgetown game in this paragraph and in the next seven paragraphs come from the following three sources:

Devin D. Gordon, "End-of-season Win has Conway 'Feeling Good,'" *Myrtle Beach Sun News*, November 11, 1989, B1 and B4.

Guy Dozier, "Tigers Win Finale," *Horry Independent*, November 15, 1989, A8.

Hank Hersch, "Choosing Sides," *Sports Illustrated*, November 27, 1989, 63.

—"I just looked down," Timbes says now, "and the ball happened to be right there."—

Michael Timbes, telephone interview by both authors, February 22, 2014.

—Robert Anderson would later write . . . if only for one night."—

Robert Anderson, "Sports Talk," *Horry Independent*, November, 22, 1989, A7.

—As Michael Timbes, the player that scored . . . "It felt like old times."—

Michael Timbes, telephone interview by both authors, February 22, 2014.

—To everybody who'd stormed the field . . . fittingly inglorious end.—

"Spring Valley Dominates Conway," *Myrtle Beach Sun News*, November 18, 1989, B4.

—Jim Kester, a man from Columbia . . . COACH OF THE YEAR.—

Guy Dozier, "Tigers Win Finale," *Horry Independent*, November 15, 1989, A8.

Hank Hersch, "Choosing Sides," *Sports Illustrated*, November 27, 1989, 63.

—A group of Conway players lifted their coach onto their shoulders . . .—

Information in this paragraph about what happened at the end of the Conway-Georgetown game comes from the following sources:

Chuck Jordan, interviewed by both authors, Conway, South Carolina, February 22, 2014.

Hank Hersch, "Choosing Sides," *Sports Illustrated*, November 27, 1989, 63.

—At that moment Sanders also happened to be looking for Jordan.—

The dialogue in this exchange between Sanders and Jordan comes from the following source:

Cleveland Sanders, interviewed by both authors, Conway, South Carolina, May 18, 2014.

—As reporter Rebecca James put it . . . many [would] be upset and outraged."—

Rebecca James, "Conway Boycott, Suspension May Leave a Bad Taste," *Myrtle Beach Sun News*, November 12, 1989, A1.

—Board member Richard Jordan . . . I have ever been in, in my life."—

Rebecca James, "School Board Puts Singleton on Hold," *Myrtle Beach Sun News*, November 15, 1989, A1.

—A few days later . . . It's a pure lose situation."—

Rebecca James, "Singleton Deadline Monday," *Myrtle Beach Sun News*, November 16, 1989, C1.

—Rev. Singleton sure didn't see the situation as pure-lose. . . .—

Information and quotations in this paragraph and in the next paragraph come from the following source:

Rebecca James, "Conway Boycott, Suspension May Leave a Bad Taste," *Myrtle Beach Sun News*, November 12, 1989, A1.

—After meeting for three hours . . . hearts of these board members."—

Rebecca James, "Board Fails to Reach Decision on Singleton," *Myrtle Beach Sun News*, November 12, 1989, A1.

—The following Thursday, Marlowe announced that the board . . .—

Information about both the board meeting and the NAACP rally in this paragraph and in the next paragraph come from the following source:

Yolanda Jones and Rebecca James, "School Board to Meet During Rally," *Myrtle Beach Sun News*, November 17, 1989, A1 and A7.

—At noon that Saturday . . . the resort hotels that lined it.—

Yolanda Jones, "1,200 Protesters Rally for Minority Rights," *Myrtle Beach Sun News*, November 19, 1989, A1.

—The Conway Movement may have begun . . . janitors, and maintenance workers."—

Andrew Shaln, "'NAACP Preach at the Beach' Coming to Strand," *Myrtle Beach Sun News*, November 10, 1989, C1 and C3.

—Myrtle Beach Chamber of Commerce . . . not neglecting it."—

Andrew Shaln, "'NAACP Preach at the Beach' Coming to Strand," *Myrtle Beach Sun News*, November 10, 1989, C3.

—**Wearing a black T-shirt that read** *Preach at the Beach 1989* ...—

Information and quotations relating to the NAACP rally in this paragraph and in the next paragraph come from the following source:

Yolanda Jones, "1,200 Protesters Rally for Minority Rights," *Myrtle Beach Sun News*, November 19, 1989, A1 and A10.

—**Meanwhile, at Conway High ... boycott for racial reasons?"**—

Rebecca James, "School Board Fires Singleton," *Myrtle Beach Sun News*, November 19, 1989, A1 and A10.

—**The vote came up 5-1 ... largely black crowd."**—

Paul A. Barra and Kathy Ropp, "Singleton Blasts Board's Decision," *Horry Independent*, November 22, 1989, A1 and A2.

—**Heath represented the lone ... Singleton in an earlier session.**—

Rebecca James, "School Board Fires Singleton," *Myrtle Beach Sun News*, November 19, 1989, A1 and A10.

—**Five votes to one. Nelson Rivers called it a "declaration of war."**—

Rebecca James, "School Board Fires Singleton," *Myrtle Beach Sun News*, November 19, 1989, A1.

—**When Preach at the Beach broke up ... people were sitting in the pews.**—

Rebecca James, "School Board Fires Singleton," *Myrtle Beach Sun News*, November 19, 1989, A1.

—**H. H. Singleton was obviously disappointed ... our day in court."**

Paul A. Barra and Kathy Ropp, "Singleton Blasts Board's Decision," *Horry Independent*, November 22, 1989, A1.

—**"I suspect," Rivers said ... in the black community."**—

Rebecca James, "School Board Fires Singleton," *Myrtle Beach Sun News*, November 19, 1989, A10.

—**That anger jelled ... in protest of Singleton's firing.**—

Rebecca James, "Black Parents Vote to Keep Kids at Home," *Myrtle Beach Sun News*, November 21, 1989, A1 and A8.

—**Over the next two days ... up for renewal in a few weeks.**—

Yolanda Jones, "Parents Pull Students from School," *Myrtle Beach Sun News*, November 22, 1989, A1 and A6.

—**Singleton had been fired ... pick up a student."**—

Robert Anderson and Kathy Ropp, "Protesting Parents Pull Students from School," *Horry Independent*, November 22, 1989, A10.

—**Over the holiday weekend ... back to school on Monday.**—

Yolanda Jones, "Black Children to Return to School," *Myrtle Beach Sun News*, November 26, 1989, A1.

—**The kids did return to classes ... displeasure with him."**—

Joseph J. Serwach, "Black Students Take Boycott to Lunchroom," *Myrtle Beach Sun News*, November 28, 1989, A1.

—**In the days after the vote to fire Singleton** ...—

Information and quotations in this paragraph relating to the board members' thoughts about the board's decision come from the following source:

Kathy Ropp, "Board Members Haven't Changed Their Minds," *Horry Independent*, November 22, 1989, A1 and A2.

—**During the week before Thanksgiving . . . adamantly oppose that."**—

Kathy Ropp, "Board Expresses Concern for Absent Students," *Horry Independent*, November 22, 1989, A2.

—**As individual board members . . . position was correct."**—

Associated Press, "Clyburn Decries Singleton Firing," *Myrtle Beach Sun News*, November 28, 1989, A5.

—**On the Tuesday after Singleton . . . First Amendment should prevail."**—

"Singleton Firing Hurts All County," *Myrtle Beach Sun News*, November 21, 1989, A6.

—**As folks flipped their calendars . . . Lawrence was named the MVP.**—

Devin D. Gordon "Conway Soars. Mitchell is MVP," *Myrtle Beach Sun News*, December 10, 1989, B1.

—**A few days later, Lawrence . . . to play football and basketball.**—

Mel Derrick, "Mitchell Picks USC," *Myrtle Beach Sun News*, December 16, 1989, B1.

—**Mickey Wilson, despite his turbulent year . . . ever had at quarterback."**—

Robert Anderson, "Four Tigers Make All Conference Team," *Horry Independent*, December 20, 1989, B6.

—**Carlos Hunt, who in his junior season . . . required preseason workouts.**—

Mickey Wilson Sr., interviewed by both authors, Conway, South Carolina, October 23, 2013.

—**The original controversy . . . virus and possibly pneumonia."**—

Joseph J. Serwach, "Dispute Quiets, but Conway Still Unsettled," *Myrtle Beach Sun News*, November 27, 1989, A1.

—**Now that he was officially fired . . . hiring him for paid engagements.**—

Hank Singleton III, interviewed by Joe Oestreich, Conway, South Carolina., March 2, 2013.

—**Early in December, Conway . . . districting was put into place.**—

Kathy Ropp, "Vote Upholds At-large Elections Here," *Horry Independent*, December 6, 1989, A1.

Joseph J. Serwach, "Conway Rejects Election Change," *Myrtle Beach Sun News*, December 6, 1989, A1.

—**A week later, three hundred people . . . black parents as a pressure group."**—

Rebecca James, "Dawsey Is Given Two More Years to Moans, Jeers," *Myrtle Beach Sun News*, December 14, 1989, A1 and A7.

—**On the heels of Dawsey's extension . . . substantive black Conwayites were.**—

Rebecca James, "Blacks to Show Economic Impact," *Myrtle Beach Sun News*, December 30, 1989, C1 and C10.

—**. . . sheriff of Richland County . . . "keep the niggers out."**—

Richard Greer, "Sheriff Blames Columbia Blacks for Shootings in Shopping Mall," *Myrtle Beach Sun News*, December 22, 1989, A1.

—**On April 1, 1991 . . . forty-five-page decision in favor of H. H. Singleton.**—

Andrew Shaln, "U.S. Judge Rules for Singleton," *Myrtle Beach Sun News*, April 2, 1991, A1.

—Hank Singleton remembers . . . "Rein*state*ment, boy."—

Hank Singleton III, interviewed by Joe Oestreich, Conway, South Carolina, March 2, 2013.

—The judge's decision boiled down . . . punishment by the school system.—

Andrew Shaln, "U.S. Judge Rules for Singleton," *Myrtle Beach Sun News*, April 2, 1991, A1.

—Three months later, on July 12 . . . $62,000 in legal fees and court costs.—

Chrysti Edge and Andrew Shaln, "Singleton May Return to Teaching," *Myrtle Beach Sun News*, July 13, 1991, A1.

—And while some members . . . coffers of the school system.—

Hank Singleton III, interviewed by Joe Oestreich, Conway, South Carolina, March 2, 2013.

—In mid-August, the earth science teacher was preparing to return to the classroom,—

Information and quotations in this paragraph and the next three paragraphs relating to Singleton's return to teaching and the 1991 "Victory March" come from the following three sources:

Robert Anderson, "200 Marchers Celebrate H.H. Singleton's Victory," *Horry Independent*, August 22, 1991, A11.

Paul A. Barra, "Conway Middle Wins and Waits," *Horry Independent*, August 22, 1991, A1.

Hank Singleton III, interviewed by Joe Oestreich, Conway, South Carolina, March 2, 2013.

EPILOGUE

—When Coach Jordan talks about . . . patience that "wasn't natural."—

Chuck Jordan, interviewed by both authors, Conway, South Carolina, March 14, 2012.

—He'll sometimes repeat a story of an exchange that happened in the early 1990s . . .—

Chuck Jordan, interviewed by both authors, Conway, South Carolina, March 14, 2012.

—Hank Singleton admits . . . "a magical time."—

Hank Singleton III, interviewed by Joe Oestreich, Conway, South Carolina, March 2, 2013.

—. . . schools are often essentially as segregated today as they were decades ago, . . .—

For more information about the current state of unofficial school segregation in America, see the following two sources:

Nikole Hannah-Jones, "Segregation Now," *The Atlantic*, April 16, 2014, http://www.theatlantic.com/features/archive/2014/04/segregation-now/359813/.

Jeff Coplon, "New York State Has the Most-Segregated Schools in the Nation," *New York Magazine*, April 23, 2014, http://nymag.com/news/features/park-slope-collegiate-integration-2014-4/.

—. . . the racist comments made by NBA owner Donald Sterling . . .—

Kyle Wagner, "Exclusive: The Extended Donald Sterling Tape," *Deadspin*, accessed May 23, 2014, http://deadspin.com/exclusive-the-extended-donald-sterling-tape-1568291249.

—When we asked Lawrence Mitchell . . . "I'm still going through it."—

Lawrence Mitchell, telephone interview by both authors, October 15, 2013.

—Like others who still call Lawrence the best athlete they've ever seen—

Information and quotes about Lawrence Mitchell in this and the next two paragraphs come from the following source:

Mickey Wilson Jr., interviewed by both authors, Conway, South Carolina, November 21, 2012.

—Lawrence ended up being academically ineligible . . .—

Information about Lawrence Mitchell's post–Conway High career and difficulties at the University of South Carolina in this paragraph comes from the following sources:

Robert Anderson, "Mitchell Could Use a Few Get Well Wishes," *Horry Independent*, September 19, 1991, A10.

Associated Press, "Gamecocks Charged with Telephone Fraud," *Sumter* [South Carolina] *Item*, October 25, 1991, B4.

"Daily Update, A," *Atlanta Journal and Constitution*, September 9, 1991, E4.

Chuck Jordan, interviewed by both authors, Conway, South Carolina, March 14, 2012.

—"Unfortunately," says Mickey Wilson . . . not a good one."—

Mickey Wilson Jr., interviewed by both authors, Conway, South Carolina, November 21, 2012.

—"I check on that Reuben Long site sometimes . . .—

This quote from Jordan about Lawrence Mitchell comes from the following source:

Chuck Jordan, interviewed by both authors, Conway, South Carolina, April 22, 2014.

—Indeed a search for . . . recent arrests for petty crimes.—

"Daily Bookings and Releases," Horry County Sheriff's Office website, accessed October 16, 2013, http://sheriff.horrycounty.org/Detention/DailyBookingsandReleases.aspx.

—A co-worker at the bar, a woman named Mary, told us, . . .—

Mary (no last name given), interviewed by both authors, Myrtle Beach, South Carolina, August 16, 2012.

—It could be said that . . . Atlanta Falcons of the NFL—

Reggie Alston, interviewed by Scott Pleasant on the team bus somewhere between Myrtle Beach and Florence, South Carolina, September 28, 2012.

—The heat on Jordan got so hot that in November—

L. Cole Smith, "Smith: Time for a Change at Conway High?" *Horry Independent*, accessed January 7, 2014. http://www.myhorrynews.com/opinion/letters_to_editor/article _10f426c0-53b3-11e3-8e4b-0019bb30f31a.html

BIBLIOGRAPHY

"30 Costliest Hurricanes, The." *WeatherUnderground*. Last modified 2014. Accessed April 2, 2014. http://www.wunderground.com/hurricane/damage.asp.

"2012 NFL Draft Results and Analysis." *ESPN NFL DraftTracker*. Accessed May 7, 2014. http://insider.espn.go.com/nfl/draft/rounds/_/round/7/year/2012.

"About Us." *Carolina Forest High School*. Accessed May 27, 2014. http://cfh.horrycoun tyschools.net/pages/Carolina_Forest_High_School/About_Us.

"Al Campanis Racist Remarks on *Nightline* (April 6, 1987)." YouTube video, 2:13. Posted by Dingo Ate My Baby! January 18, 2011. http://www.youtube.com/watch?v =O4XUbENGaiY.

Allen, Dennis J. "Singleton Is Problem." *Horry Independent*, September 13, 1989, A2.

Anderson, Robert. "200 Marchers Celebrate H.H. Singleton's Victory." *Horry Independent*, August 22, 1991, A11.

———. "Crowd Claps as KKK Goes to Courthouse." *Horry Independent*, February 7, 1990, A1.

———. "Four Tigers Make All Conference Team." *Horry Independent*, December 20, 1989, B6.

———. "Huge Second-half Comeback Gives CHS Tigers Region Win." *Horry Independent*, October 11, 2012, A7.

———. "It's Been a Rough Week for the Conway Tigers." *Horry Independent*, August 30, 1989, A8.

———. "Mitchell Could Use a Few Get Well Wishes." *Horry Independent*, September 19, 1991, A10.

———. "Resolution to Boycott Stalemated: Graffiti Sprayed at CHS." *Horry Independent*, October 18, 1989, A1.

———. "Sports Talk." *Horry Independent*, November 22, 1989, A7.

Anderson, Robert, and Kathy Ropp. "Protesting Parents Pull Students from School." *Horry Independent*, November 22, 1989, A1.

Applegate, Aaron. "The Painful Legacy of 1989's Greekfest Endures." *PilotOnline.com*. September 8, 2009. Accessed May 8, 2014. http://hamptonroads.com/2009/09/ painful-legacy-1989s-greekfest-endures.

Armand Derfner Collection, Avery Research Center for African American History and Culture, College of Charleston (South Carolina).

Assistant Democratic Leader James E. Clyburn. Accessed on August 22, 2014, http://assis tantdemocraticleader.house.gov/.

Associated Press. "Clyburn Decries Singleton Firing." *Myrtle Beach Sun News*, November 28, 1989, A5.

———. "Gamecocks Charged with Telephone Fraud." *Sumter* [South Carolina] *Item*, October 25, 1991, B4.

———. "Ronald Rouse, 18, Dies During Game." *ESPN.com*. October 6, 2012. http://espn .go.com/high-school/football/story/_/id/8468314/high-school-lineman-south-carolina -collapses-tackle-dies.

Barbree, Denise. "District Grievance Policy Similar to State Procedure." *Myrtle Beach Sun News*, May 9, 1987, A5.

Barra, Paul A. Letter to the editor. *Horry Independent*, August 30, 1989, A2.

———. "Conway Middle Wins and Waits." *Horry Independent*, August 22, 1991, A1.

Barra, Paul A., and Kathy Ropp. "Singleton Blasts Board's Decision." *Horry Independent*, November 22, 1989, A1.

"Berkeley Schools: 'Error in Transcript' Led to Goose Creek DQ." *ABCNews4.com*. November 13, 2012. Accessed April 28, 2014. http://www.abcnews4.com/story/20084671/ defending-champs-goose-creek-high-dqd-from-football-playoffs.

Blondin, Alan. "Myrtle Beach's Rally Falls Short Against Hanahan." *Myrtle Beach Sun News*, November 9, 2012. Accessed May 11, 2014. http://www.myrtlebeachonline .com/2012/11/09/3162191/myrtle-beachs-rally-falls-short.html.

Bowman, Phillip. "Goose Creek Gives Up Fight." *Charleston Post and Courier*, November 21, 2012. Accessed April 28, 2014. http://www.postandcourier.com/article/20121121/ PC20/121129908/goose-creek-gives-up-fight&source=RSS.

Broder, John M. "Thousands Stage Silent March on Capitol: Civil Rights Gathering Protests Recent Supreme Court Decisions." *LosAngelesTimes.com*. August 27, 1989. Accessed May 8, 2014. http://articles.latimes.com/1989-08-27/news/mn-1753_1_supreme-court -decisions.

Bryant, Bobby. "Conway Inquiry Finds No Racism." *Myrtle Beach Sun News*, November 4, 1989, A1.

Bryant, Bobby, and Steve Smith. "NAACP Criticizes Clyburn Hiring Consultant." *Myrtle Beach Sun News*, November 9, 1989, C10.

Burwell, Bryan. "Small-Town Football Feud Sparks Full-scale Racial Rift." *Detroit News*, October 15, 1989, C1.

Campbell, Roy M. "Why Virginia Beach Happened." *Philadelphia Inquirer*, September 10, 1989. Accessed May 8, 2014. http://articles.philly.com/1989-09-10/news/26100185 _1_greekfest-black-youths-disturbance.

"Campbell's Racism Policies Called Too Quiet." *Myrtle Beach Sun News*, September 18, 1989, A1.

Centers for Disease Control. "Morbidity and Mortality Weekly Report." *CDC.gov*. Last modified September 29, 2006. Accessed May 9, 2014. http://www.cdc.gov/mmwr/pre view/mmwrhtml/mm5538a1.htm.

Chrampanis, Rich. "Conway's Moody Picks Up SEC Offer." *CarolinaLive.com*. Last modi- fied March 2, 2012. Accessed May 7, 2014, http://www.carolinalive.com/sports/story .aspx?id=726127#.U2OX54VJW2w.

———. "Goose Creek Appeal Denied, Conway Officially Back in Post-season." *CarolinaLive. com*. November 14, 2012. Accessed April 28, 2014. http://www.carolinalive.com/sports/ story.aspx?id=825539#.U1kr2oVJW2w.

———. "MB to Use One QB, Carvers Bay Has D1 Prospect." *CarolinaLive.com*. Last modified July 3, 2012. Accessed May 7, 2014. http://www.carolinalive.com/sports/story .aspx?id=772427#.U2OuqIVJW2w.

Christopher, Andre. "Former Players Back Jordan." *Myrtle Beach Sun News*, August 27, 1989, B1.

"Chuck Jordan Fully Vindicated." *Horry Independent*, September 20, 1989, A2.

Clyburn, James. "Clyburn Gives Report on Conway." *Horry Independent*, October 4, 1989, A2.

"Coach and Player: They Need to Talk." *Myrtle Beach Sun News*, September 12, 1989, A8.

Conneff, Lawrence. "Goose Creek Removed from Playoffs; Bobcats Wait to Learn Opponent." *BlufftonToday.com*. November 13, 2013. Accessed April 28, 2014. http://www .blufftontoday.com/bluffton-news/2012-11-13/goose-creek-removed-playoffs-blufftons -next-opponent-be-determined#.U1ktqoVJW2w.

"Conway in Controversy." *Myrtle Beach Sun News*, September 7, 1989, A8.

Cook, Bob. "For Goose Creek High, Advancing in the South Carolina Football Playoffs Means Winning in Court and on the Field." *Forbes.com*. November 16, 2012. Accessed April 28, 2014. http://www.forbes.com/sites/bobcook/2012/11/16/for-goose-creek-high -advancing-in-the-south-carolina-football-playoffs-means-winning-in-court-and-on -the-field/.

Cook, Monty. "Conway Falls 42-14." *Myrtle Beach Sun News*, September 2, 1989, B1.

Coplon, Jeff. "New York State Has the Most-Segregated Schools in the Nation." *New York Magazine*, April 23, 2014, http://nymag.com/news/features/park-slope-collegiate integration-2014-4/.

"Daily Bookings and Releases." *Horry County Sheriff's Office*. Accessed October 16, 2013. http://sheriff.horrycounty.org/Detention/DailyBookingsandReleases.aspx.

"Daily Update, A." *Atlanta Journal and Constitution*, September 9, 1991, E4.

"Day the President's Commission on Education Came to Conway, South Carolina, The." *Life*. January 1989, n.p. (wraparound cover).

Dearing, Chris. "Summerville's John McKissick Is the Winningest Football Coach at Any Level." *State* (Columbia, SC), October 26, 2012. http://www.thestate.com/ 2012/10/28/2498176/summervilles-john-mckissick-is.html.

"Death Valley." *ClemsonTigers.com*. Accessed May 11, 2014. http://www.clemsontigers.com/ ViewArticle.dbml?ATCLID=205504983.

Derrick, Mel. "Another Day of Hopes and Heartbreak for Conway Team." *Myrtle Beach Sun News*, August 25, 1989, B1.

———. "Conway Loses Again, But Gains Six Suspended Players." *Myrtle Beach Sun News*, September 9, 1989, B1.

———. "Conway's Jordan Wants to Do the Right Thing." *Myrtle Beach Sun News*, August 23, 1989, B1.

———. "Conway's Mitchell Set for Basketball." *Myrtle Beach Sun News*, November 2, 1989, B1.

———. "If Mitchell Could Only Turn Back the Clock." *Myrtle Beach Sun News*, November 5, 1989, B1.

———. "In Conway, Both Sides Need to Erase the Line." *Myrtle Beach Sun News*, September 3, 1989, B1.

———. "Jordan Looks to Summerville." *Myrtle Beach Sun News*, August 29, 1989, B1.

———. "Mitchell Called Third Best in U.S." *Myrtle Beach Sun News*, August 15, 1989, B1.

———. "Mitchell Picks USC." *Myrtle Beach Sun News*, December 16, 1989, B1.

———. "'No Comment' Is Rule for Conway Players." *Myrtle Beach Sun News*, August 24, 1989, B1.

———. "Rational Thinking Needed Quickly." *Myrtle Beach Sun News*, August 27, 1989, B1.

———. "A Reunion of Football Pals." *Myrtle Beach Sun News*, August 20, 1989, B1.

———. "White? Black? No, He's Just a Teammate." *Myrtle Beach Sun News*, September 10, 1989, B1 and B12.

"Doug Shaw Memorial Stadium." *Myrtle Beach Local Government Page*. Accessed May 17, 2014. http://www.cityofmyrtlebeach.com/dougshaw.html.

Dozier, Guy. "Knights Pound Tigers." *Horry Independent*, November 1, 1989, A8.

———. "Tigers Fall to Dillon." *Horry Independent*, October 11, 1989, A8.

———. "Tigers Pull Up Short Against Archrival MB." *Horry Independent*, September 20, 1989, A8.

———. "Tigers Win Finale." *Horry Independent*, November 15, 1989, A8.

———. "Two Blocked Punts Give Socastee Win Over Tigers." *Horry Independent*, November 8, 1989, A9.

Edge, Chrysti. "Blacks Gather to Protest Singleton Suspension." *Myrtle Beach Sun News*, August 30, 1989, A1.

———. "Charleston Blacks Picket Conway's Football Squad." *Myrtle Beach Sun News*, September 9, 1989, A1.

———. "Strand Braces for Fury of Storm." *Myrtle Beach Sun News*, September 22, 1989, A1.

Edge, Chrysti, and Andrew Shaln. "Singleton May Return to Teaching." *Myrtle Beach Sun News*, July 13, 1991, A1.

Edge, Chrysti, and Yolanda Jones. "Striking Tigers Watch Team Lose." *Myrtle Beach Sun News*, August 26, 1989, A1.

Elswick, Ryan. "Conway Wins Shootout with Marlboro County." *Myrtle Beach Sun News*, September 14, 2012. Accessed May 10, 2014. http://www.myrtlebeachonline.com/2012/09/14/3059767/conway-wins-shootout-with-marlboro.html.

Fretwell, Sammy. "Conway Racial Dispute Described as One of Worst in S.C. History." *Myrtle Beach Sun News*, September 9, 1989, A5.

———. "Jordan: Not Used to Boos." *Myrtle Beach Sun News*, September 3, 1989, A1.

———. "Marchers May Have Cut Business Access." *Myrtle Beach Sun News*, September 12, 1989, A1.

Fretwell, Sammy, and David Hill. "Grand Strand Scurries to Protect Itself from Disaster." *Myrtle Beach Sun News*, September 22, 1989, A1.

"Friday's Football Jamboree Will Bring Out the Area's Best." *Myrtle Beach Sun News*, August 15, 1989, B1.

Gilmer, Jason. "Winning Traditions." *GoUpstate.com*. Last modified November 30, 2005. Accessed May 7, 2014. http://www.goupstate.com/article/20051130/NEWS/511300353.

Glass, Robert. "Caribbean Braces for Hugo Fury." *Myrtle Beach Sun News,* September 17, 1989, A1.

——. "Hugo Pummels U.S. Virgin Islands: Storm Expected to Hit Puerto Rico Today." *Myrtle Beach Sun News,* September 18, 1989, A1.

"Golson Accepts Suspension." *ESPN.com,* May 28, 2013. Accessed May 7, 2014. http://espn.go.com/college-football/story/_/id/9313557/everett-golson-banned-notre-dame-fighting-irish-poor-academic-judgment.

Gordon, Devin D. "Conway Soars. Mitchell is MVP." *Myrtle Beach Sun News,* December 10, 1989, B1.

——. "End-of-season Win Has Conway 'Feeling Good.'" *Myrtle Beach Sun News,* November 11, 1989, B1.

Greenhouse, Linda. "Justice Criticizes U.S. Court's Civil Rights Ruling." Written for the *New York Times.* Reprinted in Myrtle *Beach Sun News,* September 9, 1989, A1.

Greer, Richard. "Sheriff Blames Columbia Blacks for Shootings in Shopping Mall." *Myrtle Beach Sun News,* December 22, 1989, A1.

Guerin, Ian. "The Freshman Phenom Will Start." *Prep Talk: Inside High School Sports Blog.* August 23, 2007 (4:20 PM). Accessed March 11, 2014. http://thesunnews.typepad.com/preptalk/2007/08/the-freshman-ph.html.

——. "Conway Draws National Powerhouse Goose Creek in First Round of Playoffs." *Myrtle Beach Sun News,* November 3, 2012. Accessed May 11, 2014, http://www.myrtlebeachonline.com/2012/11/03/3151359/conway-draws-national-powerhouse.html#storylink=cpy.

——. "Conway Football Entering Pivotal Stretch." *Myrtle Beach Sun News,* October 1, 2012. Accessed April 8, 2014. http://www.myrtlebeachonline.com/2012/10/01/3091889/prep-notebook-conway-football.html.

——. "Conway Rallies to Knock Off Sumter." *Myrtle Beach Sun News,* October 26, 2012. Accessed May 27, 2014. http://www.myrtlebeachonline.com/2012/10/26/3137455/conway-rallies-back-to-knock-off.html.

——. "Conway's Season Over Regardless of Goose Creek's Fate." *Myrtle Beach Sun News,* November 16, 2012. Accessed April 28, 2014. http://www.myrtlebeachonline.com/2012/11/16/3173942/judge-knocks-conway-out-of-playoff.html.

——. "Myrtle Beach's Keane Makes Return to Carolina Forest on Friday." *Myrtle Beach Sun News,* September 13, 2012. Accessed May 27, 2014. http://www.myrtlebeachonline.com/2012/09/13/3057067/myrtle-beachs-keane-makes-return.html.

——. "Northwestern Drubs Conway 55-19." *Heraldonline.com.* August 25, 1989. Accessed March 12, 2014. http://www.heraldonline.com/2012/08/25/4213231/northwestern-drubs-conway-55-19.html.

——. "Prep Notebook: Carolina Forest Looks to Play Spoiler Against Conway." *Myrtle Beach Sun News,* October 29, 2012. Accessed May 27, 2014, http://www.myrtlebeachonline.com/2012/10/29/3142165/prep-notebook-carolina-forest.html.

———. "Prep Notebook: Conway Football Entering Pivotal Stretch." *Myrtle Beach Sun News.* Last modified October 1, 2012. http://www.myrtlebeachonline.com/2012/10/01/3091889/prep-notebook-conway-football.html.

———. "SCHSL Upholds Goose Creek Ruling: Conway Back in State Playoffs." *Myrtle Beach Sun News,* November 14, 2012. Accessed April 28, 2014. http://www.myrtlebeachonline.com/2012/11/14/3170304/schsl-upholds-goose-creek-ruling.html.

———. "Socastee Knocks Off Rival Myrtle Beach." *Myrtle Beach Sun News.* Last modified October 5, 2012. http://www.myrtlebeachonline.com/2012/10/05/3099524/socastee-knocks-off-rival-myrtle.html#storylink=cpy.

Hamilton, Brian. "Kelly: Notre Dame Offense, QB Must Improve." *ChicagoTribune.com.* September 23, 2012. http://articles.chicagotribune.com/2012-09-23/sports/chi-kelly-notre-dame-offense-qb-golson-must-improve-20120923_1_qb-golson-notre-dame-offense-everett-golson.

Hannah-Jones, Nikole. "Segregation Now." *The Atlantic,* April 16, 2014, http://www.theatlantic.com/features/archive/2014/04/segregation-now/359813/.

Hersch, Hank. "Choosing Sides." *Sports Illustrated,* November 27, 1989, 42–63.

"High School Teams Get Back on the Ball Tonight." *Myrtle Beach Sun News,* September 29, 1989, B1.

Holshouser, Gregg. "Blocks Give Braves Boost Over Conway." *Myrtle Beach Sun News,* November 4, 1989, B1.

Homegoing Celebration in Loving Memory of the Late H. H. Singleton II. January 5, 2013. DVD. Directed by Wardell Brantley. Conway, South Carolina: As-One Media and Rejoice Christian Network, 2013.

"Hugo Aiming for U.S. Coast." *Myrtle Beach Sun News,* September 20, 1989, A1.

"Hugo Trashes Grand Strand." *Myrtle Beach Sun News,* September 23, 1989, A1.

James, Rebecca. "Activist Teacher Avoids Reprimand." *Myrtle Beach Sun News,* August 26, 1989, A1.

———. "Black Parents Vote to Keep Kids at Home." *Myrtle Beach Sun News,* November 21, 1989, A1.

———. "Blacks to Show Economic Impact." *Myrtle Beach Sun News,* December 30, 1989, C1.

———. "Board Fails to Reach Decision on Singleton." *Myrtle Beach Sun News,* November 12, 1989, A1.

———. "Board to Decide Singleton's Fate Today." *Myrtle Beach Sun News,* November 11, 1989, A1.

———. "Booster Club Loan Fund Unusual in Area Schools." *Myrtle Beach Sun News,* September 15, 1989, A1.

———. "Civil Rights Activists Organize, Orchestrate to Make Their Point." *Myrtle Beach Sun News,* September 1, 1989, A1.

———. "Clyburn Finds No Evidence of Racism." *Myrtle Beach Sun News,* October 3, 1989, C1.

———. "Coach Testifies at Teacher's Suspension Hearing." *Myrtle Beach Sun News,* November 7, 1989, C1.

———. "Conway Blacks Denied Petition: Schools Chief Refuses Football Coach's Removal." *Myrtle Beach Sun News,* August 31, 1989, A1.

———. "Conway Boycott, Suspension May Leave a Bad Taste." *Myrtle Beach Sun News*, November 12, 1989, A1.

———. "Conway Coach Cuts Boycotting Players." *Myrtle Beach Sun News*, August 29, 1989, A1.

———. "Conway Football Boycott Continues." *Myrtle Beach Sun News*, August 24, 1989, A1.

———. "Conway Game Quiet; Boycott Spreads to Band." *Myrtle Beach Sun News*, September 2, 1989, A1.

———. "Dawsey Is Given Two More Years to Moans, Jeers." *Myrtle Beach Sun News*, December 14, 1989, A1.

———. "District Suspends Singleton: Boycott Organizer Calls Act Unfounded." *Myrtle Beach Sun News*, August 30, 1989, A1.

———. "No Progress Made in Conway Dispute." *Myrtle Beach Sun News*, September 1, 1989, A1.

———. "Protesters Picket School-District Offices." *Myrtle Beach Sun News*, September 19, 1989, C1.

———. "S.C. Human Affairs Chief Investigates Dispute." *Myrtle Beach Sun News*, September 8, 1989, A1.

———. "School Board Fires Singleton." *Myrtle Beach Sun News*, November 19, 1989, A1.

———. "School Board Keeping Low Profile on Racism Issue." *Myrtle Beach Sun News*, September 20, 1989, C1.

———. "School Board Puts Singleton on Hold." *Myrtle Beach Sun News*, November 15, 1989, A1.

———. "School Board to Review Coach's Actions." *Myrtle Beach Sun News*, September 21, 1989, A1.

———. "Singleton Deadline Monday." *Myrtle Beach Sun News*, November 16, 1989, C1.

———. "Singleton Hearing Brings Out Best, Worst in Folks." *Myrtle Beach Sun News*, November 12, 1989, A6.

———. "Singleton Suspension Case Assigned to Judge." *Myrtle Beach Sun News*, September 13, 1989, A1.

———. "Singleton's Fate Could Be Decided Today." *Myrtle Beach Sun News*, November 10, 1989, A1.

———. "Singleton's Fate to Wait Until Monday." *Myrtle Beach Sun News*, November 4, 1989, A1.

———. "Star Player Returns to Boycott." *Myrtle Beach Sun News*, September 12, 1989, A1.

———. "Star's Return to Boycott Explained." *Myrtle Beach Sun News*, September 14, 1989, A1.

James, Rebecca, and Ettie Newlands. "Parents Seeking Boycott of Singleton's Classes." *Myrtle Beach Sun News*, August 29, 1989, A1.

James, Rebecca, and Sammy Fretwell. "Boycott Shows Tension." *Myrtle Beach Sun News*, August 27, 1989, A1.

James, Rebecca, and Yolanda Jones. "Conway Coach Asks Blacks to Rejoin Team." *Myrtle Beach Sun News*, September 8, 1989, A1.

James, Rebecca, Ron Morrison, and Sammy Fretwell. "Conway Mayor Forms Committee to Look at Race Relations." *Myrtle Beach Sun News*, September 2, 1989, A1.

"Joe Montana—Career Stats." *NFL.com*. Accessed May 7, 2014. http://www.nfl.com/player/joemontana/2502166/careerstats.

Johnson, Mark. "Hillcrest Outmans Tigers 34-6." *Myrtle Beach Sun News*, August 26, 1989, B1.

———. "No Foolin'—Tigs' Mitchell Is For Real." *Myrtle Beach Sun News*, August 13, 1989, B1.

———. "Prep Football." *Myrtle Beach Sun News*, August 24, 1989, B1.

———. "Seahawks Dump Testy Tigers." *Myrtle Beach Sun News*, September 16, 1989, B1.

———. "Seahawks Hope to Hear a Bell Friday Night." *Myrtle Beach Sun News*, September 14, 1989, B1.

———. "Tigers Fall to Hartsville." *Horry Independent*, October 25, 1989, A8.

———. "Wanted: Experience; Contact Conway." *Myrtle Beach Sun News*, August 13, 1989, B8.

Jones, Joyce. "Racist Acts, Many In, Out of Schools." *Myrtle Beach Sun News*, September 7, 1989, A8.

Jones, Yolanda. "1000 More Join NAACP's Weekly March." *Myrtle Beach Sun News*, September 17, 1989, D1.

———. "1,200 Protesters Rally for Minority Rights." *Myrtle Beach Sun News*, November 19, 1989, A1.

———. "Black Children to Return to School." *Myrtle Beach Sun News*, November 26, 1989, A1.

———. "Football Jamboree Annual Family Event." *Myrtle Beach Sun News*, August 19, 1989, A1.

———. "NAACP Boosts Membership, and S.C. Disputes Are Helping." *Myrtle Beach Sun News*, September 14, A1.

———. "NAACP Files Lawsuit to Bar Action Against Singleton." *Myrtle Beach Sun News*, September 10, 1989, A1.

———. "NAACP Pledges Weekly Marches." *Myrtle Beach Sun News*, September 10, 1989, A1.

———. "Parents Pull Students from School." *Myrtle Beach Sun News*, November 22, 1989, A1 and A6.

———. "Singleton Suspension Targeted: Human Affairs Official Seeks Probe Regardless of Decision." *Myrtle Beach Sun News*, November 9, 1989, A1.

Jones, Yolanda, and Rebecca James. "School Board to Meet During Rally." *Myrtle Beach Sun News*, November 17, 1989, A1.

Jones, Yolanda, and Sammy Fretwell. "Some Blacks Rejoin Conway Team." *Myrtle Beach Sun News*, September 9, 1989, A1.

Jordan, Chuck. "Jordan's Statement." *Myrtle Beach Sun News*, August 29, 1989, B1.

Joyner, Charles. Foreword to *Horry County, South Carolina: 1730-1993*, by Catherine H. Lewis. Columbia: University of South Carolina Press, 1998.

"Junior Hemingway Bio." *Go Blue.com*. Accessed May 7, 2014. http://www.mgoblue.com/sports/m-footbl/mtt/hemingway_junioroo.html.

King, Martin Luther, Jr. "I Have a Dream" (transcript). August 28, 1963. Accessed May 10, 2014. http://www.archives.gov/press/exhibits/dream-speech.pdf.

"Knights Zap Conway; Aynor Blanks GSF." *Myrtle Beach Sun News*, October 28 1989, B5.

Krausz, Tony. "No QB Controversy for Irish." *Fort Wayne* [Indiana] *Journal-Gazette*, September 23, 2012. Accessed April 7, 2014. http://www.journalgazette.net/article/20120923/BLOGS02/120929804/0/blogs.

Kudelka, Bob. "Vandals Write on Conway High Walls." *Myrtle Beach Sun News,* Oct 14, 1989, C2.

Kunerth, Jeff. "Small-town Bar Runs into Some Big-time Trouble." *Orlando Sentinel,* October 8, 1989. Accessed May 8, 2014. http://articles.orlandosentinel.com/1989-10-08/news/8910082910_1_salter-buffalo-room-naacp.

Latimer, George, Jr. "Newspaper is Racist" (letter to the editor). *Myrtle Beach Sun News,* August 31, 1989, A13.

"Letter to Readers." *Myrtle Beach Sun News,* September 14, 1989, A15.

Lewis, Catherine. *Horry County, South Carolina 1730-1993.* Columbia: University of South Carolina Press, 1998.

"Life of Hurricane Hugo, The." In *Hurricane Hugo and the Grand Strand.* Struby, Cynthia J., ed. Myrtle Beach: Sun Publishing, 1989.

Long, Gary. "No Joy in Conway as Tigers Are Shut Out." *Myrtle Beach Sun News,* October 14, 1989, B5.

———. "South Florence Runs Roughshod Over Conway." *Myrtle Beach Sun News,* September 30, 1989, B1.

Mann, Judy. "Putting Racism to Rest." *Washington Post,* February 3, 1988, D3.

Moniz, Dave. "Reconciliation Under Way in Conway Football Spat." *Spartanburg* [South Carolina] *Herald-Journal,* September 9, 1989, C2.

Moniz, Dave. "Some Who Boycotted Team Return." *State* (Columbia, SC), September 9, 1989, A1.

———. "Struggling Against Racism's Shadow, Conway Still Trying to Heal Wounds of '89." *State* (Columbia, SC), August 18, 1990, A1.

Moore, Mary E. "Out of Skins; Less Racism." *Myrtle Beach Sun News,* September 7, 1989, A8.

Morrison, Ron. "Strand Takes Precautions Against Hugo." *Myrtle Beach Sun News,* September 19, 1989, A1.

"Myrtle Beach 33, Irmo 27." YouTube video, 2:20. Posted by WPDE NewsChannel 15, August 25, 2012. http://www.youtube.com/watch?v=-X8aYFBCZ-U.

"Myrtle Beach Area History: History and Local Folklore." *VisitMyrtleBeach.com.* Accessed May 7, 2014. http://www.visitmyrtlebeach.com/about/history/.

Myrtle Beach Football (on *HomeTeamsOnline.com*). Accessed on multiple dates, http://www.hometeamsonline.com/teams/?u=MYRTLEBEACHFOOTBALLCOM&s=football&t=c.

"NAACP March." *Myrtle Beach Sun News,* September 8, 1989, A1.

National Oceanic and Atmospheric Administration (NOAA). *National Disaster Survey Report.* Silver Springs, MD: U.S. Department of Commerce, 1990. Accessed April 2, 2014. http://www.nws.noaa.gov/om/assessments/pdfs/hugo1.

"No. 20 Notre Dame Beats No. 10 Michigan State 20-3." *SportsIllustrated.CNN.com.* Accessed April 7, 2014. http://sportsillustrated.cnn.com/football/ncaa/gameflash/2012/09/15/49664/.

Page, Clarence. "Thanks for Being Honest, Jimmy 'The Greek'—Too Honest." *Chicago Tribune,* January 20, 1988. Accessed May 27, 2014. http://articles.chicagotribune.com/1988-01-20/news/8803230751_1_thighs-black-professional-sports.

Page, D. W. (Associated Press). "NAACP Faults Va. Beach Actions." *Myrtle Beach Sun News*, September 5, 1989, A1.

"Palmetto's Finest Record Book: Football." *South Carolina High School League*. Accessed May 12, 2014. http://www.schsl.org/2012/PFfb.pdf.

Papanek, John. "The Odyssey of Little Homer." *Sports Illustrated*, December 28, 1981. Accessed March 12, 2014. http://sportsillustrated.cnn.com/vault/article/magazine/MAG1125121/index.htm.

Pope, Lamond. "Suspended Irish QB Everett Golson admits cheating on test." *Chicago Sun-Times*, October 29, 2013. Accessed September 8, 2014. http://www.suntimes.com/sports/colleges/23420462-419/suspended-irish-qb-everett-golson-admits-cheating-on-test.html#.

Program for the Rev. H. H. Singleton's "Homegoing Ceremony," 5 January 2013.

Ravo, Nick. "Marchers and Brooklyn Youths Trade Racial Jeers." *New York Times.com*. August 27, 1989. Accessed May 8, 2014. http://www.nytimes.com/1989/08/27/nyregion/marchers-and-brooklyn-youths-trade-racial-jeers.html.

Remember the Titans. Directed by Boaz Yakin. Walt Disney Pictures, in association with Jerry Bruckheimer Films. Buena Vista Home Entertainment, 2006. DVD.

Ropp, Kathy. "Blacks Continue Boycott, Protests: Hundreds Parade in Conway." *Horry Independent*, September 13, 1989, A1.

——. "Board Expresses Concern for Absent Students." *Horry Independent*, November 22, 1989, A2.

——. "Board Members Haven't Changed Their Minds." *Horry Independent*, November 22, 1989, A1 and A2.

——. "Clyburn Traces Racial Problems to Reagan Era." *Horry Independent*, September 13, 1989, A5.

——. "District Attacks Singleton." *Horry Independent*, November 8, 1989, A1.

——. "Jordan Explains Causes for Replacing Hunt." *Horry Independent*, November 15, 1989, A1.

——. "Vote Upholds At-large Elections Here." *Horry Independent*, December 6, 1989, A1.

Rosenberg, I. J. "A Change at QB Tears Town Apart—Black-White Switch Spurs Boycott, Rally." *Atlanta Journal-Constitution*, September 2, 1989, E7.

Rubillo, Tom. *Hurricane Destruction in South Carolina: Hell and High Water*. Charleston: History Press, 2006.

Serwach, Joseph J. "Black Students Take Boycott to Lunchroom." *Myrtle Beach Sun News*, November 28, 1989, A1.

Serwach, Joseph J. "Conway Marchers Resume Picket." *Myrtle Beach Sun News*, September 27, 1989, C1.

——. "Conway Rejects Election Change." *Myrtle Beach Sun News*, December 6, 1989, A1.

——. "Conway Strike Looms Over First Day of School." *Myrtle Beach Sun News*, August 28, 1989, A1.

——. "Dispute Quiets, but Conway Still Unsettled." *Myrtle Beach Sun News*, November 27, 1989, A1.

Serwach, Joseph J., and Yolanda Jones. "Former Conway QB Tells His Story." *Myrtle Beach Sun News*, September 11, 1989, A1.

Shaln, Andrew. "'NAACP Preach at the Beach' Coming to Strand." *Myrtle Beach Sun News*, November 10, 1989, C1.

———. "U.S. Judge Rules for Singleton." *Myrtle Beach Sun News*, April 2, 1991, A1.

Shannon, Lesia J. "Dawsey Looks into Complaints of Singleton's Role in Protests." *Myrtle Beach Sun News*, May 16, 1987, A1.

———. "NAACP: Principal Bowed to Whites in Squad Additions." *Myrtle Beach Sun News*, May 8, 1987, A7.

———. "School Officials Agree to Trim Conway JV Cheerleader Spots." *Myrtle Beach Sun News*, May 14, 1987, A1.

Shannon, Lesia J., and Denise Barbree. "Conway Racial Dispute Escalates into Student Protests." *Myrtle Beach Sun News*, May 13, 1987, A1.

Shannon, Lesia J., and Lisa Greene. "Evacuation Urged for Some Areas." *Myrtle Beach Sun News*, September 21, 1989, A1.

Sherman, Jimmy. "Justice Should Prevail" (letter to the editor). *Myrtle Beach Sun News*, August 31, 1989, A13.

"Singleton Firing Hurts All County." *Myrtle Beach Sun News*, November 21, 1989, A6.

Singleton, H. H. "Remarks at Press Conference Outside Cherry Hill Baptist Church on August 22, 1989." From a non-commercial DVD privately owned and loaned to the authors by Hank Singleton III.

Singleton, H. H., and Cleveland Fladger. "Singleton, Fladger Write: The Boycott Shall Continue." *Horry Independent*, October 25, 1989, A2.

Smith, L. Cole. "Smith: Time for a Change at Conway High?" *Horry Independent*. Accessed January 7, 2014. http://www.myhorrynews.com/opinion/letters_to_editor/article_10f426c0-53b3-11e3-8e4b-0019bb30f31a.html.

South Carolina High School Football History Page. Accessed on multiple dates. http://www.scfootballhistory.com/index.aspx.

"Spring Valley Dominates Conway." *Myrtle Beach Sun News*, November 18, 1989, B4.

Stepping Stones to Excellence: Conway High School Mirror 1989. Susan Timmons and Sarah Young, eds. Conway, SC: Conway High School, 1989.

"Story of 'Fired Up! Ready to Go!'—Obama for America 2012, The." YouTube video, 4:31. Posted by BarackObamadotcom, April 4, 2012. http://www.youtube.com/watch?v=QhWDFgRfiiQ.

"Super Bowl XIII: Dallas Cowboys' Jackie Smith's Key Drop Helps Steelers Win." *NYDailyNews.com*. Last modified December 29, 2013. http://www.nydailynews.com/sports/football/super-bowl-xiii-sickest-man-america-article-1.1561166#ixzz2y9HzdWal.

"Teams Tune Up in Football Jamboree." *Myrtle Beach Sun News*, August 19, 1989, B1.

"Today's NAACP March." *Myrtle Beach Sun News*, September 9, 1989, A1.

"Tommy Rees Comes Off Bench to Engineer Notre Dame's Winning Drive." *ESPN.com*. Last modified September 8, 2012. http://espn.go.com/ncf/recap?gameId=322520087.

"Tyler Keane" [bio]. GoCCUSports.com. Accessed April 9, 2014. http://www.goccusports.com/sports/m-footbl/mtt/tyler_keane_858584.html.

United States Census Bureau. *Census.gov*. Accessed on multiple dates. http://www.census.gov/.

Wagner, Kyle. "Exclusive: The Extended Donald Sterling Tape." *Deadspin*. Accessed May 23, 2014. http://deadspin.com/exclusive-the-extended-donald-sterling-tape-1568291249.

"Week 0 Georgetown 25 Conway 42." YouTube video, 2:57. Posted by WPDE NewsChannel 15, August 17, 2012. http://www.youtube.com/watch?v=meLGMnmmYYA.

"Week 2 Rock Hill 34 Conway 13." YouTube video, 1:20. Posted by WPDE NewsChannel 15, August 31, 2012. http://www.youtube.com/watch?v=IG_cFohEvG4.

"Week 7 Conway 35 Conway 42." YouTube video, 2:13. Posted by WPDE NewsChannel 15, October 5, 2012. http://www.youtube.com/watch?v=LkIrX2isXbo.

"Week 9 Conway 29 South Florence 36." YouTube video, 6:11. Posted by WPDE NewsChannel 15, October 19, 2012. http://www.youtube.com/watch?v=qdfhV2HPNSo.

"Week 10 Sumter 24 Conway 34." YouTube video, 3:40. Posted by WPDE NewsChannel 15, October 26, 2012. http://www.youtube.com/watch?v=kZh-nUYuoy4.

"What People Are Saying." *Myrtle Beach Sun News*, August 28, 1989, A5.

INDEX